Amnesty and Reconciliation in Late
Fifth-Century Athens

New Approaches to Ancient Greek Institutional History

Series editors: Mirko Canevaro, University of Edinburgh; Edward Harris, Durham University; David Lewis, University of Edinburgh

This series will showcase new trends in the study of Greek political, legal, social and economic institutions and institutional history. It will create a fruitful dialogue between Greek institutional historians and the political and social sciences – and in particular the New Institutionalisms.

Books in the series will go beyond a traditional approach to offer theoretical and methodological reflection on the importance of institutions and on how we should study them. They will appeal to Greek historians and to political and social scientists alike.

Books available in the series
The Ideology of Democratic Athens: Institutions, Orators and the Mythical Past
Matteo Barbato

The Politics of Association in Hellenistic Rhodes
Christian A. Thomsen

Amnesty and Reconciliation in Late Fifth-Century Athens:
The Rule of Law under Restored Democracy
Christopher J. Joyce

Visit the series web page at: edinburghuniversitypress.com/new-approaches-to-ancient-greek-institutional-history

Amnesty and Reconciliation in Late Fifth-Century Athens
The Rule of Law under Restored Democracy

Christopher J. Joyce

EDINBURGH
University Press

Edinburgh University Press is one of the leading university presses in the UK. We publish academic books and journals in our selected subject areas across the humanities and social sciences, combining cutting-edge scholarship with high editorial and production values to produce academic works of lasting importance. For more information visit our website: edinburghuniversitypress.com

© Christopher J. Joyce, 2022, 2024

Edinburgh University Press Ltd
The Tun – Holyrood Road
12(2f) Jackson's Entry
Edinburgh EH8 8PJ

First published in hardback by Edinburgh University Press 2022

Typeset in 11/13 Bembo Std by
IDSUK (DataConnection) Ltd

A CIP record for this book is available from the British Library

ISBN 978 1 3995 0634 2 (hardback)
ISBN 978 1 3995 0635 9 (paperback)
ISBN 978 1 3995 0636 6 (webready PDF)
ISBN 978 1 3995 0637 3 (epub)

The right of Christopher J. Joyce to be identified as the author of this work has been asserted in accordance with the Copyright, Designs and Patents Act 1988, and the Copyright and Related Rights Regulations 2003 (SI No. 2498).

Contents

Preface and Acknowledgements	vii
List of Abbreviations	x

1	**Introduction: The Athenian Reconciliation in Modern Scholarship**	1
	An Overview since Antiquity	3
	Democracy and Justice: The Athenian Reconciliation as a Moral Principle	12
	Sources and Methodology	20
	Structure and Outlay	29
2	**Civil Strife at Athens, 404–403**	38
	Athens on the Eve of the Thirty	40
	The Subversion of Democracy at Athens in Autumn 404	47
	The Reign of Terror	54
	The Victory of Thrasybulus and the Democrats	62
3	**Oaths and Covenants**	68
	The Athenian Reconciliation: Definitions and Chronology	69
	The Covenants of Reconciliation	75
4	**The Legal Scrutiny and the Resurrection of the Rule of Law**	90
	The Rule of Law: Its Definitions and Characteristics	93
	The Trial of Nicomachus, c. 399 (Lys. 30)	98
	The Amnesty and the Scrutiny of the Laws (And. 1.71–105)	107

5	**The Amnesty Applied (I): The Trials of Agoratus and Eratosthenes**	126
	The Trial of Agoratus, 402–398 (Lys. 13)	129
	The Trial of Eratosthenes, Late 403, or Possibly after 401 (Lys. 12)	142
6	**The Amnesty Applied (II): The Trials of Callimachus and Socrates**	158
	The Trial of Callimachus, 403–400 (Isoc. 18)	160
	The Trial of Socrates, 399 (Pl. *Ap.* with X. *Mem.*)	170
7	**The Athenian Reconciliation as the Paradigm for the Greek World in the Classical and Hellenistic Ages**	180
	The Meaning of μὴ μνησικακεῖν	183
	Legacy and Paradigm: Amnesty in the Classical and Hellenistic Ages	195
8	**The Rule of Law Restored: The Legacy of the Reconciliation in the Fourth Century**	205
	The Rule of Law in Action in the Fourth Century	207
	Conclusions	212

Bibliography	227
Index Locorum	244
Subject Index	250

Preface and Acknowledgements

What do we mean when we talk about amnesty? In the modern world, amnesty is understood as an initiative to reconcile two or more sides in a political conflict, where vindictive action for offences dating from an internal conflict is forbidden below a certain level. Since the Second World War, such conceptions of amnesty have been witnessed in West Germany, post-Apartheid South Africa and in the former Soviet satellite countries after the end of the Cold War. In all those examples, there was an injunction to make litigation against past offences inadmissible, excepting the most notorious and egregious crimes. In recent times, classical scholars have asked whether the modern paradigm finds a comparable example in Greek antiquity. The purpose of this study is to show that it does. In 404 BCE, the Athenian democracy was abolished and replaced by an oligarchy which ruled for eight months, leading to civil war and the eventual reassertion of democracy in 403. To reconcile the two warring sides, legal measures were required to ensure that Athens did not relapse into civil war, or *stasis*. The Treaty of Amnesty successfully banished civil war and ensured that the losing side would not be subject to recrimination at the hands of the victor. Recent efforts to deny that Athens measured up to the standards of amnesty which the modern world holds essential have, by that estimation, been flawed. The present study argues that the Athenian example of 403 was the paradigm not only for later amnesties in the ancient world, but also for modern amnesty agreements.

This study is the product of over ten years of separate, freestanding publications on the Athenian Reconciliation of 403. Most of my earlier articles addressed technical matters of legal and semantic interpretation. This study aims to understand events of that vital year in a broader historical setting. It begins with the circumstances which led to the overthrow of democracy in 404 and moves, in turn, to the oligarchy, the democratic resurgence of 403, the legal measures which put an end to civil conflict, and the trials which ensued. Whilst it has become current in some quarters to deny that Athenian democracy functioned according to the rule of law, this study shows that without the rule of law, the Athenian Reconciliation of 403 would not have been impossible but would have taken a very different course from the one it did. I have tried to consign disagreement to footnotes and, in the main body of my text, to present the arguments as lucidly, and with as little unpleasant polemical residue, as possible. Inevitably, some readers will take different theoretical approaches to ancient democracy and will disagree with many of my conclusions. Nevertheless, I make no apology for my own theoretical approach or for siding with scholars who see law and democracy as inextricably intertwined. The evidence on which modern reconstruction is grounded is often difficult and controversial, and my interpretation of it will by no means prove unassailable. Since 2008, when I first published on the Athenian Amnesty, my own views have, on several key details, shifted. As new evidence comes to light and as old ways of examining existing evidence come under review, my ideas will continue to transform. I have already had to admit fault in some of my earlier writing.

This study forms part of a series of New Institutionalist perspectives on Greek history, law and society. It belongs to a tradition of thinking originating with Douglas North, James March and Johan Olsen, which views institutions as mechanisms through which individual choices are influenced, regulated and channelled. Though New Institutionalism, as a theory, is broad and incorporates many different strands and variants, this study focuses on the role played by the democratic Athenian lawcourts in guaranteeing that political society in the aftermath of civil war and reconciliation could cohere. 'Forgetting the past' entailed much more than just a moral commitment to bear no grudges. The evidence for the years which followed the Reconciliation of 403 BCE shows that bitter feelings still ran deep, and that an emotional or ethical appeal to the goodwill of citizens to bury the hatchet would alone have been insufficient to constrain underlying vindictive feelings which, if left legally unchecked, would have plunged Athens into renewed internal conflict. The triumph of the Athenian Reconciliation Agreement was to ensure that the rule of law, enforced through the democratic courts, was reinstated after 403 and provided a secure and stable means to forestall potential backsliding into civil war.

My deepest gratitude is to Professor Edward Harris, without whose encouragement, advice, discussion, honesty and insight I would never have found the impetus or courage to write this book. I became acquainted with Edward some ten years ago, when I approached him for advice on the quoted decrees in Andocides' first speech *On the Mysteries*. Little did I know at the time that he was about to demolish the authenticity of all three inserted documents. These articles opened the road to a new and more coherent reading of

Andocides' self-defence and of the Amnesty itself. Intricate problems which for years had racked my brain vanished overnight. Since that time, Edward has become a close friend and ally, full of sage advice, a fountain of knowledge and expertise, and a reference point in all matters related to the classical world and beyond. In addition, I would like to thank Professor Peter Liddel, who read an earlier draft and who offered excellent advice and admonition; and Professor Mirko Canevaro and Dr David Lewis, who both steered me clear of many errors which I would, no doubt, have made without their scrupulous readings of earlier drafts. Acknowledgement is due to the anonymous referees for Edinburgh University Press, who identified areas where the initial draft had been defective. In addition, I would like to thank Dr Jane Burkowski for her committed work in helping me to prepare the final MS of this book for publication, without whose acute eye for detail innumerable errors and inconsistencies would have remained in the text. I would also like to thank Fiona Conn and Isobel Birks at Edinburgh University Press, the former for overseeing the proofreading process and for the efficiency with which she helped to iron over any remaining inconsistencies in the text, the latter for facilitating requested changes in the paperback edition.

Finally, it remains for me to acknowledge my wife, Sophia, for her patience with me during this lengthy process. Without her love and support, this book would not have seen the light of day. If my endeavours to comprehend the Athenian Reconciliation have been at all successful, success is due to the care and inspiration of all who have known me throughout the writing process. If they have been only partially successful, that is due, in totality, to my own failings and shortcomings.

Author's note to the second edition.

Since the release of the first (hardback) edition in October 2022, new bibliography has appeared, in response to which two short addenda have been added to Chapters 4 and 6. A small number of changes has been made to the wording of the text in places where I felt that changes were necessary, or where my original phraseology was, in retrospect, misleading; otherwise, this second edition is a near exact replica of the first.

Abbreviations

For ancient authors and their works, I follow the conventions of the LSJ. Modern journals and periodicals, where abbreviated, use the conventions laid out in *L'année philologique*. The text and notes contain other abbreviations when referring to volumes of published inscriptions and fragments of Greek historians, which are listed below for reference:

DK	*Die Fragmente der Vorsokratiker*, ed. H.A. Diels, W. Kranz, 5th ed. Berlin, 1934–7
FGrHist	*Die Fragmente der griechischen Historiker*, ed. F. Jacoby, Berlin–Leiden, 1923–58.
IC IV	*Inscriptiones Creticae*, ed. M. Guarducci, Vol. 4, *Tituli Gortynii*. Rome, 1950.
IEleusis	*Eleusis: The Inscriptions on Stone. Documents of the Sanctuary of the Two Goddesses and Public Documents of the Deme*, 2 vols in 3 parts, ed. K. Clinton, Athens, 2005–8.
IG I²	*Inscriptiones Graecae, I: Inscriptiones Atticae Euclidis anno (403/2) anteriores*, 2nd ed., F. Hiller von Gaertringen, Berlin, 1924.
IG I³	*Inscriptiones Graecae, I3: Inscriptiones Atticae Euclidis anno anteriores 3, Fasc. I*, ed. D. M. Lewis, Berlin, 1981.
IG II²	*Inscriptiones Graecae II et III: Inscriptiones Atticae Euclidis anno (403/2) posteriores*, 2nd ed., parts I–III, ed. J. Kirchner, Berlin, 1913–1940.

IG II³	*Inscriptiones Atticae Euclidis anno posteriores 3, I: Leges et decreta. Fasc. 2: Leges et decreta annorum 352/1–322/1*, ed. S. D. Lambert, Berlin, 2012.
IG XII, 2	*Inscriptiones Graecae, XII: Inscriptiones insularum maris Aegaei praeter Delum, 2. Inscriptiones Lesbi, Nesi, Tenedi*, ed. A. W. Paton, Berlin, 1909.
IG XII, 5	*Inscriptiones Graecae, XII: Inscriptiones Cycladum, 5, I–II*, ed. F. Hiller von Gaertringen, Berlin, 1903–9.
IG XII, 8	*Inscriptiones Graecae XII 8: Inscriptiones insularum maris Thracici*, ed. Carl Friedrich, Berlin, 1909.
I.Magnesia am Sipylos	*Die Inschriften von Magnesia am Sipylos*, ed. T. Ihnken, Bonn, 1978.
Inscr. Eryth.	*Die Inschriften von Erythrai und Klazomenai*, 2 vols, ed. H. Engelmann and R. Merkelbach, Bonn, 1972–3.
IPArk	*Prozessrechtliche Inschriften der griechischen Poleis: Arkadien*, ed. G. Thür, H. Täuber, Vienna, 1994.
ML	*Selection of Greek Historical Inscriptions to the End of Fifth Century B.C.*, ed. R. Meiggs, D. M. Lewis, Oxford, 1969, 2nd ed. 1988.
Michel	*Recueil d'inscriptions grecques*, ed. C. Michel, Brussels, 1900.
Milet I	*Inschriften von Milet*, 1, ed. A. Rehm and P. Hermann, Berlin and New York, 1997.
*OCD*⁴	*Oxford Classical Dictionary*, ed. T. Whitmarsh and S. Goldberg, 4th ed., Oxford, 2012.
OGIS	*Orientis Graecae inscriptiones selectae*, ed. W. Dittenberger, Leipzig, 1903–5.
RO	*Greek Historical Inscriptions 404–323 BC*, ed. P. J. Rhodes, R. Osborne, Oxford, 2003.
SEG	*Supplementum Epigraphicum Graecum* (1923-present). Leiden (until 1971), Aalpen aan den Rijn and Germantown, MD (since 1979).
*Syll.*³	*Sylloge Inscriptionum Graecarum*, ed. W. Dittenberger (ed. F. Hiller von Gaertringen, J. Kirchner, H.R. Pomtow, E. Ziebarth, 4 vols, Leipzig, 3rd ed.,1915–1924.

When referring to Greek authors and historical figures, I have used Latinised names (e.g. Isocrates, not Isokrates; Pericles, not Perikles) throughout. Key words transliterated from the Greek (e.g. *polis, stasis*) are always italicised. When transliterating a Greek word, I have followed the closest natural equivalent in English (e.g. *dokimasia*, not *docimasia*; but *echthros*, not *ekhthros*).

For Sophia, and for all my pupils, past and present

CHAPTER I

Introduction: The Athenian Reconciliation in Modern Scholarship

The Athenian Reconciliation of 403 BCE is one of the most complex and disputed episodes from Greek history. Contracted following a desultory civil war, when Athens had been split between supporters of democracy and oligarchy, the purpose of the Reconciliation Agreement was to rebuild the city and reunite the citizenry. To accomplish that end, legal measures needed to be put in place to guarantee peace. But how far it was effective, and what precisely it sought to achieve, are matters upon which modern scholarship remains sharply divided. Much of the difficulty lies in the source material, often contradictory and unreliable. Scholarship moreover has reached no consensus as to what democracy in ancient Athens was or why the legislators of 403 decided to revive democracy, when other forms of government were available. Besides reconciling the citizens, the commissioners of 403 redevised the democratic constitution. As the evidence for the Athenian Reconciliation Agreement of 403 is scattered, there is never going to be agreement over every one of its details. One of the chief objectives of this study is to show that the period of recovery from the brutal and divisive civil war which followed Athens' defeat in the Peloponnesian War (431–404) was expertly overseen and managed, resulting in a community which was coherent, workable, lawful and democratic. The revival of democracy in 403 was possible only because Athenians were willing to bury the past. This entailed more than a moral commitment: the pledge 'not to revisit past grievance', in Greek μὴ μνησικακεῖν, was a legal commitment not to prosecute in court crimes committed before 12 Boedromion 403, the date of the treaty to which both sides swore. Though a superficial reading of the orators might give rise to the impression that the Oath of Reconciliation was not adhered to in earnest, a more careful analysis will show that its terms were carefully laid out and strictly applied thereafter. Athens reconciled in 403, and the spectre of civil war which could have resurfaced in the years that followed never reared its head again until the Macedonian involvement towards the end of the fourth century when, in the wake of the Lamian War, Athens experienced revolutions and *stasis* owing to foreign intervention.

This is a study of the Athenian Reconciliation Agreement. It begins with the events which led to the overthrow of democracy in autumn 404, when Athens capitulated to Sparta after twenty-seven years of exhausting conflict in what has come to be widely known as the Peloponnesian War (431–404). This disastrous war meant that Athens tore down her walls and accepted a Spartan-backed junta of thirty men, known in subsequent historiography as 'the Thirty Tyrants', or more simply, 'the Thirty'. When installed in power, these oligarchs embarked on a reign of terror which lasted some eight months before democracy was restored in the summer of 403. Modern estimates have put the death toll somewhere around 5 per cent of the total population, but that can only be a rough guess. When democracy was restored, the legislators faced the dual task of restoring the rule of law and ensuring that Athens would not revert to a state of incessant civil conflict provoked by the memory of what had taken place in the months preceding. This meant, above all, that a statute of limitations was required barring litigation for any untried offences which predated the democratic restoration. As experience from modern times has shown, such measures are never easy to put into effect, and the test of a durable system is whether it can resist the tendency to backslide into civil conflict. Some cities in the ancient Greek world went so far as to institute cults of *Homonoia* (literally, 'like-mindedness') to enforce a sense of social cohesion among their citizens in the aftermath of a conflict. Athens, however, never went that far, and the evidence of the orators shows that despite the measures put in place to prevent a re-escalation of civil war, feelings of resentment seethed beneath the surface. As far as we can tell, there were no legal prohibitions to resentful grudges; the oath 'not to vent grudges' was a promise not to deny that vendettas existed, but rather not to use the courtroom as a battleground to carry out those vendettas. This is to be understood in the light of what had happened in the period leading up to the defeat of 404, when for some three decades the authority of the courts had been abused by politicians for sycophantic goals, as well as in the light of what took place subsequently under the Thirty, when in retaliation the authority of the courts was completely subverted. To restore the rule of law in 403, the victorious democrats had to guarantee against two principal tendencies, on one side the abuse of the courts to vent personal or political feuds, and on the other the unaccountability of public officials which had resulted from the suppression of the courts under the Thirty. The juggling act was therefore to restore the authority of the courts to bring public officials to account and to guarantee that courts would serve a legal, rather than a political, principle.

Studies to date of the Reconciliation of 403 have varied between those which have recognised the rule of law in operation from 403 and those which have not. The present study is written in the conviction that the rule of law was not only a reality at Athens, but the key ingredient which allowed democracy to function at all. For a democratic system to be under the rule of law, four essential criteria are required. First, there needs to be equality before the law.[1] Secondly, public officials need to be accountable.[2] Thirdly, the laws must be applied in the courts, and court verdicts must turn on legal principle.[3] Fourth, decisions must be made according to a system of fixed rules.[4] These criteria will be explored in greater detail in the pages that follow.[5] In brief, restoring democracy in 403 was about restoring the sovereignty of the courts and the rule of law. But, before launching into the main body of the argument, it will be worth surveying modern scholarly treatments of the Reconciliation, if only to draw points of similarity and contrast between this and previous treatments. In so doing, this chapter falls in two initial parts, one of which surveys modern scholarship on the Athenian Amnesty, and the second of which makes some more general remarks on prevailing intellectual themes which have surfaced over the past forty years in discussion. The final two sections discuss issues of methodology and source material, as well as the prevailing themes with which the study deals.

AN OVERVIEW SINCE ANTIQUITY

The Reconciliation Agreement which ended the bitter civil conflict at Athens in 403 has been the subject of a long-standing discussion since classical antiquity. Terminological problems, which will be treated more comprehensively in Chapter 3, have often bedevilled discussion. In modern times, various terminologies have been used to refer to the process by which the democracy of Athens was restored after the expulsion of the Spartan-backed oligarchy,

---

[1] Dicey 1885; Bingham 2010: 55–9; Harris 2013: 5.
[2] As defined by the World Justice Project at http://www.worldjusticeproject.org; see also Harris 2013: 6. For examples of this principle in action in Athens in the fourth century, see Aeschin. 3.12–27; *Ath. Pol.* 48.4–5. For a list of generals and politicians in the fourth century held to account and convicted, see Hansen 1975: 60.
[3] Bingham 2010: 90–109. For a more complete discussion of the Judicial Oath and its reconstruction from ancient sources, see Harris 2013: 101–37.
[4] Bingham 2010: 73; Raz 1977: 198–9; Harris 2013: 9–10. The principle that laws could not apply retroactively is recognised at D. 24.43. The principle that officials could only use written laws is articulated at And. 1.87.
[5] For a broader overview and discussion of the operation of the rule of law in the Greek city states, see Canevaro 2017.

which came to power eight months earlier on the back of defeat at the end of the Peloponnesian War. Those have included concepts and phrases such as 'amnesty', 'restoration', 'reconciliation', 'treaty', 'peace agreement', 'democratic resurgence', to name but a few. All the above overlap in their implications, but they are potentially misleading nonetheless, because each presupposes a theory as to what the historical processes were which led to the ending of civil conflict and re-establishment of democratic government at Athens. To call it an amnesty would be to imply that the only point that mattered was to reunite two sides of a civil war, but as we will see, the accounts illustrate that much more was entailed. A restoration implies a return to a *status quo ante*, but there is widespread disagreement about the relationship of the restored democracy of 403 to the one which had fallen a year earlier, in 404. Reconciliation could imply a standpoint of equality between two negotiating sides in a conflict which had ended inconclusively, and there is ongoing disagreement as to whether the events of 403 can be characterised purely in terms of horse-trading between two ends of a bargaining table, bartering an agreement based upon equality of power relationship. A treaty implies a legal ratification, upon which not all scholars agree. The meaning of a peace agreement is often vague, as this could simply imply that the two sides swore to lay down arms, without further undertakings as to how the peace was to be enforced in law. To call it a democratic resurgence could imply that no concessions were made to erstwhile oligarchs, or that those who had taken the winning side were now free in practice, if not in law, to pursue retaliatory actions in the courts. All those approaches would be mistaken. The terms in which the legal process which ended civil war in 403 was described at Athens will be surveyed more extensively in Chapter 3. Suffice it for now to use the modern terms 'reconciliation' and 'amnesty', even though these terminologies entail slippage and must be applied with an awareness of their potentials for misrepresentation and misunderstanding.

Discussion should begin with a famous remark of the Roman orator Cicero, who four hundred years after the event described the Athenian Reconciliation Agreement as the *Atheniensium vetus exemplum* (Cic. Phil. 1.1.1). Cicero lived through two brutal civil wars and, towards the end of his life, grew increasingly anxious about Rome's prospects of survival as a unified and lawful society. The harking back to Athens at the start of his *First Philippic* reveals something crucial about how the events of 403 were perceived in subsequent antiquity: this was not just a makeshift bargain, backed up by force, but a conscientious effort to reconcile a bitterly divided political community on a principle of law and justice. If Rome could enact that example for itself, the dying Republic might stand a chance. The historical context in which Cicero recalls the Athenian Reconciliation is here significant because he implicitly identifies the events of 403 with the restoration of legality. Modern scholars of Athens, especially in the English-speaking world, have furiously debated whether Athens possessed anything to compare with what in modern times, since the European Enlightenment, could be characterised as a society presided over by legal principle, rather than just mob rule. Though this debate goes back to Greek antiquity, noteworthy is that in fifth- and fourth-century Athens, those who liked to lambast democracy as 'ochlocracy', or the 'rule of the mob', often tended to be oligarchic polemicists whose accounts were slanted, and thus unreliable.[6] If Cicero's opinion is taken at face value, such an approach would be mistaken. Nonetheless, it has become increasingly common in recent times to claim that Cicero was merely romanticising about a golden past which he did not fully understand, and whose details had become obscured in the mists of time. That current of scepticism goes hand in hand with a tendency to downgrade Athenian democracy as a lawful institution and, indeed, the Reconciliation as a moral commitment.

Scholarship on the Athenian Reconciliation begins in the middle of the nineteenth century. Before the discovery of the Aristotelian *Athenaiôn Politeia* (from now on referred to by its abbreviation, the *Ath. Pol.*) on papyrus scrolls, discussion of the Amnesty was limited to the evidence provided by ancient historians, such as Xenophon, Diodorus (drawing on Ephorus) and Justin's epitome of Trogus, and the Attic orators. Scholars of the nineteenth century were understandably mystified as to when the Reconciliation occurred, because the evidence available to them was so conflicted. Knowing nothing of the Covenants of Reconciliation spelled out at *Ath. Pol.* 39, R. Großer predicted accurately that the lacunose and sketchy narrative of Xenophon, which mentions an Oath of Reconciliation between Athens and the oligarchic enclave at Eleusis in 401 but nothing of a treaty in 403, had severely abridged events, and that a reconciliation agreement must have been sworn by the two sides in 403, not least because the orator Andocides refers to one in the speech *On the Mysteries* (on this, see Chapter 4). Against Großer, the Xenophontine version won favour with J. Luebbert, who argued that there was no general amnesty in 403 and that Andocides referred to events of 401.[7] The difficulty for the nineteenth century is that it possessed no ancient document upon which to reconstruct a reliable narrative of the Amnesty. Without the account of *Ath. Pol.* 39, which scholars since have regarded to be authoritative, the matter of when the Amnesty took place or what it contained could only have been a matter of speculation. The discovery of the *Ath. Pol.* in the last decade of the nineteenth century was therefore paradigm-shifting.

---

[6] For a modern discussion of oligarchic dissent at Athens in the fifth and fourth centuries, see Ober 1998. Ober's treatment has the merit of covering a wide range of oligarchic literature, but his view of Athenian democracy as a conversation between 'mass' and 'elite' is often based on the biased views of these self-same oligarchs. For a critique, see Harris 2000 and 2005b.
[7] Großer 1868; Luebbert 1881.

Writing some twenty-five years after the first edition of the *Ath. Pol.*, P. Cloché argued that the success of the Reconciliation lay not with the democratic resurgence but with the moderate oligarchs, whom he identified with the City Party, and sought to reconcile the evidence by claiming that though there was an effort in 403 to bring the factions together, the actual Decree of Amnesty did not take place until 401, when the oligarchic enclave at Eleusis was finally dissolved. Cloché's view was challenged by A. Dorjahn, who discounted the notion that the oath came about by decree and preferred instead to speak of μὴ μνησικακεῖν as a moral commitment which never found official legal expression, but which carried the same force as law. In contrast to Cloché, Dorjahn understood the commitment not to dredge up the past in terms of 'political forgiveness' whereby one side in a former conflict pledged to 'forgive' the other and let bygones be bygones.[8] The idea of forgiveness is always difficult. In a moral sense, to forgive an enemy is to relinquish all claim to retribution for a crime committed in the past. More recently, scholars have even debated how far it is appropriate to attribute to the ancient world the modern idea of forgiveness, but what is clear from the orators is that anger over what had happened in the past was sharp in the years which followed the conclusion of the Amnesty.[9] If the Oaths of Reconciliation demanded forgiveness, it was only in the narrow sense that legal recrimination for acts committed prior to 403 was blocked in the courts. Nevertheless, feelings of hatred and recrimination continued to bubble beneath the surface, and the trials which followed on from the Amnesty illustrate that no quantity of legislation could ever banish those emotions. Some scholars more recently still have suggested that the moral prohibition on retaliation was never fully developed in Greek popular morality and that vengeance was seen to be a noble motive.[10] I argue in Chapter 7 that such an approach is problematic and ignores evidence that in the moral sensibilities of Greeks, vengeful retaliation was reckoned ignoble.[11]

T. C. Loening understood μὴ μνησικακεῖν as a legal term which prohibited action in a court of law for earlier offences and, pointing out that the oath expressly provided against frivolous litigation, argued against any formal covenant which spelled out the rule. Loening's study was an important milestone in the modern historiography surrounding the Amnesty of 403, and his insight into μὴ μνησικακεῖν as a ban on vexatious litigation in the courts remains fundamental. Democracy is often taken for granted, but what it was and how the process of legal redaction which followed on from the Amnesty related to the Amnesty itself are matters which do not have an easy resolution. Yet respect

---

[8] Cloché 1915; Dorjahn 1946.
[9] See Konstan 2010; Cairns 2011.
[10] See Chaniotis 2013, with the discussion in Chapter 7.
[11] Thus Harris 2017.

is due to his analysis of the Covenants of Amnesty, which, though incorrect in various details, was insightful and illuminating.[12] The key to reading the Amnesty Agreement was to understand it in its legal parameters. Placing a priority on the account of *Ath. Pol.*, Loening carefully analysed every clause which can be reconstructed from chapter 39, elaborating and improving upon the older, outdated commentary of Cloché, whose reconstruction of the terms was at times questionable. Unlike Cloché, Loening showed that the treaty cited at *Ath. Pol.* 39 derived from a single document. The purpose of the Amnesty Treaty was to guarantee a peaceful relationship between the restored democracy at Athens and the oligarchic enclave at Eleusis and to iron out difficult legal matters involving access to the homicide courts and to the Eleusinian cult. Loening saw the treaty of 403 as a deal or contract between two sides, bargained from a standpoint of pragmatism so that Athens and Eleusis could coexist side by side without war resurfacing. Though reserved on the question of its moral significance, his study has become the textbook for the 403 Amnesty.

Since Loening, scholars have contested the scope and intent of the Athenian Amnesty. Claiming that the courts in democratic Athens operated as battlegrounds for feuding political rivals, S. C. Todd has argued that whilst the oath formally forbade offences committed in the time of civil conflict, political show trials rapidly ensued which violated the spirit of the oath, and which were allowed to take place while Sparta occupied its attention elsewhere.[13] Others have focused on μὴ μνησικακεῖν as an ideological commitment which sought to enshrine the idea, fictitious in origin, that the triumph of democracy was the triumph of the whole of the *dêmos*, sweeping under the carpet the unpleasant reality that oligarchy had its adherents among the citizenry. N. Loraux understood μὴ μνησικακεῖν to imply an attitude of oblivion to the past which, since Homeric times, was essential to the cohesion of society and which granted forgiveness for offences committed before the Amnesty.[14] From different angles, A. Wolpert and J. L. Shear have argued that, within the prevailing ideology of the restored democracy, blame was attributed to a small and defined group of outstanding criminals who did not come to terms and that a blame culture was, paradoxically, avoided by heaping blame on a small group of miscreants. Consequently, the only people who committed 'wrong' in the eyes of the restored democracy were the Thirty and their immediate cohorts who were not covered.[15]

Over the past thirty years, the emphasis of scholarship has been away from the idea of political 'forgiveness' and has embraced the idea that the Amnesty

---

[12] Loening 1987.
[13] Todd 1996.
[14] Loraux 1997.
[15] Wolpert 2002; Shear (J. L.) 2011: 295–301.

was a contract between two sides in the interest of restoring political stability, leaving aside whether there was a moral principle at stake. That approach has been canvassed by E. Carawan, who takes to an extreme the idea that the Amnesty of 403 was purely contractual and disengages from any consideration of its underlying moral principles. Questioning the authority of the Aristotelian tradition, Carawan argues that the Covenants of Reconciliation came about in two separate packages, one in 403, the other in 401, and divides the terms between those sworn with Eleusis in 403 and those sworn at Athens in 401. According to his view, the account of *Ath. Pol.* 39 is unreliable and presents an amalgamation of two individual treaties concluded at different times, between different signatories. Most significantly, he seeks to disengage the amnesty treaty of 403 from received notions of 'political forgiveness' and argues that as a legislative measure, its use and scope was limited to a group of written covenants (συνθῆκαι), which the Oath of Reconciliation embodied and the phrase μὴ μνησικακεῖν simply reinforced. This was by no means a universal amnesty, and thus should be understood not in the Ciceronian sense of *oblivio*, but as a tightly controlled measure to reconcile opposing sides under a limited set of terms. The scrutiny of the laws which followed was the mechanism by which the terms of amnesty were translated into law.[16] Carawan's approach to the Athenian Amnesty is in keeping with more recent trends which have made similar claims about the practice and application of amnesty in other portions of the Greek world.[17] The thrust of recent scholarship has been to challenge the idea that the practical application of amnesty in the ancient world in any real sense amounted to *Staatsnormalisierung*, or a turning back of the clock, which resulted in the reinstatement of affairs prior to a given conflict. Amnesty was simply a bargain, an exchange of agreements between two sides which may, in some cases, have brought about a lasting reconciliation, but which in many others asserted partisan political dominance.

The approach is in evidence in studies of amnesty agreements elsewhere in the Greek world in the classical and Hellenistic periods. In a survey of amnesties dating from archaic times to the end of the fourth century, M. Dreher has pointed to a tendency not to bring about reconciliation and argues that in some notorious cases, amnesty was a politically weighted mechanism which promoted a staunchly partisan interest.[18] L. Rubinstein makes similar observations in

---

[16] Carawan 2002; 2012; 2013; *contra* Joyce 2008; 2014; 2016.

[17] See, for example, Thür *RE* (2) 1997: col. 215 s.v. Amnestia: 'Gesetzmässig festgesetzter Verzicht auf Anklage, Wiederaufnahme von Verfahren, Urteils-vollstreckung und Strafvollzug als Mittel, die streitenden Parteien nach internen oder externen Krisen zu versöhnen.' Implicit in this definition is the claim that amnesty measures are there to alleviate crisis and to bring about reconciliation.

[18] Dreher 2013.

respect of amnesty measures in the Hellenistic period, where often larger power structures interfered in the internal affairs of cities and enforced the claims of one party or grouping for reasons of self-interest.[19] From a different angle, but with overlapping implications, C. La'da has argued that, whilst often a means of reconciliation, amnesty in Ptolemaic Egypt was not so much a peace deal between competing factions as an act of grace bestowed by royal edict, and the concentration of amnesties toward the close of the Ptolemaic dynasty might indicate the ineffectiveness of the central power to restore law and order locally.[20] From a different angle, the most recent treatment of *stasis* and its resolution by H. Börm has argued that, in the Hellenistic age, and down until the time of Augustus, civil conflict in Greece was structurally recurrent in the Greek cities, that, far from being occasional or incidental, *stasis* is what defines and drives the history of the city states of the mainland and beyond. His study envisions *stasis* almost exclusively in terms of the self-interested political agency of conflicting elite groups, interpreting the political grounds for *stasis* and reconciliation purely in utilitarian terms, as the result of elite competition for power and prominence, and therefore bracketing out any reference to higher moral principle and to competing conceptions of the requirements for a functioning political community.[21] Though their perspectives are different, these studies analyse amnesty agreements in terms of their practical function, placing a greater degree of consideration on the utilitarian question of how *stasis* should be remedied and resolved than upon the moral and political principles which those contractual agreements sought to enshrine. To follow that line, amnesty in the ancient world was less a principled enactment, designed to uphold and guarantee a set of normative political ends, and more an instrument of utility serving, above all else, survivalist objectives.

Other approaches, while not entirely disengaging from the issue of moral principle, are nevertheless heavily influenced by this line of argument. B. Gray, for instance, envisions two alternative models of reconciliation in the aftermath of *stasis*: one (the 'Nakonian' one) concerned with the actual pacification and reintegration of the community; the other (the 'Dikaiopolitan' one), in line with the recent trends I have described, a utilitarian measure designed to secure the survival of a community through bargaining and contractually accommodating conflicting interests.[22] F. Carugati analyses the collapse and overthrow of democracy in 404 in terms of a 'crisis of legitimacy rooted in the Assembly's inability to credibly commit to policy'.[23] According

---

[19] Rubinstein 2013; 2018; 2023 (to the last of which I respond on p. 179).
[20] La'da 2013.
[21] Börm 2019. For a summary and review of Börm's recent monograph, see Fabiani 2021.
[22] Gray 2015.
[23] Carugati 2019. For a detailed critique of her analysis, see Harris 2022.

to her view, the rise of the Thirty in 404 was an incidental consequence of two major political mistakes made in the final decades of the fifth century, the execution of the inhabitants of Mytilene in 427 by popular decree (Th. 3.36–49) and the trial *in absentia* of the Arginusae generals in 406 (X. *HG* 1.6.27–7.35). In both episodes, the Athenian people underwent a *volte-face* of policy. Carugati uses these test cases to argue that Athenian democracy was unable in the fifth century to hold its nerve in political decision-making and was characterised by institutional and legal instability. This basic instability – and the corresponding desire for more stable and reliable political decision-making – was at the basis of the support gained by the oligarchic solution towards the end of the century. And, accordingly, the Reconciliation Agreement and the restored democracy were primarily concerned with securing the survival of the city through providing a more stable and viable system of democratic decision-making.

It would be tempting in the light of this paradigm shift to argue that the Reconciliation Treaty of 403 at Athens was something less than a measure of annulment. It cannot be denied that many so-called 'amnesties' in the ancient world did not live up to the modern expectation of political forgiveness, but care should nonetheless be taken not to overstate the point. Due consideration of the Athenian Amnesty and its application shows that even if Greeks did not understand forgiveness as a moral concept in the post-Christian sense, the legislators of 403 put measures in place which made it impossible to pursue in the courts any but the most egregious criminals of the former oligarchy. Objections that the Athenian Amnesty was not about political principle are in fact aligned with wider claims that the democracy which the Amnesty revived was, in origin, also fundamentally an unprincipled and lawless institution which was not founded on values such as liberty, equality, justice (akin to modern liberal values), and which did not understand or enforce anything akin to a modern understanding of the rule of law.[24] Because of institutional estrangement from liberal norms, Athenian democracy was therefore incapable of framing itself in moral language or in terms of the rule of law. To argue thus is to make prior assumptions and claims about what democracy in the ancient sense was. If, on the other hand, democracy in the ancient world enshrined law and justice, the revival of democracy in 403 must have been

---

[24] The treatment of ancient democracy as 'pre-liberal' goes back to B. Constant and A. de Tocqueville in the early nineteenth century; see Constant 1819; Tocqueville 1835–40. For a discussion of the influence of de Tocqueville's ideas, see Blaug and Schwarzmantel 2004. For the claim that modern paradigms fail as useful points of comparison for ancient institutions, see Rawls 1971; Finley 1973; Ober 2017.

driven by a desire to restore a law-abiding regime which respected law and justice.

Increasingly, however, this is being denied. A good example of the entanglement of interpretations of the Reconciliation Agreement in purely transactional, 'survivalist' and utilitarian terms with wider approaches to Athenian democracy that underplay its commitment to the rule of law can be found in the work of A. Lanni, which describes the Reconciliation in morally neutral language, avoiding any claim that the democratic restoration was about political principle. Lanni presents as a case study of political amnesty in the ancient world the trials which took place in the wake of the Amnesty, claiming that political forgiveness to which they collectively allude in the Treaty of Reconciliation represents a trumped-up ideology geared at fostering an illusion of unity and togetherness in the aftermath of the Reconciliation. She starts from the position that the treaty of 403 which heralded in the democratic restoration was forged on a principle of raw utility, and that it is mistaken even to think of a democratic favour, which was an *ex post facto* concoction. The impression of a democratic favour and a principled act of benefaction from one side to the other is nothing more than sentimentalised fiction at a time when Athenians needed to do all in their power to forget past strife and join shoulders against a common menace.[25] Lanni eschews any normative understanding of the Athenian democracy and appears to treat it as a brute fact, lacking justification beyond survival, not a political and constitutional system which enshrined moral norms and values which were preferable to those of oligarchy or other non-democratic alternatives. Such an approach holds that the restored democracy eradicated division after the fall of the Thirty and Ten but speaks of 'selective and exemplary' punishment, as if the limits set down by law as to who was really covered under the terms of the Amnesty were blurred. This was necessary to ensure that 'the flexibility of the Athenian legal system mitigated tension between ordinary, rule-of-law justice and expedient political settlement', so that the trials which came after the Amnesty were less about legal principle than about expediency.[26] Lanni confesses as a point of doctrine that there was no rule of law and that the trials of Eratosthenes and Agoratus belong to a heritage of sycophancy which the Amnesty did little to remedy. This is to believe that ancient democracy had no moral value and that it is futile to see the Amnesty in moral terms, despite the encomiastic attitudes of later antiquity.

---

[25] Lanni 2010. For a more complete expression of the doctrine that rule of law was absent from Athens, see Lanni 2016, which fails to take adequate account of ancient sources which show that the rule of law was important; see (e.g.) S. *OC* 913–19; Th. 2.37; Lys. 2.19; D. 24.215–16; Aeschin. 1.179; 3.6.

[26] Lanni 2010: 589–90. Lanni's effort to downplay the principled character of the Amnesty influences both Carawan (2013) and Carugati (2019).

DEMOCRACY AND JUSTICE: THE ATHENIAN RECONCILIATION AS A MORAL PRINCIPLE

One of the key points of dispute is whether we should interpret the rationale of given arrangements and institutional set-ups, and the motivations of the agents that brought them about, in purely utilitarian terms or rather as aimed at actualising higher political principles.[27] Beyond the brute question of survival, democrats in Athens were committed to ideals of justice, rule of law, political stability, banishment of feuding, the right of all citizens to a fair trial and equal participation in the share of government, which, regardless of whether Athens was placed in a stronger position to ward off internal and external threats to its survival thereby, were from a *normative* standpoint considered to be desirable, and which made democracy preferable to other systems of government which did not guarantee those ideals.[28] There was nothing in antiquity that corresponded to a modern Bill of Rights. Ancient societies took no objection to the appalling practice of slavery which was integral to their economic efflorescence.[29] But whilst it is true that the idea of inalienable human rights was lacking, what is also clear is that ancient democracies, with Athens in the vanguard, had a refined understanding of citizen rights which they expressed as a key component of their ideologies and conscientiously applied to practice. The terms in which ancient authors spoke of democracy, from the start, show that principle was important.

In Book 3 of the *Histories*, Herodotus refers to a debate between three Persian notables over which type of government – democracy, oligarchy or kingship – was the most desirable (Hdt. 3.80–3). Most scholars regard the debate as fictitious, but whether it took place or not, it illustrates crucially that ancient discussion over which political system was the most suitable did not operate in some moral vacuum. Otanes, the proponent of democracy, begins by proclaiming that monarchy is 'neither pleasant nor good' (οὔτε γὰρ ἡδὺ οὔτε ἀγαθόν). To put the matter thus is already to transcend the mere question of utility. Cambyses was not a desirable ruler, not because Persia could not survive under monarchy, but because Cambyses' behaviour was arrogant and morally reprehensible. Cambyses possesses insolence (ὕβρις), which in combination with absolute power breeds within him extreme evil. In contrast,

---

[27] For a recent critique of some modern utilitarian conceptions of political motivation, see Cairns et al. 2022.

[28] For a full discussion of these ideals and how Athenian democracy sought to enshrine them, see Harris 2013, whose arguments I develop further in the following chapters. The Amnesty of 403 can only be understood properly against the backdrop of a society which recognised and respected rule of law as a cardinal feature of the restored democracy.

[29] See Lewis 2018; Porter 2019. Porter argues that slavery did much more than enable Athenians to 'get by'; for their economy to grow, slaves were essential, especially in the silver mines.

equality before the law (ἰσονομίη) is the finest of all political systems, because it does none of the things which a monarch does. Otanes proceeds then to describe the components of democracy, which include sortition, accountability and public deliberation. Notable about the argument proposed is that the question of survival does not enter the equation. Democracy is preferable to its non-democratic rivals not because it has a better survival prospect, but because morally speaking, it was considered far superior and preferable. The first known political tract from the ancient world to discuss the merits and demerits of different types of government uses moral language to anchor its claims. This must warn against modern efforts to underplay normative concerns and overplay utilitarian self-interest in explaining political action, and, most of all, democratic political action.[30]

To reduce the rationale of (and motivations behind) the Reconciliation Agreement and the restoration of democracy to utilitarian considerations of mere survival is to misrepresent what was attempted and achieved. The commissioners of 403 achieved far more than the appeasement of two sides in a civil war, not that appeasement as a goal is to be underestimated. If the one and only aim in 403 had been to achieve political stability, there is no obvious reason why democracy should have been preferred over any other form of government. The resuscitation of democracy after the disruptive and bloody period of the oligarchy in 404/3 was due to a recognition that higher principles were in the scales, which entailed above all the re-establishment of justice and the rule of law, which in the dark days of the Thirty Tyrants had fallen by the wayside. This – from the point of view of the democrats – would have been impossible under any other form of government. Once the legislators had drafted a treaty to which Athenians swore, the next test was to build a society which recognised the rule of law as the guarantor of everything which democracy upheld, including legal justice, equality, freedom and universal participation in the political process (though only, of course, among the male citizenry) regardless of status, wealth, position, education or social influence. The fact that the practice and application of democracy at Athens preceded the formulation of a written democratic tract or theory is of far less importance than scholars in the past have made out.[31] Unlike modern democracies

---

[30] For further discussion and debate, see Miller 2019; Cammack 2019b; Mansbridge 2019; McCormick 2019; Urbinati 2019; Ober 2019.

[31] For the view that the absence of a counterweight democratic apology, balancing out the oligarchic theories of pseudo-Xenophon in the theoretical literature, signals a bias among literate Athenians towards anti-democratic systems, see Ober 1989 and 1998. As argued in Chapter 2, such an approach underestimates the degree of support which democracy had from much of the wealthy elite and, conversely, the degree to which oligarchic systems could draw upon the support and political sustenance of the poorer members of society.

which drew on theoretical literature from the seventeenth and eighteenth centuries, the Athenian democracy did not appeal to a written tract in which its principles and ideals were formulated. But that does not mean that it had no underlying moral and political principles that were enshrined in its institutions.

Even though Athenians did not, as far as we know, refer to a tract comparable to the American Declaration of Independence, which expressly stated and laid out the purposes for which their democracy was founded, nevertheless their democratic literature is infused with abundant reference to political and moral principle.[32] In the Funeral Oration put by Thucydides into the mouth of the Athenian statesman Pericles, the beauty of Athens' political heritage was that it spoke of equality before the law, included all citizens in the deliberative process regardless of wealth or status, and engendered respect for law, officials and customs (Th. 2.37).[33] In the *Suppliant Women* by Euripides, king Theseus eulogises the virtues of democracy, which include equality in the political process, equal access to the courts and the freedom to speak one's own mind (E. *Supp.* 404–7, 433–41).[34] Even Plato's *Republic*, often seen as an anti-democratic tract, speaks of democracy as a pleasant thing, with a superabundance of liberty (Pl. *R.* 8.557a–d, 562a–d).[35] Later in the century, Aeschines reminded the judges that democracy embraces equality and the law (Aeschin. 1.5).

The arguments for democracy proceeded from the question of principle, which is why Aristotle later in the fourth century pitted the question of what was natural against what was virtuous. Yet, it would be misleading to claim that the values proclaimed by democracy were unique to democracy.[36] As P. A. Cartledge has pointed out, at Sparta citizens were called *homoioi*, or 'equals', even if Sparta lacked any of the egalitarian principles upon which Athens was founded.[37] As other scholars have observed, Athenians valued equality of political privileges, *isonomia* ('equality before the law'), *isêgoria* ('equality of speech') and *isogonia* ('equality of birth').[38] These were all principles which recommended themselves upon their own merits, not upon the question of whether a community which practised and reified those values was better at surviving than one which did not. M. H. Hansen has emphasised a considerable degree

---

[32] For the view that Athenians did not need to refer to such a document, see Brock 1991: 169.

[33] See Loraux 1986; Samons 2004: 55–7 and 187–95. Th. 2.37.1 has often been interpreted to entail a critique of democracy by rotation; see most recently Mitchell 2019. But this misinterpretation rests on a mistranslation by Rhodes (1988: 81, 220). For a refutation, see Harris 1992, which shows that far from being a critique, Pericles' oration praises Athenian democracy.

[34] On the relationship between tragedy and democracy, see Henderson 2007; Carter 2007.

[35] On Plato's interaction with Athenian democratic culture, see Monoson 2000; Wallach 2001.

[36] See here especially Canevaro 2017.

[37] Cartledge 2001: 55–67, 72–3.

[38] Loraux 1986: 193–4; Rosivach 1987; Raaflaub 1996; Hansen 1991: 84–5; Lévy 2005.

of overlap between the ancient and modern principles which held democracy together, though other scholars have also given a salutary warning of some of the stark differences, such as religious freedom, which was not recognised or embraced in any corner of the ancient Greek world, including Athens, socio-economic equality, which the state did little to promote, or the idea that all humans were created equal, which is a foundational doctrine on which the Enlightenment view of democracy relies.[39] As E. M. Harris has now shown, key to understanding democracy's existence is recognition that its chief purpose was to enshrine the principle of justice, which was what democracy's opponents, most notoriously the Thirty, subverted.[40]

One of the main threads of this study is to show that the rule of law was a reality in the fifth and fourth centuries, and that the chief aim of the Reconciliation was to reinstate the rule of law and sovereignty of the courts after its submersion under the Thirty. It has become increasingly widespread to claim that the Athenian Reconciliation Agreement was limited or defective and did not end division. This study argues to the contrary, that the oaths and covenants of the Reconciliation Agreement successfully reconciled the two sides of an ugly civil war. The exercise of democracy depended on the rule of the law enforced and applied through the courts. The recent effort of Lanni to argue that there was no rule of law in democratic Athens claims little evidential justification, and a closer study of the Reconciliation proves the opposite conclusion.[41] The Athenian Reconciliation was held up as the moral and legal paradigm of all amnesty treaties in the ancient world by Cicero for good historical reason, that it succeeded because it was grounded in law and because its effect was to limit vindictive action in the courts for offences which predated 12 Boedromion 403.[42]

---

[39] Hansen 1991: 81–5 2005; Roberts 1996; Rawls 2001: 64–6; Blaug and Schwarzmantel 2001: 120–41. Some scholars, notably Grote (1845–56: vi.6–15) and Ober (1989), have argued that socio-economic tensions at Athens were defused through the democratic political process, but with the one major exception of Syracuse (see Consolo Langer 2005), there is little evidence that Greek democracy was founded upon the premise that citizens should be equal in terms of wealth and property. See further Harris 2006: 121–40, which shows that Athenian democracy did not depend on any notion of economic equality. For wider discussion, see also Liddel 2009.

[40] Harris 2013; *contra* Lanni 2016. The successive chapters seek to throw further light upon Harris's fundamental observation that democracy and rule of law were two sides of the same political coin, by showing that the revival or democracy in 403 could not have worked without the sanctification of legal principle, and that once the two sides had been brought together it was of paramount importance to place Athens under the rule of law.

[41] Lanni 2016. As I argue to the contrary, the most important bequest of the Amnesty was to restore the rule of law to Athens; see below, especially Chapters 4, 5, 6, and 8.

[42] The thrust of this study aligns with the New Institutionalist thinking of March and Olsen 1989, and with some of the more recent approaches to ancient democracy and law outlined in the opening chapter of Harris 2013. See also Barbato 2020: 1–20.

At the Syracusan assembly, Athenagoras is represented to have said that the masses were better than anyone else at listening to speeches and judging between them (Th. 6.39.1). Cleon proclaimed that the people, not the privileged elite, was best at administering the city (Th. 3.37.3–4). A similar argument was used by Demosthenes a century later when he extolled the merits of a system which allowed political experts to offer advice, make speeches and enact laws (D. 18.320–2). Xenophon spoke of the improvement of the state finances under the institution of a state protector (X. *Mem.* 3.6). To be sure, the pros and cons of democracy could be and often were discussed in terms of what was best for the city, but to recognise this is not to concede that there was no ulterior moral or ethical principle for which democracy stood. To overturn the bald, depressing, utilitarian accounts of what Athens was and stood for, we need evidence to harness a contrary viewpoint. If a fresh study of the available evidence can show that the Athenian Amnesty of 403 was driven by a moral purpose, and that democracy was chosen in place of oligarchy because it was by its nature morally desirable, we might feel less bashful about citing Cicero, who, though separated from the events by four hundred years, was historically better positioned than we. The pervasive idea in much scholarship, that democracy at Athens was a lawless institution, claims no justification in the evidence.[43] The idea that the lawcourts were legal battlegrounds for feuding politicians which took little account of legal principle is rooted in events which took place from the time of Cleon until the fall of democracy in 404 but which the democratic restoration did all in its power to rectify.[44] The idea that the Amnesty was not taken seriously, or that the trials which followed did little more than pay token lip service to it, must be rejected on a closer analysis of the major trials which followed, those of Agoratus and Eratosthenes, of Callimachus and Socrates. The idea that amnesty agreements in other parts of the Greek world did not respect the principle to let bygones be bygones depends on distorted and biased misreading of important inscriptional evidence from the fifth and fourth centuries, which together shows that the rule μὴ μνησικακεῖν attested at Athens in 403 is attested with the same force elsewhere, to forbid frivolous pursuit of past offences.

Comparative studies in recent times of the Athenian Reconciliation and other treaties of amnesty in the Greek world have given rise to the claim that the principle of political forgiveness was not systematically applied in antiquity and that

---

[43] In addition to Lanni, cited above, who is the most extreme example, others who have proposed that Athens took no interest in the rule of law include Cohen (D.) 1995: 34–58; Christ 1998: 160–224; and Allen 2000. Of those cited, Cohen takes the most nuanced view.

[44] Against the notion that Athenian justice can be understood in terms of feuding, see Harris 2013: 60–98.

the ancient conception of amnesty did not entail forgiveness as a foundational principle.[45] Some scholars have gone as far as to claim that forgiveness as a concept did not exist in any sense understood in a post-Christian world. This study shows that whilst those approaches are not wholly mistaken, those claims have at times been overstated.[46] More specifically, it presents the documentary debate over the meaning of the clause μὴ μνησικακεῖν as presented in many ancient treaties, arguing that the purpose was more than just to seal off pre-agreed terms, and its effect was to prohibit legal action in the lawcourts for crimes which took place in the time of *stasis*. Civil conflict, or *stasis*, has been analysed from a wide range of theoretical angles, from the Marxist[47] to the non-Marxist.[48] The collapse of democracy in 404 and the imposition of an oligarchy has often been seen as the result of a class struggle between rich and poor, where the cause of the rich found temporary ascendency in the Thirty. More recently, that view has been challenged by scholars who have drawn attention to the opportunistic circumstances of the struggles of the late fifth century.[49] A recent analysis of the oligarchy at Athens has questioned the assumption that its main supporters were necessarily rich or opponents necessarily poor.[50] This entails a different view of the fall and reassertion of democracy in 404 and 403 respectively, that the historical processes which led to both were less to do with socio-economic factors and more to do with matters of political principle, whether authority should rest with the magistrates or the courts. The Thirty came to power on the back of the disgrace which the sycophantic misuse of the courts at the end of the fifth century had brought about; conversely, democracy was re-established a year later, on the back of the disgrace which the suppression of the rule of law under the Thirty had caused. To reassert democracy after the civil war, the enforcement of the rule of law through the courts was vital. Reconciling division was all about reinstating the sovereignty of the lawcourts.

Some Marxist approaches have argued that the great war between Athens and Sparta was all about the forces of progress against those of reaction, the cause of the poor versus that of the rich.[51] Such an approach invariably prejudices discussion of the events of 403, because if the Peloponnesian War was all about 'rich' versus 'poor', the establishment of the Thirty in 404 and their fall a year later should then be traced back to a 'class conflict' in which the

---

[45] This assumption is implied in varying degrees by Rubinstein (2013), Dreher (2013), Chaniotis (2013), and Carawan (2013).
[46] Contrast Konstan 2010 with Cairns 2011. *Pace* Konstan, Cairns argues that the concept of forgiveness was present and evident in the pre-Christian world of classical Greece and Rome.
[47] Ste Croix 1981; Rose 2012.
[48] Ruschenbusch 1978; Lintott 1982; Gehrke 1985.
[49] Brock 2009.
[50] Németh 2006.
[51] See especially Ste Croix 1972.

poor throughout Greece sought to emancipate themselves from the oligarchic fetters of the rich, and the cause of democracy which triumphed in 403 was a triumph for the poor and oppressed. That approach is, however, problematised by the sheer absence of evidence, outside oligarchic literature itself, that democracy in Greece conceived itself in terms of the 'rule of the poor'. Thucydides is plain that by 427, those states that favoured democracy were siding with Athens, while those that sided with Sparta were favouring Sparta (Th. 3.82.2). The history of the Greek city states is replete with episodes of *stasis*, to which subject numerous modern studies have been devoted. The theoretical perspectives of modern authors range from the Marxist, which seeks to explain human conflict in terms of 'class struggle', to the anti-Marxist, which argues that class struggle is not a useful or relevant idea when seeking to analyse the origin and cause of the great majority of wars and struggles throughout history.[52] The early poets of Greece knew of *stasis* but say relatively little about its antidotes. In Solon's case, we know from later evidence that he did not go in for a radical solution, which would have been to abolish debt-bondage altogether, but took the more targeted step of abolishing debt-slavery. Later sources make it clear that debt-bondage continued right down until the end of the classical age and into Hellenistic times, but the one feature of archaic practice which Solon undoubtedly abolished was enslavement for debt.[53]

Ironically, the earliest known prescription for *stasis* in Greek cities was tyranny. There is widespread disagreement as to whether the tyrants of Greece were ideologically motivated. When we read the fourth-century accounts, particularly those influenced by the Aristotelian school, it rather seems that the classical age looked back upon the archaic through the lens of its own experience.[54] By the time of the Peloponnesian War, the causes of *stasis* most certainly were ideological, as Thucydides' description of the *stasis* at Corcyra shows. Thucydides famously characterised the Corcyran crisis as a historical watershed which divided the Greek world down ideological fault lines, with democrats relying upon the support of Athens and oligarchs on the support of Sparta (Th. 3.82). The new power alignments followed ideology.[55] If read

---

[52] For examples of Marxist treatments see Ste Croix 1981 and Rose 2012. For a thoroughly anti-Marxist treatment see Ruschenbusch 1978. For more intermediate treatments, see Lintott 1984 and Gehrke 1985.

[53] For a full survey and discussion of the evidence, see Harris 1997 and 2002.

[54] For the Aristotelian view of the Peisistratid tyranny as championing the popular cause, see *Ath. Pol.* 13.4. For the view that the early tyrants of Greece did not put forward politically progressive programmes, see Cawkwell 1995.

[55] The best known and most complete statement of the Marxist analysis of the causes of the Peloponnesian War is Ste Croix 1972. On the disputed question of when and whether oligarchy was established at Samos between 439 and 412, see Legon 1972; Meiggs 1972: 43; Ostwald 1993. On the use of democracy as an instrument of imperialism, see most recently Brock 2009.

without the hindsight of fourth-century theoretical perspectives, it would seem from the record of Herodotus, who produced the first continuous historical narrative, that *stasis* in the archaic age was often less about political ideology than about dynastic feuding within the political hierarchies, though Herodotus also wrote about conflicts between tyranny and the rule of law. The regional nature of *stasis* is attested with the rise of Peisistratus at Athens, who rose to power on the back of factional allegiance in what was a regionally based conflict, and Cypselus at Corinth, whose successful efforts to topple the ruling Bacchiad family may have originated in a family squabble invoking parentage.[56] At the same time, we should be open-minded to the possibility that both axes of conflict – that is, intra-elite infighting and the struggle between rich and poor – operated in concert in archaic Greece.

Once we get into the fifth century, the origin of *stasis* in Greek cities was undeniably ideological. As Thucydides recognised, one of the disastrous effects of the Peloponnesian War was to range the city states of Greece into opposing alliances, one led by Athens, whose member states were mostly democratic, the other by Sparta, whose member states were predominantly, though not exclusively, oligarchic.[57] As he also recognised, this polarisation wielded a divisive influence upon the cities themselves. The best documented example was Athens herself, who at the end of the fifth century succumbed to Sparta and accepted a pro-Spartan oligarchy which lasted only eight months, during which time the city descended into a nasty civil conflict. But the practical realities of Athenian democracy in the late fifth century were that it was riven by faction, and recognition of the virtues of democracy as a political system should not override acknowledgement of the internal difficulties and threats which Athens' democracy in the last two decades of the Peloponnesian War faced. Nevertheless, care should be taken before claiming that Athens gave way to oligarchy in 411 and 404 *because of* internal strife, even if internal factors played a role in the overthrow of democracy in those years. To be sure, both in the fifth and in the fourth centuries Athens harboured critics, and the evidence relating to the fifth century reveals the existence of political clubs called *hetaireiai*,[58] consisting mainly of men of noble birth whose purpose was to provide mutual support in the courts and in politics. Until the end of the fifth

---

[56] For Peisistratus see Hdt. 1.59–60; Sealey 1960; Anderson (G.) 2003: 13–84. On Cypselus see Hdt. 5.92; *FGrHist* 90 F 57; Oost 1972; Drews 1972; McGlew 1993: 61–3; Mitchell 2013: 93–4.

[57] An exception in the Spartan-led Peloponnesian League was democratic Elis; see Legon 1968: 212; Kagan 2013: 272. For the anti-tyranny stances of both alliances, see Joyce 2022.

[58] The term ἑταιρεία has a wide number of connotations in Greek and can encompass military, social, educational and political organisations. For its meaning as a 'political club', see Th. 3.82.6; Lys. 12.55; Isoc. 4.89; Eup. 8.6D; *Com. Adesp.* 22.31D; Pl. *R.* 2.365d; *Tht.* 173d; Arist. *Pol.* 2.27.1272b34; 1305b32; Plu. *Arist.* 2; *Cim.* 17; *Per.* 13.

century, these clubs did not exist for subversive purposes.[59] Athens' democracy was able to absorb and to incorporate such associations, and some of the great names such as Cimon and Pericles belonged to them.[60] To an important degree, it can be argued that their existence was integral and necessary to the functioning of democracy, and we should not be schematic or reductive in the assumption that champions of democracy were necessarily poor, whereas those who came from more privileged and moneyed backgrounds were disposed automatically to favour oligarchy. At any rate, the evidence for the existence of political clubs and associations among the wealthier members of society indicates that, far from alienating the interests of the rich and wealthy, the democracy created circumstances under which the wealthy and educated were able to thrive politically.[61] As a political entity, democracy at Athens guaranteed an equal participatory share to all regardless of wealth.

The study is not without its methodological difficulties, and before proceeding, it would be useful to make some preliminary statements about available source material and its uses.

SOURCES AND METHODOLOGY

One of the most intriguing facets of this period is that no continuous surviving narrative exists to which we can defer to check our understanding of the facts, and so modern scholars need to rely upon scattered sources of varying generic category and historical quality. The narrative of Thucydides breaks off in 411, and the last eight years of what later came to be known as the Peloponnesian

---

[59] For a general survey of these clubs and their functioning in the late fifth-century democracy, see Sinclair 1988: 142–3; Connor 1971: 25–9. For a more recent discussion as to whether the democracy ever produced associations comparable to our political 'parties', see Hansen 2014.

[60] The later perspective of Plutarch turns these clubs into ideological organisations, whereby the *hetaireia* of Thucydides son of Milesias was a group of oligarchic conspirators who opposed the more democratic Pericles (*Per.* 11–14). But this is likely to result from a later theoretical schematisation of Athenian politics, where theorists divided politicians into 'democrats' and 'oligarchs'. As modern studies have shown (see above), political clubs need not have been subversive or undemocratic. In probability, this perception developed retrospectively after 404, when the *hetaireia* of Critias overthrew democracy.

[61] It was only at the end of the Peloponnesian War when one political club, that to which Critias belonged, became openly subversive. The pseudo-Aristotelian account blames the overthrow of democracy on the *hetaireiai* which were made up of the nobles (*Ath. Pol.* 34.3), but the evidence must be read with care. The more contemporary evidence of Lysias indicates that the *hetaireiai* were responsible for the election of the five ephors and ten phylarchs at Athens once the democracy had been overthrown (Lys. 12.43–6). The involvement of the political clubs in the instalment of the oligarchy came about when the overthrow of democracy was already a *fait accompli*.

Epicerdes (D. 20.41–5; cf. *IG* I³ 25). These are among some examples where it is evident that the orators had access to genuine texts of legal documents which they could cite and upon which they were able to construct coherent legal arguments. If an inserted text does not fulfil the criteria for consistency outlined above, we should not *a fortiori* assume that its inconsistency with the summary of the orator implies the ignorance of the orator. There is just too much independent evidence to suggest that Attic orators were fully *au fait* with the texts they cited. The more reliable course of action is simply to remove the document from consideration as a forgery. As we will see (Chapter 4), the documents inserted into the text of the first speech of Andocides, *On the Mysteries*, do not satisfy the basic criteria for authenticity. Vast quantities of scholarly ink have been spilled trying to reconcile them, or indeed to suggest that Andocides was less familiar with his legal documentation than might be desirable. Those methodologies are flawed. If and where the documents do not match up with the orator's description, they must simply be expunged.[76]

A third orator to feature in the narrative is Isocrates (436–338), a near contemporary of Lysias and Andocides, whose longevity became proverbial in Greece. Isocrates is remembered for his anti-Persian stance and efforts to encourage Greeks to put aside their internal differences to unite against a common enemy. By 387/6, the year of the swearing of the King's Peace, Persian power had reasserted itself convincingly on the western shores of Asia Minor and was not to be challenged again until the 330s, the period of the conquests of Alexander the Great. For Isocrates and his contemporaries, the inordinate tragedy of the Peloponnesian War and the Corinthian War which followed on from it (395–386) was the division it sowed among the Greeks of the mainland and, in turn, the resolve which they sapped among them to come to the aid of their kinsfolk on the Asiatic coast. The eighteenth speech of Isocrates, *Against Callimachus*, does not touch upon that larger theme but prosecutes the defendant for violating the terms of the Amnesty by introducing a special plea called *paragraphê*. The speech has been subject to repeated misinterpretation, because scholars have often tried to infer from it special loopholes in the

---

[76] Recently, it has been argued that the inserted documents come from collections of Athenian decrees compiled by Craterus at the end of the fourth century. The hypothesis was initially floated in the nineteenth century (see Ladek 1891: 64), but it has been revived in more recent years; see MacDowell 1990: 46; Scafuro 2006: 180; Sommerstein 2014: 56; Faraguna 2015; Carawan 2016: 47–8; 2017; 2019. The problem with the 'Craterus' theory is that the fragments of Craterus' work show that its author compiled a collection of imperial decrees all of which dated from the period 480–410, and closer analysis of the inserted documents found in Andocides, Aeschines and Demosthenes illustrates that Craterus could not have been the source for the texts either of genuine or forged documents. For a more detailed refutation of the 'Craterus' theory, see now Harris 2021.

Amnesty which permitted certain types of case coming to light. As argued in Chapter 6, that approach is mistaken because it fails to observe the reasons why Isocrates referred to the Amnesty at all. Careful use of the orators shows that all too often they referred to historical events as moral examples, rather than to construct a strict point of law. Isocrates' *Against Callimachus* is a good example where reference to the Amnesty serves a rhetorical purpose rather than a strictly legal one. Here, we observe another key feature of methodology. When using orators, it is crucial to separate rhetorical talking points from legal issues which affected the case in hand. As will be shown, the eighteenth speech of Isocrates, though it does refer to the Amnesty, deals with legal matters largely irrelevant to, and unaffected by, the terms of the Reconciliation. Orators harked back often to the Amnesty as a moral example.

To supplement knowledge of how amnesties in the ancient world operated, inscriptions provide a fruitful supply of comparanda. These texts are often fragmentary and in a poor state of legibility, but collectively they show that the ancient concept of amnesty was, despite the assertions of some modern scholars to the contrary, not far removed from modern ideas. Inscribed fragments feature also in the discussion of the legal redaction. The key difficulty with inscribed texts is that they often lack historical context, which must be supplied, if possible, from extraneous sources, and for that reason they can be wildly misinterpreted. A case in point is the so-called 'sacrificial calendar', surviving on twelve opisthographic fragments. It is so tempting to build a historical argument upon those fragments by combination with other historical material relating to the republication of the laws after 403, but here, another crucial point about methodology arises. It is only appropriate to seek to understand inscribed texts with reference to extraneous material supplied in literary sources if there can be no doubt that the literary source in question provides a suitable historical context in which to locate the inscribed text under examination. All too often, scholars have tried to infer more than can legitimately be inferred by assuming a connection with an external source, when in fact the two are entirely unconnected. Remarks of Quintus Curtius about the Exiles Decree of Alexander give a very useful point of entry to understand the historical background of the Tegea decree which granted restoration to erstwhile fugitives (see Chapter 7), but that is only because the connection can be established beyond any reasonable doubt. What is not permissible, however, is the claim, for example, that because a 'wall' is obliquely referenced in a forged document in the first speech of Andocides, the twelve opisthographic fragments *a fortiori* formed a single coherent unity which abutted on to the back wall of the Stoa Basileios. Where a historical connection cannot be made with certainty, special care must be taken not to read into evidence conclusions which, on the part of the modern historian, are already preconceived and therefore prejudicial.

Finally, our understanding of the rule of law in Athens in the fourth century is drawn from a huge range of oratorical and inscribed evidence, and in Chapter 8 we examine the range of sources from the fourth century which show, beyond reasonable doubt, that the rule of law was a reality both before and after 403. As far as the legal trials are concerned, the one great anomaly is the trial of Socrates, dated to 399, which resulted in his execution. The difficulty here is that we lack an official transcript of the trial and are thrown back upon sources of very dubious historical reliability, Plato's *Apology* and Xenophon's *Memorabilia*. The first is a philosophical reconstruction of Socrates' speech in self-defence, but scholarship has shown that it does not conform to any of the legal requirements of a court speech, as typical in forensic oratory, and must therefore be read as a philosophical rather than a historical work (see Chapter 6). The second is a collection of vignettes pertaining to the philosopher's life and moral example, which are interesting in themselves, but which throw little light on the nature of the trial, beyond that the outcome was an outrage. As the next seven chapters show in detail, piecing together the Reconciliation and its historical aftermath is a fascinating, if daunting, task which involves difficult problems of ancient evidence and its interpretation. The aim of this study is to make the best sense available of the evidence which survives. No interpretation is ever going to be free of difficulties, and any effort to reconstruct this controversial period from the fragmentary traces which it leaves is never going to win over universal consensus. For this reason, an element of modesty is, perhaps, needed on the part of the modern historian who attempts to make sense of the confused tradition which comes down. This study aims to understand the evidence in the light of a broader conviction about the rule of law upon which a functioning democracy depended. Those who do not accept that Athens was governed lawfully will never agree with its main tenets, but as this study will show, the rule of law is the only suitable historical framework within which to interpret the Athenian Reconciliation, without which the democracy of the fourth century would never have emerged.

STRUCTURE AND OUTLAY

This study has a complex theme. The Athenian Reconciliation of 403 BCE refers to a legislative process sworn into effect in autumn 403, on the twelfth day of the Attic month Boedromion, the third month of the Athenian lunar calendar. From the time of Cleisthenes at the end of the sixth century BCE, who crafted the foundations of Athenian democracy after the overthrow of the tyranny of the Peisistratids, Athens had gone by two parallel calendrical systems, the older lunar calendar consisting of twelve equal months of twenty-eight days, and the new prytanic, or solar, calendar which divided the revolution of the earth around the sun – or the sun around the earth, if we think in geocentric terms – into ten artificial divisions of varying lengths, called 'prytanies'. It always used to be held that Athenians kept the old lunar system for religious and cultic purposes, whereas the newer calendar they adopted for purposes of state. This creates a false distinction, because religion was an integral component of ancient societies, and the separation of 'Church' and 'State', which came about in modern times with the Enlightenment, found no ancient parallel. The prytanic system was introduced to correspond to the needs of the new democratic institutions which Cleisthenes superimposed upon Athens, whereas the older constitutional structures which survived, such as the nine annual archons, continued to operate according to the older lunar, or Attic, method of reckoning time. For this reason, though to us it might seem confusing that Athenians operated according to a lunar and a solar calendar simultaneously, from a historical perspective this fits well with what else we know of the evolution of Athenian democracy. Democracy evolved not by cancellation of what had existed previously, but by adding on to, or refining, older institutions and moulding them to the pattern of a new democratic ideology. The Athenian Reconciliation Agreement, which ended eight months of bitter civil war which had raged in the interval between the defeat of Athens by Sparta and her allies in late summer 404 and the overthrow of a foreign-imposed oligarchic junta, the infamous Thirty Tyrants, the following year, is no exception the rule. The archonship of Eucleides, which on our reckoning refers to the lunar year 403/2, was no year zero. From an Athenian perspective, the resurrected democracy was a continuance of the democracy which had existed in the fifth century, with one or two important constitutional innovations.

The lunar year at Athens began mid-summer, around July. To calculate from summer to summer, this would place the Oath of Reconciliation in September 403, or thereabouts. When the oaths were sworn, Athenians committed not revisit in the courts untried cases which predated the Reconciliation. Yet, as the various trials which ensued shortly after the swearing of the oaths into effect show, the commitment was not as easy as it appeared on paper. Bitter feelings still rankled, and extra measures were needed to ensure that the Reconciliation was duly observed. There can be little doubt that clever prosecutors often operated from motives of vengeance but, in law, what mattered was not the underlying motive of a litigant but the legal principle on which the case turned. The rule of law entailed that court trials should be decided purely on legal, as opposed to partisan or political, principle. Modern interpreters have often spoken of 'political' trials in the aftermath of the Reconciliation, though this is to place a false spin on the problem. Many have doubted that the rule of law, such as we understand the concept in modern times, existed at all in ancient Athens and, for that reason, have been tempted to argue that the terms of the Reconciliation were either not legally observed or, at most, were half-observed. As argued in the following pages, that approach is altogether mistaken. The evidence shows that when democracy was revived at the end of the fifth century, for the commissioners who devised a new constitution it was of paramount importance to enshrine the rule of law. This must explain why, in the immediate wake of the Reconciliation, a complex process which had begun in the last decade of the fifth century was revived to scrutinise and publish the entire corpus of valid Athenian law. The trials which followed, in every case, turn on a legal principle. Though some trespassed into what we might call a legal grey area, in no example would it be fair to allege that the law was disregarded or taken lightly. The evidence of litigation in these years indicates that the Reconciliation, far from casually applied, was scrupulously observed. The scope of this study therefore incorporates not only the clauses of the Reconciliation in 403, but their application in the early years of the restored democracy, from 403 to 398.

Scholars have discussed the Reconciliation and its aftermath from a variety of angles and perspectives (see above), but a common thread of recent discussion of the democratic restoration at the end of the fifth century is the doctrine that the legislators of 403 cared only about how to make restored democracy survive and did not seek to enshrine underlying moral or political principles which gave democracy legitimacy. This trend underestimates what Athenian democracy said about itself, as well as ancient theoretical discussions of the merits of democracy over those of rival political systems. The present chapter has surveyed past and current scholarship about the Reconciliation and detailed the pitfalls of the relevant source material and the methodological principles that will be followed in the following chapters. It has identified a trend in recent years to underplay the normative goals of those who restored democracy – the principles and ideals behind the restoration – and overplay the centrality of bargaining between competing interests and a utilitarian concern for mere survival. The following chapters make a comprehensive case for identifying different priorities behind the Reconciliation, to do with restoring legality and the rule of law as basic conditions of democracy.

Chapter 2 argues that democracy collapsed at the end of the fifth century because of a military crisis, in part, but also because its credibility had been damaged by the misuse of the courts in the last three decades of the fifth century. In the time of Pericles and before, we hear of few if any politically motivated court actions, when such rivalry was played out through the practice of ostracism. From the time of Cleon until the death of Cleophon, a fundamental change occurred, where the courts for the first time became political battlegrounds for rival generals and politicians. The reasons are multifarious, but the primary cause was the psychological stress and paranoia which the unprecedented circumstances of the Peloponnesian War brought about at Athens.

The undermining of the courts as the guarantors of the rule of law meant that the mainstay of democracy was brought into disgrace. This gave detractors the political ammunition to reduce the sovereignty of the courts and to assert the power of the magistrate over the courts. This proved devastating to democracy, which in 404 collapsed under pressure from the Spartan Lysander and succumbed to the rule of the Thirty. Externally, there were contingent reasons also why democracy did not survive the defeat of Athens in 404, which were a shift in Spartan policy from championing the freedom and self-determination of the Greeks (with Sparta nevertheless as the leading military power) to a posture of installing pro-Spartan oligarchies in the city states which fell within Sparta's military sphere. Lysander and his policy of forced political imposition were devastating not only for Athenian freedom but also for Sparta's long-standing credibility as the champion of Greek liberty. The historical sources which shed light on the democratic collapse are fraught with contradiction and inconsistency, but what they collectively reveal is that Athens gave way to Lysander under pressure and accepted an oligarchy of thirty commissioners against its deeper wishes. When in power, the Thirty behaved with ruthless efficiency eliminating or exiling political opponents in kangaroo courts which made no reference to the rule of law. The political ascendency of the Thirty is to be explained as a sharp reaction against the authority of the courts and the assertion of the rule of the magistrate, whose power was not curtailed by legal reference or principle. Marxist scholarship has understood this historical process in terms of class struggle, but as recent studies have shown, the Thirty's supporters were not necessarily rich, and their opponents not necessarily poor. Socio-economic explanations are indeed less powerful in explaining the rise of the Thirty than legal and political ones. The Thirty were eventually toppled because their rule became unendurable, but also because Sparta became aware that the situation which had been created was unsustainable. The trial and execution of Theramenes was the nadir of the crisis, but also its turning point. The sources disagree on how far Theramenes can be described as an oligarch, and some, like Lysias, had a vested interest later in eroding all perceived ideological distinctions between radical and moderate oligarchs. But other historical sources suggest that the distinction was real, and that Theramenes, for all his faults as a politician, tried to keep at bay the worst excesses of the oligarchy led by Critias.

Chapter 3 examines the terms of the Reconciliation which resulted from the defeat and exile of the Thirty and Ten in 403. It shows that the Reconciliation was a comprehensive legal enactment which, with the noted exception of the Thirty, Ten and Eleven, barred legal action for crimes which predated the democratic restoration. At the heart of its provision was the guarantee that the victorious democrats would not wreak vengeance on those they had defeated. Of course, there were guarantees to the victors as well, but the most important of its stipulations was that vindictive litigation in the courts for crimes committed in the time of the Thirty, and untried offences dating from before that, should be impossible. The Amnesty, with its stated exceptions, was a blanket measure of political reconciliation. By making past offences unactionable, it reinstated the courts as the guarantors of the rule of law, not just as feuding battlegrounds for rival political factions and aggrieved parties. From 403, the only cases admissible in the courts were those which concerned offences post-dating the democratic restoration. As the next two chapters show, that commitment was dutifully honoured, even though there were some notorious grey areas, such as the trial of Agoratus. Scholars in the past have mistakenly assumed that the Reconciliation Agreement drew a legal and conceptual distinction between different categories of homicide, some of which were still actionable after 403 if committed prior to the date of reconciliation. Closer examination shows that this involves a misreading of Athenian homicide law, which made no distinction between own-hand killing and other types, and this rectification will be crucial to bear in mind when we turn to examine the legal issues at stake in the trial of Agoratus, which is often miscited as 'evidence' that the amnesty terms were either incomplete or ineffectual. The chapter presents a schema for the Reconciliation along a twenty-point system of legal clauses. Against those who have argued for two separate treaties, one concluded in 403 and another in 401, when the oligarchic enclave at Eleusis was dissolved, this chapter shows that the terms of the Reconciliation given in the Aristotelian tradition are reliable and derive from a single, unified legal document.

The fourth chapter argues that the Reconciliation of 403 enshrined the rule of law, which it defines more thoroughly. It shows that the much-debated 'scrutiny of the laws' which took place in the aftermath of the Reconciliation was the clearest evidence of the resurrection of democracy according to legal principle. The greatest difficulty in studying this event is that we see it through the eyes of two very difficult and unreliable representatives, Lysias and Andocides, the second of whom was put on trial shortly after the democratic restoration for violating a decree passed in 415 of *atimia*, restricting the rights of movement of those tarred with the desecration of the Herms. Andocides argued that the decree of Isotimides was now invalid because it was a decree which predated the re-establishment of democracy in 403, not a law according to the new definition of what distinguished a law, whose effect was permanent, and a decree, whose effect was impermanent. Andocides rightly argued that the amnesty of 405 had annulled *atimia* and that he was no longer liable under the terms of Patrocleides. However, the reference to the 403 amnesty amounts to legalistic sophistry. If Andocides is believed, the scrutiny eliminated the efficacy of statutes, such as the decree of Isotimides, passed before the Reconciliation, but a more detailed analysis will show that he slurred over events to argue that he was not liable under the terms of Isotimides after 403. In fact, the legal scrutiny did not nullify the effect of earlier decrees but clarified in concrete terms the distinction between decrees and laws, so that the restored democracy could know what its laws were. This was essential to the reassertion of the rule of law at Athens after 403. The thirtieth speech of Lysias, *Against Nicomachus*, is difficult to evaluate, as the exact nature of the plaint against the defendant is unclear. All the same, it shows that at the end of the fifth century and into the fourth, conscientious efforts were under way at Athens to present a clear and cogent statement of the valid and up-to-date law, so that the courts had at their disposal a transparent legal criterion by which court trials could take place. Some have identified a collection of inscribed stone fragments with a sacrificial calendar put together by the redactors of 403, but that is to place faith in the so-called 'decree of Teisamenus' preserved in the speech of Andocides, which has now been shown to be a forgery, and to ignore the fact that none of the preserved fragments contains a prescript. The opisthographic format of the inscribed fragments makes it very unlikely that we are even dealing with laws, and there are no good internal grounds to identify any of the epigraphical material with the alleged 'wall' to which the forged decree of Teisamenus refers. As Lysias shows, Nicomachus was prosecuted in 399 for adding material from spurious authority. Whether or not the prosecution had a good case, the redactors of 403 aimed to produce a coherent statement of the valid law of Athens.

Chapter 5 is the first of two which study the application of the Amnesty provisions. It deals with two trials which came to light in the immediate aftermath of the Reconciliation, those of the oligarchs Agoratus and Eratosthenes. The easier of the two to understand, in the light of the Amnesty provisions, is the second, that of Eratosthenes, who had served on the board of the Thirty and, according to the terms of exception, was culpable after 403 for crimes committed in the time of oligarchy. The more difficult of the trials is that of Agoratus, who, not a member of the Thirty but a close accomplice, stood trial after 403 for his part in the oligarchy. The trial of Agoratus has caused endless puzzlement. Some have argued that Agoratus' crimes were actionable because his claims to citizenship were in doubt and, if not a citizen, he was not covered under the terms of amnesty. That is to make two crucial assumptions, first, that non-citizens were not covered by the Amnesty, and secondly, that Agoratus was not a citizen. The matter of citizenship comes up in the trial, but for none of the reasons traditionally given. The prosecution makes much of the idea that the decrees awarding citizenship to those who had fought on the side of the democrats at Phyle did not apply to Agoratus, not because that would have exempted Agoratus from cover under the Amnesty's provisions, but because by arguing that Agoratus had not been awarded citizenship, his claims to having fought on the side of democracy were not believable. Others have argued that Agoratus' crime of murder was still actionable because, according to the prosecution, it was own-hand, rather than causally indirect. This is to misunderstand Athenian homicide law, as well as to misread the vital clauses of the Reconciliation Agreement touching homicide. Nothing in the terms of reconciliation exempted 'own-hand' homicides from the terms of provision. The crime of Agoratus, which was homicide, was actionable because it was a public, not a private, act. The focus of the prosecution is to show that the action against Agoratus was not partisan, because it represented the case of the entire city against a conspirator, not the grievance of a private individual. This explains the unusual process by *endeixis*, rather than the usual *dikê*, or private suit, for homicide. Of all the trials, this is still difficult, because Agoratus was not a member of the Thirty and therefore, by the letter of the law, not liable. The intriguing question was how much to read beyond, whether underlying legal principles could be extrapolated from the exemption clauses which might be thought to apply to egregious criminals, like Agoratus, who technically were only accomplices under the oligarchy. Though this is a legal grey area, what the trial shows is that prosecutions turned on a legal, not a vindictive, issue. Both the trials of Agoratus and Eratosthenes illustrate the working of the rule of law in action after 403.

Chapter 6 turns to the trials of Callimachus and Socrates. It argues that much of the modern discussion surrounding the trials is misplaced, and that neither violated the principle of amnesty, which was to grant protection to those who had committed crimes under the oligarchs. The first of those trials, that of Callimachus, has often been misread as a violation of amnesty because it refers to events which took place prior to 12 Boedromion 403, but a careful reading shows that the trial was in full accordance with the terms of amnesty, because the legal issue turned on a legal settlement which occurred after the democratic revival, not beforehand. Because this trial happened by means of the newly created process of *paragraphê*, which turned the tables on the prosecution in the courts, scholars have casually assumed that it was related to the Amnesty. To be sure, the new legal process was designed to deal with vexatious litigation in the wake of amnesty, but it remained as a process throughout the fourth century and was not limited to cases which arose from the Reconciliation. Thus, the fact that Callimachus was the defendant in the case, rather than the plaintiff, has no bearing upon whether the matter arose from the Reconciliation or not. The speaker alludes to the Reconciliation, but for rhetorical effect, to show by way of contrast with the magnanimous example of the democrats of 403, Thrasybulus and Anytus, how mean-spirited and churlish the defendant Callimachus was. The trial of Socrates, though fascinating on its own merits, is another red herring upon which scholars in the past have latched to advance the case that the Amnesty was taken half-heartedly. The plaint against Socrates had no bearing on events predating the revival of democracy in 403, even though the prosecution smeared him with association with Critias. The vast problem here is that our understanding of the trial comes through philosophical channels, and we lack a transcript of the trial from either point of view. The trial of Socrates has gone down as one of the worst miscarriages of justice in history, but that is chiefly because the judges made a fatally erroneous judgment, not because, in some broader systemic way, the rule of law at Athens was not followed in full earnest. The chapter draws on recent studies of *paragraphê* to show that the aim after 403 was to reduce frivolous litigation by turning the tables on the prosecutor.

Chapter 7 examines other amnesty agreements throughout the classical and Hellenistic ages, showing that Cicero was right to hold Athens up as the paradigm. Though many of those amnesty agreements and treaties did not turn on a legal principle, this should not subtract from our view of the standard of historical comparison which Athens set. Recent scholars have argued that because many of those amnesty agreements did not demonstrate a coherent legal or moral principle, we should therefore divest ourselves of the notion that lawful amnesty was the paradigm in antiquity. This is a vast overstatement. Many city states failed to reconcile on the same terms as Athens in 403, but to recognise this should not reduce our perception of Athens as the gold standard of what a successful amnesty entailed. This chapter examines a wide range of inscribed texts over a large period of history, from the time of the Peloponnesian War in the last third of the fifth century, down to the Hellenistic period. It shows that whilst amnesty treaties could and often did fail to observe legal principle, those which succeeded did so because they observed the law. Athens was exemplary because the law, rather than force, was the binding principle which held the restored community together and prevented it from relapsing into a state of civil conflict. Those cities and communities which followed Athens' example in the wake of division or civil war were those which effected lasting amnesties. Those which did not tended to be those which rapidly slid back into a state of division, or else could only guarantee 'reconciliation' by application of brute force, often sponsored from outside.

Finally, Chapter 8 examines the rule of law at Athens under the restored democracy. It traces the constitutional mechanisms of *nomothesia*, or 'law-making', from 403 onward and shows that a society could be reliably democratic only if it was governed by law. There has been a habit of thought to date which claims that the fourth-century democracy was 'less democratic' than the democracy of the fifth century, which preceded it. This is to make a chain of erroneous claims and assumptions. There was nothing undemocratic – to the Athenians –about the rule of law. On the contrary, those societies which governed themselves under the rule of law were more democratic than those which did not. As the fourth century shows, Athenian justice upheld the rule of law in the courts, and this was the most important legacy of the Reconciliation. Whereas the end of the fifth century had witnessed the rule of law break down, with the result that the magistrate became unaccountable, the purpose of the Reconciliation was to reverse what had taken place under the Thirty by ensuring that the rule of law was applied throughout.

The reassertion of democracy was, primarily, about the reassertion of due legal process. The result was a system in which justice referred to legal principle, and where vindictive action in the courts was placed under severe restraint through the application of the terms of the Reconciliation.

The overriding argument of this study is that democracy was able to be restored in 403 because the rule of law was restored. If rule of law had not been restored, there would have been no hope for the resuscitation of a society which could govern itself according to legal or democratic principle. The Reconciliation Agreement of 403 was all about reinstituting the rule of law at Athens. The triumph of democracy in 403 was the triumph of law over lawlessness.

CHAPTER 2

Civil Strife at Athens, 404–403

The Athenian Amnesty Agreement of 403 BCE is the best-known treaty of its kind from Greek antiquity and was hailed in later ages as the paradigm of reconciliation. A full understanding of the difficulties and challenges faced by Athens in 403, when the Thirty were defeated and overthrown, in reinstalling the ancient and prized democracy is impossible without exploration of the period which preceded it. It would be tempting to begin with the victory of the democratic Thrasybulus in Piraeus over the oligarchs and the Reconciliation that followed. As Cloché realised, however, the magnitude and scale of what the democrats achieved after regaining control of the city in the summer of 403 is to be measured against the scale and size of the calamity which gripped Athens during the eight intervening months between her defeat at the hands of the Spartan general Lysander in autumn 404 and the resurgence of the democratic resistance the following year.[1] Crucially, the regime of the Thirty Tyrants, or simply 'the Thirty', signalled a suspension of law and order alongside systematic suppression of the principle of legal justice. To rebuild democracy in the wake of these calamities, it was essential for the victorious democrats in 403 to re-establish justice and the rule of law. The restored democracy of the fourth century is viewed by some as a democracy 'tempered' by legal restraint, in contrast to fifth-century Athens, often caricatured as 'lawless' democracy, but

---

[1] For an overview of Cloché's approach and how it fits into the development of modern historiography surrounding the Reconciliation, see Chapter 1, pp. 6–7. For Cloché's treatment of the Thirty, see Cloché 1915: 1–250.

a closer look at the evidence will show that democracy and rule of law were two sides of the same coin, and that in order to re-establish democratic principle, it was of paramount importance to reaffirm the sovereignty of law as the final authority through and under which democracy and justice could be guaranteed.

Some critics may object to a chapter on the Thirty, on the grounds that it presents merely a sideshow. I wish to argue otherwise. The thirty-ninth chapter of the Aristotelian *Ath. Pol.* gives a nearly complete and compendious summary of the Reconciliation terms, which the Athenians contracted on the twelfth day of the Attic month Boedromion, in the archonship of Eucleides (403/2). These contracts or covenants are of vital historical importance, and modern scholars have rightly prioritised them in their reconstruction of the Athenian Amnesty Agreement. Yet, at the same time, they tell only part of the story. In various ways, the Covenants of Reconciliation drawn up between the warring parties of 404/3 together constitute a rider to the much more important achievement, namely the rebuilding of democracy, law and justice. The oaths sworn by the opposing sides on 12 Boedromion incorporated more than a swearing to abide by the covenants of the Reconciliation Agreement, but beyond that, to observe the sacred principles of law and justice, without which a renascent democracy could not have hoped to survive. These were crucial, since the Thirty had risen to power on the back of subversion of those same principles upon which democracy itself rested. Required of the democrats in summer 403 was the mirror image of what had been required of the Spartan-backed oligarchy in autumn 404 in building a regime founded upon arbitrary government and application of brute force. Just as the Thirty had put themselves in power by annihilating every bastion of law and justice at Athens to date, the resurgent democracy needed to re-establish legal and judicial principle, which is why the Judicial Oath was of such vital importance in the process of the rebuilding of democracy at Athens. The Covenants of Amnesty detailed in *Ath. Pol.* 39, in one sense, are the least illuminating components of the democratic restoration. Of course, they tell much about the relationship between restored Athens and the newly created oligarchic enclave at Eleusis, set up between 403 and 401 as a 'state within a state' to home erstwhile supporters of the ousted regime unwilling to live within the restored democracy. But beyond that, they say relatively little about what the restored democracy amounted to or about the legal and political principles upon which it relied. A closer look at the events under the Thirty will throw a clearer light on the mess which the victorious democrats in 403 inherited and the enormity of the task they embraced in reconstructing a political system not only under which both sides of a bitter civil conflict could coexist, but which would prove internally and constitutionally durable.

ATHENS ON THE EVE OF THE THIRTY

When Athens capitulated to Sparta, she was left with no realistic choice but to accept whatever regime was imposed upon her. Thucydides characterised the Peloponnesian War as a polarising event dividing Greece between democrats and oligarchs, whose watershed was the *stasis* at Corcyra, which exemplified the principle that democrats enlisted the support of Athens, oligarchs the support of Sparta.[2] As always, there were exceptions: democratic Elis on the west coast of the Peloponnese remained loyal to the Spartan-led Peloponnesian League, while the Athenian-led Delian League contained member states, such as Samos, which may not have had democracies.[3] Nonetheless, the vast majority of cities within the alliances appear to have conformed to Thucydides' paradigm, which has led many to understand the Peloponnesian War as a conflict between the forces of democracy on one side, of oligarchy on the other.[4] On defeating Athens in 404, Sparta's first move was to overturn democracy. Though democratic for well over a century, Athens nevertheless had numerous internal dissenters, most notorious among them a pamphleteer known by the nickname of 'Old Oligarch',[5] who wrote a choleric work entitled *Constitution of the Athenians* (not to be confused with the Aristotelian treatise of the same title), which was little more than a rant against the evils of mob rule. As this notorious anti-democratic tract shows, in the ideology of its critics democracy equalled the rule of the mass,[6] but it is important to recognise that

---

[2] Th. 3.82–3. For modern treatments of this episode, see Fuks 1953; Price 2001: 1–78.

[3] On democratic Elis in the Peloponnesian League, see Legon 1968: 212 and Kagan 2013: 272 n. 40. On the establishment of democracy at Samos in 441–439, see Th. 1.115.3. For the vexed question of Samos' ideological status before 412, see Legon 1972; Meiggs 1972: 43; Ostwald 1993.

[4] Thucydides at 3.82.1 phrases the matter thus: οὕτως ὠμὴ <ἡ> στάσις προυχώρησε, καὶ ἔδοξε μᾶλλον, διότι ἐν τοῖς πρώτη ἐγένετο, ἐπεὶ ὕστερόν γε καὶ πᾶν ὡς εἰπεῖν τὸ Ἑλληνικὸν ἐκινήθη, διαφορῶν οὐσῶν ἑκασταχοῦ τοῖς τε τῶν δήμων προστάταις τοὺς Ἀθηναίους ἐπάγεσθαι καὶ τοῖς ὀλίγοις τοὺς Λακεδαιμονίους. Recently, it has been argued (see Brock 2009) that democracy was something of a flagship policy and that provided cities were prepared to remain subordinate to the empire, Athens was less concerned than Thucydides perhaps implies about the form of government which they used.

[5] See [X.] *Ath. Pol. passim*. For the variant dating of the pamphlet between the 440s and the penultimate decade of the fifth century, see Gomme 1962a: 68; Bowersock 1967: 33–8; Ste Croix 1972: 307–10; Ostwald 1986: 188–91; Yunis 1996: 46–50. For a recent edition of the text with introduction, see Osborne 2004.

[6] This point is made most clearly by the Old Oligarch at [X.] *Ath. Pol.*1.6–8. For a general discussion of how the term *dêmos* was used in the rhetoric of oligarchs, see Donlan 1970; Raaflaub 1983: 524; Petrey 1988: 43–6; Ober 1989: 4 with n. 2.

this was not how the Athenian democracy saw itself.[7] When used in the most commonly attested legal formula introducing decrees of the Athenian legislature ('resolved by the Council and People'), the term *dêmos* denoted not 'the mass' in a socio-political sense, but the citizenry in its legal and constitutional entirety.[8] Greek distinguished between *dêmos* in a strict legal sense, to mean 'the citizenry' regardless of social rank or status, and *plêthos* in a sociological sense, to mean 'the mass', or *ochlos* in a pejorative sense, to mean 'the mob'. If the Athenian democracy is to be understood in terms of the political dominance of one faction over another, in this case the poor over the rich, then the ideological contest between democracy and oligarchy at the end of the fifth century can perhaps be understood in terms of a contest between different ideological groupings defined by wealth and education.[9] If this is true, then the return to democracy in 403, and the Amnesty which ensued, was nothing more than a shifting of the political scales, whereby one social class or group reasserted dominance over another. The victory of the democrats would, on

---

[7] The definition of *dêmokratia* as the rule of the entire citizenry, as opposed to a distinct part of it, is made clear in a speech which Thucydides puts into the mouth of Athenagoras of Syracuse during his account of the Athenian military expedition to Sicily (6.39.1). In the famous Funeral Oration Pericles outlined what this meant in practice (Th. 2.35–43): freedom for all, regardless of social position or status, to serve the state, and equal justice for all under the law. Importantly, Pericles praises democracy not as the 'rule of the lower orders'; such a view is completely absent in the official democratic rhetoric of the Athenian state but finds voice only in the critical and distorted political pamphlets of the Old Oligarch and others who might have shared his anti-democratic opinions. Some (e.g. Sealey 1973: 280–2) have gone so far as to claim that this meaning of *dêmokratia* can only be construed as an apology, but there is no need to hold that interpretation; against such a position, see Thomas 1989: 234 and Harris 1992. For a more recent evaluation of the Athenian democracy as a society governed under the law, rather than a form of mob rule as has been alleged by both ancient and modern critics, see now Harris 2013: 60–98; Filonik 2019.

[8] This formula spread throughout Greece among those cities which practised democracy; see Robinson 2011: 214.

[9] Perhaps the best example in Anglo-American scholarship of the Marxist view of ancient Greek democracy is the classic work of De Ste Croix (1972), which understands the rise of democracy as the outgrowth of class struggle. Unfortunately, the evidence from Greek antiquity conspicuously fails to support such a theory. As argued below, the sources suggest that the Athenian democracy was the accidental consequence of a dynastic squabble within the local aristocracy and cannot, at any point of its development, be understood as the outgrowth of an underlying social or political revolution. The Athenian democracy was the brainchild of enlightened thinkers in the sixth century who perceived that the best way to create a cohesive and lasting political community which did not depend on the brute force of a tyrant was to devise a system in which all were equal under the law. Democracy came about not by violent means but through successive waves of legislation.

that gloomy and distorted analysis, have invoked the principle of political subjection by one side of the other.[10]

Many modern scholars have read these paradigmatic distinctions over-literally and have been led to understand the democratic restoration in terms of the victory of the poor over the rich. This is to miss the fundamental point: if democracy meant 'sovereignty of the *dêmos*' in the sense in which the term is attested in legal documents, then the restoration of democracy in 403 need be seen not as the renewed political subjection of the rich by the poor, but the renewal of a system in which no one grouping in society had a right to dominate another. Put differently, a perfectly functioning democracy would have been one wherein *stasis* was totally banished. Under such a system, all citizens had equal shares in government regardless of wealth, class, education or social status. Under such a system, there was no political division, as all had an equal stake in the political process.[11] Though it can fairly be argued that Athenians got closer to perfecting the democratic principle than did any other city in antiquity, it is not the case that even Athens was ever completely shot of the divisive and polarising influences of *stasis* which, according to Thucydides, were to blame for her failure to manage the war responsibly and her final defeat at the hands of Sparta.[12] Yet Thucydides' testimony must also be read with care, since many modern interpreters have mistakenly read his comment as a critique of democracy and exposé of its weaknesses and shortcomings.[13] Thucydides was concerned not so much with the weakness of democracy as with the divisive effect of the war with Sparta.[14] The essential point he

---

[10] Wolpert (2002) has rightly argued that in the ideology of the restored democracy the victory of Thrasybulus over the Thirty in 403 was understood as a victory of the whole people, not one faction within it. This is borne out by the fact that the Oaths of Reconciliation, which promised to allay memories of past grievances, were sworn by the whole of the citizen body; see And. 1.90 with Joyce 2014: 5.

[11] The principle that the Athenian concept of democracy implies political and legal, rather than social or economic, equality is rightly stated by Hansen (1991: 64–85).

[12] Th. 2.65.

[13] An example of such a tendency is to be found in Ober (1998: 52–121), who understands the *History* of Thucydides to form part of a tradition of intellectual dissent incorporating the Old Oligarch, Aristophanes and later Plato. The problem with his approach is that it seeks to align literary texts of very different genres and aims. The main purpose of Thucydides is not to criticise democracy in principle but to show how Athenian democracy, the most stable of all political systems in Greece with the possible exception of Sparta itself, was gradually undermined by the course of the war through greed, ambition and the private quarrelling of its leaders.

[14] The principal target of Thucydides' criticism was Alcibiades, who persuaded the Athenians against their better judgement to launch the disastrous campaign in Sicily against the more conservative policies of Pericles. Significantly, the term *dêmagôgos* is used only once in the whole of the Thucydidean narrative (Th. 4.21.3 in reference to Cleon) and, unlike our modern derivative 'demagogue', does not carry with it negative moral connotations. The word

makes is not that Athenian democracy was inherently weak or faction-ridden, but that the war fostered desperate conditions whereby, in the end, rational decision-making was clouded by madness. When criticising Athens in the wake of the death of Pericles in 430, Thucydides railed not against the 'evils' of democracy, as some claim reading his commentaries in the same vein as those of the Old Oligarch, but against the destructive psychological ravages of war.[15]

What was it, then, that caused democracy at the end of the fifth century to be shaken to the core? The question is complex and must incorporate two separate, but interwoven, historical strands, innovations within both Athens and Sparta during the Peloponnesian War. By tradition, despite the awful caricature which the policies of Lysander generated in the last decade of the fifth century, Sparta had always been the defender of liberty in Greece. Xenophon (HG 2.4.30) states that the Peloponnesians only followed Spartan policy when it aimed to protect freedom. In his essay *On the Malice of Herodotus*, Plutarch (*Mor.* 858) records an anecdote dating back to King Cleomenes' attempt to reinstate the tyrant Hippias at Athens a century earlier, in 508. According to the story, Sosicles of Corinth on hearing of the Spartan ruse to bring Hippias back from exile in Sigeum reminded Cleomenes of what his own city had suffered under the tyranny of Cypselus and Periander (see Hdt. 5.90–1). Plutarch ascribes this tradition, which he dismisses as fabricated, to Herodotus' desire to rob Sparta of the glory of the liberation of Athens from the rule of the Peisistratids. Whether true or not, the objection of Plutarch is important, because it shows how Sparta was perceived in Greece, as a liberator rather than an enslaver. What is clear in 432 is that the Spartans rallied support in mainland Greece for a war against Athens on the grounds that Athens had become an enslaver, against the terms outlined in the treaty of 446 which guaranteed autonomy to the cities of the mainland, and similar tendencies are evident in the policies of Brasidas and in the Plataean debate. In context, the support for freedom meant the support for ancestral constitutions, whether those constitutions were moderately oligarchic, such as Corinth, or democratic, such as Elis. After the failure of the Athenian expedition against Syracuse, however, a new policy was introduced by Lysander, which was to install oligarchies to

---

dêmagôgos in Greek means 'leader of the people' in a neutral descriptive sense, not in the sense of 'rabble-rouser' in which our derivative is normally used. For Thucydides' attitude to the 'radical demagogues', see Cawkwell 1997: 56–74.

[15] For a clear and lucid analysis of the shift in political culture which resulted from the Peloponnesian War, see now Harris 2013: 305–44. Harris argues persuasively that the misuse of litigation in the final decades of the fifth century at Athens came about from the stresses and tensions of warfare and was analogous to the factional movements which tore Corcyra apart in 427 and exposed the weaknesses of the legal system. It would be wrong, however, to read Thucydides as saying or implying that malicious prosecutions were an integral component of the democratic system which led to its eventual demise in 404.

ensure support of Sparta. This met reproof from King Pausanias, with whom Lysander had political ructions (see below), but what is clear from the historical accounts is that Lysander's policies were out of keeping with the more traditional Spartan objective, which was to respect and uphold the traditional *status quo* among the Greek cities which acknowledged her military leadership. That policy, as Chapter 3 shows, won out a year later in 403 at the restoration.

The second strand is the change in Athenian politics after the death of Pericles, which Thucydides puts down to the ruthless ambition of Pericles' successors for political supremacy (Th. 2.65.10). Thucydides describes these leaders as slanderers who jockeyed for position with attacks on the characters of their political opponents (κατὰ τὰς ἰδίας διαβολάς).[16] Commentators have often bypassed the precise meaning of this phrase, taking it to be a moralising judgement about the political methods of the demagogues. Yet closer investigation of the orators shows that the word *diabolē* is deeply connected with litigation in the courts.[17] This connection does much to explain why one of the first moves of the Thirty was to attack the sycophants, which the sources describe as a popular step (see below). In the period until the Peloponnesian War there is no record of prosecution of generals.[18] Until then, the preferred way of getting rid of an opponent was by ostracism.[19] This all seems to have changed in the period which followed: in 430/29, Pericles was tried, removed from office (Th. 2.65.3) and fined (D.S. 12.45.4; Plu. *Per.* 32.3–4; 35.2); in 429/8, Phormio was found guilty and fined a hundred mnai (*FGrHist* 324 F 8); Paches committed suicide after his accounting (*euthynai*) (Plu. *Arist.* 26.3; *Nic.* 6.1); the general Demosthenes chose to remain at Naupactus through fear of what would happen if he returned (Th. 3.18, 25–36, 49–50); in 424 we learn of the public prosecutions of Sophocles, Pythodorus and Eurymedon (Th. 4.65.3); Aristophanes in the *Wasps* (894–1008) parodies the trial of Laches by Cleon. Though some have downdated the use of the lawcourt as a political weapon to the period after the ostracism of Hyperbolus,[20] the decade of the 420s is replete with such cases, and Aristophanes connects this change of

---

[16] For the meaning of *diabolē*, see Rizzo and Vox 1978; Rhodes 1988: 245; Rusten 1989: 213; Hornblower 1991: 213. For its connection with litigation, see Harris 2013: 305–47.

[17] See, for example, D. 18.7, 11, 225; 57.36; [D.] 59.5; Aeschin. 1.126, 152; 2.10, 11, 145; 3.223.

[18] See Harris 2013: 309–13.

[19] On the ostracism of Aristeides, see Hdt. 8.79.1 with Brenne 2001: 114–18; Siewert 2002: 193–204. On the ostracism of Themistocles, see Th. 1.135.2–3; Pl. *Grg.* 516d; D. 23.204–5; Plu. *Them.* 21.5; D.S. 11.55.1–3 with Siewert 2002: 247–57. On the ostracism of Cimon, see Pl. *Grg.* 516d with Brenne 2001: 193–5 and Siewert 2002: 350–7. On the ostracism of Hyperbolus, see Connor 1971: 79–84.

[20] For example, Rhodes (1994: 97–8), who ignores much of the evidence for its use in the period preceding; *contra* Harris 2013: 316–17.

practice to the influence of Cleon, who was the first to use prosecution to win popularity.[21] Similar tactics were employed before the Assembly.[22] Once the law was subverted and usurped to bring down public officials, Athens' ability to win the war was severely hampered. More importantly, however, the lawcourt was brought into disrepute. The most egregious abuse of the law for political gain was the infamous case of the generals at Arginusae in 406, who after winning a spectacular victory against the Spartan fleet disobeyed orders to save a shipwrecked crew (X. *HG* 1.7.1–34). In their absence, they were charged before the Assembly and convicted, a move which according to Plato the Athenians bitterly regretted (Pl. *Ap.* 32b).

The consequence was a *volte-face* in the attitude to the lawcourts. The sources make clear that the most dedicated supporters of the Thirty were those who had been brought down in the courts, which explains why the Thirty physically removed the laws of Ephialtes from the Areopagus (*Ath. Pol.* 35.2).[23] Though scholars have often understood this as an empowering measure, it was just the reverse: by removing those laws, the ancestral role of the Areopagus as the protector of the law was suspended. Accountability was a central component of the rule of law, but because Cleon had abused the procedure to harass politicians, it was easy for the Thirty to argue that the law as a restraining measure should be pushed to the margins, which does much to explain why despite their initial commission to publish the ancestral constitution by which they would govern, they rapidly ignored their remit and neglected publication of the laws (X. *HG* 2.3.2, 11). This reveals something fundamental about Athens on the eve of the Thirty, which the lawgivers of 403 nearly a year later needed urgently to remedy: because of a policy of sycophancy which had raged in Athens for nearly three decades, a wedge had been driven between the law and its enforcement in the courts on one side, and political authority on the other. Support for and opposition to the Thirty was principally over this issue, not over the issue of personal means (see further below). The sources make clear that the Thirty were just as capable of oppressing the wealthy as they were the poor (*Ath. Pol.* 35.3–4). The matter of the ideological divide between democrats and oligarchs had far less to do with economic or social status, in the conventional Marxist sense of a class struggle,

---

[21] Thus *Eq.* 235–9, 258–63, 278–9, 300–2, 304–10, 442–3, 475–9, 626–9; *V.* 288–9, 474–6, 487. See also Th. 3.38.2; 3.42.3, 43.1; Lys. 21.19. For a discussion of the evidence, see Harris 2013: 316–17.

[22] For a full discussion of the cases, see Harris 2013: 320–34.

[23] The removal of the laws of Ephialtes is often interpreted as a nod in the direction of oligarchy, as if the authority of the Areopagus were thereby being elevated. That is to miss the point. By taking down the laws from the Areopagus, the Thirty were *removing* the authority of the Areopagus as the protector of the law; for a thorough reappraisal of the evidence, and a critique of earlier scholarship, see now Harris 2019a.

and far more to do with the matter of authority: should authority reside with the public official or the lawcourt? The early success of the Thirty is surely to be explained by the disillusionment of many at the way the courts had been mishandled, though once the Thirty began to confiscate wealth without trial, the security of ownership and respect for ownership suffered violation, and the scales began to tip in the other direction again. The ascendency of the oligarchs in 404 is therefore to be seen in terms not of the failure of the *dêmos* but the revenge of officeholders on public prosecutors.

These considerations cast doubt on the claim that the events of 404 came about through the failure of democracy. To make such a statement unequivocally would be to underestimate both the extraneous and internal factors and forces which led to Athens' collapse. The complete destruction of her expeditionary force in Sicily in 413 plunged Athens into a desperate war of survival against the combined forces of Sparta and Syracuse.[24] The situation worsened when, in the following year, Sparta enlisted the support of Persia on the eastern flank of Athens' naval empire.[25] In 411 she installed an oligarchy of Four Hundred as a bid to win over Persia.[26] The effort was futile, and democracy swiftly returned.[27] In 405, the naval defeat at Aegospotami gave Sparta control of the grain route, whereupon slowly Athens was starved into submission.[28] In 404, she concluded a peace treaty on Sparta's terms.[29] Athens had found herself in a position where she had to accept any terms Sparta dictated. Though they tried to exert some degree of negotiating power, Athenians were left with no realistic choice but to accept the subversion of democracy and instalment, at Sparta's bidding, of an oligarchic government which most found repellent. But the ascendency of the Thirty requires an internal explanation also. Athens on the eve of her defeat to Sparta had seen one of the most sacred guarantors of her democracy, the lawcourts, thrown into disrepute through repeated violation and abuse for selfish political ends. The actions of the Thirty are to be explained in large measure as a reaction to this tendency, and when democracy was restored the following year, it was important for the rule of law to be reinstated as a key provision in the accountability of public officials. The period of the Thirty was not a 'counterrevolution'.[30] Provided opposition to democracy did not become

---

[24] For an account of the desperate circumstances which the collapse of the Athenian expedition to Sicily created, see Th. 8.17.4–18.

[25] Th. 8.17.4; 8.29.

[26] Th. 8.47–54, 56; Plu. *Alc.* 25.3–6.

[27] X. *HG* 1.1.14, 23; Plu. *Alc.* 28.2; D.S. 13.52–3; Plu. *Lys.* 1.

[28] *Ath. Pol.* 34; Plu. *Alc.* 36.4–37.3; *Lys.* 9.4–11.

[29] X. *HG* 2.3.2; Plu. *Lys.* 15.5; Paus. 1.2.2; 3.5.1.

[30] This mistake is made most recently by Simonton (2018), who fails to differentiate between different types of oligarchy. For a criticism of his approach, see Harris 2019b.

violent or openly subversive, Athens' democracy down to 404 was quite willing to tolerate those who did not believe in democracy; as Demosthenes later pointed out (D. 20.105–8), not to approve of democracy was a democratic right of which oligarchs took full intellectual advantage.

THE SUBVERSION OF DEMOCRACY AT ATHENS IN AUTUMN 404

In late summer of 404, Athens was brought to her knees. Sparta had cut off her food supply from the Aegean, and though the defensive mechanisms and strategies Pericles had ingeniously contrived had served her well for twenty-seven years, she had no choice but to open her gates to Spartan garrisons. The humiliation of defeat would have been indescribable, to say nothing of the anger Athenians would have harboured against those who had brought defeat upon the city. At first glance, it might be tempting to imagine that disillusionment with democracy as a political form of government set in, and that Athenians were now willing to accept an oligarchic alternative, but that would be to miss a more obvious point: Athenians accepted the overthrow of democracy not because they had ceased to believe in democracy as an institution but because circumstances presented no alternative. Anger and disapproval were directed not against the democratic constitution but against those who had led Athens into disastrous military action. Those who hated democracy saw their chance: now was the time to strike a bargain with Sparta and use the ill-fated predicament in which Athens had landed herself to bring about the political change which they had long coveted. The chief ringleader of this anti-democratic resistance was a man called Critias,[31] a pupil of Socrates and established proponent of oligarchy.[32] Critias is best remembered for his radical views about the nature of the gods, which he believed were the inventions

---

[31] Questioning the claim that Critias was in any meaningful sense a 'leader' of the Thirty, see Németh 2006: 19–27. It is of course difficult to know from the extant source material how power was distributed among the Thirty, as the evidence fails us on this matter, but the sources agree that Critias wielded far-reaching influence.

[32] The precise relationship with Socrates is difficult to extrapolate. Little vignettes from Xenophon's later writings suggest that Socrates had upbraided Critias during the time of the oligarchy for his mismanagement of the city's affairs and for harbouring an unhealthy lust for a young man called Euthydemus (X. *Mem.* 1.2.29–33). Famously, Critias was described as an 'amateur among philosophers, and a philosopher among amateurs' (schol. Pl. *Ti.* 20a). But we also know that his name was used as an interlocutor in some of Plato's dialogues (see *Chrm.* 153c; *Prt.* 316a; *Ti.* 19c). On the philolaconism of Critias, see Jordović 2014. Against the use of the term 'aristocracy', see Fisher and Wees 2015.

of men to control lawlessness.³³ There can be little doubt that Critias was the product of a training which had led him to hold disdainful views of democracy. Fragments of his writings show that he was deeply interested in political constitutions, and according to the historian Xenophon, he notoriously said that Sparta had the best of all constitutions.³⁴ Born around 460, he is known for his connection to the scandal of 415 known as the *hermokopeia*, or 'Mutilation of the Herms', in the course of which a group of nobles defaced a set of family monuments which stood in the Agora and led to fears among the populace that a conspiracy was afoot to undermine the democracy (see further Chapter 4). Critias' connection with this scandal is known to us through Andocides, who states that Critias was implicated, placed under arrest and subsequently released (And. 1.47–68). Critias also had been attached to the oligarchy of 411, though the connection is unclear. In the wake of the Four Hundred, he proposed the trial of the dead oligarch Phrynichus, and later set up a hoplite democracy in Thessaly along Spartan lines after being prosecuted in 406 by Cleophon.³⁵ A renowned Laconophile, he was one of the five 'ephors' chosen in 404 from the *hetaireiai* to subvert democracy (Lys. 12.42).

How the Thirty were installed is open to dispute. According to Xenophon, the oligarchy did not come to power until Athens was starved finally into submission.³⁶ Previous attempts to negotiate with Sparta on the terms she demanded had been thwarted, but now that affairs had reached a state of desperation, the Athenians realised that they had no choice but to accept any terms which Sparta might impose. They dispatched Theramenes, an oligarchic sympathiser and subsequently a member of the Thirty, to Sparta to negotiate peace.³⁷ The Spartans demanded that Athens tear down her Long Walls, the walls which protected the Piraeus harbour, surrender her fleet, recall all exiles and hand over affairs to a panel of thirty men empowered to devise a new constitution once they had searched out the ancestral laws.³⁸ Whereas Xenophon attests that Athenians had no choice but to tear down their walls and subvert the democracy,³⁹ Lysias puts a rather different spin on the story (Lys. 12.71–8). According to his version, the Spartans did not initially demand the tearing down of the walls; this was a bargain

---

³³ DK 88 F 25.
³⁴ X. *HG* 2.3.34; DK 88 F 32–7.
³⁵ Lyc. 1.113. For differing views as to Critias' connections with the Four Hundred, see Avery 1963; Adeleye 1974; Németh 2006: 31.
³⁶ X. *HG* 2.2.21. For general discussion of the scale and extent of Athenian population losses by the end of the war, see Strauss 1986; Hansen 1986.
³⁷ X. *HG* 2.2.16–21.
³⁸ X. *HG* 2.2.20; 2.3.2. For different ancient perspectives on the Athenian assembly which finally ratified peace with Sparta, see Lys. 12.71–6; *Ath. Pol.* 34.3; D.S. 14.3.5–7; Plu. *Lys.*15.
³⁹ For doubts about the veracity of Xenophon's account, see McCoy 1975: 136.

on the part of Theramenes, who subverted democracy for motives of his own. According to Lysias, Theramenes had been sent to Sparta with the remit to negotiate peace, but the initial demand from Sparta was that peace be formalised without destruction of walls or surrender of the fleet or subversion of the constitution. This the Athenians would have accepted had it not been for Theramenes, who, as Lysias alleges, was so bent on the destruction of the city that he was prepared to go to any length to bring it about. Lysias further claims that he prevented the Assembly from meeting to discuss proposals until the Spartan generals were present to oversee the meeting, at which point the Athenians were so overawed by Spartan military presence that they were prepared to accept any demands. When revised proposals were put before the Assembly, there was such an uproar of disapproval that the Spartan general Lysander declared that if they did not accept the terms of the peace as presented, this would be noted by Sparta as wholesale repudiation. Lysias backed his condemnation of Theramenes by pointing out that when put on trial by the Thirty, he appealed to restored exiles, saying that they owed their repatriation to him primarily.[40]

There can be no doubt that Lysias is truthful in relating the sequence of events by which the democracy fell in 404, but the claim that the subversion of democracy, along with the other crippling peace conditions, was a mere political device of Theramenes is less believable. What is clear is that Lysander journeyed from one defeated city to the next, overthrowing democracy and replacing it with commissions which kept the conquered cities in subjection to Sparta.[41] It remains unlikely, therefore, that he did not have similar designs for Athens. Furthermore, despite his unfortunate association with the oligarchy of the Four Hundred some eight years previously, Theramenes evidently was a man in reasonable standing with the Athenian people, whom the people were prepared to trust to bring about as favourable a settlement as possible with Sparta. If Xenophon is to be believed, there were many in Sparta who advocated the annihilation of Athens and enslavement of its population, but others remembered the good services performed by Athens to Greece in the days of the Persian invasion, and thus wished to spare the city on condition that it came to peace terms.[42] Theramenes spent some months at Sparta and

---

[40] For the completely contradictory tradition that Theramenes opposed the Thirty, see D.S. 14.3.5–7. Salmon (1969) argued that Theramenes made two separate speeches to the Assembly, one which advocated support for the Thirty and another which opposed them (followed by Krentz 1982: 49 n. 21). But this looks like an attempt to make sense out of nonsense. It is far easier to suppose that, as a complex and controversial figure, the tradition surrounding Theramenes in the fourth century and beyond resulted in disagreement and contradiction, as the slanderous nature of Lysias' account indicates.

[41] X. *HG* 2.2.1–2.

[42] X. *HG* 2.2.19–20.

would soon have got to know the perilous condition of his countrymen.[43] Any pragmatic politician in his position would have realised that Athenians did not have the bargaining capability to be able to resist any demand which Sparta issued. If Lysias is correct to insinuate that the timings of the meeting at Athens were orchestrated in such a way as to stun the Athenian people into acceptance, this shows that Theramenes was cunning and knew how to achieve his ends. The idea that Sparta would never have demanded the overthrow of democracy or destruction of the city's defences had it not been for Theramenes looks like facile rhetorical slander. It is central to the argument of Lys. 12 to erode the distinction which Eratosthenes in self-defence sought to make between extreme and moderate members of the oligarchy. Eratosthenes arrested the brother of Lysias but did not put him to death. To undermine the case in defence, Lysias needs therefore to present the argument that really there was no difference between the two. It has also been suggested on grounds of intertextuality that Lysias' account was a direct response to an oligarchic pamphlet known as the 'Theramenes papyrus', which relates that Theramenes was appointed by the Assembly to negotiate peace with Lysander, though others have inferred that the Theramenes pamphlet is a direct response to Lysias, and others still that it is a much later forgery dating from the Hellenistic period interested in rhetorical *bons mots*.[44]

The author of the *Ath. Pol.* tells the story in a different way.[45] On his account, the initial agreement between Sparta and Athens was that the Athenians govern themselves according to their ancestral practices. This was a middle-of-the-road offer, since the populace was divided among three factions, those who wanted democracy, those who wanted outright oligarchy and those who desired something intermediate. Almost certainly, this is simplification: Theramenes wished to limit citizenship to the hoplites as had the oligarchy of 411; unlike Archinus, Anytus and Phormisius, he chose to participate in the regime of the Thirty. The *Ath. Pol.* envisages the offer of government along the lines of the ancestral constitution as a bid to the moderate party over which Theramenes presided. By the 'ancestral constitution', this means not oligarchy *tout court*, for which no ancestral precedent could be cited, but something rather less democratic than what existed in the late fifth century. Lysander is said to have favoured oligarchy and, on the motion of Dracontides, the Athenians were cowed into voting in Lysander's demands. This version agrees with Lysias in that it suggests that Athenians were pressured into oligarchy on Lysander's initiative, but disagrees

---

[43] According to Xenophon, Theramenes was at Sparta for almost four months (*HG* 2.2.16).
[44] For the *editio princeps*, see Merkelbach and Youtie 1968. For varying theories as to the relationship between these documents, see Andrewes 1970; Peseley 1989; Loftus 2000.
[45] *Ath. Pol.* 34.3.

on the point that Theramenes did not get what he desired. If this version is believable, Lysander was initially content with the proposal that the radical democracy should be abolished and replaced with something more moderate, but when he saw that there were many oligarchs who actively desired unbridled oligarchy, he changed his mind and went along with their proposals. This would make it difficult to connect Theramenes with extreme oligarchy. In the following section, the *Ath. Pol.* states that the Thirty neglected what had been agreed as to the ancestral constitution and elected their own Council of Five Hundred, a commission of ten to govern in Piraeus and a bodyguard of three thousand men to keep the people in check, and they maintained pretence of governing in accordance with the ancestral constitution until they turned on the citizens.[46] Evidently there was an initiative to reinstate the ancestral constitution, but that proposal was not limited to Theramenes. At some point the Thirty took over, and once they tired of the pretence of legality, jettisoned the remit altogether.[47]

Reconstructing the chronology has proven an almost irresolvable task.[48] Plutarch (*Lys.* 15.1) states that Lysander entered Athens on 16 Munychion, which must refer to 404, and in a different place states that the Oath of Reconciliation was sworn on 12 Boedromion 403 (*Mor.* 349f1–3). That allows a chronological gap of some seventeen months in which to place the Thirty's eight months in power. Todd has argued recently that the sources are deliberately misleading, and, because of this, that it is methodologically impossible to get to the truth.[49] While we must acknowledge the limitations of the evidence, the following broad outline of events can be traced from the discordant material. Sparta was divided over whether to spare Athens. A more extreme party advocated its destruction, whereas a moderate voice proposed to spare the enemy on condition that it met some exacting terms. It seems highly improbable that Lysander or anyone at Sparta would have been content to let the Athenian democracy continue as before or Athens keep her defences, as Lysias alleges. Almost certainly, it was an integral part of the Spartan objective to beat Athens into total submission and overturn a system of government which the Spartans elsewhere in Greece were systematically opposing. As a result, they bargained with Theramenes to bring about a change of government and consulted his advice as to how this should be

---

[46] *Ath. Pol.* 35.
[47] Krentz 1982: 135–9 gives priority to this account by claiming that its ultimate source is the *Hellenica Oxyrhynchia* and not an Atthidographer. But there is no good reason to prioritise it over the much more complete and comprehensive account of Xenophon.
[48] For older scholarly treatments, see Lenschau RE 6 (1937): cols 1257–2361; Hignett 1952: 378–83; Rhodes 1981: 436–7; Krentz 1982: 142–4; Green 1991: 15–16.
[49] Todd 2020: 17–23, contesting the assumption of Green (1991: 15–16) that our sources are trying their best to be truthful.

achieved. Theramenes realised that the Athenians would not accept oligarchy without a fight, and so advised the Spartans to tender an offer which in some way was ideologically palatable, but which nevertheless entailed enough fluidity to allow some form of oligarchic regime to be installed. As two of the three sources state, Lysander's objective was oligarchy, and provided he got what he desired, he did not care about the language used to disguise it. Therefore, a proposal was put to the Assembly to overturn the democracy and govern according to the 'ancestral constitution'. This, it was hoped, would have a more acceptable tone than an outright proposal to install a proxy regime. But the citizens saw through the ruse, and blamed Theramenes for betraying their interests. Lysander then made it clear that, call it what they might, the Athenians must accept an oligarchy. Dracontides proposed a commission of thirty to search out the ancestral laws, among them Theramenes, who, it would appear, was playing a double game. His objective was to get Athenians to accept Spartan demands but hoodwink Spartans into granting a regime perhaps not as pernicious as the extreme oligarchies they had instigated elsewhere.

There is another component to the puzzle which the sources do not explicitly draw out, but which needs further comment. In 411, when the Four Hundred were installed, Theramenes had also been an important player in the oligarchy of those years. Thucydides simplifies the oligarchic regime, drawing very little distinction between moderate and extreme supporters.[50] But as the Aristotelian version shows (*Ath. Pol.* 30.2–5), there was a significant difference between the form of oligarchy espoused by Theramenes, which was moderate and proposed the creation of the Five Thousand, and the extremists led by Phrynichus, whose sole ambition was to rule through a council which was answerable to nobody.[51] The extremists around Phrynichus wanted peace with Sparta, whilst the moderates around Theramenes wanted to continue the war under a reformed constitution. After the Four Hundred were overthrown, it was the unauthorised negotiations with Sparta that came under fire. Because Phrynichus did not have the backing of a foreign power, his government quickly fell into disrepute and tumbled, with Theramenes in ascendance, whereas in 404 the matter was different: Critias and the extremist wing of the Thirty were backed by a foreign power in the form of Lysander, and so it was much more difficult for Theramenes to exert a moderating influence upon the nastier wing of the movement. Once again, the Aristotelian tradition clarifies (*Ath. Pol.* 34.3) that in 404 there was a very decisive contrast between the moderate and extreme factions within the oligarchy, but because the dynamics of

---

[50] For a recent assessment of Thucydides' attitude to the oligarchic interlude of 411, see Wolpert 2017.

[51] For the view that the political aims of Theramenes in 411 should be taken seriously, see Harris 1990.

politics were different, it was far less easy for the milder faction to win the day. Lysander made it clear through nods and winks that the Assembly should accept outright oligarchy without nuance. It is perhaps not surprising therefore that, in popular tradition, Theramenes became associated with something irreconcilably repugnant and evil, as the lambasting rhetoric of Lysias in the aftermath of 403 shows (see Chapter 5). But it is important from the angle of historical assessment to understand Theramenes as a moderating influence who, for reasons of circumstance, could not exercise the necessary restraint in 404 which might have prevented the oligarchy from plunging the city into the turmoil of *stasis* which resulted in the horrific events that followed and which the restorers of democracy in 403 needed to remedy through the Amnesty legislation. The sources are messy, but even though Lysias gives our most contemporary extant account, care should be taken before assuming that just because it is first in chronological order, somehow it should be given priority of credence.

As the accounts are so contradictory, inevitably we must resort to speculation. What is clear is that though they would have had internal supporters, the Thirty came to power despite vehement protest from within the citizenry. Unlike other cities, such as Corinth or Samos, which were extremely volatile and experienced successive political upheavals, Athens had, since the days of Peisistratus, been politically orderly. At all stages of history, the city had harboured those who slighted the political *status quo*, whether through lampoonery, as in the case of the famous comedian and satirist Aristophanes, through diatribe, like the Old Oligarch, or through philosophical speculation into the ideal form of government, like the Academy founded by Plato. But the nature of democracy was that it was able to absorb within it those strands of intellectual criticism. There is little evidence until the final desperate years of the Peloponnesian War that the oligarchy of the Thirty was a political tragedy waiting to happen. The events did not arise out of a struggle between 'mass and elite', supporters and critics of democracy. The Thirty gained political ascendancy in 404 for no other reason than that a foreign power had put them there. But, for the sake of appearance, it was still necessary to give the oligarchic regime the outward image of having been installed not by Lysander, though he was the one who recommended their appointment, but by the Athenian citizenry.

One of the oldest and most sorely debated questions is why Lysander chose thirty men at Athens, whereas in other parts of the Greek world he installed commissions of ten officials (decarchies). R. Loeper in the nineteenth century argued that the Thirty modelled themselves on the Cleisthenic tribal system, where each of the ten tribes was subdivided into three ridings, or *trittyes*.[52]

---

[52] Loeper 1896. Loeper argued that the list of names of the Thirty in the MSS of Xenophon do not follow the conventional tribal order but that each name came from one *trittys* (tribal, coastal, city) in regular order. But democratic precedents for this are difficult to find; see now Todd 2020: 7.

Loeper's view was rejected when prosopographical evidence came to light which made it impossible to accept the trittyal reconstruction proposed.[53] A variant was suggested by T. Lenshau, who argued on the strength of Lys. 12.76 that the Assembly which appointed the thirty commissioners chose three men from each of the ten tribes, one nominated by Theramenes, a second by the ephors, and a third by the Assembly itself.[54] Others have suggested that the oligarchy modelled itself on the pattern of Sparta, where the number thirty drew its inspiration from the number who sat on the Spartan Gerousia and the Three Thousand modelled on the assembly of Spartiates who held a privileged position within the Spartan system.[55] In contrast, G. Németh more recently has suggested that the number is not a self-conscious attempt to mimic Sparta but one drawn from oligarchic utopian literature.[56] Even more recently, Todd has argued that the number ten was deliberately avoided because of its democratic association at Athens, and that by choosing thirty instead of ten, the oligarchy was bringing to the fore its oligarchic credentials rather than masquerading as a system which claimed some putative precedent in the ancestral constitution.[57] Any one of the above theories can only be speculative, and as Todd admits, there is a weakness in his own theory, which is that the Amnesty exempted not only the Thirty and the Eleven, but also the two boards of Ten (see Chapter 3). We will perhaps never know for certain why Lysander went for thirty men, rather than the more conventional ten, but what all the literature agrees on is that the Thirty were unreconstructed political criminals who plunged Athens into its worst and most psychologically scarring civic nightmare.

THE REIGN OF TERROR

Once in power, the Thirty began a witch-hunt which resulted probably in 5 per cent of the population perishing.[58] Their first step was to bring to trial those who had profited under democracy as sycophants.[59] In reality, their objective was to wreak revenge on those who had opposed the treaty of 404, especially the generals and taxiarchs.[60] The first public show trial of its kind was before

---

[53] Whitehead 1980.
[54] Lenschau *RE* 6 (1937): cols 2363–4. For objections, see Todd 2020: 10–11.
[55] Krentz 1982: 64–5; Whitehead 1982–3: 120.
[56] Németh 2006: 68–9.
[57] Todd 2020: 13–14.
[58] Nippel 1997: 107. Ancient sources disagree on the figure, but it is thought to have been around 1,500 men; thus Isoc. 7.67; 20.11; Aeschin. 3.235; *Ath. Pol.* 35.4. For more conservative figures, see D.L. 7.5; schol. Aeschin. 1.39.
[59] X. *HG* 2.3.12; Lys. 25.19; *Ath. Pol.* 35.3; D.S. 14.4.2.
[60] Thus Lys. 13 *passim*; see Krentz 1982: 60.

the Council of Five Hundred of men accused of plotting against the people. Although in practice this would have been little more than a kangaroo court, there was still an effort made to proceed according to legal formality.[61] We know of the identity of some of those who died from the trial: Dionysiodorus, Strombichides, Nicias, Nicomenes, Aristophanes of Cholleidae, Eucrates, Hippias of Thasos and Xenophon of Kourion.[62] Once removed, they turned on others who had been labelled sycophants, bribe-takers and embezzlers.[63] According to the Old Oligarch, those who came from the higher echelons were 'good' not only in a social but in a moral sense, and thus had a right to govern; conversely, those from the masses were seen as morally bad.[64] There is, however, a difference between this type of crude oligarchic theory and the more nuanced philosophical theories of Socrates and Plato. Conventional apologists for oligarchy understood 'the good' to mean those who came from the higher social ranks as defined by wealth and status. This stands in direct contrast to the Platonic ideal, in which the ruling elite is selected from those who are best suited to govern regardless of material wealth. Though critical of democracy, Socrates was no advocate of the style of government practised by the Thirty, and it would be mistaken to envisage Platonic thought as originating in the same vein as the kinds of political theories which motivated the oligarchy of the Thirty.

The sources give the impression that in the early period of their regime, there was a relative degree of restraint, but that the oppression became worse once democratic resistance began to mount on the borders of Attica. Those who lost their lives in the reign of terror included Antiphon,[65] Leon of Salamis,[66] Niceratus the son of Nicias,[67] and Lycurgus son of Lycomedes.[68] The first is otherwise unknown. Leon had been involved in the resistance to the Four Hundred in 411 and was probably targeted by the Thirty for his democratic sympathies.[69] Niceratus was the son of the famous general who died during the Sicilian expedition and had served as trierarch in 409. The sources do not clarify why he was targeted, but in the case of Lycurgus, other evidence indicates that he was popular with the people, as he later received a public burial.[70] In addition, we

---

[61] Lys. 13.50.
[62] Lys. 13.23–41.
[63] Lys. 12.5.
[64] [X.] *Ath. Pol. passim.*
[65] X. *HG* 2.3.40; Plu. *Mor.* 833a.
[66] X. *HG* 2.3.39.
[67] X. *HG* 2.3.39; D.S. 14.5.5; Lys. 18.6; 19.47; Plu. *Mor.* 998b.
[68] Plu. *Mor.* 841ab.
[69] X. *HG* 2.3.39; *Mem.* 4.4.3; And. 1.94; Pl. *Ap.* 32cd; *Ep.* 324e.
[70] Plu. *Mor.* 843d; 852a.

know that the Thirty pursued wealthy metics who were opposed to their rule.[71] These executions may have taken place at different times, but what is clear is that in many cases the motive may simply have been greed.[72] This would suggest that those who fell victim to the Thirty were not necessarily those who came from the poorer echelons of society. In the case of Niceratus, an estate worth fourteen talents was confiscated.[73] The identity of the Thirty's victims indicates that many came from wealthy and privileged backgrounds, and if the sources are trustworthy, it is possible that ownership of significant wealth made one a ripe candidate for persecution. The other main motive behind the persecutions was fear. Especially once opposition began to mount, the primary concern of the Thirty was to purge the city of anyone who was perceived to be a threat. The civil conflict of 403 cannot therefore be analysed as a struggle between rich and poor. The dividing issue was not wealth or property, but whether one supported democracy or oligarchy. Ideology, not status, was paramount.

Some scholars have claimed that the Thirty created a comprehensive constitutional package which defined all their powers.[74] Unfortunately, we do not have sufficient information at our disposal. Inscribed fragments of a so-called 'law code' from the late fifth century bore the signs of a legal redaction under the Thirty, but there is no way of proving this, and indeed it is not universally agreed that the surviving fragments of sacrificial laws dating from that time belong to a code of any sort (see Chapter 4). But we do know from scattered references that laws were created in the time of the Thirty. Critias himself is known to have passed at least two laws, records of which survive in literary references. One of these specified that none of the Three Thousand (the elite body of citizens created under the Thirty who later became known as 'the City Party') could be executed without the vote of the Council.[75] A second law attributed to Critias outlawed the teaching of rhetoric.[76] We also know that the Thirty went about abrogating some of the fifth-century laws such as the laws of Ephialtes of 462/1 which narrowly defined the competences of the Areopagite Council under the new dispensation.[77] What the effect was of the Thirty 'taking down from the Acropolis the laws on the Areopagus' has in the last thirty years been debated, as the Areopagus was the body which

---

[71] Lys. 12.6; X. *HG* 2.3.21–2, 40; D.S. 14.5.6.
[72] *Ath. Pol.* 35.4.
[73] Lys. 19.47.
[74] Ruschenbusch 1956; *contra* Krentz 1982: 61.
[75] X. *HG* 2.3.51.
[76] X. *Mem.* 1.2.31.
[77] *Ath. Pol.* 35.2; for the so-called 'Ephialtic reforms' of 462/1, see A. *Eum.* 701–2; *Ath. Pol.* 25.2 with the cautionary comments of Harris 2019b.

tried murder, and it was murder in which the Thirty were engaged.[78] At most, this could have been a political gesture to indicate that a more oligarchic government was being instituted. We also know that some amendments were made to the laws of Solon, one of which was the law which entitled a man to leave his property to whomever he wished unless he be of unsound mind, old age or under the influence of a woman.[79] Among the changes under the Thirty was the decision to transfer judicial powers to the Council, perhaps to spare cost by reducing the machinery of the city.

Mention has been made of the Three Thousand, chosen by the Thirty to bolster their regime from a group selected by birth and by wealth.[80] In principle, the Three Thousand formed an inner core of privileged citizens who were allowed to remain in the city and who enjoyed legal protection under the oligarchy, and functioned as a bodyguard. Scholars debate their social composition. Conventionally, it has been assumed that the Three Thousand came from a relatively wealthy segment of society which naturally would have shared the oligarchic sympathies of the Thirty, but this has more recently been questioned on the grounds that we do not know enough about the nature of this Solonian census classes to know for certain whether it represented the wealthier members of society or not, and it is far from clear in any case that to be a hoplite ever implied extensive financial means.[81] Besides, many of those who were cast out of Athens who were not among the Three Thousand were property owners, perhaps some of them wealthy, and many of those who were targeted may have suffered because they were personal enemies of the oligarchs and owned property which their opponents coveted.[82] The evidence of the fifth and fourth centuries reveals a multitude of wealthy and privileged citizens who served the democracy.[83] Almost certainly the Three Thousand

---

[78] Thus Fine 1983: 389. For a more sceptical view, see Hall 1990. For a re-evaluation of the role of the Areopagus in the Athenian democracy and its role as the protector of Athens' democratic institutions, see now Harris 2019a. Harris argues that the reforms of Ephialtes did not put an end to the dominance of the Areopagus, because such dominance never existed.

[79] *Ath. Pol.* 35.2.

[80] X. *HG* 2.3.19, 51; *Ath. Pol.* 37.1–2. On the 'myth of middle-class army', see Wees 2001; *contra* Guiá and Gallego 2010.

[81] Németh 2006: 41–74.

[82] See the example of Nicaretus, above, and the discussion in Chapter 4. The fragmentary evidence of Lysias' speech *Against Hippotherses* indicates that one of the questions which arose after the restoration of democracy in 403 was the recovery of non-moveable property. If so, it would be reductive to claim that those who belonged to the Three Thousand were necessarily wealthy, while those who did not were poor or dispossessed. The division is much more likely to have been down political and ideological than economic or social lines.

[83] For a full survey of propertied families at Athens down to the end of the classical age, see Davies 1971; see also Kron 2011.

were chosen because of their loyalty to the Thirty, not because they were necessarily rich or of privileged social class.

Those not on the roll lost all civic rights, and their property was confiscated and sold.[84] Disfranchisement (*atimia*) at Athens did not mean exile.[85] In practice, some who did lose their rights did go abroad for the sake of their own protection, as had the orator Andocides after being convicted for his role in the scandals of 415 (see Chapter 4). The penalty of *atimia* tended to fall into three main categories, permanent, non-permanent and specified. Permanent disfranchisement stripped a citizen of the right to serve on embassies or in the lawcourts, to give evidence, to speak in the Assembly, to hold public office and to enter sacred areas.[86] Non-permanent disfranchisement entailed the same deprivations but accrued from public debt and was cancelled once the debt had been paid.[87] More limited disfranchisements were meted out for lesser offences and involved the loss of fewer rights.[88] Very recently, it has been maintained that verdicts of *atimia* down to the late fourth century could involve the penalty of death or exile, but that interpretation depends on a very tendentious and questionable reading of the evidence.[89] Though Lysias is clear that the Thirty put a large number of innocent citizens to death, it is probable that this would have been done by separate court verdicts.[90] Failing to make the roll of the Three Thousand probably did not condemn a citizen to death or exile, but initially meant that his citizen rights were abrogated and, if he owned property, then that would be confiscated and placed in possession of the treasury. There is no evidence to support the theory that the purpose was to follow the Spartan model,[91] and the Three Thousand were probably chosen because the Thirty needed internal support and backing.

Because the Thirty understood that they could not achieve their ends without Spartan support, they sent a request to Sparta to send a garrison (X. *HG* 2.3.13). Once it was granted, Critias began putting innocent citizens to death.

---

[84] X. *HG* 2.4.1; Lys. 25.22; D.S. 14.32.4; Just. 5.9.12.

[85] For a sharp disagreement of perspective on this crucial issue, see Dmitriev 2015 and Joyce 2018.

[86] D. 21.32, 87; 22.30; 25.30; Aeschin. 1.18–27; Hyp. *Eux*. col. 31; *Lyc*. col. 16; Hansen 1974: 63; Bruyn 1995, 25; Thür *RE* (2) 1997: col. 215.

[87] And. 1.73; D. 53.27; 22.603; 24.200; [D.] 59.7.

[88] And. 1.33, 75; D. 25.75; Paoli 1930: 307; Scafuro 2012: 923.

[89] Dmitriev 2015; *contra* Joyce 2018. My conclusions are very similar to those of Youni (2001 and 2019). For a fresh analysis of *atimia*, see now Rocchi 2022.

[90] Lys. 12 and 13 *passim*.

[91] Xenophon (*HG* 2.4.1) states that the injunction to leave Athens if not on the roll took place after the death of Theramenes, not before, at a time when Critias had lost his grasp on reason, and his verdict is echoed by Lysias (25.22); see also D.S. 14.32.4; Just. 5.9.12. The sources together indicate that exile from Athens was not one of the initial consequences of being excluded from the roll but came about later once Critias saw that he was losing support from within the city.

This new political development marked the creation of the Three Thousand and signalled the point at which a political ruction emerged between Critias and Theramenes (X. *HG* 2.3.15). The latter protested the injustice of killing men in good standing and warned that the oligarchy might not survive, but the main sticking point was the creation of the Three Thousand: Theramenes realised that if the city was to cohere under oligarchy, the number three thousand was much too small. In place of three thousand, he advocated extending the franchise to five thousand citizens, as in 411, which in practice would have involved nine thousand (X. *HG* 2.3.35–49, which meant a less narrow conception of oligarchy which did not meet Critias' approval. The latter executed resident aliens (metics) and took their goods (X. *HG* 2.3.21). When instructed to carry out the executions, Theramenes again protested to Critias on moral grounds, at which point Critias decided that Theramenes was more trouble than he was worth and voted to have him removed. Theramenes was tried for subversion; he was initially acquitted, and once Critias saw that he had been outmanoeuvred, he proposed that Theramenes be struck off the roll of the Three Thousand and executed.[92] The trial ended with Theramenes toasting the health of Critias from the cup of hemlock.[93] Unlike Lysias, implacably opposed to Theramenes, Xenophon and the Aristotelian version are more favourable. Differences in the later accounts manifest themselves in the extent to which writers were prepared to distinguish between moderate and extreme oligarchs.[94]

The trial of Theramenes plays an intriguing role in the narrative of Xenophon. Like some other political trials which Xenophon narrates, most notably the trial of the Arginusae generals, it functions as a precursor to a military defeat, in this case the victory of democrats over the oligarchs at Phyle.[95] This is in keeping with the attitude to the misuse of the lawcourts found in both Xenophon and Thucydides, which may well stem from their own personal experiences: Thucydides was exiled by Cleon in 424 after failing to stop Brasidas taking Amphipolis and remained in exile for the next twenty years (Th. 5.26.5); Xenophon in the *Anabasis* relates that while he was abroad in Asia Minor the people of Athens voted about his exile, though we do not know the outcome (X. *An.* 7.7.57). In his account of the *stasis* at Corcyra in 427, Thucydides relates that each side sought to eliminate its opponents either by malicious court action or through use of physical violence (Th. 3.82.8). In the

---

[92] *Ath. Pol.* 37.1; D.S. 14.4.5–5.4; Just. 5.9.2; Oros. 2.17.7.
[93] On the authenticity of this speech, see Usher 1968.
[94] Harding 1974; Rhodes 1981: 359–60.
[95] This is to be contrasted with its place in the Aristotelian tradition, which has a completely different chronology. At *Ath. Pol.* 37.1, we read that the occupation of Phyle by the democrats took place before the trial and death of Theramenes.

passage which follows (3.84.1), we are told that *stasis* gives rise to miscarriages of justice through avarice and desire to acquire the property of others. At the same time, unjust verdicts are themselves the cause of *stasis*, and the problem is presented as a vicious cycle. Unlike in Thucydides, who seems more interested in unjust litigation, the trials narrated by Xenophon are for the most part just. For example, when the Spartans tried Anaxilaus of Byzantium for treason, mention is made of the extenuating circumstances of which they took due account (X. *HG* 1.3.19). No explicit comment is passed on the recall of Thibron, but the implication is that the trial was justified.[96] A similar case can be made for the trials of Timagoras in 366.[97] Yet what Xenophon does share in common with Thucydides, who in his famous diatribe against the successors of Pericles at 2.65.11 links sycophancy to the defeat of Athens in 404 (see above), is the idea that political litigation can often foreshadow military disaster. After reducing the Spartan fleet at Arginusae, Theramenes charged the generals with neglect of duty for failing to rescue shipwrecked sailors, whereupon the next chapter presents the disastrous defeat at Aegospotami (X. *HG* 1.7.1–34). In the case of his own trial, what is clear in the order of narration is that Xenophon implicitly links it to the oligarchic defeat at Phyle (see Chapter 3). This connection between misuse of the courts and subversion of a political regime is vital to bear in mind when we turn to consider the ban on vexatious litigation after 403. As argued in the next chapter, the chief purpose of the Amnesty legislation as far as Athens was concerned was to ensure that vindictive actions in the courts did not destabilise the fragile political *status quo*, and so it was decided that all crimes predating the restoration of democracy should thereafter be unactionable.[98] The civil strife of 404/3 and the role of the courts in fuelling the conditions which led to the establishment of the Thirty in autumn 404 and, in the case of the downfall of the Thirty, the trial of Theramenes in spring 403 are the crucial factors which drove the commissioners of 403 to recognise that the democracy only stood a chance of survival if a restraint was imposed on the misuse of litigation. The historical background of the clause μὴ μνησικακεῖν, which forbade prosecution of any untried case predating 12 Boedromion 403 (see Chapter 3), is to be found in the conditions which led both to the end of democracy in 404 and to the failure of the Thirty to retain power.

The period of the Thirty is crucial to grasp the aims of the legislators of late spring 403 who reconstructed democracy and built the foundations of the Reconciliation. The regime of the Thirty represents the breakdown of law

---

[96] X. *HG* 3.2.1; cf. D.S. 14.38.2.

[97] X. *HG* 7.1.35; cf. D. 19.31, 137, 191; Plu. *Pel.* 30.9–13.

[98] Carawan (2013) fails to bring out these connections sufficiently, because he does not set the amnesty legislation in the context of what had immediately preceded it.

and its appropriate application in the courts, which perhaps stands as the one single reason why the regime failed. But it is not enough to speak of this in isolation. The Thirty came to power precisely because the courts themselves had been misapplied in the period prior to the fall of democracy in 404. The era of Cleon is important here in that it represents a radical departure from what had preceded it. Until the death of Pericles in 429, trials of generals were infrequent if not non-existent. The war with Sparta changed all this, and the breakdown of democracy twenty-five years later was, in large measure, the result of the misuse of law as an instrument of faction and party politics. Of course, we must not underestimate the role played by Lysander and his drastic recalibration of Spartan foreign policy which by custom had always respected the freedom of the Greeks and respect for ancestral laws, a policy which would later come to fruition again at the time of the Peace of Antalcidas in 387/6. Yet it would be facile to attribute the imposition of the Thirty entirely to fortuitous external events. As Xenophon clarified (X. *HG* 2.3.12), when the Thirty turned against the sycophants as their first political move in clamping down on democrats, their policy met the approval of many Athenians who saw their defeat as consequential on the ignoble use of the courts which Cleon and his successors had unleashed.[99] When democracy was restored, it was therefore necessary to bring the courts under control, by preventing their usurpation by political activists who merely wanted to misuse litigation for selfish and vindictive ends.

The reign of terror exemplifies a principle seen again and again: as soon as it perceives threat, invariably an unpopular dictatorship resorts to violence in a bid to hold its position. The unleashing of violence functions as a means by which tyranny holds a population in subjection, but it also lays the seeds of tyranny's unravelling. As persecutions became worse, increasing numbers of citizens took to flight. The decision to divide the Athenian civic population among those who retained full rights and those who did not proved disastrous. Whilst the motive had been to bolster support for the regime, in the long run it had the opposite effect, as those who found themselves on the outside of the favoured circle were bound to outnumber those on the inside, as Theramenes rightly predicted. Crucially, the division created among the citizenry was not long-standing, but owed its origin to the political circumstances created in 404/3. When the democrats some months later were faced with the task of reconciling the community, the issue was tantamount to ending a recent and accidental civil conflict, not mending a deeper internal division which pre-dated the end of the war with Sparta, or which arose from a long-standing historical polarity between rich and poor. The democratic victory of 403 was the

---

[99] This impression is borne out in other sources also; see especially *Ath. Pol.* 35.3, which states that the Thirty went about doing away with sycophants as an initial bid for popular support.

triumph not of poor over rich but of a rational ideology, which recognised the advantages of an inclusive political system, over an irrational oligarchy which to its own detriment alienated the majority. Key was to restore accountability of officials and to reassert trial by impartial judges.

THE VICTORY OF THRASYBULUS AND THE DEMOCRATS

Xenophon claimed that the regime of the Thirty degenerated into unbridled oligarchy after the execution of Theramenes. The sources disagree sharply on the political attitude of Theramenes, and Xenophon probably simplified matters considerably. Athens had been a democracy as far back as anyone remembered. It is unlikely that those who lost their civic rights were prepared to acquiesce for long. By creating internal division, the Thirty had sown the seeds of their own demise. It may be that Theramenes exerted a moderating influence over Critias, as Xenophon alleges, but this goes only some way to explain why exercise of power by the Thirty became untenable after Theramenes' death. The establishment of the Three Thousand in late 404 or early 403 was the point at which the community began to fall apart. Once division had been created between those who enjoyed full rights and those who did not, it was a matter of time before those who had lost their rights would start to fight back. Many of the exiles took refuge at Salamis and Thebes, but we also know from scattered sources that some refugees also went to Argos, Chalcis, Megara and Oropus.[100] Slowly, resistance began to develop. Before 403, we know relatively little of Thrasybulus' son Lycus. During the oligarchy of 411, he had served as trierarch at Samos, later had campaigned in the Hellespont with Alcibiades and Theramenes and was trierarch at Arginusae in 406. In early 403, he organised from exile at Thebes a small band of men, no more than seventy, to seize the border fortification of Phyle.[101] Of those who joined him, the name of one man is known, Archinus of Koile, whom the historian Cratippus later praised for his role in bringing down the oligarchy.[102] At some later point they were joined by Anytus son of Anthemion, one of the generals in 409, Thrasybulus of Collytus, a trierarch at Notium, Aesimus, who later led the procession from Piraeus, and Ergocles.[103] As soon as they heard that their position was under serious threat in northern Attica, the Thirty responded by sending out the Three Thousand and the

---

[100] X. *HG* 2.4.1; Lys. 12.17; 24.25; 31.9.17; Aeschin. 2.147–8; D. 15.22; D.S. 14.6.2–3; Plu. *Lys.* 27.2; *Pel.* 6.4; Just. 5.9.4; Oros. 2.17.8.
[101] X. *HG* 2.4.2; Plu. *Mor.* 345d; Nep. 2.1.
[102] D. 24.135; *FGrHist* 64 T 2.
[103] Lys. 13.78, 80–2; 28.12; D. 24.134.

cavalry to beat the rebels into submission. What followed was a pitched battle at the hill of Phyle resulting in a victory for the resistance.[104]

Sparta reacted by sending out decrees over Greece instructing cities to hand over the Athenian exiles to the Thirty.[105] The injunctions were heeded by most cities with the exception of Argos and Thebes.[106] Argos, the inveterate enemy of Sparta, was the only Peloponnesian city to have taken the Athenian side during the war; Thebes had until recently been irreconcilably opposed to Athens, but cracks were now appearing in the Theban–Spartan alliance, especially since Thebes began to fear the rising power of Sparta and the threat to her own independence. Once the democratic resistance began to establish itself, emboldened by their early successes, the democrats established themselves at Piraeus and began to make forays against the Three Thousand in the city, mainly to take vengeance for what the exiles had suffered at the hands of the Thirty (Lys. 25.22). Though they could not rely on the overt military support of Thebes or Corinth, the member states of the Peloponnesian League were tacitly willing to support them.[107] The Thirty realised that their position was no longer secure militarily, and in response appropriated the island of Salamis to the south of Attica and the land of Eleusis in western Attica, turning out the inhabitants and killing approximately three hundred of the original occupants.[108] From a rebel band of no more than seventy on the borders of Attica, the partisans of Thrasybulus had emerged as a fighting force ready to take on the combined might of the Three Thousand and the Spartan army. Later accounts turned Thrasybulus into a hero by implying that he had defeated this overwhelming opposition singlehanded, but the historical reality was almost certainly otherwise. What the sources do reveal is that Thrasybulus had the backing of Thebes, and support for the Thirty in the city was rapidly disintegrating. Though it would be wrong to underestimate the achievement of the democratic resistance, the likelihood is that the tenure of the oligarchy at Athens was now rapidly crumbling. In spring 403 the Thirty sent out feelers to Thrasybulus inviting him back to Athens and even extending the offer to replace Theramenes on their panel.[109] After the latter refused, the Thirty sent to Sparta begging help, in response to which request Lysander sent out seven hundred hoplites under Callibius.[110] These arrived at Athens and fortified the Acropolis.[111] The sources clarify that the resistance which the rump of the

---

[104] X. *HG* 2.4.2–3; *Ath. Pol.* 37.1; D.S. 14.32.2–3; Just. 5.9.10; Oros. 2.17.10.
[105] Lys. 12.95, 97; Din. 1.25; D.S. 14.6.1; Plu. *Lys.* 27.2; Just. 5.9.4; Oros. 2.17.8.
[106] Din. 1.25; D. 15.22; D.S. 14.6.2; Just. 5.9.4–5; Plu. *Lys.* 27.2–4; *Pel.* 6.3.
[107] Thus Loening 1987: 13.
[108] X. *HG* 2.4.8–10; Lys. 12.52; 13.44; D.S. 14.32.4.
[109] Just. 5.9.13; Oros. 2.17.11.
[110] *Ath. Pol.* 37.2; D.S. 14.4.3–4; Just. 5.8.11; Oros. 2.17.5.
[111] *Ath. Pol.* 37.2; Lys. 12.94; 13.46.

resistance put up was fortified by Sparta.[112] A detachment of men from the city fortified Acharnae but were defeated.[113] The increased numbers of Thrasybulus' army laid siege to the Piraeus. The Thirty counterattacked at Munychia, where Critias fell.[114]

The Three Thousand realised that they could not trust the Thirty and the following day voted to depose them and elect ten men, one from each voting tribe, to govern in their place. The official mandate of the Ten was to contract peace with the Piraeus Party, though it seems that they shared the oligarchic principles of the Thirty and, rather than observing the mandate under which they had been elected, chose instead to continue the policies which they inherited for the ousted regime.[115] The names of four of the Ten survive: Pheidon, Epichares of Lamptra, Hippocles and Rhinon son of Charicles.[116] Nothing is known of Hippocles. Andocides refers in passing to one Epichares who served on the Council of Five Hundred during the oligarchy, though we cannot be certain that this is the same man (And. 1.95). Rhinon is known in connection with the treasurers of Athena in 417/16 and also stood up to public accounting after the restoration of democracy, thereafter reaccommodated in the new political dispensation (ML 77 lines 26–7). Pheidon was probably identical with the Pheidon who had served on the board of the Thirty.[117] As far as we can tell, the machinery of government continued under the Ten as it had under the Thirty, since Lysimachus remained as hipparch (X. HG 2.4.26). Political witch-hunts continued under the Ten as they had previously. Among the victims was Demaretus, a man of means (Ath. Pol. 38.2). As a further impediment to the partisans of Thrasybulus, Sparta sent out Lysander to blockade Piraeus.[118] Sparta's military engagement was more limited than what the Three Thousand had been expecting, but the force was nevertheless formidable and resulted in some men deserting through fear from Thrasybulus' army.[119] At this time, however, Sparta was preparing a campaign in the East, and there had emerged to boot political

---

[112] Ath. Pol. 37.2; D.S. 14.4.3–4; Just. 5.8.11; Oros. 2.17.5.
[113] D.S. 14.32.6.
[114] X. HG 2.4.11–19; D.S. 14.32.6–33.1; Ath. Pol. 38.1; Just. 5.9.14–10.3; Oros. 2.17.11–12; Nep. 7.2.5–7.
[115] The sources disagree as to the selection of the Ten. The Aristotelian tradition has it that they were selected by the Thirty themselves (Ath. Pol. 35.1; Nep. 3.1), but this is contradicted by other sources, which claim that they were elected by the Three Thousand (X. HG 2.4.23). As seen in Chapter 5, the sources also conflict on the question of whether the Ten were excluded from the amnesty or not.
[116] Lys. 12.55; Isoc. 18.6.
[117] Krentz 1982: 93.
[118] X. HG 2.4.28; D.S. 14.33.5; Lys. 12.59–60; Plu. Lys. 21.2.
[119] See, for example, Callimachus (Isoc. 18.49).

ructions between Lysander and Pausanias (Plu. *Lys.* 19.4). Lysander was replaced by Pausanias, who was more favourably disposed to Athens (X. *HG* 2.4.31).

Scholars have been inclined to doubt that Pausanias was as favourably inclined to the men of Piraeus as Xenophon alleges.[120] If he had been friendly, it seems strange that he should have laid siege to the Piraeus and killed over 180 men (X. *HG* 2.4.32–3). What is more likely is that there was a change of policy at Sparta during this period, where it must have become clear that the oligarchy at Athens had descended into an irreparable mess, and that it lay more in the interest of the alliance to unify the Athenian citizenry than to tolerate an ongoing civil war which was bound to absorb Spartan money and effort. Spartan hesitation might also be understood in the broader history of tension between the impulse to preserve freedom on the one hand and to install puppet governments on the other, one which can be documented as early as the period from 510 to 508, when King Cleomenes won the support of the Peloponnesian League by throwing out tyrants, but in the years that followed alienated goodwill by threatening to reinstate Hippias (see above). A hundred years later, this same basic tension is in evidence, between Spartan policy of restoring liberty to Greece on the one hand, and Lysander's policy of ensuring loyalty to Sparta by installing decarchies. The political fallout between Lysander and Pausanias is to be explained in terms of that contradiction, where Pausanias recognised that the only way to secure Athenian loyalty and Peloponnesian allegiance was to abandon support of the rump oligarchy. Furthermore, by this stage both the Corinthians and Thebans were refusing to support the Three Thousand (X. *HG* 2.4.30). Suspicions had arisen at Thebes and Corinth that Sparta sought to reduce the whole of Attica to an imperial possession, and support was given to the democrats who, they argued, were not acting in violation of the treaty of 404. After an indecisive battle in the Halipedon plain to the north of Piraeus, Pausanias realised that his best manoeuvre was to reconcile the two parties (X. *HG* 2.4.33). And so, instructions were delivered to the Three Thousand to come to terms with the Piraeus Party and accept new peace proposals on condition that Athens remain loyal to the Spartan alliance. No doubt, the Spartans were aware that their fragile alliance with Corinth and Thebes was under strain and that their best hope of retaining an alliance against Persia was to defuse fears about Spartan expansionism. Besides, it had become plain that the oligarchy had lost all credibility among the Athenian citizens. According to one anecdote, Diognetus brother of Niceratus, who had previously been executed under the Thirty, placed his son on the knees of the Spartan king in an appeal to restore democracy (Lys. 18.10). Whether true or not, the story indicates that

---

[120] See, for example, Krentz 1982: 98–9.

the Spartans had realised the hopelessness of the regime they had inaugurated and saw it to be in their interest to win Athens over in a renewed alliance.

In the years after the democratic restoration, patriotic Athenians liked to characterise the democratic victory as their own unique achievement. Reality was almost certainly more complex. The historiographical tradition agrees that the Spartan king Pausanias was largely to be credited for ending the war between the two factions, mainly because of mounting jealousies between himself and Lysander, whose power was becoming too great, and who had started to treat the oligarchic regimes he had established as his own vassals.[121] He persuaded the ephors to make an expedition to Athens to bring about peace in the interest of all. This meant that a new treaty needed to be drawn up between Athens and the member states of the Peloponnesian League, her former enemies. Unlike the treaty nine months earlier, on this occasion Thebes and Corinth refused to take part, as suspicions had by now mounted about Spartan ambitions, and cracks had appeared in the anti-Persian alliance.[122] In order to cement a new alliance, Pausanias saw the need to send representatives of the City Party, the rump of the Three Thousand who had remained loyal to the Thirty, to Sparta and for the ephors to send ambassadors to the Piraeus Party (consisting of those who had taken sides with Thrasybulus, in many cases exiles from the Thirty) to forge peace (X. HG 2.4.35–8); Sparta responded by sending out ten commissioners (or fifteen), to oversee the ratification of a treaty.[123] Given that Pausanias had used force against the Piraeus Party, his attitudes are difficult to extrapolate. But the best explanation is that through the use and display of military force he cowed the democratic resistance into accepting whatever arrangement the Spartans had in store for both sides.[124] In reality, this was a Spartan settlement. The Reconciliation was in principle a renewal and modification of the peace treaty between Athens and Sparta nine months earlier and therefore entailed a trilateral pledge.

This marks the start of the Reconciliation. The Thirty had been a disaster from the outset. In origin they had been pawns for Sparta, but their incompetence above all resulted in the loss of faith among those they governed. The Ten originally appointed by the oligarchs to govern in Piraeus were overthrown and replaced by a more democratic panel of ten to take charge of affairs while the Piraeus Party started parleys with the City Party. Tensions between Sparta, Thebes and Corinth no doubt played to Athens' favour: though Thebes had been an inveterate enemy during the Peloponnesian War, after Athens had finally been beaten attitudes changed rapidly. Sparta's

---

[121] Lys. 18.10; X. HG 2.4.38; Ath. Pol. 38.4; D.S. 14.33.6; Just. 5.10.7; Nep. 3.1; Plu. Lys. 21.3–4.
[122] X. HG 2.4.29–30; 3.5.8–10; Lys. 12.60; Just. 5.10.12–13; Plu. Lys. 27.2.
[123] X. HG 2.4.38; Ath. Pol. 38.4. The Aristotelian version puts the number at fifteen.
[124] Thus Loening 1987: 14.

decision to reconcile the two parties must have arisen from the realisation that a political implosion at Athens would not operate ultimately to the advantage of the alliance, and already Spartan troops had been called upon to prop up a failing proxy regime. The internal rivalry between Lysander and Pausanias must also have had a role to play.[125] The government of the Thirty was the brainchild of Lysander, and Pausanias, perhaps as a diplomatic gambit, saw that by launching a truce and by bringing Athens back into the Spartan-led alliance as a unified city he would do much to discredit his political rival. Even so, though external politics were important, it would be mistaken to imagine that reconciliation was wholly imposed from outside. Understandably, the Athenian ideology of reconciliation downplayed the role of Sparta in bringing it about, but the fact that Sparta did not oppose it should not be read to imply that Sparta achieved it single-handed. Both Xenophon and the author of the *Ath. Pol.* clarify that a Spartan commission oversaw the negotiations, but the talks which resulted in reunification and the restoration of democracy occurred on the initiative of Thrasybulus. Despite all they had suffered, the Reconciliation was an Athenian, not a Spartan, achievement. Sparta had imposed it by threat of force, but it was down to the wisdom of Athenians that the Reconciliation lasted.

---

[125] On the nature of Spartan internal politics, see Hamilton 1970; Thompson 1973.

CHAPTER 3

Oaths and Covenants

When the disputants came to terms in summer 403, the task they faced was daunting. Athens had been rent apart by the most gruesome civil conflict in memorable history, and the impulse for revenge on both sides must have been fierce. Had it not been for the interventions of the Spartan king Pausanias, civil unrest would have continued indefinitely. Lysias is clear that the democratic forays around the walls of the city were motivated by revenge, and the Three Thousand were not prepared to come to a settlement without a fight (Lys. 25.22). Though scholarly convention has been to speak of a 'democratic victory', the reality was somewhat different.[1] Though this was a democratic victory in the sense that a line was drawn under eight months of oligarchy, it would be mistaken to imagine that one party was the victor in a military sense. Athenians reconciled under a Spartan mandate not because one party had decisively beaten the other, but because Spartans had by now understood that unless measures were taken to unite the Athenian citizenry under a tenable government, her allies Thebes and Corinth would get dragged into the military fray, jeopardising chances of a united campaign against Persia in the East. It was therefore essential that Sparta ensure that the basic tenets of the Spartan-led alliance of 404 were reinforced, with the important exception that she was now prepared to recognise that Athens would best be governed under her traditional democracy, and that any attempt to back further the imposed oligarchy of 404 was destined to end in disaster. The treaty of 403 was overseen by a board of ten (or fifteen) Spartan officials.[2] The sources refer to these as *diallaktai*, cognate

---

[1] For the development of the ideology of reconciliation in the fourth century, see Wolpert 2002: 41.
[2] X. *HG* 2.4.38; *Ath. Pol.* 38.4.

with the Greek for a negotiated settlement, *diallagê*, whose remit was to ensure that the two sides reconciled and enforce this in law.[3]

As noted in Chapter 1, modern discussions of the Athenian Amnesty of 403 have been hampered by definitional problems. It has become a commonplace in scholarship to speak of an 'amnesty' which followed on from the victory of Thrasybulus, but the difficulty here is that the terms of the Reconciliation entailed much more than a commitment from one side to the other to discontinue hostilities. A careful study of the terms of the agreement will show that, far from being just a promise to lay down arms, the treaty of 12 Boedromion was a comprehensive package which laid out detailed provisions for the relationship between democratic Athens and the hub of the oligarchs who had taken up residence in a special enclave at Eleusis. In this respect, it is appropriate to think of the treaty as bargaining or horse-trading. But that is true only if we take the terms of the whole treaty, which set down provisions for Eleusis which the democrats needed to respect, and *vice versa*. As for the clause of amnesty, which represents only one clause of a possible twenty in the agreement, this was not in the nature of an exchange contracted on a theoretical principle of equality. The commitment 'to forget wrongs' was a unilateral pledge to guarantee that crimes committed in the time of oligarchy could not now be revisited in the courts. Of course, it would be reductive to understand this purely in partisan terms, as one could argue that, in theory, those who had taken the side of the democratic resistance might have benefited from this also, seeing that events were messy and ill-defined. In principle, however, as far as the Reconciliation Agreement entailed a clause of amnesty, it was a pledge which ensured that those who would otherwise have stood to lose most from the victory of the democrats and the re-establishment of democracy would not lose provided they came to terms and ceased hostilities. Our principal source is *Ath. Pol.* 39. Before we engage in analysis of its clauses, some problems of definition and chronology must be addressed.

THE ATHENIAN RECONCILIATION: DEFINITIONS AND CHRONOLOGY

One of the chief problems we face when grappling with the treaty is the sequence of events by which the treaty passed into law. Here, the account of *Ath. Pol.* 39 is not especially helpful, and we are thrown back on to other, more contemporary, sources. The speech of Andocides *On the Mysteries*, to which much more attention will be devoted in Chapter 4, is key to establishing

---

[3] For a general overview, see Joyce 2015; 2016.

the chronology by which the different phases of reconciliation took place. In §§81–90 of the speech, Andocides differentiates between at least two separate and self-contained stages of legal enactment, the earliest being the διαλλαγαί, or 'exchanges', that preceded the oath-taking, the second being the νόμοι enacted after the oaths were sworn. At §90 Andocides states that the oaths were sworn μετὰ τὰς διαλλαγάς, which cannot be identical with the laws to which he alludes in the previous sections. Andocides' chronology shows that those νόμοι were additional measures taken after the ratification of amnesty, and not before. The laws cited cannot have been part of the agreement concluded after the democrats returned. In some sense, they added to, refined or nuanced the agreement, but they cannot be regarded as identical or synonymous with it. Xenophon (*HG* 2.4.38) refers to fifteen men sent from Sparta to Athens to negotiate (διαλλάξαι). The verb implies the same διαλλαγαί to which Andocides and Lysias allude,[4] arbitrated by the ten (or fifteen) arbiters, or διαλλακταί. He tells us that the arbitrations brought about peace between the warring factions, but *Ath. Pol.*'s account is more substantial: the covenants listed at 39.1–5 pertain to oligarchic émigrés to Eleusis and focus on property rights. The term used is not διαλλαγαί but διαλύσεις. Other evidence indicates that some of those covenants addressed matters of property rights. The pledge μὴ μνησικακεῖν is part of the treaty but functioned as a clause *sui generis*. Andocides (1.81) specifies that the oath was sworn once the negotiations had taken place. Its terms are not to be confused with the earlier covenants between Athens and Eleusis, as its provisions were relevant only to Athens.

The διαλλαγαί, συνθῆκαι or διαλύσεις cannot therefore have been the same legislative enactments as those which Andocides calls νόμοι. The etymology of the relevant terms attested militates against such an identification: with διαλλαγαί, some exchange or bargain is implied, whereas συνθῆκαι, on the other hand, implies ratification of a treaty between two sides of a negotiating table.[5] The implication is that the covenants were brokered with Sparta and the remnants of the oligarchy over property and citizenship. In contrast, the subsequent νόμοι were carried unilaterally by newly created lawgivers, and their concerns were mainly separate from those of the covenants (συνθῆκαι).[6] The issue of criminality in the time of Thirty, and

---

[4] And. 1.90; Lys. 12.53; see also *IG* II² 10 (= *SEG* 30.54) line 8.
[5] For the etymology of διαλλαγαί, see Yarlan 1965. Carawan (2013: 100–3) suggests that the legal understanding of contract in Greek law amounted to something different from *consensus in idem*, though his arguments are difficult to follow.
[6] This is clearly implied by Andocides (see Chapter 4). The speech of Isocrates *Against Callimachus* is aware of a conceptual distinction, as it refers to the law of Archinus on παραγραφή in a separate sense from the συνθῆκαι (Isoc. 18.2; see Chapter 6).

how to quash civil and criminal action against oligarchs, was handled after the oaths were sworn. In his account of the negotiations of early summer 403, the historian Xenophon omits to include an oath. The first time Xenophon mentions a clause μὴ μνησικακεῖν in his account is in relation not to 403, but to two years later, in 401, when Eleusis was reintegrated into the Athenian polity and new oaths were sworn (X. HG 2.4.43). Nevertheless, it seems most likely that this was a reaffirmation of an oath sworn two years earlier, which Andocides cites *verbatim*, and which resembles the wording of the terms spelled out in Xenophon's narrative for 403 barring the Thirty, Ten and Eleven from the city (X. HG 2.4.38; cf. And. 1.90). Andocides attests that μὴ μνησικακεῖν was sworn after the compacts. He does not say that the clause reinforced every covenant but seems to think that the pledge not to nurse grudges was taken after the initial bargaining. The chief aim of the διαλλαγαί was to reverse the decrees of the Thirty which had driven opponents into exile and to provide circumstances whereby partisans of the Thirty need not fear future reprisals. The evidence indicates that the initial purpose of the διαλλαγαί was to provide for the return of the democrats and the recovery of some, but not all, of their sequestered goods. This then developed into a further discussion about Eleusis and provisions there for the settlement of oligarchs and anyone who chose not to reintegrate with the democratic city. The promise 'not to bear grudges' was included among the Covenants of Reconciliation, and Andocides clarifies that it was reiterated in a separate oath (And. 1.90).

When the democrats returned to Athens, their principal concern was to ensure that the decrees of the Thirty under which they had been exiled were annulled and that measures should be taken to specify relations between the two semi-independent political communities. *Ath. Pol.* 39 shows that the compacts of the Reconciliation pointed mainly to future arrangements, whereas only one of its provisions, the clause not to dredge up old grievances, had anything to say about the past. As we will see presently, the narratological structure of *Ath. Pol.* 39 is organised in such a way that arrangements for the future, which we might call 'innovations', counterbalance traditional arrangement, which we might call 'conventions'. The clause μὴ μνησικακεῖν is framed as an innovation, but it links a future provision, not to bear grudges, with a historical reality, which is the civil war just fought and lost by the oligarchs. One recent suggestion has been that the clause μὴ μνησικακεῖν was a mere formality which bound the terms of the rest of the treaty. This has been backed by legal comparisons with the clause as attested in other legal treaties, to which greater attention will be devoted in Chapter 7. Suffice it to say for now that to regard μὴ μνησικακεῖν as a sealing provision for earlier covenants, rather than a covenant *sui generis*, is to ignore the fact that this was one clause of the agreement and cannot therefore be read as a byword for the agreement *in toto*.⁷ The oath μὴ μνησικακεῖν reaffirmed, though perhaps without as much verbal detail, the covenant spelled out at *Ath. Pol.* 39.6, and its purpose was to reaffirm *that covenant alone*. The fact that it began with καί, as reported by Andocides, indicates that it was preceded by at least one other oath, if not more than one, which affirmed other covenants of the agreement. When the orators refer in a blanket way to what we tend to mean by the 'Amnesty', they use the standard expression 'covenants and oaths', but do not refer to one single amnesty clause within the agreement. In this respect, it is vital to observe the distinction between the 'Amnesty' and the Reconciliation.

These observations should warn against recent efforts to suggest that the Amnesty came about through a series of legal covenants which the oath μὴ μνησικακεῖν merely formalised. If the oath did nothing more than ratify preexisting covenants, a separate Decree of Amnesty would have been redundant. But for that reconstruction to work, some serious tampering with chronology is required. In those sections of his self-defence (§§81–90), Andocides differentiates between the stages of the Reconciliation. First came the negotiations which preceded the conclusion of the peace (90); then followed the oath μὴ μνησικακεῖν (81); next arose objections by citizens liable under old laws (82), so a scrutiny and publication of the laws followed (82–5). The historical implications of this are enormously complex and will be treated separately, and in much greater detail, in the next chapter. Once revised laws were written up, new laws were passed (85–9). The order is clear: discussions, oaths, republication of old laws, passing of new laws. The revisionist view of the evolving Reconciliation Agreement, in contrast, draws no clear distinction between the Covenants of Amnesty and the additional laws ratified after the oaths were sworn, ignores the etymology of μὴ μνησικακεῖν, which must refer to past, not to future matters, and maintains, without good supporting evidence, that the covenants entailed or implied legal principles which the laws spelled out at And. 1.85–9 simply restated. Unless Andocides muddled his chronology beyond redemption, the oaths cannot have referred to or reaffirmed any of the laws spelled out in §§85–9 of the speech *On the Mysteries*.

The treaty of 403 survives not in an inscription but in scattered literary sources. There can be little doubt that the treaty was inscribed and set up in a visible location after the terms were contracted and sworn to on 12 Boedromion.⁸ Xenophon, saying little of worth about the Reconciliation, in a cursory summary omits to list those who were exempt from the terms of the Amnesty, most notably the Ten of the City (X. *HG* 2.4.38). If this had been the only surviving source, we might have been excused for concluding

---

⁷ Thus Joyce 2015: 30; *pace* Carawan 2002; 2012.
⁸ Thus Shear (J. L.) 2011: 209; Scheibelreiter 2013: 101.

that the Reconciliation involved no more than a pledge not to vent grievances.[9] But other sources supplement our knowledge, and it is clear from the incomplete summary in the *Ath. Pol.*, as well as from later allusions in Lysias, Isocrates and Nepos, that the treaty's most important aim was to create circumstances whereby two political communities could live side by side, a restored democracy at Athens and a rump oligarchy at Eleusis, where oligarchs had seized land and possessions in the spring of 403; moreover, a secondary motive was to lay out provisions whereby former oligarchs who chose not to join the partisans at Eleusis after 403 should be protected from further legal reprisals. Taken in entirety, the treaty's overriding aim was to provide for those who otherwise would have stood the most to lose in the event that democracy was restored and those who had suffered under the oligarchy took vengeance on those who had sided with the Thirty in the period of *stasis*.[10] Of the provisions about which we know anything, there is not a single surviving clause of the treaty which said anything about the rights of the democrats. Though papyrus fragments of Lysias' speech *Against Hippotherses* make clear that the restoration of non-moveable property to those who had been stripped under the oligarchy was guaranteed, no clause reversing earlier verdicts of *atimia* is known.[11] Because the regime of the Thirty was now regarded as null and void, the cancellation of *atimia* under its rule may have been automatically implied. The fact that no clause stating this explicitly has survived may be explained by recourse either to the theory that the Thirty did not enshrine their acts in any legal framework, as Xenophon implies, or that the democratic bias of the sources and of the treaty itself cast the treaty as a benefaction of the democrats towards the oligarchs. If the latter, the treaty enshrined in law the principle of forgiveness, which was the founding doctrine upon which democracy was restored in 403.[12] This should discourage faith in the recent and methodologically arbitrary attempt to understand the treaty in terms of a cancellation of verdicts of *atimia* issued under the oligarchy, an approach which depends on one solitary allusion in the first speech of Andocides, *On the Mysteries*, whose underlying motives are entirely skewed and distorted, to earlier examples where decrees stripping citizens of their rights were reversed (And. 1.107–8).

---

[9] Until the discovery of the Aristotelian *Ath. Pol.* towards the end of the nineteenth century this was the main source from which earlier scholars reconstructed the Athenian Amnesty; see Mitford 1829; Grote 1846–56: vi; Großer 1868; Luebbert 1881. The discovery and subsequent editions of the Aristotelian papyri from Oxyrhynchus has since rendered those accounts outdated.

[10] Joyce 2008: 512–14.

[11] Carawan 2002; 2013: 81–90 has argued that this was the primary focus of the treaty.

[12] For evidence that the Thirty were not interested in legal protocol, see X. *HG* 2.3.11.

The Reconciliation Agreement of 403 came about in a single legislative package.[13] Our two principal accounts, those of Xenophon and pseudo-Aristotle, put a rather different spin on the measures. The abbreviated account of Xenophon indicates that the principal focus was the restoration of exiles, excepting the Thirty, who were permitted to migrate to Eleusis. This may have included an official clause abrogating earlier decrees of *atimia*, but there is no conclusive evidence that the Reconciliation Agreement had anything to say about those who had had their civic rights limited in the period before the collapse of democracy in 404. When referring to the agreement, orators used the phrase ὅρκοι καὶ συνθῆκαι ('oaths and covenants'),[14] but the sources conflict over whether the treaty included a specific amnesty clause. The most complete account, that of *Ath. Pol.* 39, states that it did (§6), but the later writer Nepos appears to believe that an amnesty came about by a separate law passed when Thrasybulus returned from Piraeus.[15] Xenophon is aware of an Oath of Amnesty but dates it to 401 after the fall of Eleusis, and his version is followed by Justin and Orosius.[16] Nineteenth-century scholars, who knew nothing of the *Ath. Pol.* except for chance fragments, favoured the view that the final Oath of Amnesty was not sworn until 401, but the discovery of the papyri in Egypt brought that position into disrepute.[17] When the London papyrus was published in 1891, attempts were made to reconcile the discrepant evidence by positing the existence of two amnesty agreements, one in 403 and a later one in 401.[18] But as the twentieth century progressed, scholars rightly began to speak of only one amnesty arrangement in 403 reaffirmed two years later in 401.[19] This agreement, or set of agreements, was legislated, inscribed and guaranteed by a series of sworn oaths.

What happened to the oligarchs at Eleusis until 401 after the political division between Eleusis and Athens was eradicated is uncertain. If the last of the oligarchs were reintegrated into the community at that time, we might well

---

[13] Cloché (1915: 239–44) suggested that there were two separate peace proposals, one between Athens and Sparta and a separate one which reconciled the two parties at Athens. His argument rested on the variation of terminology between X. *HG* 2.4.38–9 and *Ath. Pol.* 39.1, but there is no good reason to accept this suggestion; thus Loening 1987: 23; Shear (J. L.) 2011: 190–1; Scheibelreiter 2013: 101; Joyce 2015: 29–30.

[14] Lys. 13.88; 25.23; 28.34; [Lys.] 6.39; Isoc. 18.29.

[15] Contrast *Ath. Pol.* 39.6 with Nep. 3.2. The Aristotelian version wins the support of And. 1.81–90, whose chronology makes it clear that an Oath of Amnesty was sworn in 403.

[16] X. *HG* 2.4.43; Just. 5.10.11; Oros. 2.17.15. Isocrates (7.67) has sometimes been cited as following this tradition, but all he says is that amnesty was concluded after the oligarchs were deposed; there is no reason to think that Isocrates was alluding here to the fall of Eleusis.

[17] See Großer 1868: 21–3; Luebbert 1881: 12.

[18] Stahl 1891: 277–8; Cloché 1915: 294.

[19] Dorjahn 1946: 22–3; Kühn (J.-H.) 1967: 45; Krentz 1982: 104; Loening 1987: 27.

suppose that, like the rest of the citizenry two years earlier, they were expected to swear the oath. But that supposes that the oligarchs did not swear in 403, despite the indications of Andocides that they did (And. 1.90). There is further disagreement as to whether the Reconciliation came about by a decree, or whether instead it was no more than a moral commitment.[20] Andocides appears to think that a decree prefaced it, though this has been disputed on the grounds that the term ἔδοξε is used informally to indicate a public decision rather than an official psephism.[21] Though covenants did not themselves come about by popular decree, when the agreements had been formulated and were ready to be sworn in, the Assembly may well have issued a decree sanctioning an Oath of Amnesty, which is what Andocides implies. There are plenty of examples in the historical record of laws whose publication was authorised by a separate free-standing decree, one of which comes from 409/8, when the Assembly decreed to have a copy of Draco's homicide law which they got from an *axôn* inscribed on stone.[22] The stone copy of the law is prefaced by the decree which authorised its republication, and there is no reason to think that in 403 the Athenian Assembly could not have decreed an Oath of Reconciliation. Even if the covenants themselves did not come about by decree, the oaths by which those covenants came into effect must have had the backing of a decree, as the whole of the people were expected to swear the oaths. The terms were never referred to as *nomoi*; the laws which followed were individual enactments.[23] The agreements were legally binding, because if Athenians acted in contravention, they were acting illegally.

THE COVENANTS OF RECONCILIATION

Our principal source for the Reconciliation is *Ath. Pol.* 39. This is not without its difficulties, one of which is a serious textual corruption in §5 relating to homicide, for which various restorations to date have been suggested, though none of them entirely satisfactory. Before we engage in a point-by-point analysis of the terms, some preliminary remarks about the style and structure of *Ath. Pol.*'s narrative would be useful. One of the issues the drafters had to face was what needed to change and what should stay as before. At §2, the temple of Eleusis is under the jurisdiction of both communities (innovation), but the

---

[20] For the view that the Amnesty was an extra-legal commitment which never found expression in law, see Dorjahn 1946: 20–1; Loening 1987: 28–30; *contra* Joyce 2008: 508; 2015.
[21] *IG* I³ 104 lines 1–9.
[22] Thus Joyce 2015: 27.
[23] This follows Joyce 2015; 2016.

Kerykes and the Eumolpidae are to retain control of the priesthoods (traditional). Those residing at the city cannot go to Eleusis (innovation) except to attend the Eleusinian Mysteries (traditional). The same counterpoise between innovation and tradition is evident at §3, between buyers who cannot persuade a possessor to sell (traditional), with the appointment of assessors to fix a price and arrange a sale (innovation). Every one of these provisions is prospective, that is, future-looking. The provisions for homicides at §5 within the logic of the narrative are similarly prospective and do not relate to past homicides, as if this were exceptional to the Amnesty itself. The balance between innovation and tradition is here in play. The question is what to do about homicides in future which take place between Athens and Eleusis (innovation), for which standard procedures are prescribed (tradition).[24] Similarly, at §6, the rule of amnesty (μὴ μνησικακεῖν), which puts a stop on future litigation in the courts (innovation) against anyone except the Thirty, Ten and Eleven, stands in counterpoise to the standard process of public accounting prescribed for members of those boards who elected to remain in Athens and not join the rump community of oligarchs at Eleusis.

From the evidence as it stands it is possible to formulate a twenty-point outline of the covenants sworn into law on 12 Boedromion. Most of this reconstruction depends on the material of the *Ath. Pol.*, but added information is supplied by chance references in the orators.[25]

1. The Reconciliation Agreement took place in the archonship of Eucleides (403/2). (*Ath. Pol.* 39.1)
2. Those of the City Party who wish to emigrate may have Eleusis. (*Ath. Pol.* 39.1; X. *HG* 2.4.38)
3. They retain full citizenship rights with full power and authority. (*Ath. Pol.* 39.1)
4. They are entitled to draw revenues of property elsewhere. (*Ath. Pol.* 39.1)
5. The sanctuary of Demeter at Eleusis is to be common to both parties. (*Ath. Pol.* 39.2)
6. It is to be controlled by the Kerykes and Eumolpidae according to custom. (*Ath. Pol.* 39.2)
7. Those at Eleusis may not go to the city. (*Ath. Pol.* 39.2)
8. Those in the city may not go to Eleusis except for the Mysteries. (*Ath. Pol.* 39.2)
9. Those at Eleusis must contribute funds to the alliance like the other Athenians. (*Ath. Pol.* 39.2)

---

[24] Thus Harris 2015b: 46.
[25] Thus Loening 1987: 35; *contra* Carawan 2013: 72.

10. If anyone departing take a house at Eleusis, he must persuade the owner, but if they cannot come to terms each party is to choose three assessors. (*Ath. Pol.* 39.3)
11. Those natives of Eleusis whom the new settlers (or assessors?) accept may stay. (*Ath. Pol.* 39.3)
12. Rules about registration for residents in Attica and abroad. (*Ath. Pol.* 39.4)
13. No one at Eleusis may hold office in the city before being reregistered. (*Ath. Pol.* 39.5)
14. Homicide trials are to take place at Athens according to ancestral custom. (*Ath. Pol.* 39.5)
15. No one is to remember past wrongs against any except the Thirty, the Ten, the Piraeus Ten, and the Eleven (*Ath. Pol.* 39.6; X. *HG* 2.4.38; And. 1. 90)
16. If any listed above submit to accountings, they are to be protected. (*Ath. Pol.* 39.6)
17. Those ruling in Piraeus are to appear before courts in Piraeus; those in the city offering sureties, before courts of men; those who do not should migrate. (*Ath. Pol.* 39.6, with textual emendation)
18. Each party should pay off the loans contracted during the war. (*Ath. Pol.* 39.6)
19. Items confiscated under the Thirty and not sold off may be recovered (see source below).
20. Items sold off to a third party may not be recovered. (Lys. *Against Hippotherses* lines 34–48)

As reconstructed, the Covenants of Reconciliation throw up important questions. The first, and most pressing, is whether émigrés to Eleusis remained Athenians in the wake of the Reconciliation. Covenant 9 specifies that those at Eleusis were obliged to contribute to the Athenian alliance just like other Athenians (καθάπερ τοὺς ἄλλους Ἀθηναίους),[26] which might be taken to imply that a distinction between the émigrés and those who remained at Athens did not emerge. Retention of citizenship entailed the right to hold land and non-moveable property within Attica, and it also meant that the residents of Eleusis were protected as Athenian citizens under the law, but as covenants 7 and 13 illustrate, those who chose to move to Eleusis were not allowed to set foot in the city unless they reregistered, and were disqualified from holding public office. This was not a permanent arrangement, as the decision to emigrate was reversible, but it did mean that if an oligarch for protection decided that it would be better to stay away from the geopolitical centre, one of the concessions he had

---

[26] Thus, Loening 1987: 35; *contra* Carawan 2013: 72. It is reasonable to speculate that emigrees to Eleusis held on to property at Athens, as did those from Iulis half a century later; *IG* II² 111 = RO 39 lines 65–6. See also X. *HG* 4.1.35; D. 7.41; [D.] 59.102. For the older view that the possessions of oligarchs were confined to Eleusis, see Cloché 1915: 251–3.

to accept was that he could not vote in the Assembly or participate in the political process. However, this forfeiture was compensated by the guarantee spelled out in the third clause that oligarchs could be self-sufficient and self-governing. An older view was that the guarantee to retain property applied within the geographical confines of the newly created communities, but this has been rightly rejected on the strength of evidence that oligarchs retained estates in Attica and were not confined to Eleusis (X. *HG* 2.4.20–2).

How self-contained and separate were the two communities? Covenants 5–8 guaranteed geographical separateness, with the notable exception that those of the city who wished to use the shrine at Eleusis could do so without hindrance. This exception was made to honour the traditional religious rites associated with the sacred precinct of Demeter and Persephone, controlled by the *genê* of the Kerykes and Eumolpidae. Xenophon mentions that among the partisans of Thrasybulus was Cleocritus, who was a herald of the Mysteries.[27] The democrats knew that if a complete boundary was drawn between the two communities which neither side could cross under any circumstances, this was likely to create difficulties and lead to objections from those who took up residence in the city. The claims of religion were too important to ignore, and so some provision needed to be made so that religious duties could be observed without violating the principle that the two communities remain divided geopolitically.[28] It has been assumed that the Greater Mysteries alone are meant here, since the provision is for city residents to cross over to Eleusis, not vice versa.[29] Yet the Lesser Mysteries were celebrated at Agrae in the urban centre, and unless reciprocal, it is difficult to see how the Lesser Mysteries could have been included. An inscription dating from the first half of the fifth century details the period of truce in which initiates could travel to the Greater and Lesser Mysteries (*IG* I³ 6). According to sacred law, it was possible for cult members to travel unharmed to Eleusis and Agrae within a specified period. One interpretation treats the rule reciprocally, whereby during the truce there was two-way traffic,[30] but that underestimates the importance of locality. At the time of the Greater Mysteries it is easier to assume that the traffic went in the direction of Eleusis, whereas at the time of the Lesser Mysteries it went towards Agrae. If, however, the customs of the Greater Mysteries were upheld to benefit the residents of the city, it is unlikely that those of the Lesser Mysteries were not similarly upheld to benefit the residents of Eleusis. If so, the *Ath. Pol.* has been somewhat cryptic in detailing the nature of the religious

---

[27] Thus Loening 1987: 32.
[28] Kühn (J.-H.) 1967: 39–40; Lehmann 1972: 223 n. 57; Levi 1967–8: 343; *contra* Loening 1987: 33.
[29] Loening 1987: 33.
[30] This is how Loening (1987: 34) reads the text of the inscription.

provisions. Though unprovable, the hypothesis stands that those oligarchs at Eleusis who were cult members were given permission to come to the city for religious reasons.

Were both communities assessed separately for contribution of funds, or was there one overarching assessment which covered both Athens and Eleusis?[31] Covenant 18 suggests that each community was assessed separately. During the conflict, the oligarchs forcefully took homes and property away from inhabitants at Eleusis and executed over a hundred.[32] The terms of the covenants fail to clarify whether the violent occupation was now recognised in law or whether the matter of ownership of property at Eleusis needed to be assessed in its entirety. Covenant 10 indicates that assessors were required if future transfers of property were to be conducted. The provision applies to those who under the terms of the agreement from now on choose to migrate to Eleusis, not to those who in the past had sequestered goods and property from unfortunate victims of the oligarchy in the *stasis*. This raises the related question as to the arrangements made for the coexistence of the indigenous inhabitants of Eleusis and the newcomers.[33] The 'natives' of covenant 11 must refer to the old inhabitants who had been there prior to the civil conflict,[34] but the question remains to whom the pronoun οὗτοι refers: does it refer to the new settlers or to the assessors? Plain examination of the wording as preserved cannot decide the matter either way, but most modern commentators have concluded that it must refer to the new inhabitants who were being asked under the terms of the treaty to decide whether they wished to dwell side by side with the original inhabitants, or whether instead they wanted those older settlers to leave.[35] Taken together, covenants 10 and 11 indicate that under the terms of settlement, every effort was made to accommodate the needs of former oligarchs at the potential expense of those at Eleusis who had not already suffered at their hands. Covenant 12 stipulated a ten-day window in which residents of the city could emigrate under truce. As covenant 13 specifies, this roll was needed because those who emigrated could not hold office thereafter at Athens, perhaps to coincide with the timing of the Greater Mysteries.[36] Plutarch (*Mor.* 349F) indicates that

---

[31] Loening 1987: 35.
[32] X. *HG* 2.4.8–10; D.S. 14.32.5–6; Lys. 12.52; 13.44–6.
[33] *Ath. Pol.* 39.3 reads as follows: ἐὰν δέ τινες τῶν ἀπιόντων οἰκίαν λαμβάνωσιν Ἐλευσῖνι, συμπείθειν τὸν κεκτημένον. ἐὰν δὲ μὴ συμβαίνωσιν ἀλλήλοις, τιμητὰς ἑλέσθαι τρεῖς ἑκάτερον, καὶ ἥντιν᾽ ἂν οὗτοι τάξωσιν τιμὴν λαμβάνειν. Ἐλευσινίων δὲ συνοικεῖν οὓς ἂν οὗτοι βούλωνται. The last of these clauses (covenant 11 in my scheme) creates the greatest difficulty, as we do not know to whom the pronoun οὗτοι refers.
[34] Cloché 1915: 256–8.
[35] Thus Kühn (J.-H.) 1967: 40; Levi 1967–8: 343–4; Lehmann 1972: 222 n. 56; Rhodes 1981: 466–7; Loening 1987: 36.
[36] Loening 1987: 38, 69.

the treaty was sworn on 12 Boedromion, in the middle of the truce, and so the narrow window prescribed is likely to have been chosen so that after the truce the matter could be closed. Covenant 13 has given rise to the question of how far émigrés were deprived of their rights at Athens, but only the holding of public office and service in the courts was limited.[37]

Perhaps the most controversial of the covenants is the fourteenth. The text at *Ath. Pol.* 39.5 reads: τὰς δὲ δίκας τοῦ φόνου εἶναι κατὰ τὰ πάτρια, αυτοχιραεκτισιοτρωσασ. Scholars offer various reconstructions of the garbled lettering which follows τὰ πάτρια in the MSS.[38] T. Thalheim proposed εἴ τίς τινα αὐτοχειρίᾳ ἐκτείσαιτο τρώσας ('if anyone should kill anyone having wounded by his own hand'), but that is one of several possibilities, and by no means is it certain.[39] If Thalheim's reading, or a similar reading which specifies a category of own-hand killing, is accepted, it might then be the case that the Amnesty clauses isolated specific types of homicide committed prior to 403 which were still actionable. But that is not warranted. However αυτοχιραεκτισιοτρωσασ is to be read, the point of the clause is not that it made a special exemption for certain categories of killing which could be pursued after 403 dating from the period of oligarchy, but that it sets out provisions for homicide trials in the wake of the Reconciliation, so that those who belonged to the enclave at Eleusis had the same access to Athenian courts as did the democrats, according to ancestral practice (κατὰ τὰ πάτρια). The purpose of the clauses was to lay down legal regulations which provided for two newly created communities in 403; its contents pertain not to what was done previously, but what is to be done in the future.[40] Read on its own merits, nothing at *Ath. Pol.* 35.5 warrants the view that special clauses were inserted into the treaty, permitting pursuit of certain categories of killing but not others. The trial of Agoratus (see Chapter 5) shows that the matter at issue after 403 in homicide trials was not the type of homicide perpetrated but its wider political relevance. Cases of homicide were usually brought by the private process of *dikê*, but Agoratus, though not a member of the Thirty, Ten or Eleven, was prosecuted through the less common channel of *endeixis*.[41] This was because the trial of Agoratus was a public, not a private, matter and related specifically to the matter of the subversion of democracy and the installation of the Thirty.

---

[37] Stahl (1891: 484) thought that émigrés were deprived of their rights until they returned to the city, whereas Cloché (1915: 258–9) pointed out that they could practise government in their own community.
[38] For suggested reconstructions, see Rhodes 1981: 468.
[39] Endorsed by Gray 2013: 399–400.
[40] Thus Harris 2015a: 46.
[41] On the Eleven, see Harris 2006: 373–90.

Because of the provision which states that homicide trials are to take place κατὰ τὰ πάτρια, scholars have tended to assume that special exemption was created for those who had committed murder with their own hand, while accessories to murder were covered under the terms of the Amnesty.[42] A variety of explanations as to why such an exception should have been created have been proffered, but none have ever been convincing. At the heart is the context in which this clause is read. If it refers to past events, then it exempted certain types of killer, so that if someone had killed in former time with one's own hand rather than plotted a murder or assisted someone else in bringing a murder about, then he could still be prosecuted after 403. But there is no good reason to assume that it does refer to the past. Indeed, the context shows that it pertains not to past, but to potential future acts. The whole of *Ath. Pol.* 39.1–5 relates to future arrangements between Athens and Eleusis. The key point at §5, which details the clauses for homicide, is that if someone commits the crime in either community in the future, the arrangements for trying homicide will follow traditional procedures, as the courts were located within the geopolitical domain from which oligarchs were otherwise banned. One recent revision has maintained that a distinction here was being upheld between homicide committed by the hand of the killer and accessory to murder, so that homicide by own-hand was to be prosecuted at Athens, while accessory was to be prosecuted at Eleusis.[43] This suggestion has the merit of recognising that the covenant pertains to the future and not the past, but the text as preserved, which is corrupt, does not imply that distinctions were drawn between homicide by own-hand and accessory, or that a division of jurisdiction was sanctioned. Athenian homicide law drew no legal distinction between homicide by own-hand and accessory.[44] It is easiest to bracket off the letters αυτοχιραεκτισιοτρωσασ as textual corruption and conclude that covenant 14 promises to allow inhabitants of the enclave at Eleusis to use the homicide courts at Athens.

If the garbled phrase αυτοχιραεκτισιοτρωσασ is parcelled off as a later rogue editorial insertion which, over the course of time, got corrupted and removed from the text altogether, a much clearer picture of the provision emerges which, in turn, combines naturally with the legal implications of Lysias' speech *Against Agoratus* (for a much fuller discussion, see Chapter 5). Thalheim's reading of εἴ τίς τινα before the first eight surviving letters in the preserved text, which look as if they might be a corruption of the legal term αὐτοχειρίᾳ, has no textual basis to warrant it, and in any case the language

---

[42] See Cloché 1915: 259–61; Bonner 1924: 175–6; Rhodes 1981: 69–70; Loening 1987: 39–40; Todd 2007: 639 with n. 55; Carawan 2013: 271–2.
[43] Gray 2013: 385–401.
[44] See the vital discussion of Harris 2015b. See also Harris 2005a.

proposed models itself upon U. Köhler's reconstruction of line 11 of Draco's homicide law, republished at the end of the fifth century on stone (*IG* I³ 104), which recent autoptic reassessments have begun to question.[45] At no point anywhere in Athenian homicide law, as far as we can reconstruct it from the orators, was the distinction drawn between homicide committed by own-hand and homicide by accessory. If a citizen died unlawfully through a denunciation, in law this counted as homicide no less than if a person was knifed or strangled. For this reason alone, it seems most unlikely that the Amnesty made any exception for homicide which took place from a direct blow from the killer, as distinct from homicide which had been caused more indirectly. As argued at length in Chapter 5, the reason why Agoratus came to trial after 403 had nothing to do with whether he delivered the death blow himself, which is not the legal point at issue. The issue for the prosecutor is whether the crime of Agoratus was a public or a private matter. Ordinarily, homicide at Athens was a private matter and was therefore brought by a private lawsuit (*dikê*), though other legal processes were available, include *graphê* and *endeixis*. The provisions of the Amnesty ruled out any prosecution of homicide by *dikê*, that is, as a private matter between two citizens, one of whom (the defendant) had killed a close family member of the other (the plaintiff). But if the homicide could be presented in law as a public matter, that is, as a matter of criminal law which affected the entire city, the legal question now took on a broader dimension. The clauses of the Amnesty exempted the Thirty, the Ten and the Eleven (see below), but as Lysias 13 illustrates, if it could be shown that an oligarchic sympathiser not on those panels had acted in such a way as to cause directly the overthrow of democracy, this was now a public matter actionable after 403 in the same way as the crimes of the Thirty, Ten and Eleven were still actionable. The aim of the Clauses of Reconciliation was to prohibit private suits for untried disputes predating the swearing of the oaths from reaching the courts after 12 Boedromion. This meant that if a former oligarchic sympathiser had killed, raped or abused a democrat, or burnt down his house, or committed some other outrage during the war, this was a private matter between two citizens which was inadmissible after 403. The evidence of Lysias 13, however, shows that crimes with public consequences, such as the overthrow of democracy, which could be brought by public processes, such as *endeixis*, were still actionable provided it could be shown that the legal issue hinged not on a private quarrel between two citizens, but between the defendant and the people.

It has recently been argued that the clause μὴ μνησικακεῖν in Greek did not guarantee forgiveness of the past but functioned as a more limited legal

---

[45] For a discussion of the republished Draconian law and its implications for how we are to read Plu. *Sol.* 19.3–4, see Joyce 2021/2.

expression which formalised pre-existing covenants.[46] I have already expressed objection to that interpretation in independent publications, and there is not space here to survey all the extant attestations of this disputed phrase, to which more space will be devoted in Chapter 7. As argued elsewhere, in every known instance in which the clause is attested it entails a promise of annulment, usually from the victor to the defeated, though there are some outstanding examples in which the clause is contracted on a theoretical principle of equality between two sides (see Chapter 7). Though, as Andocides attests, the oath was sworn by the whole people and not by one faction, this should not be taken to imply that the principle of annulment was absent.[47] If the promise had been made by one faction within the citizenry and not by the whole people, a sense of division and future recrimination is likely to have been engendered. The purpose of the Amnesty was to ensure that any feeling of party division was eradicated, and so, by making the whole people swear, a greater sense of political unity could be fostered. Once the oath was sworn, the distinction between 'Piraeus Party' and 'City Party' vanished. In the ideology of the restored democracy, this was a victory of the whole of the people regardless of earlier attitudes toward the anti-democratic regime.[48] Crucial about the representation of the clause here is that the promise μὴ μνησικακεῖν was a covenant in its own right reinforced by an oath which Andocides partially quotes. As at Iulis fifty years later, it expressly relates back to events that happened in the past, not to future issues,[49] and so the natural interpretation of covenant 15 is that it pledged not to pursue acts committed before the Amnesty. Equally important to recognise is that it upheld the principle of *res iudicata*, whereby court verdicts reached when Athens was still a democracy remained in force, whereas any verdict reached under the Thirty was null and void and, furthermore, any action before 403 could not be pursued, unless the Thirty and Ten had committed it.[50]

Unsurprisingly, the Thirty, Ten and Eleven were not protected under the Amnesty if they chose to stay at Athens. The reasoning behind this was that, as enemies of democracy, they should answer for their crimes. At first sight this might look like a violation of the Amnesty principle, but it is important to see this clause in its legal context. As the subsequent trials of Agoratus and

---

[46] Carawan 2002; 2012; 2013; *contra* Joyce 2008; 2014; 2016.
[47] And. 1.90 with Joyce 2014: 43.
[48] Thus Wolpert 2002.
[49] *IG* II² 111 = RO 39 lines 57–61: τάδε συνέθεντο καὶ ὤμοσαν οἱ στρατηγοὶ οἱ Ἀθηναίων πρὸς τὰς πόλες τ[ὰ]ς ἐν Κέωι κα[ὶ] οἱ σύμμαχοι· *vacat* ὃ μνησικακήσω [τῶ]ν πα[ρ]εληλυθότων πρὸ[ς] Κείος οὐδ[ε]νὸς οὐδὲ ἀποκτενῶ Κ[είων] ὁ[δ]ένα οὐδὲ φυγάδα ποήσω τῶν ἐμμενόντων τοῖς ὅρκο[ις καὶ τ]αῖς συνθήκαις ταῖσδε.
[50] On *res iudicata* as a means of preventing feuds in the courts, see Harris 2013: 72–6.

Eratosthenes show (see Chapter 5), the aim in 403 was to heal the old division between the City Party and Piraeus Party by creating a new sense of 'us versus them', the 'us' being the whole of the citizenry regardless of former allegiance, the 'them' being those who sat on the boards of the Thirty, Ten and Eleven. By polarising the matter in this way, it was easier to create a belief in a common enemy to foster unity between both sides of the civil war. There is some disagreement in the sources as to who was exempted. Xenophon says that only the Thirty were left out, whereas Nepos includes the City Ten, and Andocides refers to the Thirty, the Ten and the Eleven.[51] The fullest account is the version of the *Ath. Pol.* which mentions the Thirty, the City Ten and the Eleven, and some modern editors have amended the oath preserved in Andocides (1.90) to incorporate those who held office in Piraeus. Others have deleted the City Ten on the grounds that their regime had been milder and could not have been targeted after 403.[52] But we know from other portions of the Aristotelian narrative that some members of the Ten, such as Rhinon, did submit accounts, and this would imply that unless they went through the same process as the Thirty they would have been exempt from the terms of the Amnesty.[53] Though they had been set up to end civil war, the sources tend to agree that the Ten continued the vile methods of the Thirty, from whom they took over in spring 403, and on the basis of this it seems unlikely that they would not have been targeted.[54] The Eleven were exempted for the obvious reason that they had been part of the machinery of government under the Thirty, and therefore were directly responsible for the most egregious crimes that took place under their rule.[55] The most insoluble question is whether there were one or two boards of Ten. Some commentators have chosen not to amend the Aristotelian version but to preserve the text as it stands.[56] Others have assumed on the basis of the silence in Xenophon that the Aristotelian version as preserved is in error.[57] The silence of Xenophon should not cause worry, as his account is at this point so cursory and cannot be used to correct the far more complete and precise list of covenants. More troubling, however, is the silence of Lysias, who refers to the City Ten and alludes to some of the horrors committed under their regime yet says nothing of the Piraeus Ten. Yet Lysias was primarily concerned with Pheidon, who had served on

---

[51] X. *HG* 2.4.38; And. 1.90; Nep. 3.1.
[52] Dalmeyda 1930: 45; Lenschau *RE* 6 (1937): col. 2376; Maidment 1941: 408.
[53] MacDowell 1962: 130–1.
[54] *Ath. Pol.* 38.4; Lys. 12.58–60; D.S. 14.33.5–6; Nep. 3.1; Just. 5.10.5; see Loening 1987: 43.
[55] On the function of the Eleven, see *Ath. Pol.* 52.1. For their role in the death of Theramenes, see X. *HG* 2.3.55–6.
[56] Thus von Mess 1911: 382–3; Beloch 1922: 12.
[57] Thus Cloché 1915: 184; Fuks 1953: 199.

the board of the City Ten, and therefore did not need to mention the Ten of the Piraeus.[58] Another solution is that only one board existed but that its membership over time changed once it became clear to the Three Thousand that the initial board, henceforth known as the City Ten, were not willing to fulfil their remit of ending the war and were then substituted.[59] That solution gets around the silence of the extra-Aristotelian sources, but is not powerful enough to rectify the papyrus reading. The easiest conclusion is that there were two boards, and that the reason the elusive Piraeus Ten are not mentioned is that there was no need subsequently to do so.

Covenants 17–18 confirm the existence of two panels.[60] What is not clear is how the judges were composed. Is the implication that the judges at Piraeus would be made up of members of the Piraeus Party, and the judges in the city from members of the City Party, or were the panels to comprise a mixture of judges from both parties? There is no modern consensus on the question, and a further difficulty is presented in the fact that we do not know what is meant in context by τὰ τιμήματα παρεχομένοις, for which there is no known parallel in Athenian legal documents.[61] Scholars vary between 'offering securities', 'offering penalties' and 'producing rateable property' as possible ways to translate this obscure and elusive clause.[62] If covenant 17 states that judges provide a property qualification, as has sometimes been assumed, the composition of the judges might have been weighted in favour of the oligarchs, as those sitting on them would have been men of financial means.[63] But there are plenty examples of rich and wealthy citizens who opposed the oligarchy and indeed who fell victim to it, and it is far too simplistic to envisage a distinction between men of wealth who supported oligarchy and men of limited means who did not. Aristotle elsewhere uses the term *timêma* to refer to a property qualification, and in other contexts the expression ὅπλα παρεχόμενοι may refer to census classes from archaic times, though even here the meaning is far from certain.[64] But the grounds for thinking that this otherwise unattested

---

[58] Thus Loening 1987: 45.
[59] Thus Dorjahn 1946; Kühn (J.-H.) 1967: 38–9.
[60] This is made clear from references to the courts in the Piraeus and the city.
[61] For different textual editions of these clauses, see Kenyon 1892: 125; Wilamowitz 1893: 217; Kaibel 1893: 198; Cloché 1915: 268–71; Krentz 1982: 106.
[62] For different renditions, see Reinach 1891: 70; Wilamowitz 1893: 217–18; Cloché 1915: 268–71; Fuks 1953: 202; Rhodes 1981: 470.
[63] The wording of covenant 17 at *Ath. Pol.* 39.6 runs thus: εὐθύνας δὲ δοῦναι τοὺς μὲν ἐν Πειραιεῖ ἄρξαντας ἐν τοῖς ἐν Πειραιεῖ, τοὺς δ' ἐν τῷ ἄστει ἐν τοῖς τὰ τιμήματα παρεχομένοις. εἶθ' οὕτως ἐξοικεῖν τοὺς ἐθέλοντας. τὰ δὲ χρήματα ἃ ἐδανείσαντο εἰς τὸν πόλεμον ἑκατέρους ἀποδοῦναι χωρίς.
[64] Arist. *Pol.* 6.31.1318b30–2. For ὅπλα παρεχόμενοι see *Ath. Pol.* 4.2; Th. 8.97; *IG* I³ 21.

expression refers to a property qualification of any kind are exceedingly slim.⁶⁵ Why should Athenians after the restoration of democracy have wished to limit adjudication in the courts to men of property in a way that contravened the principles of the democracy for which they had fought so hard? No convincing explanation of that reconstruction has ever been proffered. It has been objected that the phrase cannot refer to penalties, since this would merely affirm an existing practice.⁶⁶ But if the judges were empowered to adjudicate cases, they would have been empowered to assess damages, and covenant 17 defines the competences of two extraordinary commissions. For want of a better explanation, τὰ τιμήματα παρεχομένοις must be textually corrupt, and the participle should be amended to παρεχομένους to agree with τοὺς δ' ἐν τῷ ἄστει.⁶⁷ If so, τὰ τιμήματα can be translated as 'securities', and those offering them would have been the governors standing trial.⁶⁸ This is important because, as the trial of Eratosthenes shows (see Chapter 5), the judges in the trial, though all members of the former City Party, were not necessarily men of means, as is clear from the democratic register of the language used by Lysias in the speech for the prosecution. The idea that the City Party comprised only the rich or reasonably well-to-do has been a feature of earlier scholarship, but there is little evidence to sustain this, not least since the Thirty made a habit of targeting rich influential citizens who were, by sympathy, democrats (see Chapter 2).

If παρεχομένοις is taken as read from the MSS, the understanding should be that it is those who judged the trials who provided τὰ τιμήματα; on such a reading, it would be natural to suppose that those who adjudicated in trials over the Thirty, Ten and Eleven were expected to be men of property. Two problems arise here. The first is that the City Party did not necessarily comprise wealthy citizens, and conversely, many who opposed the Thirty were from moneyed families, as Lys. 12 indicates.⁶⁹ It is much too schematic to argue that supporters of the oligarchy were men of wealth, supporters of the democracy men of lower social standing. Secondly, and more crucially, key passages in Lys. 12 indicate that the social composition of the judges in the trial of Eratosthenes was broad (see further Chapter 5); at §43 there is a reference to 'your democracy' (τῷ ὑμετέρῳ πλήθει) and again at §67 (τῷ ὑμετέρῳ πλήθει), indicating that the judges in this trial cannot have been limited to men of means. The democratic language of the speech tells against the MSS

---

⁶⁵ Thus Loening 1987: 48–9.
⁶⁶ Krentz 1982: 106.
⁶⁷ I am grateful to Edward Harris for having suggested this to me in private conversation. On this, see further in Chapter 5.
⁶⁸ On τίμημα as the short version of ἀποτίμημα see Harris 2006: 207–39.
⁶⁹ See Chapter 2, with Németh 2006: 41–74.

at *Ath. Pol.* 39.6, which imply that the body τὰ τιμήματα παρεχομένοις are those of the City Party who sit in judgement at the trial. If, on the other hand, my suggested emendation is acceptable, so that παρεχομένοις, as we have in the MSS, is altered to the accusative case, παρεχομένους, there is an easier way of making sense of the reference: those who provide τὰ τιμήματα, interpreted here not as 'property qualifications' but 'securities', are not panels of judges among the City Party, but those among the oligarchs who consented to undergo audit as per agreement.

Later references indicate that the Ten of the City had borrowed money for their war against the men of Piraeus to the tune of one hundred talents.[70] The democrats had also got themselves into a considerable war debt.[71] The purport of covenant 18 was to ensure that each side paid off its loan. But if the distinction between the City Party and Piraeus Party was now at a close, what indeed did that mean in practical terms? Are we to suppose that those who had fought on the side of the democracy were in some sense registered as having done so after 403 for the purposes of debt repayment, and similarly those who had sided with the Thirty and the Ten? If this was a genuine reconciliation, such a suggestion seems very unlikely. From the conclusion of the peace treaty on 12 Boedromion, the distinction between the two parties of the civil war vanished, but a new division was created between those who chose to live in the city and those who chose instead to migrate to Eleusis. In the legal language of the treaty the term ἑκατέρους must refer to the new distinction.[72] The main purpose of this covenant was to present to those who wished to migrate to Eleusis the very serious proposition that, if they did choose to leave, their liability to indemnity was probably going to be far greater than if they chose to stay. This indeed may have been a capping clause on the benefits lavished on the oligarchs in the earlier covenants where they were guaranteed not only property in Eleusis but freedom from recrimination if they stayed at Athens. Except for the most egregious criminals, it remained in the interests of the restored democracy to ensure that as many citizens as possible chose of their own will to join the democracy and abandon oligarchy. The ingenuity of this was that it gave citizens a choice: do you want to be part of democracy, or would you rather leave? This free decision was a crucial component in rebuilding the political community, so that those who stayed were there by their own volition rather than by legal or political imposition.

---

[70] X. *HG* 2.4.28; Lys. 12.59; 30.22; Isoc. 7.68; Plu. *Lys.* 21.2; D. 20.11–12.
[71] Lys. 30.22; *Against Hippotherses* line 168; D. 20.149; Plu. *Mor.* 835F.
[72] I am not convinced by Loening's suggestion (1987: 50) that more than two parties were involved here. The comparative nature of the pronoun ἑκατέρους must in Greek indicate a binary distinction.

Covenants 19 and 20 are known from the orators. The fact that they appear in the record shows that even the *Ath. Pol.*, which offers the best and most complete account of the treaty, is deficient, and the possibility remains that the treaty had other clauses of which nothing is known. Covenants 19 and 20 guaranteed that goods bought in the time of the Thirty would remain in the possession of the new owner, whereas anything confiscated and not sold on would be restored to the former owner. The purpose here was to ensure against the interminable pursuit of sequestered property, which was bound to hatch a further civil war if it was not controlled in some way. If a citizen had had his goods confiscated, presumably because he had not made it on to the roll of the Three Thousand, he could only reclaim if those goods remained in the possession of the treasury. If they had been passed on through sale, the legal implications of recovery would have been enormous, especially if transaction chains were long. Scholars have debated what kinds of property were involved here: does the clause apply only to moveable possessions or to land also? The majority rightly thinks that both moveable and non-moveable property is meant.[73] At any rate, covenants 19 and 20 illustrate that even if grievances against the regime of the Thirty were huge, in the interest of preserving civic and political unity after 403 it was required that they give up their old claims. For many this may have been the bitterest pill of all to swallow: dead relatives could not be resurrected, but if a returning citizen saw a former partisan of the oligarchy sitting on land which he used to own and calling it his, the feeling of resentment must have been overwhelming.

Isocrates in the speech *Against Callimachus* (§20) implies the existence of a covenant protecting those who had denounced under the Thirty. Other references in Lysias suggest that the oligarchy had relied upon sycophants, and when the democracy was restored one of the big tasks was to ensure that they were properly protected from further prosecution.[74] There is no doubt that denouncers were protected by the Amnesty, but it remains questionable whether this needed to be spelled out in a separate covenant (see Chapter 6). Some have suggested that this was not a genuine clause in the agreement, as such a covenant was rendered unnecessary by covenant 15.[75] As the *Ath. Pol.* does not mention it specifically, it is possible that the covenant to which Lysias here referred was a sub-clause of covenant 15, which defined all the ways in which raking up the past was forbidden; a law of Archinus was passed subsequently which imposed a penalty of a sixth of the claim in the event that litigation contravened the terms of the Amnesty,[76] and one would think that

---

[73] Kühn (J.-H.) 1967: 35; Loening 1987: 52–3; Todd 1993: 234; *contra* Sakurai 1995: 177–80.
[74] Lys. 6.45; 12.48; 13.1–61.
[75] Thus Loening 1987: 56; *pace* Dorjahn 1946: 24; Rhodes 1981: 468–9.
[76] For the law of Archinus, see Isoc. 18.1–4 and Chapter 6.

the various ways in which civil or criminal action could undermine the peace terms were legally spelled out in the covenants of the treaty. In my earlier work I had taken the view that the covenant mentioned at Isoc. 18.20 was a separate clause of the treaty, but I am less certain of this now. On reflection, Loening was correct to suppose that the accuser of Callimachus was drawing out the implications of covenant 15, which was the rule against dredging up the past. But whether it was spelled out as a separate rule or not, what seems clear is that those who had committed wrong under the Thirty were protected. The Treaty of Amnesty was a blanket measure of annulment, whose universal efficacy is evident from the trials which followed on from the Treaty of Amnesty in 403.

The Covenants of the Athenian Reconciliation shine out as a paradigm of amnesty. The trials which followed are often caricatured in modern scholarship as detrimental to the spirit of the Amnesty, but as the next three chapters show, the Amnesty Agreement of 403 was sanctified and respected. When litigants went to court subsequently, their aim was to ensure that the terms of the Amnesty were applied rather than violated. It has been tempting in the past to speak of a spate of 'political' trials arising from the issue, but as the next three chapters show, that is to miss the point. To be sure, some of the trials, especially those of Agoratus and Eratosthenes, employed the language of retaliation, but it is important to read this in context: if vengeful measures were to be sought out and applied, these could only operate through the channel of the law. In this sense, the trials were not 'political' so much as legal. More importantly still, the cries for justice after 403 were never packaged in factional language, as vengeance by one party upon another. Lysias appealed to the judges to avenge the democracy, but the point here is that justice is to be won for the whole of the citizenry, not just a portion of it. As with the *Panegyricus* oration of Isocrates, which on the surface looks very much like a battle cry of retaliation but on closer reading is a call for unity among the Greeks (see Chapter 7), so did the language of vengeance employed by Lysias after 403 find its context within a broader political culture of peace and reconciliation. At first sight, this might appear paradoxical, and scholars have sometimes questioned the degree to which the spirit of reconciliation was observed (see Chapter 5). But it is important to observe the cries for retaliation in the broader framework of the arguments in which they are presented. Athenian justice was about the application of a legal principle, nothing more. Though Lysias harboured a personal vendetta against Eratosthenes, he was at pains to show that this was *not* the reason why the prosecution was taking place. As the trials of Agoratus, Eratosthenes, Andocides, Nicomachus, Callimachus and Socrates show in their different ways, the Amnesty was enshrined in the hearts and minds of citizens after 403.

CHAPTER 4

The Legal Scrutiny and the Resurrection of the Rule of Law

Once the Covenants of Reconciliation had been contracted and sworn into effect, it remained for the legislators of 403 to rebuild democracy. Modern scholarship has often distinguished the democracy of the fourth century from its fifth-century prototype on the basis that whereas the one was built on the principle of the rule of law, the other prioritised popular sovereignty. The decision of the legislators in 403 to publish a comprehensive list of valid laws, as distinct from decrees, is rightly understood to dovetail with a concept of democracy which anchored itself in the sovereignty of law, and in the process of that legal redaction, clarification was given that no decree of the popular assembly should have higher authority than a law (And. 1.87). In a famous summary of how the Athenian democracy evolved, the *Ath. Pol.* states (ch. 41) that the democracy of the fourth century was the last and final phase of the evolution of democracy at Athens. Apart from the rule of law, however, this paltry narrative provides little indication of the differences between the final democracy and the penultimate phase, which prevailed from the mid-fifth century down until the subjection of Athens by Sparta in 404 and the installation of the regime of the Thirty. The democratic restoration did not pronounce a wholesale return to the *status quo ante*. In its most important outline, democracy from 403 was very similar to what had preceded it, but it contained one very crucial innovation, the process of law-making and, implied in this, a redefinition of what a 'law' was. The habit of much scholarship to date has been to see fourth-century democracy as a more 'conservative' version of the fifth-century model, but this chapter will argue that that approach is mistaken from its foundations.[1] The aim of the republication of laws in 403 was

---

[1] For a persuasive refutation of the idea that the eleventh phase of constitutional development summarised at *Ath. Pol.* 41 refers to a more 'conservative' form of democracy post-403, see

to assert the primacy of legal principle in the new constitution, yet that assertion went hand in hand with a fervently democratic objective: to guarantee that Athens did not backslide into civil war, it was paramount that democracy should be protected by legal principle. Democracy and rule of law were bedfellows.

Due recognition of the truth of this statement has been obstructed by the belief that, in Greek theoretical circles, democracy and rule of law were somehow antithetical.[2] Much of the confusion arises from a misreading of some key passages in Aristotle, which *prima facie* might be understood as claiming that democracy in its most fully realised state did not obey the rule of law.[3] Aristotle's critique of 'lawless' democracy in fourth-century Greece is not necessarily a critique of Athens, and efforts to find a common meaning between 'lawless' and 'extreme' democracy have been coloured by loose translations of the controversial phrase ἡ τελευταία δημοκρατία (Arist. *Pol.* 4.14.1298a28–35; 5.31.1319b1–3), misread as if meaning 'most developed' or 'extreme' democracy.[4] The victory of democracy in 403 over the oligarchs was hailed in the fourth century as a triumph of democracy unqualified, not 'moderate' or

---

Harris 2016, with references to earlier scholarship which mistakenly believes that the democracy installed in 403 was a less democratic type of constitution than what had existed prior to 404. Against the view of a lawless democracy, see now Filonik 2019.

[2] The notion of Athenian democracy as unconstrained by any higher legal principle, in various ways, goes back to Hume in the eighteenth century and persisted through much of the nineteenth; see Hume 1742; Goodell 1893; Bryce 1889. When the London papyrus was published in 1891, however, scholars became aware of two procedures, the *graphê paranomôn* and the *graphê nomon mê epitêdeion theinai*, which pointed to a legal system which seemed to constrain arbitrary decision-making. On the strength of the assumption that there was no concept of 'law' higher than 'decree' before 403, twentieth-century scholars concluded that the procedures for constraining politicians to observe legal principle predated the idea of a body of law which stood separate from, and higher than, the decrees of the Assembly; see Kahrstedt 1937–8; Wolff 1970. Yet, whilst it is true that a new democratic procedure for law-making came into effect after 403, it is false to assert that, until the time of the democratic Restoration, Athenians had no concept of a higher system of laws. For a further discussion of the distinction between laws and popular measures going back to Homer, see Joyce 2021: 153–4.

[3] An example of this conceptual confusion is to be found in the most recent monograph of Carawan (2020), which argues for a sense of democratic 'lawfulness' as corresponding to whatever was fitting to popular whim at any given point in time. Carawan's case takes little cognizance of the ample discussion in Arist. *Pol.* Books 5 and 6 of the distinction between lawful and lawless democracy. For a critique of Carawan's approach, see Esu 2021.

[4] This is not the place to engage in an extensive discussion of Aristotle's *Politics*. Often, translators have taken *teleutaia* ('last') as synonymous with *teleia* ('pure'), and furthermore have understood 'last' in a chronological rather than an analytical sense. In those passages, when criticising lawless democracy, Aristotle most probably refers to the democracy under Cleon. Moreover, it is far from clear that he had Athens primarily in mind when criticising democracy, as the city most mentioned in *Politics* V and VI is not Athens, but Syracuse.

'slightly more conservative than before' democracy. More importantly, the interlude of the Thirty had illustrated what happened when the rule of law broke down. In the eyes of the fourth century, the absence of legal restraint was a feature not of democracy in its purest state, but of its purest and vilest antithesis, tyranny. It would therefore be strange if the project in 403, which was to re-establish a democratic constitution founded upon the principle of the sovereignty of law, had been accompanied by the conviction that the society which the lawgivers of 403 were seeking to create was to any real degree less democratic than that which had capitulated to the Thirty. Quite the contrary: the understanding was that the legislators of 403 laid the foundations of a society which was *even more* democratic than the one before 404 by guaranteeing the additional protection of a new legislative process, recognising a conceptual distinction between a law (νόμος), namely a statute with permanent and universal application, and a decree of the Assembly (ψήφισμα), which had a more specific and temporary application.[5] The distinction was substantive and procedural: from now on, a special process of law-making (*nomothesia*) was set up through *nomothetai* (lawgivers; see below), commissioned to update and revise the body of laws currently relevant and applicable.[6]

The Amnesty of 403 was one component of the restoration of democracy. As argued in this chapter, what followed on from the Covenants of Reconciliation was, in various ways, even more significant as Athens put behind itself eight months of oligarchic rule, during which the rule of law had been systematically flouted. To restore democracy after 12 Boedromion, the reinstatement of the rule of law in 403 was thus paramount. The trials of Nicomachus and Andocides, discussed below, though difficult to handle because of the slipperiness of the evidence upon which modern discussions are based (see Chapter 1), nevertheless indicate that the rule of law was consistently applied after 403, as do those of Agoratus and Eratosthenes (Chapter 5), Callimachus and Socrates (Chapter 6). But before we turn to those cases, a vital theoretical question needs to be addressed. It is easy to speak about the rule of law in some casual fashion without a clear definition of what it entails, and though a fuller treatment of the problem can be found in Chapter 8, it will here suffice to lay down some essential criteria.

---

[5] For modern scholarly discussions of the distinction between laws and decrees, see Rhodes 1980; Sealey 1982; Hansen 1983; Rhodes 1984; Ober 1989: 96. For recent convincing arguments that the democracy of the fourth century was, contrary to the assertions of many, even more democratic than the democracy of the fifth, see now Harris 2016.

[6] For a complete and persuasive reassessment of how the new legislative process of *nomothesia* in the fourth century worked, see Canevaro 2015; Canevaro and Esu 2018: 127–36.

THE RULE OF LAW: ITS DEFINITION AND CHARACTERISTICS

The trials which followed on from the Reconciliation have been extensively debated in modern times. As argued below, these trials were legal, and less 'political', because they adhered to the principle of the rule of law which the democrats reinstated at Athens in 403. The rule of law encompassed the idea that there should be equality of all citizens before the law. Demosthenes famously said that Athenians enjoyed equality through their laws (D. 21.67, 188). One of the supplementary laws cited at And. 1.87, though partially corrupt, specified that no law could be passed against individuals unless it applied to all citizens (μηδὲ ἐπ' ἀνδρὶ νόμον ἐξεῖναι θεῖναι, ἐὰν μὴ τὸν αὐτὸν ἐπὶ πᾶσιν Ἀθηναίοις). The rider which comes after this, that the rule should apply unless it met the vote of six thousand people, has been excerpted by editors rightly on the grounds that no example can be found of the operation of such an exception.[7] Though the principle was spelled out explicitly in 403, it is implicit in Draco's homicide law, the oldest sample of legislation which is extant (*IG* I³ 104 lines 10 and 27; cf. D. 23.24, 38, 45 and 60) and is visible both in Pericles' Funeral Oration and in fifth-century tragedy.[8] All officials were accountable for their actions, submitting their conduct to judicial review (Aeschin. 3.12–27; *Ath. Pol.* 48.4–5). The law needed to be universally accessible, which was why in 403, as in the period which preceded (411–404), efforts were made to publish all the laws of Athens in a conspicuous location.[9] Demosthenes later stated that the aim of *nomothesia* was to ensure that there were no opposing laws (D. 20.93). In the fourth century, copies of all laws were kept in the Metroon for the consultation of anyone.[10] That of course did not invalidate or negate the need to display them on stelae also, but it is important to recognise that inscribed texts of laws, which are relatively few in extant number, were not the only records. Inscribed texts of laws which we do possess often make express reference to the public location of their intended display, such as the law of Nicophon of 375/4 (*SEG* 26.25 lines 44–7).[11] The process of *nomothesia* demanded that all proposed laws be displayed before the Eponymous Heroes in the centre of the Agora (D. 20.94; 24.18).[12] The rule

---

[7] Canevaro and Harris 2012: 117–18. For efforts to find such examples, see Hansen 1979; *contra* Rhodes 1984. For other fourth-century references, see D.
[8] Th. 2.37.1; cf. [Arist.] *Rh. Al.* 2.21.1424b15–16; E. *Supp.* 433–4, 437; cf. D. 51.11.
[9] Thus Fuller 1964; Sickinger 2004; *pace* Todd 1993: 55–8.
[10] Lyc. *Leocr.* 69 with Sickinger 1999: 149–52.
[11] For a study of those formulae, see Liddel 2003.
[12] See Shear (T. L.) 1970.

of law also implied that there should be no punishment without the law, as recognised at D. 24.43, which mentions that no law should be applied retroactively,[13] and at And. 1.87, which forbade officials to use an unwritten law. Though there were differences between the Athenian and the modern concept of rule of law as understood in post-Enlightenment societies, especially over the use of torture, the fundamental principles of universality and accessibility were central.[14] This is why it is vital to understand the legal redaction in and after 403 in the full historical light of what the Reconciliation was trying to achieve. Democracy could function only if the law was supreme, and that could only be achieved if the laws of Athens were completely and comprehensively published in a central location near the Stoa, as Andocides states (1.85). The Amnesty brought reconciliation, but after the Reconciliation, it was required to lay the foundations on which democracy could thrive.

The first reference to lawgivers (*nomothetai*) appears in Thucydides, who describes the events which followed the overthrow of the Four Hundred in 411. Their identification is crucial but also problematic. The Athenians met on the Pnyx and voted to hand the government of the city over to the Five Thousand, at which point they chose lawgivers to lay out the blueprint for a new constitution: ἐγίγνοντο δὲ καὶ ἄλλαι ὕστερον πυκναὶ ἐκκλησίαι, ἀφ' ὧν καὶ νομοθέτας καὶ τἆλλα ἐψηφίσαντο ἐς τὴν πολιτείαν (Th. 8.97.2). How this is to be translated is debatable, as it is not obvious what ἀφ' ὧν means. The normal assumption has been that the assemblies met in 411 to appoint a separate commission of lawgivers to give Athens a new constitution. Philologically, this admittedly is possible, because there are attested instances in Greek where ἀπό can denote agency.[15] But the reason this has been assumed is that, with very few exceptions, scholars have imagined that the *nomothetai* of the fourth century were different in kind from the Assembly which passed decrees. This is because it has been assumed that democracy and rule of law were conceptual polarities, that the 'lawful' democracy from 403 was one in which the sovereignty of the Assembly was 'tempered' by a higher authority in the shape of a separate panel of lawgivers, which created the law. The difficulty here is the silence of the *Ath. Pol.* as to the existence of a legislative process called *nomothesia* which was separate or distinct from the legislation of the Assembly. The most common explanations are that the author of the *Ath. Pol.* was either careless or selective,[16] but they miss a much more fundamental point: the second half of the *Ath. Pol.*, devoted to

---

[13] On this formulation, see Harris 2006: 425–30.

[14] For a broader discussion of the differences between ancient and modern constructions of 'the rule of law', see Harris 2013: 10–12.

[15] See, for example, Hdt. 1.14; 2.54; Th. 1.17; 6.61; Pl. *R.* 528a; E. *Tr.* 74; S. *OC* 1628.

[16] Thus Ingravalle 1989; Wallace 1993: 34–45; Bertelli 1993: 61; Bravo 1994: 237–8; Poddighe 2014: 123–5.

the constitution in the fourth century, is organised around the three functions of deliberation, magistrates and the judiciary; the first of these three comes under the umbrella of the Council and the Assembly, which is in keeping with what Aristotle elsewhere states, that the constitutional function of councils and assemblies is to deliberate concerning the laws (*Pol.* 4.14.1298a3–5; *Rh.* 1.4.1319a–b). The author of the *Ath. Pol.* had no pressing need to write separately about *nomothesia*, because it fell under the bracket of the authority of the Council and Assembly, to which chapters 43.2–49 are devoted. The silence of the *Ath. Pol.* about *nomothesia* is problematic only if it is assumed that the lawgivers, first attested in 411, were constitutionally distinct.[17] But there is no good reason to infer from Th. 8.97.2 that the assemblies on the Pnyx appointed lawgivers who were separate or distinct from the people sitting in a legislative capacity. The natural reading is that *as a result of the assemblies* they voted in lawgivers for a new constitution. Even so, the evidence as it stands is insufficient to determine if the lawgivers in 411 were distinct from the Assembly.

The importance of this nuance will become clearer when we reflect on the relationship between democracy and the rule of law. The eleventh stage of constitutional development at Athens, the democracy of 403 which followed the defeat of the oligarchy, is not represented in the narrative of *Ath. Pol.* 41.3 as a backward step away from extreme democracy. Quite the contrary: it is democracy in its most developed state, as the wording makes clear (ἁπάντων γὰρ αὐτὸς αὑτὸν πεποίηκεν ὁ δῆμος κύριον, καὶ πάντα διοικεῖται ψηφίσμασιν καὶ δικαστηρίοις, ἐν οἷς ὁ δῆμός ἐστιν ὁ κρατῶν).[18] The Aristotelian tradition did not see the democracy of 403 as less democratic than the fifth-century democracy, but more so. But who were these lawgivers whom the *Ath. Pol.* omits to mention? The next reference comes in 403 after the exchange of the Oaths of Reconciliation. According to Andocides (1.82; see further below, pp. 107–8), a new council was chosen and lawgivers selected (νομοθέτας τε εἴλεσθε) to search out the laws of Draco and Solon. On the strength of a document inserted into the MSS of D. 24.20–3, it has been argued in the past that these lawgivers were selected from those who swore the Judicial Oath, in other words that they were judges. But recent studies have made a convincing case that that text is a forgery, as its contents find no confirmation in any other sources.[19] Their identity can be established from Aeschin. 3.38–40, which refers to a requirement that every year the thesmothetai must reconcile the laws after scrutiny, whereupon irregularities are to be posted at the statues of the ten Eponymous Heroes, after which the *prytaneis*

---

[17] Thus Canevaro and Esu 2018: 130–1.
[18] 'For the people has made itself master of everything, and governs itself through its decrees and the courts, in which the people is the dominant power.'
[19] Canevaro 2013a: 150–6; 2013b: 94–102; 2018.

must hold an assembly ἐπιγράψαντας νομοθέτας and the people by show of hands vote upon the laws.[20] What this shows is that the laws were voted on by the *dêmos*. In the conviction that the *nomothetai* to which this passage of Aeschines refers were distinct from, and above, the Assembly, modern commentators have downscaled its implications. Seeking to reconcile it with the document at D. 24.20–3, R. Schöll suggested deleting τῷ δήμῳ and amending νομοθέτας to νομοθέταις, so that the Assembly called by the *prytaneis* was there to appoint nomothetai.[21] In contrast, M. Piérart retained the MSS and interpreted Aeschines to mean that 'the *prytaneis* call an assembly labelling it nomothetai'.[22] With a rather different set of implications, P. J. Rhodes also argued against Schöll's emendation, but claimed that ἐπιγράψαντας νομοθέτας meant 'putting the nomothetai on the agenda'.[23] The final vote on the laws before the *dêmos* is the consequence of the *prytaneis* ἐπιγράψαντας νομοθέτας, so that the vote of the *nomothetai* was itself the vote of the Assembly. This is consistent with *Ath. Pol.* 41.3, where the people is sovereign through its decrees and the courts. *Nomothesia* is not included because it is not envisaged as a separate or 'higher' process.[24]

When democracy was restored at Athens in 403, the task was to build a society which respected the rule of law. If those two categories are regarded as antithetical, it becomes natural to envisage a constitutional process of lawgiving, *nomothesia*, operating independently from the Assembly. If so, the process of legal scrutiny which followed on the heels of the Oath of Reconciliation in 403 was, on that interpretation, undemocratic and operated outside the purview of the Assembly itself. Andocides states that once Athenians had sworn to the Reconciliation, they set about reviewing and publishing the laws of Athens (And. 1.81–2). The verb is ἀναγράφειν, often (but not always) read to mean 'to inscribe', as is the case, for example, in the preface to Draco's homicide law, inscribed on stone at the end of the fifth century (*IG* I³ 104 = ML 86 line 5). Thanks to the influence of S. Dow (see below, pp. 106–7), it has often been held that the reference is to the creation of a 'law code', that

[20] Harris 2013: 225–33.
[21] Schöll 1886: 116–17 with n. 4, 118 with n. 1.
[22] Piérart 2000: 229–50.
[23] Rhodes 2003: 126.
[24] Thus Canevaro and Esu 2018: 135–6: 'The procedures of *nomothesia* quite simply piled up different institutional stages with different functions, enlisting the work, in turn, of Council, Assembly, and lawcourts (all manned by the *demos*). Aristotle duly provides an account of the workings of the various institutions that played a role in the procedure but does not recognise [in] the procedure any specificity – any distinctiveness or higher function – and as a result he does not select it for inclusion, as there were, within his framework, no compelling reasons, neither from the point of view of his theoretical edifice nor from that of the organisational structure of the *Ath. Pol.*, that made its inclusion particularly meaningful.' Against the view that Draco codified laws, see Joyce 2021/2.

is, a single comprehensive statement of all the valid laws of Athens in a single inscribed text.[25] More recently, the objection has arisen that such a 'code' is not referred to at any point in the fourth century, which has led some to infer that Andocides was not telling the truth, or that the redaction in question was less extensive than he implies, or that the process of 'writing up' was not tantamount to one of inscribing in a permanent record, but writing up for temporary display laws which were scrutinised and then carried into effect, whereupon the texts would be written down on scrolls and given over to an archive.[26] In all probability, the laws were displayed in multifarious locations in the fourth century, and even if the lawgivers of 403 had enjoined a complete redaction of the laws in or near the Stoa, as Andocides implies, there is no particular reason to rule out that other stone copies of the laws were displayed around Athens. But there is a much more fundamental point which previous discussion has missed: the process which Andocides describes in 403 was not one which ended in or shortly after 403, as those who have sought to align it with Lys. 30 have maintained, but one which continued down into the fourth century to the time of Aeschines, who commented on the same process. The scrutiny of laws which began in 403 was not a legal 'codification' *sensu stricto*, whereby it aimed within a short interval of time to generate a definitive and exhaustive statement of the law of Athens which could not be amended or supplemented subsequently, but the beginning of an ongoing process which was to continue into the next century. This is confirmed by the prescript to Draco's law (lines 3–8), which shows that the law was presented to the people and that the people voted to have the law displayed in the vicinity of the Stoa Basileios, and is consistent with the view that the process of *nomothesia*, which began in 411, was interrupted by the Thirty and resumed in 403 at the time of the restoration, was a democratic process overseen by the Assembly.

Our two main inroads into the scrutiny of laws are the trials of Nicomachus in 399 (Lys. 30) and Andocides around 400 (And. 1). Both cases are notoriously difficult to interpret, as they present events in a stilted and often dishonest fashion. Nicomachus was the lead member of the board of transcribers, or *anagrapheis*, commissioned in the last decade of the fifth century to write up the laws of Athens from 410–404, and again from 403–399. The relationship between his two terms has been debated, as has the precise role which Nicomachus played. Some have characterised Nicomachus as a legal expert with a special commission to interpret and redevise the laws of Athens, whereas others have

---

[25] False analogies are sometimes made with the laws at Gortyn (*IC* IV 72) which has been described as a 'code', even though there are many laws outside this collection which happens to be the largest surviving collection of its kind. For an overview of the Gortynian laws, see Davies 1996.

[26] For an overview of the scholarship, see nn. 37–8.

understood him to have been little more than a state functionary who followed orders and performed the mechanical task of writing up laws from transcripts handed to him by a higher authority.[27] Despite its slanderous bombast, Lys. 30 when carefully analysed confirms the picture of the *dokimasia* as a democratic process, under the strict oversight of the people. Laws were sought out, presented before the Assembly, approved or rejected, and those voted in handed to the *anagrapheis* to inscribe on a stone slab. There is no reference anywhere in the speech to a unified 'code' of laws.[28] The idea that Nicomachus and his colleagues wrote up the laws in a single display is a modern inference based on reading of a forged document in the text of And. 1 (the so-called 'decree of Teisamenus') and the effort of scholars ever since Dow to relate the thirteen inscribed fragments of the so-called 'Sacrificial Calendar' to the commission of Nicomachus, for which there is no trace of supporting evidence. As argued below (pp. 105–7), the inscribed fragments detailing the costings of state sacrifices probably have nothing to do with Nicomachus' commission, as none contains a prescript comparable to the prescript at *IG* I^3 104 lines 3–8. And. 1, meanwhile, though it sheds important light on the process of legislation in 403, presents events disingenuously, as if the aim of the scrutiny was to eliminate older statutes under which Andocides was probably liable. As argued in the next section, that picture of the legal scrutiny is irrelevant and underestimates its real purpose, which was to enshrine the principle of the sovereignty of law, unified and fused with popular sovereignty. Above all, the restoration of democracy in 403 was about the restoration of the authority of the law, the central bastion of democratic government which the Thirty in 404 had undermined.

THE TRIAL OF NICOMACHUS, C. 399 (LYS. 30)

Outside the thirtieth speech in the Lysianic corpus, little is known about legal transcriber (or *anagrapheus*) Nicomachus. In around 399, he was tried for impiety and malfeasance, though the exact nature of the charge laid against him is not clear from the speech of prosecution. In all probability, the trial was conducted before the ten *logistai*, or accountants, whose task was to investigate activities and financial dealings of public officials enjoined to carry out specific tasks by the Athenian state. Scattered references from within the speech provide an outline of the chronology: after the fall of the first oligarchy in 411, the scribes (*ana*-

---

[27] For the first view, see Todd 1996; for the second, see Robertson 1990.
[28] The notion of a law 'code' is overused in modern scholarship, often without any effort to define what is meant by it; for an example of such a tendency, see Rhodes 1991, which speaks of a 'code of laws' without clarification as to what is meant by the term in practice, or how we should understand the arrangement of laws within that 'code'.

grapheis) began the task of began to write up on freestanding stone slabs the valid laws of democratic Athens; this task was originally to take only four months, but as it transpired, it took the better part of six years, cut short by the oligarchic coup of the Thirty in 404 (Lys. 30.2). How that first period of office was conducted, and how the laws were published at that time, is open to speculation. The most likely suggestion is that originally the task had been to transcribe the historical laws of Draco and Solon which had come down from the seventh and sixth centuries on monuments called *axones* and *kyrbeis*, but the remit snowballed to include every valid law of Athens.[29] Until we get to 403, we have little indication as to the shape of transcription. The partial survival of a stone copy of Draco's law on homicide (*IG* I^3 104 = ML 86) republished in 409/8 might suggest that the laws during this period were displayed on free-standing stelae, yet notable about the re-edition of Draco's law is that it was prefaced by an enabling decree, suggesting that the legal transcribers did not have a blank cheque to write up all the laws, and that every law that was transcribed was sanctioned by a separate ordinance of the people. Unfortunately, too little is understood about either term of office to know for certain the full nature of Nicomachus' remit. The implication of Lys. 30.3 is that in the last desperate years of democracy before 404, the city had descended into legal confusion, with litigants producing contradictory laws in the courts which they had obtained from the *anagrapheis*. Most importantly, this implies that in the first term, Nicomachus had been charged with the transcription of all the valid laws of Athens.

When democracy was restored in 403, the work of Nicomachus continued. It is often held on the strength of And. 1.82 that the work begun in 410 and interrupted in 404 was started afresh in 403, invalidating everything that had been accomplished in the first term. As shown below (pp. 113–15), Andocides was simply being dishonest. The reference at And. 1.82 to 'laws under which citizens were liable' which the lawgivers aimed to eliminate is made in the flow of the argument to look as if the aim of the scrutiny in 403 was to eliminate specific statutes under which citizens stood guilty after the democratic restoration. That impression has been bolstered by what Andocides later states at 1.87, that a blanket statement was issued that the laws could only be applied from the archonship of Eucleides (403/2). A law of Diocles (D. 24.42) shows that laws dating from before 404 were as valid after the return of democracy as those passed after 403, and so the meaning of the 'application of the laws

---

[29] Scholars have debated the relationship between these two sets of monuments, some (e.g. Ruschenbusch 1966) claiming that they were identical, others (e.g. Stroud 1979) arguing that the *axones* of Solon contained the 'secular' laws, the *kyrbeis* the sacred, and that their shape and form were different. For the view that the task of the *anagrapheis* from 410–399 expanded accidentally from a much narrower and specific remit, see Rhodes 1991: 100. For more recent treatments, see Davis 2011; Meyer 2016.

from Eucleides' is not quite as Andocides implies. More simply, it meant that after democracy was restored, citizens could not be prosecuted for untried offences predating 403. Thus, the implication is not that the work completed in Nicomachus' first term was invalidated by the decision in 403 to write up 'all the laws', as if this meant a clean bill, but that in 403, Nicomachus and his colleagues were enjoined to complete the work they had begun in 410, which had been interrupted by the interlude of the Thirty. According to Lysias, the second period of office was initially expected to take just thirty days, but the enormity of the administrative task before the *anagrapheis* had perhaps not been grasped adequately, and so, like the first period, it spiralled beyond the initial time expectation to extend to four whole years (Lys. 30.4–5). If the prosecution is believable, the second term was little better than the first: Nicomachus, despite being given specific instructions as to the texts he was expected to transcribe (διωρισμένον ἐξ ὧν ἔδει ἀναγράφειν), made himself master of everything (αὐτὸν ἁπάντων κύριον ἐποιήσατο), and did all this without submitting to a single audit during those four years of office (μόνος οὗτος τῶν ἀρξάντων εὐθύνας οὐκ ἔδωκεν). Rather than adhering to the specific remit he had been given, he inserted laws here, removed laws there, and though a servant treated Athens as if it were his own (ἀλλὰ τὰ μὲν ἐγγράφεις τὰ δ' ἐξαλείφεις, καὶ εἰς τοῦτο ὕβρεως ἥκεις ὥστε σαυτοῦ νομίζεις εἶναι τὰ τῆς πόλεως).

How much of this invective is to be believed is, of course, open to speculation. Because we do not know the details of the plaint against Nicomachus, it is difficult to grasp what the audit was to which the speaker alludes. What the passage does show, however, is that the task given to Nicomachus and the board was tightly regulated and under popular jurisdiction. It was the people who voted on what the *anagrapheis* were to write up and what was to be rejected. This is exactly in keeping with the prescript of Draco's homicide law (see above), where the *anagrapheis* are presented as dutifully following out instructions given to them by the people. Their initial job was to seek out laws to be presented to the Assembly, which, in a legislative capacity, that is, in the capacity of *nomothetai*, voted them in or out, and those approved were handed back to the transcribers to write up in a public location in the vicinity of the Stoa. The effort in various places to cast the defendant as an oligarchic sympathiser is relevant in this connection. At Lys. 30.11–14, the accused is charged with having conspired with the oligarchs by bringing about the trial of Cleophon in 405. According to the claim, Nicomachus had presented a law to the Council requiring it to preside over the prosecution of a popular leader in the wake of the naval disaster at Aegospotami, which had led to the grain route to the Black Sea being closed off, a trial that resulted in a number of leading democrats being convicted and executed. The purpose behind this tarnishing is clear: if the accused was oligarchic by sympathy, it is thus hardly surprising that he should flout the normal auditing procedures laid out under democracy. But there is a broader relevance still to the oligarchic connection, namely that by disobeying the will of the people, Nicomachus was acting on oligarchic impulses. The point is just that the *nomothesia* begun in 411 and continued into the fourth century was, in its whole conception, a democratic process. If Nicomachus had at any point departed from what he had been charged to carry out, he stood in violation of a democratic edict. However far we may wish to believe whatever is being alleged against him, the character of this speech is vital, because it proceeds from the foundational assumption that the scrutiny and writing up of laws were democratic.

A related question is the identity and character of the accuser. We do not know who led the prosecution of Nicomachus, but glimpses in the speech indicate that he too had been tarred with an oligarchic brush. At an earlier hearing before the Council of Five Hundred, the accused had alleged that the prosecution had been implicated with the oligarchs (Lys. 30.7–8). It remains questionable which oligarchic regime is meant. The extant MSS connect him with two groups, the Three Hundred and the Three Thousand. Since the early sixteenth century, editions of the Lysianic speeches have, in almost all cases, emended this to mean the Four Hundred and Five Thousand, to make the allusion refer to the first oligarchic revolution of 411, mainly because until the discovery of the *Ath. Pol.* a body called 'the Three Hundred' was unknown. Since the first edition of the London papyrus in 1891, however, we now know that such a body did exist during the second and far worse oligarchy of 404/3, known as the three-hundred whip-bearing attendants (*Ath. Pol.* 35.1: μαστιγοφόρους τριακοσίους ὑπηρέτας).[30] It is possible, therefore, that the oligarchy to which the accused referred was not the somewhat milder of 411, but the more hated and dreaded of 404/3. Much has been made recently of this historical distinction, mainly in an effort to identify the leader of the prosecution with a member of the recently dissolved enclave at Eleusis (403–401), who for oligarchic motives took a critical stance towards the re-edition of the sacred calendar which, in its earlier formats, omitted key sacrifices enjoined on the *kyrbeis* of Solon to make way for sacrifices which had accumulated in the later years of the democracy.[31] The problem here is that neither do we have an indication in the speech as to the identity or provenance of the speaker, nor is it clear from the poverty of the evidence that those who were reintegrated into the democratic system after the suppression of Eleusis in 401 took an oligarchic posture in politics or the courts thereafter; the account of Xenophon, at any rate, indicates that the main troublemakers were eliminated in the field and

---

[30] See Carawan 2010; 2013: 234–5.
[31] Carawan 2013: 243–50.

that those who chose to lay down arms reconciled with the remainder of the civic body under oath (X. *HG* 2.4.43).[32]

Even if the accuser had been associated with either oligarchy, the crucial point is that he was immune from prosecution after 403. This is made abundantly clear at Lys. 30.8–9:

[8] ἐγὼ δὲ οὕτω πολλοῦ ἐδέησα τῶν τετρακοσίων γενέσθαι, ὥστε οὐδὲ τῶν πεντακισχιλίων κατελέγην. δεινὸν δέ μοι δοκεῖ εἶναι ὅτι, εἰ μὲν περὶ ἰδίων συμβολαίων ἀγωνιζόμενος οὕτω φανερῶς ἐξήλεγχον αὐτὸν ἀδικοῦντα, οὐδ᾽ ἂν αὐτὸς ἠξίωσε τοιαῦτα ἀπολογούμενος ἀποφεύγειν, νυνὶ δὲ περὶ τῶν τῆς πόλεως κρινόμενος οἰήσεται χρῆναι ἐμοῦ κατηγορῶν ὑμῖν μὴ δοῦναι δίκην. [9] ἔτι δὲ εἶναι θαυμαστὸν νομίζω Νικόμαχον ἑτέροις ἀδίκως μνησικακεῖν ἀξιοῦν, ὃν ἐγὼ ἐπιβουλεύσαντα τῷ πλήθει ἀποδείξω. καί μου ἀκούσατε· δίκαιον γάρ, ὦ ἄνδρες δικασταί, περὶ τῶν τοιούτων ἀνθρώπων τὰς τοιαύτας κατηγορίας ἀποδέχεσθαι, οἵτινες τότε συγκαταλύσαντες τὸν δῆμον νυνὶ δημοτικοί φασιν εἶναι.

[8] But for my part, so far was I from being one of the Four Hundred that I was not even included in the list of the Five Thousand.[33] And I consider it monstrous that, although in a suit concerning private contracts, had I convicted him as plainly as here of wrongdoing, he would not even himself have expected to obtain an acquittal by resorting to such a defence, he now, on his trial for matters of public interest, is to count on escaping punishment at your hands by accusing me. Moreover, I find it astonishing that Nicomachus should think fit to stir up resentment against others in this criminal way, when I mean to prove that he hatched mischief against the people. And now listen to me; for it is justifiable, judges, to admit such accusations in the case of men who, having combined at that time to subvert the democracy, would represent themselves today as democrats. (tr. R. W. G. Lamb, modified)

The meaning of the reference to μνησικακεῖν at §9 is self-evident: by alluding to any possible earlier association with oligarchy, Nicomachus stands in

---

[32] The attempt of Carawan (2013: 234) to support his reading of Lys. 30.7–8, in keeping with the MSS on the basis that the speaker states that 'some were boys at the time', is unconvincing. To be sure, no one under the age of thirty could have served among the Four Hundred or Five Thousand, whereas the Three Hundred certainly would have incorporated youths. Yet the point Lysias makes is just this: do not believe all the slander you hear, because similar slander has been issued against those who could not have been members of the oligarchy on the merits of their age.

[33] Or 'Three Hundred...Three Thousand'; see above note.

breach of the law, which had made it illegal after 403 to stir partisan leanings by allusion to events which preceded the democratic restoration. As argued in Chapter 3 and again in Chapter 7, μὴ μνησικακεῖν was a pledge not to pursue in the courts untried offences predating the democratic restoration. Recently, it has been argued that here, violation of the rule μὴ μνησικακεῖν refers to overturning a specific clause in the agreement affecting private contracts.[34] That misses the larger point: the speaker is not claiming that the Amnesty contained clauses governing private legal obligations. Rather, the situation being presented here is hypothetical: *if* it were the case that Nicomachus were being pursued for violation of a contract, for instance, even in such a private lawsuit he would not have dared to try to bring discredit upon the character of his opponent by mentioning the unmentionable; therefore, it is a matter of public disgrace and outrage that in a political trial of this kind, whose ramifications extend so much further, he should have the audacity to call to mind a political association which, even if true, should have no bearing upon the merits of the case under investigation. By bringing up Cleophon, the speaker comes close to violating the rule himself, but he does this for a specific purpose, to show that despite the horrific record of Nicomachus, this was not actionable after 403. Thus, if Nicomachus wanted to make an issue of old associations now irrelevant, his raking over the past could only backfire.

What was the actual charge against Nicomachus? The interpretative problem is that the prosecution mentions two types of violation, one of deleting old laws, another of inserting new. Until the epigraphical remnants of the sacrificial calendar came to light, the standard view had been that Nicomachus stood in the dock for lavish and gross expenditure of public moneys.[35] When assembling and publishing the inscribed fragments, Dow reached the conclusion that the principal delict had on the contrary been one of omission.[36] On the strength of the so-called 'decree of Teisamenus' at And. 1.83–4, Dow concluded that the wall referenced in Teisamenus was the same as a 'wall' of adjoining stelae from which the inscribed fragments came, and this led to speculation that the erasure detectable on one of the faces (see below) was the result of a reworking of the law code, either before the Thirty came to power, or after their defeat and exile in 403.[37] In a reappraisal of the problem, N. Robertson observed that the 'wall' of Teisamenus at And. 1.84 cannot

---

[34] In his reconstruction of the Covenants of Amnesty, Carawan (2013: 88, 237) asserts the existence of a special covenant in 403 upholding private contracts under the democracy, despite the total absence of attestation to such a clause.

[35] Blass 1887: 466–7; Gernet and Bizos 1999 [1926]: 158–9.

[36] Dow 1959: 18; 1960: 275.

[37] For variant explanations of the erasure, see Dow 1961; Fingarette 1971; Clinton 1982; Kühn (G.) 1985; Shear (J. L.) 2011: 175.

reasonably be identified with the 'wall' of stelae which Dow and others had reconstructed, mainly because the language of the preserved decree does not seem to support a permanent mode of publication, and instead inferred that the inscribed sacred calendar was incidental to the task laid upon Nicomachus and his colleagues in 403, and that the erasure took place not in 403 but in 399, after Nicomachus had been prosecuted, to be completed by a different commission.[38] Robertson was doubtless correct in his comments about the language of Teisamenus but, like almost all scholars at that time, believed in its authenticity. The problem, as Robertson himself observed, is that the terms of the preserved decree do not combine with what Andocides states at §85, where the mode of public display understood by the orator was one of permanence, not a temporary publication as envisaged in the terms of the quoted decree. Since Robertson, Canevaro and Harris have shown that both Teisamenus and the other two documents quoted in the speech *On the Mysteries* are later forgeries. If so, there is no need to base the process of legal review and republication on Teisamenus. The meaning of Lys. 30 is clear: Athenians in 403, as before in 411, decided to publish *in permanent form* all their laws.

The implications for how we read Lys. 30 are far-reaching. As Dow recognised, if the commission had been to publish *all* the laws, then Nicomachus cannot have been charged with including laws not listed among the archaic ordinances of Draco and Solon. Lys. 30.17 indeed lists the sources of authority upon which Nicomachus and his commission drew: the re-edition of the sacrificial calendar was to be drawn from the *kyrbeis* and the stelae (τὰς θυσίας τὰς ἐκ τῶν κύρβεων καὶ τῶν στηλῶν κατὰ τὰς συγγραφάς), which implies two sources, the historical laws of Solon and more recent additions to the calendar in the fifth century, presumably through decrees of the people.[39] The nature of this remit would suggest that the task was comprehensive, not just limited to the archaic calendar. Yet the prosecution also states that Nicomachus stepped beyond his remit by adding sacrifices not part of ancestral practice (§§18–19). Thus, the charge against him was not only that he had omitted ancestral laws but that he had included regulations for which there was no ancestral precedent. From this, it has been suggested recently that the task in 403 had not been to transcribe all the laws, but only a limited number, and that the prosecutor of Nicomachus was an Eleusinian oligarch who advocated wholesale return to the less democratic constitution of the early sixth century.[40] This is simply to ignore the explicit statements of Lysias to the contrary. At §19, we

---

[38] Robertson 1990.
[39] The *syngraphai* are most probably the instructions of the commission which authorised the sources of the law upon which the *anagrapheis* were expected to draw; thus Rhodes 1991: 95; Parker 1996: 44–5.
[40] Carawan 2013: 243.

are told quite explicitly what Nicomachus had failed to do: (1) to observe the ancestral rites; (2) to promote the interests of the city; and (3) to follow the will of the people. The last is crucial, since if the commission referred only to laws from the *kyrbeis*, we would not expect reference to what the people had voted (ἃ ὁ δῆμος ἐψηφίσατο). The etymology could not speak more eloquently: *in addition to* the Solonian laws, Nicomachus and his panel were tasked to write up other statutes from the decrees (ψηφίσματα) of the fifth century. The objection levelled against him is not that he had included in the calendar post-Solonian statutes, a job which stood expressly in keeping with the remit, but that he had added laws which *neither* Solon *nor* the citizen assembly had sanctioned. In this regard, he had placed himself above the law, not because the revised laws contained sacrifices which had not appeared in the laws of Solon, but because they authorised sacred rites for which no established precedent could be found, either in the *kyrbeis* or in the public decrees of Athens.

Discussion of Lys. 30 has been supplemented by some intriguing epigraphical finds which are usually thought to belong to a code of sacrificial law inscribed by Nicomachus and his board at two separate and self-contained intervals. Of the identifiable portions, some thirteen fragments in total survive.[41] These come from a series of joined marble stelae joined together at the top by clamps. The writing on the fragments suggests that both faces were inscribed, one side (Face B) in Attic script, the other (Face A) in Ionic; the variance in the style of the lettering most naturally indicates that each side was inscribed at a different time in relation to the Thirty, Face B in Attic letters before 404, and Face A in Ionic letters after 403, when it became standard practice to write all public inscribed documents in the new Ionic lettering. On Face A, there may be evidence of an erasure across the surface, which has suggested to the scholarly majority that it had initially been inscribed with Attic letters but was eradicated and reinscribed in the period following the democratic restoration.[42] The Ionic letters reveal that the stelae were meant to be joined, not clamped together at a later date, as the text spills over the edges.[43] Face A, which post-dates 403, was arranged in sequences, an annual sequence for yearly contributions, followed by two biennial sequences for items funded by the state in alternate years. Within each sequence, the sacrifices are arranged under chronological headings as well as by provenance, i.e. which of the official texts the list of sacrifices was taken from: fragment 3A line 77 attests the preface ἐκ τῶν στ[ηλῶν], which may correspond to the evidence

---

[41] For an edition of the fragments and general overview, see Lambert 2002. This does not include *IG* I³ 240K, a tiny fragment on which no word survives, which Dow tentatively included within the code. For the view that it more probably belongs to *IG* I³ 1185, see Lambert 2002: 355 n. 12. Another new fragment has more recently been published; see Gawlinski 2007.

[42] Thus Clinton 1982: 35; Rhodes 1991: 94–5.

[43] G. Kühn (1985: 216) suggests that the stelae were clamped only after 403, when the Ionic lettering was added.

of Lys. 30.17 about the transcripts which the redactors used.[44] Individual festivals are not named, but the description of the sacrifice is often enough to be able to locate the festival to which a sacrifice belongs. Face B survives in too scant a state to be able to determine with any certainty the nature of the earlier arrangement, but the main body of text on both faces shows essentially the same structure and organisation, the deity or hero in whose honour the sacrifice is performed, the animal slaughtered, the extras such as barley or wine, and the official to whom money is to be paid. Together, these thirteen or so fragments have been taken to support the impression derived from the text of Lys. 30, that a comprehensive and up-to-date codification of the sacrificial law was aimed at by Nicomachus and his panel in the years of his second commission (403–399), and that the commission with which they had been charged in 403 entailed significantly more than merely the reinscription of the Solonian laws.

In recent years, J. L. Shear has reassessed the archaeological material and has argued that the two fragments displaying the erasure (frr. 2–3 Lambert) came from stelae which stood originally in the south-west corner of the Stoa Basileios and abutted directly on to the Stoa, and which were later fashioned for the sacrificial calendar after 403; originally, neither face of those stelae was used for sacrificial laws, and therefore the stelae in question date from the period of the first commission. According to her argument, after 403 the stelae were erased and reused in the wall, newly clamped during the second commission, and inscribed on just one side in Ionic lettering with the new sacrificial calendar. Unlike Dow, who imagined that the stelae had already been clamped together as a 'wall' in 411/10, Shear proposes instead that their initial purpose had nothing to do with the sacrificial laws, and that the period of clamping came about at a time when Nicomachus was charged with the more specific task of inscribing the sacrificial law.[45] Behind all of these arguments is one driving assumption, that the adjoining stelae present a 'wall' upon which the redactors of 410–399 wrote up the laws. The originator of that claim was Dow, who argued from the reference in Teisamenus to a wall that the 'wall' was the row of adjoining stelae from which the thirteen or so inscribed fragments come. That has only ever been a supposition, and even if such an association can be made, it depends vitally upon the authenticity of the document. But recent studies have shown that the document is in fact false, and so there is no basis to the assumption that the adjoining stelae which the inscribed fragments signify had anything to do with Nicomachus' commission. There is the further problem that none of the fragments contain evidence of a prescript, in which case it is difficult to align their engraving to the activities of the board of

---

[44] This reconstruction is not certain; see Lambert 2002: 378, who indicates a possible alternative reading of σ[υμβόλων].
[45] Thus Shear (J. L.) 2011: 241.

anagrapheis from 410–399. There is no trace of lettering beneath the so-called 'erasure', which makes it difficult to postulate that anything was erased, or that the Ionic letters had been superimposed upon older texts in Attic lettering of which we have no evidence. It remains unclear why the redactors would have inscribed clamped-together slabs on both sides, as there is no evidence that this was ever done in the case of other inscribed laws which have come down to us. But most importantly, the fact that the text was written in opisthographic format makes it extremely improbable that these were even laws, as no laws or decrees from the fifth or fourth century of which we know otherwise were inscribed in such a way. There is no way of knowing for certain what these fragments represent, but it is as likely as not that they were records of costings for sacrifices and have nothing whatsoever to do with a 'code of laws' as modern scholars have assumed. Scholars have argued from the reference in fragment 3a either to the stelae or the *symbolai*, and from the formula ἐκ τῶν φυλοβασιλικῶν on Face A, a reference to an archaic institution which did survive the Cleisthenic reforms at least in the sacred sphere, that the picture is one of a coherent programme of sacrifices which took into account the historic laws taken from the archaic lawgivers and more recent additions which, despite their relative novelty, were still regarded as 'ancestral', in virtue of the fact that they were recognised and practised at Athens. But the reasons to associate any of this with the activities of Nicomachus are paper-thin.

The legal review which took place at the time of the democratic restoration tells a vivid story of a city, emerging from civil war and conflict, which strove as far as it could to grapple with the vast quantity of law which had amassed over the previous century and to present it in a clear, consistent, coherent and articulate fashion. This process goes hand in hand with the resurrection of a democratic political system which recognised, above all, the rule of law and its central importance in guaranteeing the preservation of a society which was able to function fairly, justly and democratically. The legal redaction was of greater importance even than the covenants which regulated the relationship between Athens and Eleusis in 403. Once the law had been clarified, it was possible for the Athenian people to return to political normality by banishing any obscurity and ensuring that the law was applied consistently and evenly. The rule of law was the key ingredient which made fourth-century democracy efficient and durable.

THE AMNESTY AND SCRUTINY OF THE LAWS (AND. 1.71–105)

The covenants, or συνθῆκαι, according to which the warring parties came to terms in 403, as argued already, represent one stage of the democratic restoration. But as the orator Andocides notes, the process did not end there.

It is tempting to think of the reinstalment of democracy in 403 as a measure which brought an end to the conflict between the two sides and thereby to limit discussion of the restoration to the Covenants of Reconciliation (see Chapter 3). But the ending of conflict, and the laying out of terms for peaceful coexistence in two communities, was the first step in a much longer and more painstaking process of political recovery. In order to make democracy work, conditions needed to be created whereby democracy and rule of law could thrive. Banishing the evil scourge of civil conflict meant more than expecting each side to swear not to revisit old grievances in the courts (μὴ μνησικακεῖν; covenant 15 in my scheme). Beyond that, it was necessary to ensure that all manner of feuding in the courts was forbidden, and that legal cases be judged according to the issue at hand, and not in keeping with factional loyalties or political cliques. The only way to guarantee this was to ensure that (1) the law was sovereign, (2) citizens knew what the laws of Athens were, and (3) they swore to uphold them.

One of the difficulties we face in evaluating this episode is that Andocides, our chief authority, is somewhat oblique in his description. Extensive quotation is needed (1.81–7):

[81] ἐπειδὴ δ᾽ ἐπανήλθετε ἐκ Πειραιῶς, γενόμενον ἐφ᾽ ὑμῖν τιμωρεῖσθαι ἔγνωτε ἐᾶν τὰ γεγενημένα, καὶ περὶ πλείονος ἐποιήσασθε σῴζειν τὴν πόλιν ἢ τὰς ἰδίας τιμωρίας, καὶ ἔδοξε μὴ μνησικακεῖν ἀλλήλοις τῶν γεγενημένων. δόξαντα δὲ ὑμῖν ταῦτα εἵλεσθε ἄνδρας εἴκοσι· τούτους δὲ ἐπιμελεῖσθαι τῆς πόλεως, ἕως ἂν οἱ νόμοι τεθεῖεν· τέως δὲ χρῆσθαι τοῖς Σόλωνος νόμοις καὶ τοῖς Δράκοντος θεσμοῖς. [82] ἐπειδὴ δὲ βουλήν τε ἀπεκληρώσατε νομοθέτας τε εἵλεσθε, εὑρίσκοντες τῶν νόμων τῶν τε Σόλωνος καὶ τῶν Δράκοντος πολλοὺς ὄντας οἷς πολλοὶ τῶν πολιτῶν ἔνοχοι ἦσαν τῶν πρότερον ἕνεκα γενομένων, ἐκκλησίαν ποιήσαντες ἐβουλεύσασθε περὶ αὐτῶν, καὶ ἐψηφίσασθε, δοκιμάσαντες πάντας τοὺς νόμους, εἶτ᾽ ἀναγράψαι ἐν τῇ στοᾷ τούτους τῶν νόμων οἳ ἂν δοκιμασθῶσι. καί μοι ἀνάγνωθι τὸ ψήφισμα . . . [85] ἐδοκιμάσθησαν μὲν οὖν οἱ νόμοι, ὦ ἄνδρες, κατὰ τὸ ψήφισμα τουτί, τοὺς δὲ κυρωθέντας ἀνέγραψαν εἰς τὴν στοάν. ἐπειδὴ δ᾽ ἀνεγράφησαν, ἐθέμεθα νόμον, ᾧ πάντες χρῆσθε. καί μοι ἀνάγνωθι τὸν νόμον. "Νόμος· ἀγράφῳ δὲ νόμῳ τὰς ἀρχὰς μὴ χρῆσθαι μηδὲ περὶ ἑνός." [86] ἆρά γε ἔστιν ἐνταυθοῖ τι περιελείπετο περὶ ὅτου οἷόν τε ἢ ἀρχὴν εἰσάγειν ἢ ὑμῶν πρᾶξαί τινι, ἀλλ᾽ ἢ κατὰ τοὺς ἀναγεγραμμένους νόμους; ὅπου οὖν ἀγράφῳ νόμῳ οὐκ ἔξεστι χρήσασθαι, ἦ που ἀγράφῳ γε ψηφίσματι παντάπασιν οὐ δεῖ γε χρήσασθαι. ἐπειδὴ τοίνυν ἑωρῶμεν ὅτι πολλοῖς τῶν πολιτῶν εἶεν συμφοραί, τοῖς μὲν κατὰ νόμους, τοῖς δὲ κατὰ ψηφίσματα τὰ πρότερον γενόμενα, τουτουσὶ τοὺς νόμους ἐθέμεθα, αὐτῶν ἕνεκα τῶν νυνὶ ποιουμένων, ἵνα τούτων μηδὲν γίγνηται μηδὲ ἐξῇ συκοφαντεῖν

μηδενί. καί μοι ἀνάγνωθι τοὺς νόμους. [87] "Νόμοι: ἀγράφῳ δὲ νόμῳ τὰς ἀρχὰς μὴ χρῆσθαι μηδὲ περὶ ἑνός. ψήφισμα δὲ μηδὲν μήτε βουλῆς μήτε δήμου νόμου κυριώτερον εἶναι. μηδὲ ἐπ' ἀνδρὶ νόμον ἐξεῖναι θεῖναι, ἐὰν μὴ τὸν αὐτὸν ἐπὶ πᾶσιν Ἀθηναίοις, ἐὰν μὴ ἑξακισχιλίοις δόξῃ κρύβδην ψηφιζομένοις." τί οὖν ἦν ἐπίλοιπον; οὑτοσὶ ὁ νόμος. καί μοι ἀνάγνωθι τοῦτον. "Νόμος: τὰς δὲ δίκας καὶ τὰς διαίτας κυρίας εἶναι, ὁπόσαι ἐν δημοκρατουμένῃ τῇ πόλει ἐγένοντο. τοῖς δὲ νόμοις χρῆσθαι ἀπ' Εὐκλείδου ἄρχοντος."

[81] When you returned from Piraeus, though it lay within your power to wreak revenge, you decided to let go of the past, and you made salvaging the city a higher objective than your own vengeance, and you decreed[46] not to recall grievances against each other for what had passed. Once you had decreed these things, you chose twenty men entrusted with the care of the city, until such time as laws had been passed. In the meantime, it was decided to use the laws of Solon and ordinances of Draco. [82] When you had selected a council by lot and chosen lawgivers, finding that there were many laws of Draco and Solon under which many citizens were liable for what had happened previously, forming an assembly you deliberated concerning them and voted to vet all the laws and to write up in the Stoa those of the laws which had been vetted. Read out for me the decree . . . [85] The laws were scrutinised, gentlemen, according to this decree, and those of the laws which passed scrutiny they wrote up at the Stoa. When they were written up, we made a law which you all use; read it out to me: 'Law: The magistrates are not to use any unwritten law concerning any matter.' [86] Is there anything left out? Can any case be brought to court by a magistrate or initiated by you, except in accordance with the laws written up? Therefore, if it is illegal to enforce an unwritten law, surely it is illegal to use an unwritten decree. When we saw that very many citizens were in straits because of previous laws and previous decrees, we enacted the following laws to

---

[46] As at Joyce 2008: 508, I give ἔδοξε μὴ μνησικακεῖν as 'you decreed not to . . .', contra Shear (J. L.) 2011: 199 n. 34 and Carawan 2012: 185 n. 25 (see also Chapter 3). The argument that there was no separate decree of amnesty was made by MacDowell (1962: 120 and 128), who argued that the decree to which And. 1.81 refers was the enabling decree for the government of the Twenty installed after the return from Piraeus, and that Andocides refers here to a resumptive clause, not a separate measure. But MacDowell's argument was predicated on the claim that the Oath of Amnesty was brought into effect by the law cited later, barring litigation for crimes predating 403. As argued here, that statute was part of a legislative package which gave further definition to the Amnesty but did not bring it into existence. For Carawan, MacDowell's interpretation is crucial, as Carawan claims that μὴ μνησικακεῖν formalised the Covenants of Reconciliation and required no separate enabling measure.

prevent what is happening right now; we wanted to prevent this very thing from taking place, that is to say, and make it impossible for anyone to pursue action from grudgeful motives. Read out the laws: 'Laws: Under no circumstances are magistrates to apply a law which is unwritten. No decree of the Council or People may override a law. No law shall be applied against an individual without applying it to all citizens alike, unless resolved by an assembly of six thousand by secret vote.' What else was needed? Only the following, which I ask the secretary to read out to you. 'Law: All private suits and arbitrations in the time of democracy shall be valid. The laws shall be applied from the archonship of Eucleides (403/2).' (tr. K. J. Maidment)

Scholars have puzzled over this passage, mainly because of the cryptic connection it provides between the Amnesty and the scrutiny of the laws which followed. It had already been decided that untried cases predating the Amnesty should not be pursued, and so it remains unclear why an additional scrutiny was needed to expunge older statutes under which citizens were liable. Possibly, the laws needed to be adapted with inserted riders referring to the Amnesty to limit their applicability after 403, but that would have entailed a painstaking and needless task. There must be some other, more slanted, reason why Andocides chose to refer to the scrutiny.

To see why Andocides harped on the episode, it is worth bearing in mind that he had a personal point to prove: the religious scandals of 415 had resulted in a decree being moved by one Isotimides, placing limitations on the rights of those who had confessed to Profanation of the Mysteries and Mutilation of the Herms (§71). The legal issue at stake in 400, or whenever the trial was heard, is whether the decree of 415 was valid after 403. His accusers had brought a case against him for trespassing in a sacred precinct earlier that year in violation of the rule of Isotimides. Andocides argues that he was not liable under the rule because he did not commit impiety, and that the earlier amnesty of 405 (And. 1.73–6) had cancelled out the ban. Rather disingenuously, Andocides seeks a route around his conundrum by insinuating that the aim of the legal scrutiny in 403 was to remove any statute from the record which made offences committed before the democratic restoration actionable after 403. This distorts the issue, because the matter for which Andocides was being tried in 400 post-dated the Amnesty. Andocides would have the court believe that because Isotimides did not appear among the laws of 403, it was no longer binding. But this is to put a special spin on the legal compilation, as if its purpose were to rule out the efficacy of any statute which did not appear in it. That was not the point at all. At this stage, a technical distinction was emerging in Athenian conceptual vocabulary between laws (*nomoi*) and decrees (*psêphismata*), and so it was important for Athenians to understand what the city's laws were, as distinct from other forms of legislation, in the form of an archival compilation which stated: 'These are the *nomoi*.' The rule 'not to use an unwritten law' meant, simply, that a statute not in the list could not qualify as a 'law', not that it was necessarily invalid after 403. If the *atimia* annulment of 405 was universal (see addendum, p. 125), Andocides in 400 was no longer liable; however, the arguments he draws from the legal scrutiny are a sideshow.[47]

The background of the trial is important to grasp. The occasion was a scandal in which Andocides and other youths from prominent families had been implicated in 415, the year when Athens embarked on her disastrous expedition to Sicily.[48] The Mutilation of the Herms, or *hermokopeia*, is related by Thucydides and is told in various ways by subsequent authors.[49] Modern historians have debated the nature of the crime of which Andocides was accused, but most now agree that unlike Alcibiades, who was convicted in absence for parodying the Eleusinian Mysteries, the charge against Andocides was the Mutilation of the Herms, which involved destruction of carved genitalia on stone monuments which stood in the Agora and in other public places to ward off evil spirits and bad luck.[50] Each Herm contained a bust of the god Hermes, an inscription on its column honouring the family which had paid for dedication, and a phallic representation beneath.[51] The earliest literary account of the affair is preserved in Thucydides, who states that Athens woke up one morning in 415 to find that all but a few had been defiled, whereupon a decree was issued instructing anyone who knew the identity of those who had participated to declare it publicly. Thucydides states that the reason the incident was taken so seriously was because Athens had just launched the invasion of Sicily, and many understood it to presage disaster to come. It was linked in the public imagination to a conspiracy to overthrow democracy and replace it with alternative government (Th. 6.27). The Mutilation led to investigations into the affairs of Alcibiades, who in the privacy of his own home had been imitating the Eleusinian Mysteries, one of the most sacred cults of antiquity.

The parodying of the Mysteries resulted in Alcibiades' immediate recall. There were many in Athens who suspected the influence which Alcibiades wielded on the opinions of the people and wanted to have him removed (Th. 6.28). For reasons not immediately obvious, Thucydides proceeds to liken false perceptions of the religious scandals to the mistaken notions of how

---

[47] I no longer accept the explanation of MacDowell (1962: 200–3); For a detailed analysis of the 405 amnesty, see now Rocchi 2022: 109–128 and the addendum on p. 125.
[48] On the meaning and scope of *atimia* in the fifth and fourth centuries, see Dmitriev 2015; *contra* Joyce 2018.
[49] For a full survey and analysis of the literary and epigraphic evidence, see Furley 1996; Hamel 2012.
[50] As argued convincingly by Marr 1971.
[51] For an example of archaeological representations of Herms on Athenian vases, see Berlin F 2298.

the democracy had been set up a hundred years earlier. Athenians associated democracy with the assassination of Hipparchus, younger son of Peisistratus, but as Thucydides comments this was impossible since his elder brother Hippias was reigning as tyrant when the tyrannicides removed the younger brother.[52] Whatever Thucydides' motives in linking the two episodes, he evidently thought that the public reaction to the scandals of 415 was fuelled by internal rivalries among those who wished to hold dominant political positions. Thucydides implies that this was no oligarchic conspiracy, as many people at the time had suspected, but was more likely to have been a prank which, in the heat of the moment, got magnified out of proportion. It is unsurprising that Thucydides held religion and its symbols in suspicion, and thus degraded a religious scandal in historical importance. Yet the public reaction shows that there was general belief in a conspiracy afoot. Though Andocides protested his innocence, the evidence points to his guilt, as his was the only Herm to remain undefiled.[53] Pythonicus had informed on Alcibiades for deriding the cult at Eleusis. An investigation resulted in ten, including Alcibiades, being pronounced guilty, all except one of whom went into voluntary exile. Some of the names are confirmed by extant fragments of inscriptions known as the 'Attic Stelae' listing men whose property was then confiscated (*IG* I³ 421–30), but the lists provided in the MSS of And. 1 are questionable, as the Attic Stelae give names not included in the MSS, such as Cephisodorus, Oenias and Hephaestodorus.[54] The reason Andocides lists names is to show that he was not among those implicated in the Profanation (And. 1.11–14).

The trial of the conspirators gave way to a second round of investigation. Eighteen men were denounced, but once again Andocides' name was not included on the list (And. 1.15, 35). Two more pieces of information came to light, the last of which implicated Andocides' father, who was subsequently acquitted (And. 1.17). As for the Mutilation, Andocides argues that the public linked it to an oligarchic conspiracy through machinations of two ringleaders, Charicles and Peisander, the second of whom is indeed no surprise, as he was a driving force behind the oligarchy of the Four Hundred in 411.[55] In a general mood of disquiet, Diocleides brought an impeachment before the Council, which in the climate of emergency had been granted supreme authority. Diocleides claimed to have caught sight of about three hundred men near the Theatre of Dionysus on the night of the Mutilation before riding out by moonlight to Laurium. On the next day, when he heard that the Herms had

---

[52] Th. 6.56–9; also 1.20. For a recent discussion of these excurses see Meyer 2008.
[53] And. 1.62.
[54] Compare And. 1.13, 15, 35 and 47 with *IG* I³ 421 lines 10 (Hephaestodorus), 33 and 217 (Oenias), 317 (Cephisodorus).
[55] And. 2.13–15.

been defaced, he rode back to Athens, where he encountered Andocides and was bribed not to turn informer (And. 1.40–1). According to his story, he at first accepted the bribe but later, when defaulting on the bargain, denounced him to the Council (And. 1.42). Forty-two were named, including two on the Council, whereupon Peisander moved to submit to torture all those whose names were on the list. Orders were given for Andocides' arrest, as well as that of members of his close family (And. 1.43–7). According to Andocides, to save his own kinsmen he turned informer in order that they and three hundred others be acquitted (And. 1.51). Andocides testified that a former associate, Euphiletus, had proposed the Mutilation, which he had opposed. His story to the Council was confirmed by slaves under torture (And. 1.61–8). Thus, he claims, he was never involved in the Mutilation.

Andocides canvassed a two-pronged attack. In addition to protesting his innocence, he argued that the decree of 415 against all who participated in acts of impiety was now invalid. No record of the decree survives outside Andocides, and as far as we can glean it did not name specific persons but made a general proclamation against those who had committed impiety and admitted it. Andocides protests that Isotimides' decree did not apply to him, as he had been complicit neither in the Profanation nor in the Mutilation. Beyond this, he claims that it could not be cited because the Reconciliation barred issues predating 403. His accusers declared that he had acted illegally because, as a participant in the Mutilation, he was guilty of impiety and liable to restrictions imposed in 415 from temples and sanctuaries. Andocides alludes to events of 403 to show that the decree cited against him was no longer valid and could not be used in evidence (And. 1.72–105). The earlier amnesty of 405 cancelled out liabilities under Isotimides; this, and not the events of 403, clinched the issue in his favour. A further point in his support is that the Amnesty had declared unactionable all untried cases predating 403, and because Andocides had not been tried for his role in the Mutilation, it was open to question whether the matter could be brought against him now. As argued below, the case probably was legal because the legal point at issue was not an action predating the Amnesty but a later event, the laying of a branch in the temple of Demeter. If Andocides was *atimos*, his behaviour in 400 was illegal and actionable. The difficulty for the prosecution was that to bring a case against him, it needed to bring up an old issue.

Did the Athenians vote in 403 to publish all their laws? This is certainly the implication of §82, but the reference has provoked an enormous quantity of scholarly disagreement. Most importantly, there is no reference anywhere in the fourth century to a single legal redaction, or 'code'. Further, it is questionable just what Andocides means by 'all the laws' at §82.[56] Some,

---

[56] For an exchange of interpretations, see Carawan 2012; *contra* Joyce 2014.

on the grounds that the Stoa Basileios did not have sufficient room to display every current law of Athens, have taken this to mean the historical laws of Draco and Solon transmitted on the *axones* from the seventh and sixth centuries.[57] Others take the 'laws of Solon' to be a shorthand for 'all valid laws of Athens' including those passed after Solon.[58] A variant of that view holds that 'all the laws' meant all the current laws, but that rather than inscribing every one of those laws in a narrow location, more probably the decision was to write those laws up in some temporary medium and to commit to an archival repository, perhaps the Metroon archive, those which passed muster.[59] Each of those positions supposes that the scrutiny of laws bore little relation to the Amnesty itself and that Andocides just jumbled events. To add to this, the cited decrees, as preserved in Andocides, make little sense as they stand; strong arguments, though not universally accepted, have now come forward that those texts are forgeries and cannot be trusted.[60] Even before those arguments were formulated, problems with the so-called 'decree of Teisamenus' were already acknowledged; Robertson, who believed in its authenticity, claimed that it was not the cited decree that was at fault, but Andocides' interpretation of it. A fourth interpretation has been proffered by Carawan, who holds, in contrast, that the laws in question were limited to those regulating seizure and arrest, and that a complete redaction of the laws of Athens makes no sense for the case which Andocides means to advance.[61]

The claim that 'all the laws' as an expression limited itself to laws covering arrest and summary punishment is pure speculation, as there is not a trace of justification for such an interpretation anywhere in the speech of Andocides or in any other text relating to the period.[62] More fatally, it sidesteps what Andocides explicitly says at §81 about the background to which the legal scrutiny belongs: Andocides states that after the victory of the democrats in late winter 403 the Athenians elected a commission of twenty to govern the city until new legislation was carried; in the meantime, Athens was to be governed

---

[57] Clinton 1982: 28–30; Rhodes 1991: 97.
[58] Volonaki 2001: 141–6.
[59] Robertson 1990.
[60] Canevaro and Harris 2012 and 2016–17; for a different interpretation, see Hansen 2014; 2015; Sommerstein 2014.
[61] Carawan 2012: 568–9; *contra* Joyce 2008.
[62] Carawan (2013: 188) reinterprets And. 1.88 to mean: 'All the laws for *graphai*, *phaseis*, *endeixeis*, and *apopogai* … are to be scrutinized in the assembly. Those confirmed in this process (and only those) are to be written up in the stoa (82). The officers are not to admit any claim that is not based on a law listed from the Scrutiny.' This, however, fails to grasp the point of the lawgivers; the rule to apply the laws on public offences from 403 was not tantamount to an injunction that the laws on arrest and impeachment be revised and written up in the Stoa. The point is simply that public process for untried offences which predated the democratic restoration was from now on blocked.

by the *nomoi* of Solon and *thesmoi* of Draco. The administration of twenty men was established as a temporary provision while *nomothetai*, or lawgivers, deliberated on new laws which could be added to existing ones when democracy was finally restored, and Athens given a constitution. Who these twenty were is open to speculation, though a scholium to Aeschin. 1.39 attests that twenty were chosen from among the people in 403 to seek out and reinscribe dilapidated laws. But then, their remit was modified. It was soon discovered that many citizens were liable under the terms of old laws because of what had taken place in the past. Thus, instead of restricting their activities to new legislation, the decision was taken to revise and publish *all* the laws. If the Amnesty cancelled only specific liabilities but left others open, in order to close down loopholes an additional scrutiny of the city laws was required so that old liabilities which were ordinarily subject to forcible seizure and arrest, such as the crime which Andocides had allegedly committed in 415, could not now be cited against him, and so laws on arrest and seizure now incorporated the rider that they were applicable only from 403. In a series of free-standing articles, I have presented arguments against such a view, but a quick summary of my refutation is required.[63] Most importantly, it takes for granted that Andocides presents the issues honestly. Andocides presents no coherent argument that the decree which banned *atimoi* from sacred locations in 415 had been overruled in 403, and so by trespassing in a sacred precinct in 400, he stood in violation of the law so long as he had been guilty of profanation, which he denied.[64]

More widely, there is little justification for the view that the democrats in 403 should have wished to rework the law to suit those in Andocides' position. Athens had emerged from the worst conflict in living memory; the task before the city was to rebuild civic concord and to devise means whereby the citizen body would not relapse into *stasis*. It seems most unlikely that lawgivers would have devoted their energy in 403 to remedying the quandaries of those, like Andocides, who had fallen foul under democracy. The Amnesty and the scrutiny of laws which followed provided a framework in which Athens would survive as a democracy and banish the scourge of civil conflict. As D. M. MacDowell argued eloquently in several places, the cases of those who were pronounced *atimoi* in the time of democracy were irrelevant to the issue in 403.[65] The methodological difficulty for modern interpreters is that we see the events through the lens of a speech which is itself stilted and which seeks desperately to present the historical issues in such a way as to make it look as if the legislators in 403 had the slightest interest in Andocides' case. This trial,

---

[63] See Joyce 2008; 2014; 2015; 2018.
[64] The question boils down to how we interpret the law at D. 24.56; see below.
[65] Thus MacDowell 1962: 201; 1963: 138; 1978: 121–2.

indeed, furnishes a good example not of how the Amnesty was violated, but of how it could be disingenuously cited by defendants to bolster legal arguments. Nowhere is this clearer than in two later sections (And. 1.108–9) where the orator, referring to historical prototypes, appears to suggest that the purpose of the Reconciliation was to cancel verdicts of *atimia*, and from that smears his accusers with the charge of violating the oath μὴ μνησικακεῖν. Yet, as seen in Chapter 3, the Covenants of Reconciliation did not contain a single clause on *atimia*; the matter to which Andocides referred in 400 or thereabouts had no bearing at all upon the matter of the Amnesty.[66] The argument which Andocides presents before the court in 400 amounts to little more than a rhetorical rant: how can we possibly go ahead with this trial when (1) the defendant was innocent all along, and (2) when Athens has a noble tradition of restoring *atimoi* in times of political emergency? Here, we see Andocides distorting history to suit his own private purposes: the chief aim of the Amnesty in 403 was not to protect those who returned to the city at the end of the civil conflict, but conversely, to give protection to those who had stayed behind under the Thirty, in particular to the Three Thousand (the City Party), who, without the legal protection of amnesty legislation, would have stood to lose.[67]

The tortuous passage of Andocides allows for a more natural and plausible interpretation. After democracy was restored, lawgivers were selected initially to create laws affecting the governance of Athens, which already suggests a much broader remit than some are willing to allow. Their initial task was to supply a constitutional framework for the restored democracy, but their legal purview was enlarged once the problem of vexatious litigation came to light. There is no reason to suppose that their job was restricted to laws on arrest and seizure; more widely, they carried on the process of revision which began in 410 or thereabouts so that Athenians knew which laws were valid. In addition, the scrutiny guaranteed that other statutes could remain effective after 403, with the proviso that they not be applied retrospectively to offences predating the Reconciliation. The aim was to reinforce the distinction between laws (νόμοι), which were universally valid, and decrees (ψηφίσματα) of the Assembly, which were not. Passages of the orators in the fourth century suggest that the laws of Athens were organised: for example, Hypereides (*Eux.* 5–6) states that laws were enacted to deal with different offences and lists each of the offences along

---

[66] See Joyce 2008: 513–14; *pace* Carawan 2002: 3.
[67] Thus Joyce 2008: 514. Carawan at various places (e.g. 2013: 117 n. 5) has misunderstood me to infer from this that only members of the City Party were covered in the terms of amnesty, which I have never in fact claimed, and which I have expressly gone out of my way not to say (see above, p. 83).

with the magistrate appointed for each;[68] Aeschines (1.7–8) mentions that the lawgivers had issued laws regulating children, private individuals and politicians; Demosthenes (54.17–19) refers to laws covering abuse, assault and slander. The fact that later orators were able to access laws by category indicates that the lawgivers in 403 did not publish laws randomly or haphazardly, but that they were arranged by substance and category, in a coherent and accessible way.[69] Thus, whether or not it is appropriate to think of a 'law code', an effort by the *nomothetai* was made to have the laws of the city published compendiously in an accessible way, either on stone slabs or in an archive (or both), so that those who wished to access them knew where to look. More importantly, the 'law which you all apply' (And. 1.85), to use 'no unwritten law', must, in context, have meant that any law not included in the compilation could not qualify as a 'law'. This has been denied by some, on the grounds that the laws posted in the Stoa were those which had not been adapted and amended in the scrutiny.[70] But that stilted view rests on an over-literal reading of the preserved 'decree of Teisamenus', quoted at And. 1.83–4, whose authenticity has since been rightly called into question, not least for the fact that its terms fail to combine with the account which Andocides provides in the following section (§85).[71]

Many have objected that an inscribed code in 403 of all the valid laws of Athens is unattested in later sources. This might have been a problem if we are to believe that Andocides and Lysias lay testimony to a law code. But if the list compiled by the lawgivers in the wake of the re-establishment of democracy was the beginning of a process which continued into the fourth century, those objections become irrelevant. More important was that Athenians had access to records of the city's laws, and the evidence of the fourth century indicates that the most important repository for such records was the Metroon archive. As J. P. Sickinger has argued, inscriptions of legal texts and other official documents of state were not necessarily the only records, or even the primary records. If an orator wanted to find out the text of a law, he need not have researched an inscription, even though the convention when reading out a legal text was to say, 'Read me the stele', or some such formula.[72] None

---

[68] Whitehead 2000: *ad loc.*
[69] On the priority of substance over procedure, see Harris 2013: 144–9.
[70] See, for example, Kühn (G.) 1985.
[71] For a convincing rejection of the decree of Teisamenus, alongside Demophantus and Patrocleides, see the articles of Canevaro and Harris listed at Chapter 1, p. 25, n. 73.
[72] For an excellent discussion of the evidence for the Metroon as the main repository of state records in the fourth century, see Sickinger 1999. Even though non-inscribed records were a vital method of record-keeping, this does not preclude the importance and value of public inscriptions. Though we have no physical survival of the inscribed 'laws' to which Andocides refers, the onus of proof is still on those, like Carawan, who deny their existence.

of this alters the probability that a comprehensive list of laws was maintained in the fourth century as a feature of a well-organised democracy. Some statutes post-dating Solon but predating 403 were regarded in the fourth century as νόμοι; a good example would be the citizenship law of Pericles of 451/0, which, when carried, must have taken the form of a decree; it continued to apply after 403 but was replaced in the fourth century by the law of Aristophon.[73] If the *nomothetai* were established with the sole purpose of limiting the effect of statutes that provided for arrest and seizure, the question arises as to how and when fifth-century statutes, which bore no relation to this marginal matter, were entered into the state record as 'laws'. The citizenship law of Pericles remained, though under a different name, and there are other examples of laws, such as ones affecting qualifications for citizenship and inheritance entitlements, which were applied from 403 (D. 43.51; 57.30). At some point, lawgivers would have needed to make it known to the citizen public what those laws were and where they could be accessed. It would not have been enough simply to have a statute limiting validity of laws to the period after 403. In addition to this, a list of those laws was required to ensure not only that those laws were appropriately applied, but that from 403 the confusions which had arisen in previous years as to what the laws amounted to did not resurface. The republication of laws was designed to ensure that Athenians knew what their current laws were, and although Andocides connects the δοκιμασία of laws to the Amnesty, Lysias' speech *Against Nicomachus* shows that this was part of a longer process of review begun around 410 and continued down to the time of Aeschines.[74]

It might be argued on the strength of Andocides' self-defence that the main purpose of the legal scrutiny in 403 was to supplement the Amnesty Agreement of that year by proclaiming public liabilities, including ones delivered by democratic courts, null and void. The rule is attested outside Andocides, a more complete and reliable formulation of which is given at D. 24.26: τὰς δίκας καὶ τὰς διαίτας, ὅσαι ἐγένοντο ἐπὶ τοῖς νόμοις ἐν δημοκρατουμένῃ τῇ πόλει, κυρίας εἶναι. ὁπόσα δ' ἐπὶ τῶν τριάκοντα ἐπράχθη ἢ δίκη ἐδικάσθη, ἢ ἰδίᾳ ἢ δημοσίᾳ, ἄκυρα εἶναι.[75] The wording shows that the aim was to override any judicial decisions, public or private, taken by the Thirty. The corollary entailed

---

[73] On the citizenship law of Pericles, see Carawan 2008: 383–406. The evidence for the law and its use and application into the fourth century is compiled and discussed more fully by Patterson (1981). A similar case can be made for the law of Demophantus, passed initially as a decree.

[74] See Lys. 30 and the chronological reconstructions of Rhodes 1991.

[75] 'Private judgments and arbitrations which were given in keeping with the laws when the city was under democracy shall be valid, but whatever was done in the time of the Thirty or judgment given, either private or public, shall be declared invalid.'

that all decisions, private or public, taken in the time of democracy, stood firm. To be sure, the phrase τὰς δίκας καὶ τὰς διαίτας is used, which on a casual reading might be taken to limit itself to private matters alone, but if we combine it with what is said subsequently, it must also include public verdicts. The point is that any δίκη which was ἐδικάσθη, whether the nature of that trial was public or private (ἢ ἰδίᾳ ἢ δημοσίᾳ), under the Thirty was now cancelled. The aim of the rule spelled out in 403 is twofold: (1) to uphold judicial verdicts taken by democratic courts, whether public or private, and (2) to annul any verdict of an oligarchic court, whether in the realm of private or public law. The key implication is that the scrutiny of laws was not designed with the express purpose of building into the law protective clauses to cover those convicted in former time by democratic process. Rather, it was to uphold the sanctity of democracy by declaring its court verdicts valid.[76] The legal scrutiny had one simple objective, to enshrine the sanctity of the law in the new constitution. We have every reason to believe, as Andocides states, that the laws were inscribed and set out in a conspicuous location, probably in or near the Stoa, as would be expected of important legal documents, but where they were located precisely is a matter that cannot be decided on the poverty of the evidence as it stands. Certainly, it is easier to believe that the laws were republished and displayed in a public place than it is to imagine that a society which reified the law could have survived or functioned without a clear statement of the law. The fourth century created, updated, observed and governed itself by the laws. The sanctification of law, which the redaction to which Andocides attests embodies, was above all a radically democratic measure, which accompanied the revival of democracy as the antidote to civil war.

The text of Andocides contains three inserted documents, attributed to Patrocleides, Teisamenus and Demophantus, none of which can be genuine. The orator cites the decrees in support of his claim that he was no longer liable after 403. The first and third are not strictly relevant to his case, since the first refers to events in 405, after the naval loss of that year at Aegospotami, when specified and listed categories of *atimoi* (those who had had their civic rights restricted) had their stripped rights restored in that year, not in 403, and the third to the period after the overthrow of the first oligarchy, in 411. Andocides cites Patrocleides to show that some verdicts of *atimia* in 405 had been cancelled and infers from this that his *atimia* under the terms of Isotimides in 415

---

[76] See, in contrast, Carawan 2013: 192: 'Thus reconstructed, "the law that … all apply" was something to this effect: For public offences, one can invoke the established laws as listed here, and one can only enforce public liabilities beginning in the year of Eukleides.' Carawan's reconstruction, however, depends wholly on speculation and draws no ancient textual support.

was no longer in effect.[77] He cites Demophantus to show that had it not been for the Amnesty clauses, his accuser Epichares would be liable under an old law which condemned any official who had held office when Athens was not a democracy. Both citations are problematic because the historical inferences which the orator draws from them are unsound. The decree of Isotimides, which proclaimed anyone convicted for participation in the religious scandals of 415 *atimos*, was now invalid.[78] The injunction 'only to use the laws from 403' meant, in context, that any *untried* crime predating 403 could not now be prosecuted, not that all previous court verdicts were overturned. The fact that Andocides cites documentary evidence is not reason enough to accept his interpretation of that evidence, and The fact that Andocides cites documentary evidence is not enough to accept his interpretation of that evidence, and there are many good reasons to reject the interpretation of the Amnesty which Andocides provides. The second of those documents, the so-called 'decree of Teisamenus', had generated endless discussion and misconception about the process of legal review. Most recently, an elaborate argument has been built on the edifice of the inserted document of Teisamenus, that the laws of Athens were published in a single location, on a 'wall' of adjoining stelae. However, the identity of the wall referred to is mysterious, and everything which Andocides himself says about the decree of Teisamenus visibly conflicts with what appears in the MSS of And. 1.83–4.[79]

For our purposes, the decree which concerns us most is the one ascribed to Teisamenus, to which Andocides refers at the end of §82 and, again, at the start of §85. A transcript of the decree is inserted into the MSS at §§83–4. At §82, the orator states that in the wake of the Reconciliation, the Athenians decided to scrutinise and publish their laws, and cites Teisamenus as his authority. However, the content of what follows (§§83–4) militates against what Andocides says in the earlier portions. This led Robertson to infer that Andocides had wilfully misinterpreted the decree he cited in support, but that approach is hardly convincing, as it fails to explain why the orator would deliberately have referred to a text which, on any reading, contradicts the very

---

[77] Recently, and in the light of discussions of the documents which appeared subsequently to the publication of his monograph on the Athenian Amnesty, Carawan (2017) has adjusted his older position on the authenticity of Patrocleides, acknowledging that all the documents in the speech of Andocides *On the Mysteries* are probably forgeries but contain genuine material which surfaces from the compilation of Attic decrees by the late fourth-century Craterus. Carawan's case has been sufficiently and persuasively answered most recently by Harris (2021). I should only add to Harris's points that if the so-called decree of Patrocleides contains any genuine material, it must surely undermine all the conclusions Carawan reaches about the meaning of the Oath of Amnesty, since the language of Patrocleides would indicate that 'to recall past grievances' amounts to the retention of old legal documents, a claim which finds no parallel in any external literary or inscribed source. On the meaning of the clause, see further Chapter 7.
[78] My thinking has changed since the first edition; see addendum, p. 125.
[79] See Shear (J. L.) 2011: 89–105.

position he sought to argue. Two separate processes are mentioned in the cited decree, the formulation of new laws and the vetting of old. The old laws are those of Draco and Solon which, in the language of the document, are not to be examined. This contradicts And. 1.82 and 85 as well as Lys. 30.2–5, as well as the rule spelled out at And. 1.89 that the Athenians are to apply the laws from 403/2, the archonship of Eucleides, confirmed in other places (Isoc. 6.47; 8.43; Aeschin. 1.39). The provisions in the document for *nomothesia* involve not pre-existing laws but additional ones, that is, innovations to the existing laws which the Athenians are to continue to use. Yet Andocides is clear that the process was to include pre-existing laws, as is Lysias. Either the orator has misinterpreted the decree he cites, or the decree is a forgery.[80]

It was long believed that the document was authentic, yet I am persuaded by Canevaro's and Harris's arguments that the documents must be a forgery. The reference in 'Teisamenus' to the two boards of *nomothetai*, one chosen by the Council and another by the demesmen, finds no external confirmation. The process of *nomothesia* of fourth-century Athens took place before the Assembly sitting in a legislative capacity, and the reason that the Aristotelian tradition does not refer to a separate process, constitutionally superior in authority to the legislative capacities of the Assembly, is that there was no higher process.[81] The vetting procedure outlined in the document does not combine with what Andocides states, that laws carried in the Assembly were to be inscribed, implying that some were to be rejected. The document, on the other hand, begins with the laws of Solon and Draco, commissioning those to be written up. This makes little sense of the fact that the publication process had begun in 410, as the epigraphical record for 409/8 shows.[82] Why would that process have needed to start afresh in 403? According to Andocides, the Assembly elected *nomothetai* in the capacity of proposers, and the Assembly ratified what was proposed to them. According to the document, however, the first board of *nomothetai* proposed and the second in conjunction with the Council vetted the laws. This is out of keeping with what we know about *nomothesia* in the fourth century. Andocides speaks of publication at the Stoa,

[80] ἔδοξε τῷ δήμῳ, Τεισαμενὸς εἶπε: πολιτεύεσθαι Ἀθηναίους κατὰ τὰ πάτρια, νόμοις δὲ χρῆσθαι τοῖς Σόλωνος, καὶ μέτροις καὶ σταθμοῖς, χρῆσθαι δὲ καὶ τοῖς Δράκοντος θεσμοῖς, οἷσπερ ἐχρώμεθα ἐν τῷ πρόσθεν χρόνῳ ὁπόσων δ᾽ ἂν προσδέῃ, οἵδε ᾑρημένοι νομοθέται ὑπὸ τῆς βουλῆς ἀναγράφοντες ἐν σανίσιν ἐκτιθέντων πρὸς τοὺς ἐπωνύμους, σκοπεῖν τῷ βουλομένῳ, καὶ παραδιδόντων ταῖς ἀρχαῖς ἐν τῷδε τῷ μηνί τοὺς δὲ παραδιδομένους νόμους δοκιμασάτω πρότερον ἡ βουλὴ καὶ οἱ νομοθέται οἱ πεντακόσιοι, οὓς οἱ δημόται εἵλοντο, ἐπειδὰν ὀμωμόκωσιν: ἐξεῖναι δὲ καὶ ἰδιώτῃ τῷ βουλομένῳ, εἰσιόντι εἰς τὴν βουλὴν συμβουλεύειν ὅ τι ἂν ἀγαθὸν ἔχῃ περὶ τῶν νόμων. ἐπειδὰν δὲ τεθῶσιν οἱ νόμοι, ἐπιμελείσθω ἡ βουλὴ ἡ ἐξ Ἀρείου πάγου τῶν νόμων, ὅπως ἂν αἱ ἀρχαὶ τοῖς κειμένοις νόμοις χρῶνται. τοὺς δὲ κυρουμένους τῶν νόμων ἀναγράφειν εἰς τὸν τοῖχον, ἵνα περ πρότερον ἀνεγράφησαν, σκοπεῖν τῷ βουλομένῳ.

[81] See Canevaro and Esu 2018.

[82] The prescript to the republished Draconian homicide law on stone, in 409/8, gives a *terminus ante quem*.

whereas the document speaks of a 'wall'. The reference to 'where they were before' led Dow to suppose that it alludes to an erasure, which he believed he could identify on the inscribed fragments of the sacrificial calendar, but that is wholly suppositional and fails to account for the fact that there is no epigraphical trace beneath the *rasura*. In contrast to Dow, Robertson argued that the 'wall' was a free-standing structure near the Eponymous Heroes for temporary display and that the process of 'writing up' was temporary, perhaps in ink. That was also speculation and fails to account for the fact that the verb ἀναγράφειν is used in the prescript to the Draconian law on homicide, inscribed on stone in 409/8 (*IG* I³ 104 = ML 86 lines 1–10). Andocides does not think that the laws written up at the Stoa were ones written for temporary display. If there had been an extra procedure for writing the laws up in the Stoa, it would have been normal and expected for Teisamenus to have laid out provisions for that.

There are other features of the document which rule out authenticity. Unlike other decrees from the period, there is no prescript. The document uses the first-person form ἐχρώμεθα, which is extremely unusual, the only exception being oaths (*IG* I³ 40 lines 4–16, 21–32). Demesmen are usually referred to in deme decrees of other types of dedication, but never in decrees of the Council and Assembly. The normal way of enjoining magistrates to act is αὐτίκα μάλα (*IG* I³ 61, 71, 76, 93; *IG* II² 28, 43, 111, 174, 204), but never in the way seen in the document. The reference to the weights and measures of Solon makes no sense and fails to combine with what Andocides says, that the Athenians were to use the laws of Solon, without reference to other features. There is no precedent for the use of ἀναγράφειν to refer to writing on a wall, where all other decrees from the period mention inscription on a stone stele. Besides, we have the explicit statements of Lysias that the *anagrapheis* wrote the laws up on stelae, so any attempt to make sense of the 'wall' in the document fails.

Recently, Hansen (n. 60 [2016] above) has sought sense in the document, but his efforts rest on misleading grammatical assumptions about the language which cannot be defended. One prong of the attack launched against scepticism has been to claim that because Andocides is unreliable, it is misleading to use his authority to refute the authenticity of an inserted decree. The problem with such an approach is that it leaves open the question why Andocides should have wanted to cite a legal text in support of his case whose terms are so palpably incompatible with the way he describes it. Of course, Andocides misrepresents elements of the Amnesty, as if the purpose in 403 were to cancel *atimia*. That is a separate issue. How an orator referred to a historical event to bolster a case varied from one example to the next. But if it is to be argued that Andocides deliberately misrepresented Teisamenus, motives for doing so need to be advanced. None, however, have been proffered. The purpose of the citation is to show that the Athenians wrote up laws and that the decree of Isotimides was not among them. The grey area is whether it was now applicable, and whether an untried offence committed prior to the Amnesty could be brought before the court. Misrepresentation of the text of Teisamenus would have achieved nothing in driving home the point. The easiest and most economical explanation is that the inserted text is a forgery and that no further time should be devoted to making sense of it in the broader flow of Andocides' argument in self-defence.

For the sake of completeness, it is only fair to summarise the most recent defence of authenticity and to list some objections in reply. Perhaps most difficult is the understanding of And. 1.82, which is vague because he appears to believe that the subject of εὑρίσκοντες are the addressees of the speech. The grammar is unclear, as the participle εὑρίσκοντες could just as easily refer to the *nomothetai* as to the subject of the main verb in the second-person plural, but it is most unlikely historically that the implied subject is anything other than the lawgivers who were chosen specifically for the task. Internally, the subject of the verb 'you voted' cannot be the lawgivers themselves, because lawgivers cannot select lawgivers. There must be a distinction between the lawgivers chosen to carry out the task and the judges at Andocides' trial. Hansen claims that it is 'not clear from Andokides' account, to whom and by whom the inspection of the laws was to be entrusted and by whom they would be approved and published'. But the syntax shows that the subject of δοκιμάσαντες is the same as the subject of ἐψηφίσασθε, which incontrovertibly means the Assembly. In symbouleutic and forensic oratory, the verb can never refer to the activities of a body other than the Assembly. We have further confirmation in Xenophon (*HG* 2.4.42) that the decision was taken in the Assembly and not anywhere else, as well as at And. 1.89 and in the prescript to *IG* I^3 104, which shows that the *anagrapheis* obeyed the verdict of the people to write up laws which the people had approved. It has been argued that there is no contradiction between the document and Andocides' account, but this is untrue, as the document enjoins the scrutiny of 'anything needed in addition' rather than the laws of Draco and Solon, which the Athenians were to continue to use as in former time, according to its language. This is clearly incompatible with what Andocides states, because both he and Lysias attest to the scrutiny and inscription of older as well as newer laws. Refuge has been taken in the idea that there may have been a distinction between what was prescribed by Teisamenus and what was undertaken, but this underestimates the fact that Andocides' description of the process is very different from what the text of Teisamenus, as preserved, prescribes. If there had been a difference, we might have expected Andocides to comment on the fact, but it is clear at And. 1.85 that the laws were inscribed near the Stoa *in accordance with the decree*. Some of the discussion of earlier scholars, including Robertson, about publication, has been revived, but other references in the orators show that the intention of the legal scrutiny was to write laws on stelae (Lys. 30.21; D. 47.71).

Above, it was noted that the identification of the wall in Teisamenus with the 'wall' of adjoining stelae is problematic. There are further problems with this archaeologically. Lambert has noted variations in the thickness of the fragments, making it less probable that they formed part of one adjoining 'wall'. This is further problematised by a more recent fragment of different thickness attributed to the same 'law code'. As T. L. Shear noted in his preliminary report on the excavation of the Stoa Basileios, the thickness of the walls on either side of the Stoa makes it impossible to identify the inscribed fragments with one of its walls. Shear further notes the existence of slots in the intercolumniations which were suitable for the insertion of large marble stelae, which is fully compatible with the evidence of the orators cited above that the laws were written on monumental free-standing stelae and inserted in or near the Stoa.[83] What is clear from Lys. 30 is that the task of writing up the laws was handed to the *anagrapheis*, yet this panel is not mentioned by Teisamenus. This might be held unproblematic if Teisamenus were prescribing only the process of scrutiny and not the redaction itself, but that would stand in contradiction to what Andocides states at §85. Without good archaeological grounds to believe that these fragments belonged to a 'wall', it would be vain to try to defend the authenticity of Teisamenus by pointing to an archaeological framework. As noted above, none of the fragments contains a prescript, and the opisthographic writing is out of keeping with any legal publication known epigraphically from the fifth or fourth centuries. The 'wall' of Teisamenus is an anathema, one more reason why authenticity must be rejected.

The implications of this are far-reaching. Once the so-called 'decree of Teisamenus' is removed, we gain a much clearer picture of the legal review process after 403. While it was assumed that Teisamenus was genuine, scholars puzzled whether the review entailed old laws, news laws or both, and concluded that whatever the *anagrapheis* came up with in their second term was published in a single location, on a wall of some kind. Robertson, in contrast, who accepted the authenticity of Teisamenus, did not identify the opisthographic fragments with the 'wall' of Teisamenus, but to get around the problem was forced to argue that Andocides either did not have access to a genuine document or did, but for some reason refused to be honest about its meaning. Once the document is removed, however, a clearer picture of the scrutiny emerges based upon Andocides' statements about the decree. This was no injunction to publish the laws in a single inscription, or 'code'. Instead, it was a simple injunction to seek out the laws, vet them, and once ratified, reinscribe them one by one in a visible location in the city. With each law vetted, the *anagrapheis* followed the instructions of the people, sitting in a nomothetic capacity, and inscribed each on a free-standing slab. The process exactly conforms to what we can reconstruct from the thirtieth speech of Lysias and

---

[83] Lambert 2002; cf. Shear (T. L.) 1971.

from the prescript to the Draconian law on stone, discussed above. The fact that Andocides reads into this process legal arguments of dubious merit should not detain us long (see Chapter 1, pp. 24–7). There is little justification to claim that because Isotimides' decree was a decree and not a law, it was now no longer valid. The legal scrutiny did not invalidate documents not included in that scrutiny, provided they were not laws. The rule of law was reinstated in 403, and the first stage in its reinstatement was the transcribing of the valid laws of Athens. The aim was to publish a coherent list of laws to which Athenians could subsequently refer. Together with this process, the authority of the courts was reinstated, and it is to this that the next two chapters turn.[84]

ADDENDUM (to chapter IV)

In the first edition, I took the view that the decree of Isotimides was valid after 403 because the beneficiaries of Patrocleides' decree listed by Andocides in 1.73–6 did not explicitly list those, like himself, who had been banned from temples and sacred areas. Since then, I have adjusted my thinking on this key issue. The first example we have in the historical record of a general annulment of *atimia* is the famous 'amnesty law' of Solon (Plu. *Sol.* 19.3–4), which spelled out exceptions but did not list specific applications; cancellation of *atimia* was universal, with the few listed exceptions. This is consistent with what else we know of the measures of 403, which listed the Amnesty's exceptions, not its beneficiaries. The examples given at And. 1.73–6 of those who benefited from Patrocleides' decree of 405 are listed *exempli gratia*; Andocides does not mean to imply that these were the only beneficiaries; that cannot be his argument, because he refers to the earlier amnesty as proof that the decree of Isotimides was no longer effective. Thus, Andocides had a good case in law, because if the earlier amnesty of 405 had been a general cancellation of *atimia*, the decree of Isotimides was not valid thereafter. It was that earlier amnesty in 405, and not the one in 403, which was more germane to his defence.

Andocides refers to the events of 403 as a rhetorical buttress: the spirit of the measures of 403 were to draw a line in the sand with the past. As argued in this chapter, those arguments are misleading because the concern in 403 was not with *atimia*, and the scrutiny which followed did not annul earlier decrees. His self-defence, though heavily rhetorical when speaking of the Amnesty of 403, demonstrates the efficacy of law in Athens after the democratic restoration. It was the law, and how it was to be interpreted, that forms the backbone of his case.

---

[84] It is only fair to add that Hansen's defence of the Teisamenus decree has won more recent support; see Lasagni 2018: 341–2, where it is asserted that Hansen has successfully argued for authenticity and that the great majority of scholars since have sided with Hansen against the skeptical position. For an even more recent affirmation of the conclusions of Canevaro and Harris with reference to other scholarship which has taken the skeptical line, see now Faraguna 2021: 235; Boffo and Faraguna 2021: 152 and 208.

CHAPTER 5

The Amnesty Applied (I): The Trials of Agoratus and Eratosthenes

The Amnesty of 403 was followed by several famous court cases which have captured modern attention. Because of a common misconception in scholarship to date that Athenian litigation paid scant attention to legal principle, some have asserted that in the high political temperature of 403–398, Athenians from various political motives used the courts to vent their anger.[1] These trials are thereby dubbed 'political' trials, as if the principle at stake had been a political and not a legal one. As argued in Chapters 2 and 4, the misuse of the courts in the decades leading up to the establishment of the Thirty resulted in the politicisation of Athens' legal and judicial machinery, which, in turn, gave the Thirty once in power the political excuse to suppress and undermine the authority of the law. Once democracy was restored, however, the reverse needed to happen. Chapter 4 argued that once the Oaths of Reconciliation were sworn, the most pressing and urgent need was to rebuild a city which respected the rule of law. This meant above all that the courts should not be used as political venues to discredit opponents or nurse grudges. The rule μὴ μνησικακεῖν, discussed at Chapter 3 and again in Chapter 7, first and foremost forbade reference to events predating 403 in the courts, but beyond that it sought to ensure that never again would the ghastly caricature of the law

---

[1] This claim is especially in evidence in Todd 1993. The main problem with Todd's approach is that it does not distinguish between the rules of an institution, which were to enforce legal norms and ensure fairness, and the strategies of individuals to use an institution for personal vindictive or political ends. Against Todd's interpretation, see Harris 2006: 171–7 and 2013: 60–98. Harris shows from a wide range of evidence, including Lyc. *Leocr.* 6; D. 21; 27; 29; 30; 36; 39; 40; [D.] 53, that trials at Athens in the fourth century turned on a legal principle, and that it was by reference to law, not to the whim or personal favour of judges hearing the cases, that legal trials were decided. Examination of the two legal cases here illustrates this principle.

which Cleon and his successors had initiated after the death of Pericles in 429 resurface. In order to guarantee against this, it was vital that legal cases structure themselves around a legal, and not a political, issue. One of the chief aims of the present chapter is to show that the trials hinged on a legal principle, and that the scourge of sycophancy which had bedevilled Athens before 404 was now banished.

The scrutiny of the laws in 403 was the key moment when the rule of law was affirmed. Once Athenians had worked out a way to prevent civil war reigniting, the paramount task was to ensure that the newly resurrected democracy was governed under a system of law which was coherent, unified, accessible and universally recognised. Without such a system, the freshly constituted democracy would have degenerated into the legal quagmire which had prevailed in the last years of the fifth century when, as Lys. 30.3 attests, Athenians encountered the problem that their laws had become complex and, in many cases, that there was little unity or coherence between them. This had led to litigation in the courts, where citizens cited statutes whose terms appeared to contradict one another. Thus, when democracy was restored in 403, the priority was to get the mess sorted out. The purpose of the scrutiny was to guarantee that when litigation reopened, the courts were governed under a body of law not only which was coherent, but also where litigants could point to laws displayed and organised in a readily accessible compilation. From 403, litigants were empowered to know what the laws of the city were because they were published and displayed unambiguously in the vicinity of the Stoa Basileios, and thus the resumption of litigation after 403 was made smoother by the publication of those laws. That being the case, it becomes harder to speculate that the litigation of 403–398 was not driven by legal principle. To ensure that the lawless period of the Thirty would not resurrect itself, the rule of law and the authority of the courts were of paramount importance. But the efficacy of the courts in upholding and applying the rule of law could only be felt if the courts were used wisely, fairly, without the taint of vindictiveness, and in accordance with legal principle.

The paramount role of the Athenian courts in upholding democracy is affirmed in 331 by the orator Lycurgus, who mentions three main elements in the survival of democracy: the system of laws, the vote of judges and the trial. The law sets out what is to be done, the accusers denounce those subject to the penalties set out in the law, and the judges punish those whose acts have been brought to their attention (Lyc. *Leocr.* 4). Most importantly, an accuser must not act from vindictive motives (*Leocr.* 6).[2] Nevertheless, a cluster of

---

[2] Allen (2000) regards this as an innovation, but her dismissal of the authority of the passage depends entirely on the assumption that most litigation in the fourth century was driven by sycophancy. For discussion of other passages in the orators, which Allen overlooks but which uphold and affirm the principle set out by Lycurgus, see Harris 2013: 61–3.

scholars believes that the agonistic ethos was of greater weight in Athenian litigation than the legal principle itself. D. Cohen has pointed to what he sees the abundance of references in forensic speeches to enmity and argues therefrom that to prosecute from a motive of enmity and rivalry was normal in the fourth century, so that the role of the court was not to uphold the rule of law but to provide an arena wherein political feuding could operate without resort to violence.[3] Cohen's view of the Athenian court is shaped by the assumption that the driving moral maxim was to harm one's enemy and aid one's friends.[4] That view is backed by some passages in Aristotle which might support the idea that Greeks saw vengeance in a rather more positive light than we do,[5] but as I argue in Chapter 7, those passages which appear to endorse vengeance as a popular ethic need to be balanced against others which expressly condemn it. Against Cohen, Harris more recently has drawn attention to the absence of reference to vindictiveness in the great majority of the speeches of Demosthenes, who even criticises Aeschines for bringing a charge from the motive of personal enmity (D. 18.12, 15).[6] The passages of Aristotle which have often been cited to sustain the idea that Greek popular morality endorsed vengeance must be read in context, as Aristotle describes traits of human nature without necessarily giving them a stamp of approval.[7] Other evidence from the orators shows that Athenians prided themselves on their gentle character, and often litigants to show their good character mention that they have never been in court previously.[8] This speaks against the assumptions of some, that the litigation which came about in the wake of the Amnesty was driven by vengeance or that the sacred principle μὴ μνησικακεῖν was not taken with utmost seriousness and observance.

Apart from those most directly complicit in the crimes of the oligarchy, the rule of 403 forbade revisiting offences committed in the time of oligarchy in the courts (see Chapter 3, my covenant 15). Many have inferred from this that in the ideology of the restored democracy, the notion of wrongdoing was confined to those not covered by the clause μὴ μνησικακεῖν, so that a sense of political justice could be served by downgrading the wrongs committed by

---

[3] Cohen (D.) 1995: 70, 82; Hansen 1991: 195. For strong arguments against Cohen's approach, see Herman 2006.
[4] Blundell 1989: 24. For similar claims, see Dover 1974: 182; Christ 1998: 161; Fisher 1998: 82–3.
[5] See, for example, Arist. *Rh.* 1.9.20.1367a24–5; 1.11.3.1370b13; *EN* 3.8.12.1117a7; 5.5.5.1126a8–9.
[6] Harris 2013: 68; see also Rubinstein 2000: 179–80; *contra* Phillips 2008: 15–29.
[7] Many passages in Aristotle speak against vengeance; see, for example, *Rh.* 2.4.12.1381b; 2.4.17–18.1381b; 1.13.18.1374b; *EN* 5.10.1138a1–3, with discussion at Harris 2013: 65.
[8] For an overview and analysis of the relevant evidence, see Harris 2013: 69–71. See also Herman 2000: 8; *contra* Christ 2005. On *philanthropia*, see now Canevaro 2015.

others.⁹ It is tempting to infer from the legal trials which ensued that the terms of the Amnesty Agreement were driven by a principle of vengeance. Certainly, the opening chapters of Lys. 13 give a very strong impression that this was the case, but it is important to analyse those trials carefully to measure just what was at stake. Whilst the Amnesty did give rise to difficult and treacherous cases, the extent to which the evidence for litigation should undermine faith in the tenability of the Amnesty Agreement has been generally overstated. In fact, the number of *causes célèbres* in the interval that followed amount to few more than half a dozen, and thus to speak of a welter of vexatious cases where the terms and conditions of the Amnesty arrangement were overlooked or violated would be to exaggerate the matter considerably. The next two chapters cover four major trials, of Agoratus, Eratosthenes, Callimachus and Socrates, which in their different ways all shed light on the period following the Amnesty and which, if analysed carefully, show that the Amnesty Agreement of 403, far from being flimsy or hole-ridden, was largely successful in putting an end to activity in the courts which might, if uncontrolled, have destabilised Athens.

THE TRIAL OF AGORATUS, 402–398 (LYS. 13)

At some point between 402 and 398, a case relating to the period of the Thirty was brought by *endeixis*.¹⁰ The defendant was one Agoratus, a man, we are told, from humble beginnings, the son of a slave, and originally a non-Athenian. Agoratus had been smeared with murder in the time of the oligarchy because, during the escalation of political events leading to the overthrow of democracy in 404, he had informed against citizens loyal to democracy and brought about their executions by laying information (μήνυσις) before the Thirty. The prosecutor was the cousin and brother-in-law of Dionysodorus, one of the victims tried by the Thirty and executed at the trial where Agoratus had

---

⁹ For the tradition of thought which states that the democratic restoration isolated the notion of 'wrongdoing' to the exiled oligarchs, banishing any sense of past wrongdoing among the citizenry, see Dorjahn 1946; Thomas 1989: 132–8; Loraux 1997; Wolpert 2002; Dössel 2003: 110–12, 141–2; Forsdyke 2005: 262–3; Shear (J. L.) 2011: 295–301.

¹⁰ Nineteenth-century scholars rejected the title as an erroneous scribal insertion on the grounds that the term *endeixis* is used nowhere in the speech itself, whereas the term *apagôgê* is used four times (§§85–6; see also its cognates at §§44 and 68); for the rejection of the term ἔνδειξις found in the Palatinus MS both at the start of the speech (fol. 66r) and in the table of contents (fol. 1r.) see Dobree 1831: 221; Stevens 1882: 82, 142; Frohberger and Thalheim 1892–5: 79; Rauchenstein and Fuhr 1899: 64. Earlier scepticism has been rejected more recently, however, because the reference to *endeixis* is found in two surviving external testimonia to the speech in the grammarian Priscian; see Albini 1955: 94; Todd 2020: 307–8 with n. 4.

informed, who saw the indictment of the defendant as an act of retribution for the evils he had committed against his kinsman and other leading supporters of democracy. An outline of events is supplied by the prosecution. In 404, when Theramenes was plotting against the democracy, the Athenians appointed Theramenes to represent their interests at Sparta. In the interim, fellow conspirators brought to trial the popular leader Cleophon, who had spoken against tearing down the city defences in the wake of the disaster at Aegospotami. When Theramenes returned, he presented the Spartan proposal to destroy the Long Walls in their entirety. At this time two Athenian generals, Strombichides[11] and Dionysodorus, protested the proposed action on the grounds that better peace terms were available. When the oligarchs realised that their plans were being thwarted, they contrived to have these men arrested and brought to trial, persuading Agoratus to posture as a defendant in the trial so that he could be seen to give information against the generals under duress, with the promise that he would be immune to the fate of death reserved for the others convicted. Further information was laid by the oligarch Theocritus, a confidant of Agoratus, who subsequently took refuge at Munychia and made an escape by sea after making a deposition of the names of democratic sympathisers. Later, he took sides with the resurgent democracy at Phyle and became a member of the Piraeus Party in the final months of the struggle ending with the downfall of the oligarchs.

The trial of Agoratus has puzzled modern interpreters mainly because, on the surface, it appears to violate the terms of Amnesty, which outlawed prosecution of crimes dating from the time of oligarchy (see Chapter 3, covenant 15). D. D. Phillips put forward the explanation that, as a non-Athenian, Agoratus did not enjoy the same degree of protection in law as a full citizen, and though offences predating the democratic restoration were dredged up, under the special circumstances this did not constitute a violation of the oaths and covenants, because the defendant was not protected in the same way as a fully fledged Athenian citizen would have been under the oaths.[12] The problem here is that several unknown variables are at play. A decree preserved on stone, dating from the period after the fall of the first oligarchy in 411, moved by Erasinides, rewarded Thrasybulus of Calydon as chief assassin of the oligarch Phrynichus (*IG* I³ 102 = Tod 86) and entailed other benefactions for those who had served as accomplices. It is possible that this was the same decree cited at §§70–2, according to which Agoratus was granted limited rights, such as the right to hold property, without gaining the full rights of an Athenian citizen. Later, in 401/0, another decree was issued granting honours to non-citizens who had joined the demo-

---

[11] Known also from Th. 8.30.
[12] Thus Phillips 2008: 194–8.

cratic resistance at Phyle (*IG* II² 10). If the trial had taken place after this event, then Agoratus might have been entitled to full citizenship under the decree of 401/0 (if indeed it did grant the franchise), in which case the allegation made against him of not holding citizenship would have been subject to an easy refutation by the defence. More controversially, it has been claimed that Agoratus fell through the gaps left by the provisions of the Amnesty in covenant 14, widely believed to have made an exemption for own-hand killing (*autocheir*). As argued in Chapter 3, there is no evidence that this is true, and the linkage of the phrase ἐπ' αὐτοφώρῳ to particular categories of homicide committed by the blow of the killer himself is based on a misunderstanding of the Athenian homicide law, which omits to make such distinctions in categorising homicide. Moreover, it cannot make sense of the trial here, given that Agoratus, who was accused of having murdered ἐπ' αὐτοφώρῳ, nevertheless did so by means of denunciation.

A related question is where the trial stood in relation to the law of Archinus, establishing the special plea of *paragraphê* (on which, see Chapter 6). If the trial had taken place after the passage of Archinus' law, then it would have been blocked before the prosecution even had the opportunity to lay a claim. If, on the other hand, it predated that law, the reference back to the pledge μὴ μνησικακεῖν could only happen in the subsequent speech, the speech for the defence. The new rule of *paragraphê* inverted the usual order of litigation, so that the defence became the prosecution and the prosecution the defence, in the event the trial violated the Amnesty or the rule of *res iudicata*. Since the trial appears to violate the terms of the Amnesty, it is conceivable that the plaint was lodged against Agoratus at some point before it became possible for the defendant to turn tables and become the plaintiff. Here again, we depend on some very tenuous chronology, where the dating of the speech in relation to the passage of Archinus serves the preconceived idea that Agoratus, prior to the institution of *paragraphê*, could have blocked the trial after the prosecution had spoken and not before. But it seems unlikely that the court should have allowed its time to be wasted by vexatious litigation if a special plea could be put forward at a preliminary hearing which rendered the trial inadmissible, even if the trial happened before Archinus, which made it possible for victims of unlawful litigation to sue for damages, not merely to block an inadmissible case. Loening argued from §§77–82, where no mention is made of the decree honouring non-citizens at Phyle (RO 4), that the trial must predate 401/0, but the argument is unconvincing, as there may have been no need to allude to that decree if Agoratus had already been made a citizen under the earlier measures honouring him for his part in the assassination of Phrynichus.[13] Using different arguments, Carawan points to And. 1.94, which alludes to the rule that the

---

[13] Loening 1987: 74; *contra* Todd 2020: 259.

laws can only be applied from Eucleides (403/2), to argue that this particular provision was put in place not in the immediate wake of the Amnesty, but at the time of the trial of Andocides, in around 400. On the strength of that suggestion, he claims that the rule not to apply the laws for offences predating 403 had not yet been introduced at the time of the trial of Agoratus, for which the only defence is that the speaker of Lys. 13 does not mention such a rule. The argument is even flimsier because, for rhetorical reasons, it is hardly surprising that the prosecution in the trial of Agoratus should have omitted mention, whereas the defence in the trial of Andocides would naturally have referred to it as his legal linchpin.[14] Even more recently, Todd has drawn attention to the similarities between Lys. 13.7–8, 12 and Lys. 30.10–13, arguing that a plausible though not conclusive case could be made to downdate the trial of Agoratus to the period of Nicomachus' trial in 399, perhaps within a few months.[15] The dating, however, has little material consequence for the question of why the trial was admissible. Even if it predated Archinus, a claim which cannot be established with confidence, that should not affect why, in apparent violation of the Amnesty, it was permitted to come to light.

The speaker of Lys. 13 repeatedly tarnishes the defendant as a fraud and imposter. This has led some to date the trial before the decree of enfranchisement in 401/0, on the grounds that otherwise the allusions in the speech to his non-citizen status would have made no sense.[16] But there are various ways to interpret this. It may well be true, as Phillips maintained, that it would have been easier to bring a charge which ostensibly violated the Amnesty against a non-citizen than against a citizen, but there are indications that the enfranchisement decree of 401/0 had been delivered by the time of the trial. At §79, the speaker seeks to refute the defendant's claim to citizenship on the grounds that, as an erstwhile oligarch, he had been shunned by every self-respecting supporter of the democratic resistance at Phyle and that the taxiarch at the time had not assigned him a place in the tribe, as one polluted of the crime of murder. The reference to Phyle both in the prosecution and, as we might suppose, in the defence is surely significant: why would the speaker have taken the trouble to repudiate the matter of Phyle if there was not some important legal matter at stake? These final sections are not mere window-dressing but contain weighty implications for the status of the defendant and his claim to citizenship. If he was a citizen, the traditional explanation cannot work. Even if Agoratus was not a full citizen, the claim that his defective legal status

---

[14] Carawan 2013: 123–4; *contra* Todd 2020: 259–60 with n. 87.
[15] Todd 2020: 260–1.
[16] See, for example, Loening 1987: 74; Bearzot 1997: 74–6. Carawan (2013: 119–25) accepts the earlier dating of the trial but argues that Agoratus did exercise full citizenship, despite the lambasting rhetoric of the prosecution.

exposed him to litigation which, if levelled against an Athenian, would have been blocked by a special plea makes the further assumption that the clause μὴ μνησικακεῖν in the covenants applied only to citizens. Indeed, we have no conclusive proof that this was so. The exceptions (Chapter 3, covenants 16–17) to the rule against recalling past wrong were clearly spelled out in the Treaty of Amnesty. There is no word about exempting metics or other prominent figures who did not claim citizen status. If such an exemption had been implied, a hidden impracticality might have been a rush of non-citizens to claim citizenship in the wake of the Amnesty, yet no such event is recorded in the sources. Further, there is no sign anywhere in the literature that non-citizens were exposed to vindictive litigation in the wake of the Reconciliation for their part in the oligarchy. The citizen population was a fraction of the total population of Athens, and if the project in 403 was to effect reconciliation, what applied to the citizen population would certainly have applied to its non-citizen population also. Importantly, Lysias nowhere states expressly that by asserting citizen status, Agoratus could lay claim to protection under the Amnesty Agreement in such a way as would have been impossible had he not been a citizen, which is a modern interpretation.

The trial of Agoratus was a homicide case brought by the unusual process of *endeixis*.[17] Scholars have debated in the past what this rarely attested procedure amounted to precisely, as the evidence is slender. Older scholarship saw a clear procedural distinction between *endeixis* (literally 'pointing out' offenders to the appropriate official) and *apagôgê* (literally, 'leading away', commonly rendered 'summary arrest'), restricted to certain categories of offender.[18] What is striking in this speech, however, is that the former term is never used outside the title of the Palatinus MS, whereas the latter is used four times (§§85–6). More recently, Hansen has shown that the sources fail to support a hard and fast distinction between the two, and that both terms probably refer to different stages of the same overarching process.[19] This is supported by a parallel at Antiphon 5.9, where the defendant describes his arrest as *endeixis* but refers to the main body of the trial as *apagôgê*. As far as the evidence indicates, trials of *apagôgê* were linked to offenders who had been caught ἐπ' αὐτοφώρῳ, the meaning of which scholars have debated. Two renditions of the phrase have been given. According to Hansen, it meant 'caught in the act', originally in connection with theft, as the etymology of the term would tend to imply, though it is used also in reference to *kakourgoi* (meaning 'malefactors') and clothes-stealers. On that view, it originally had a narrow meaning which was

---

[17] Thus Phillips 2008: 120–31; Carawan 2013: 115–19; Todd 2020: 307–8.
[18] See, for example, Lipsius 1905–15: 319, 331.
[19] Hansen 1976: 9–24; for a more recent discussion, see Todd 2020: 255–8.

expanded later on to categories of offence beside theft, but Harris, in contrast, has drawn attention to evidence from the Digest which shows that the phrase, in Greek, corresponded more or less exactly to the Latin *furtum manifestum* and suggests 'manifest guilt' as a more likely rendition.[20] *Pace* Hansen, there is little evidence that the phrase changed its meaning over time and that ἐπ' αὐτοφώρῳ from an early stage applied to many different areas of criminal activity, not just stealing. For this reason, it should come as no surprise that a homicide case could come to light by *apagôgê/endeixis* provided the charge ἐπ' αὐτοφώρῳ was applicable. We know of one other example only of a homicide trial by *apagôgê*, the trial of Euxitheus for the murder of Herodes (Antiphon 5), though an abortive trial was also brought against Thrasybulus and Apollodorus for the murder of Phrynichus (Lyc. *Leocr.* 112). The evidence for classical homicide procedure at D. 23.63–81 indicates that trials by *apagôgê* were a later development, tacked on to the five archaic courts established by Draco, where the standard legal process would have been by private suit (*dikê*).[21]

In the opening section (§1), the judges are called upon to punish (τιμωρεῖν) a man who had been responsible for the deaths of citizens through complicity with the Thirty (ὑπὲρ τῶν ἀνδρῶν οἳ ἀπέθανον εὖνοι ὄντες τῷ πλήθει τῷ ὑμετέρῳ). Superficially, this looks like a partisan trial, of a kind which the covenants and oaths forbade. A little later (§3), the accuser appeals to justice and righteousness (δίκαιον καὶ ὅσιον) to bring down a man who had hatched grief upon honest citizens, had worked to undermine democracy, and had conspired to bring disaster on Athens. The matter of homicide was crucial, but contrary to much modern assertion, Athenian homicide law did not draw distinctions between own-hand killing and the type with which Agoratus had been tarnished under the Thirty via denunciation.[22] Before 404, homicide cases could be brought against those who had given an order to kill (Antiphon 1) or who had administered a portion resulting in a victim's death (Antiphon 6). In tragedy, Theseus is held responsible for the murder of his son Hippolytus by the circumstances under which Hippolytus was driven out, even though he did not deliver the blow by his own hand (E. *Hipp.* 1148–50; cf. also A. *Ag.* 1613–14). In the historical period, Andocides clarifies that in homicide law, no distinction was drawn between homicide committed by proxy and homicide delivered directly from the hand of the killer (And. 1.94: τὸν βουλεύσαντα

---

[20] Hansen 1976: 48–53; *contra* Harris 1994: 177–80 (= 2006: 373–90). For a confused understanding of this terminology in reference to homicide, see Carawan 2013: 125–7; against which, see further below.

[21] This militates against Carawan's understanding of trial by *apagôgê* as having been instituted by Draco (1998: 164–6), a claim which he backs with no evidence; see now the refuting remarks at Todd 2020: 255–6.

[22] On this, see the important discussion of Harris 2006: 398–404; also, Harris 2015b: 47.

ἐν τῷ αὐτῷ ἐνέχεσθαι καὶ τὸν τῇ χειρὶ ἐργασάμενον). What little survives on stone from the seventh-century law on homicide (*IG* I³ 104 lines 11–13: δ]ι- κάζεν δὲ τὸς βασιλέας αἴτιο[ν] φόν[ο] ε[ἴτε τὸν αὐτόχερα εἴτ?]ε [β]ολ- εύσαντα) indicates that from early times, Athenian law had treated own-hand homicide and planned homicide as conferring equal responsibility. In this trial, Agoratus had not delivered the fatal blow. Legally, that made no difference, because what was important was that through the act of denunciation, Agoratus was responsible for the deaths of innocent citizens. The covenants drew no distinction between own-hand homicide and accessory; the provisions of covenant 14 relate not to what had taken place previously but to how future homicide jurisdiction should be ordered between the democrats who had been restored to Athens and the oligarchic renegades at Eleusis.

The Amnesty drew no distinction between those who had delivered the blow and those who were responsible further down the causal chain. The normal assumption has always been that accessories to homicide were covered in the Clauses of Amnesty, whereas own-hand killers were not. Chapter 3 showed that such a theory depends on a misreading of *Ath. Pol.* 39.5. Yet on the strength of the claim that the Amnesty did draw such a distinction, it has been maintained recently that the aim of Lys. 13 was to elevate in the perception of the judges the crime committed by Agoratus to the level of own-hand homicide, so that the crime was still actionable under the clauses of the Amnesty which permitted certain actions against homicide to proceed.[23] Nothing in the prosecution refers to own-hand homicide, which is irrelevant to the matter at hand. The point at law in Lys. 13 is not whether the homicide was this type or that type, but whether homicide had been committed. The defence claimed that the denunciations could not have happened because the defendant had few oligarchic sympathies, which affords an insight into why the matter of citizenship was brought into play. The reason had nothing to do with the limited applicability of the Amnesty to citizens only, as Phillips claimed, but rather to do with claims which the defence had made to solidarity with the democratic cause in effort to refute the charge of complicity. It was important for the defence to prove citizenship, not because the matter of protection from vexatious litigation was at stake but, more simply, because if citizenship could be proved, that would indicate that Agoratus had been rewarded in 411/10 and 401/0 for service to democracy, and that, in turn, would have cast doubt on allegations against him of having conspired in 404 to bring about the downfall of the people. These connections are made explicit later, at §§74–6: if he had been a loyal democrat, the Thirty would never have trusted him. The matter of citizenship was important in establishing not

---

[23] See Carawan 2013: 125–35.

the claim of the defendant under the Amnesty, but his character. If he could point to a citizenship grant, that would have shown the court that his services to the democracy had been recognised, and so it would have been easier for him to refute some of the charges made against him by claiming that he had never harboured oligarchic sympathies. If, on the other hand, those claims had resulted from bribery (Lys. 13.70), the arguments of the defence would have been deflated.

If it could be shown that Agoratus had caused the deaths of citizens through the act of denunciation, he was in the eyes of fifth-century Athenian homicide law a murderer and, under ordinary circumstances, punishable. But there is a further legal point. The covenants and oaths forbade prosecution of crimes predating 403. The acts with which Agoratus was being smeared dated from 404, and so even if he had performed all the misdeeds alleged against him, under the terms of the Amnesty none of those crimes were actionable after the democratic restoration. If Agoratus had been a murderer under the Thirty, it would have been impossible to bring action after 403, regardless of whether the cause had been direct (i.e. own-hand) or indirect. It is tempting to try to reconstruct the Covenants of Amnesty in the light of the trials which followed. Because the trial of Agoratus came to the fore after 403, it is often argued *a fortiori* that the treaty contained special exempting clauses which allowed the pursuit of certain categories of killing which predated the Amnesty, but not others.[24] References in the prosecution indicate that the defendant *did* appeal to the clauses of Amnesty to argue that the trial was illegal. Lys. 13.88 seems to imply that the rule of *paragraphê* had not yet been legislated, since it states that the defendant *would* object to the trial by reference to the rule of amnesty, but the same passage places a slanted interpretation on the matter: the terms of amnesty, so it claims, cannot apply to the defendant, because the trial did not cut across party lines. If Agoratus had been a member of the Piraeus Party as he maintained, then he could not presume protection from prosecution from another member of his own faction. The point is reiterated at Lys. 13.90: the oaths were sworn between the City Party and the Piraeus Party, not between the Piraeus Party and the Piraeus Party (οὐδένα γὰρ ὅρκον οἱ ἐν Πειραιεῖ τοῖς ἐν Πειραιεῖ ὤμοσαν).[25] This is the loophole which the prosecution sought in self-justification. The plea is weak. Though the purpose of the amnesty was to protect those who had stayed in the time of the oligarchy from future vindictive action, it would be reductive to read this to mean that democrats were

---

[24] For examples of this scholarly tendency, see Cloché 1915: 259–61; Bonner 1924: 175–6; Rhodes 1981: 468; Carawan 2013: 125–7; for a more extensive bibliography of those who have taken the approach, see Gray 2013: 385 n. 49.

[25] The MSS read ἄστει, which makes no sense in the context. Modern editors have rightly emended this to read Πειραιεῖ; for different possibilities, see Todd 2020: 450 n. 439.

not also protected.²⁶ If the point had been enforceable, we would not have expected the prosecution to make extraordinary efforts in other places to argue that the defendant had not been a committed democrat. Nothing in the Covenants of Reconciliation seems to merit the suggestion that actions between members of the same democratic faction were admissible after 403. To read events in this way would be to underestimate the messiness of the historical circumstances which led to the collapse of democracy, as if the Attic population could be divided schematically between supporters of oligarchy and supporters of democracy: Chremon, Charicles and Eratosthenes, for example, big names among the oligarchs of 404, had in each case formerly served under the democracy and had oscillated at the time of the establishment of the Four Hundred in 411.²⁷

The vexing question remains: if the Oath of Reconciliation forbade the prosecution of crimes predating 12 Boedromion 403, some other reason needs to be adduced as to why this trial was admissible. The explanation that it was allowed because it did not cut across party lines seems most disingenuous. Of all the trials which post-date the Amnesty, this is undoubtedly the most difficult and the least explicable on the evidence as it stands. What this trial may indicate is that even in cases where a defendant had not served on the boards of the Thirty, Ten or Eleven but where the crimes were so serious and widespread that anger and desire for retaliation could not be restrained, grey areas remained whereby notorious and truly egregious criminals were dragged into the limelight, even if court action against them was subsequently quashed. The statement at Lys. 13.88 that Agoratus would put in a special plea surely indicates not that the Amnesty was not working, or that its terms were not being systematically applied, but that they were acknowledged to exist and were thus adhered to. Just as Andocides' self-defence entailed a dishonest citing of the Treaty of Amnesty (see Chapter 4), so was it possible on the other side of the ledger for clever litigators to sidestep the requirement not to prosecute for offences predating 403, using slippery excuses such as the one which the speaker of Lys. 13 proffers at §§88–90. The trial of Agoratus furnishes, perhaps ironically,

---

²⁶ At Joyce 2008: 513–14, I made the point that there was much more to the Amnesty than a series of measures to protect *atimoi*, and that its principal aim was to save the city, as Andocides clarifies (1.81). Carawan has since caricatured my arguments, as if I had claimed that no one except the defeated stood to gain anything from the terms, though I have never made such a claim; for my reply to Carawan on this point, see Joyce 2014: 43–4. Carawan (2013: 117 n. 5) writes: 'This would be in line with Joyce (2008), who treats the oaths and covenants as a unilateral commitment by the victors (though he does not cite this passage in evidence).' But at Joyce 2008: 514, I was clear that the Amnesty did entail benefits to both sides.

²⁷ On Chremon, see Lys. 30.14; on Charicles, see Davies 1971: 502; on Eratosthenes, see Lys. 12.42.

evidence that the Amnesty was working, because it illustrates the lengths to which prosecutors had to go to get around the legal prohibitions which made cases like this unactionable. We do not know the result of the trial, just as there is no indication in the evidence as to how the trial of Andocides materialised. As a piece of litigation, this is flimsy in construction and indicates that emotive rhetoric was used by litigants whose legal case may have been weaker than the language in which it was couched.

The public character of Agoratus' crime is the key to understanding why this trial was permitted to take place and why it was brought by *endeixis*, and not by private suit.[28] If this had been a private action for homicide, it would have been inadmissible by the very same clauses of the Amnesty Agreement. The ingenious loophole through which the speaker of Lys. 13 crawls is the grey area which arose subsequently as to what to do about criminals whose acts were so public that, even if they did not sit on the boards of the Thirty, Ten or Eleven, the principle in law which exempted members of those boards needed to be extended to other public criminals also. The point is summed up succinctly at §84: the only way the defendant can avoid condemnation is either if he can prove that he did not cause the deaths of the victims or that those victims were oligarchs and that he was acting in the capacity of a loyal democrat doing his duty by the city. This comes close once again to partisanship, but it is important to understand what precisely partisanship here entails. The law cleanly forbade vengeful acts waged by democrats against oligarchs and vice versa but, on the understanding of Lys. 13, those same criminal acts could only be unactionable if they did not have a wider, more public, consequence. The whole aim of the prosecution is to show that Agoratus' crimes are actionable for the very reason that they were *public*, not private, crimes; that is, crimes which led to the subversion of democracy and the installation of the Thirty. The reason Lys. 13 is so difficult to interpret is that this principle is not expressly stated in the covenants. The account of *Ath. Pol.* 39 does not put it quite in these terms. On a literal reading of the Treaty of Amnesty, all crimes committed under the oligarchy were unactionable except for those committed by the reigning oligarchs themselves, and even those were protected if their perpetrators submitted to public accounting. Therefore, by a literal reading, Agoratus' crimes were unactionable. But the intriguing legal question which this trial raises is whether the underlying legal principle of the treaty could be bent and then extended to others not named in the exempting

---

[28] The public nature of this case is brought out by the complex interplay in the proem (§§1–4) between first-person singular and the second-person plural pronouns, on which see Grau 1972: 60–1. By casting the crime as an offence against the city, rather than a crime against private individuals alone, the speaker elevates the case to a matter of public interest, thus circumventing the objection that this could be a trial arising from a private grudge.

clause, but whose crimes were of such a nature that, by their legal implication, they fell within the zone of exemption. If Agoratus' liability was to the family of Dionysodorus alone, the matter would have been inadmissible. The unknown issue here, however, is whether he had a liability to the city and, if so, whether that *public* liability placed him in the same category of exemption as the Thirty, Ten and Eleven, who were exempt by the democratic principle of accountability.

The next section of the speech (§85) proceeds to a legal point which has generated vast discussion: whether Agoratus had been caught ἐπ' αὐτοφώρῳ.[29] Agoratus protested that the warrant for his arrest added the clause ἐπ' αὐτοφώρῳ and that because he had not been caught with a knife or club in his hand, the action against him was inadmissible. The speaker refutes this by showing that ἐπ' αὐτοφώρῳ does not mean that Agoratus had delivered the fatal blow. The first attested appearance of this phrase comes at Hdt. 6.72, where Leotychidas was accused of receiving bribes and convicted when found to possess coins up the sleeves of his tunic. His trial and condemnation proceeded from the principle that because he had been caught ἐπ' αὐτοφώρῳ with coins on his person, that was evidence enough that he had committed the crime of which he had been accused. The term, attested in the fourth century in the orators, is relatively uncommon but meant no more than 'clearly' or 'manifestly'.[30] The defendant argued against the admissibility of the trial on the grounds that the accusation ἐπ' αὐτοφώρῳ had been added into the plaint by the Eleven but, according to the prosecution, the Eleven had acted appropriately, since by adding this phrase to the plaint it was now legally permissible to bring a case by *endeixis*.[31] Whether Agoratus delivered the fatal blow is indeed immaterial. To say that he had been caught ἐπ' αὐτοφώρῳ means no more than that his guilt was incontrovertible: Agoratus denounced, democrats died, democracy was subverted. In law, it made no difference whether the physical act had been perpetrated by the defendant, if the defendant was causally responsible for the deaths of innocent democrats because he had denounced to the Thirty, and if the same acts of denunciation had led to the show trial which resulted in their murder and the subversion of Athens' democracy. The law may have been loosely phrased and allowed for interpretative slippage. The important point

---

[29] Carawan (2013: 125–7) seems to understand the existence of a clause in the covenants exempting own-hand homicide and identifies that with ἐπ' αὐτοφώρῳ. As Harris (1994) has shown, however, that these two concepts are entirely distinct and that to be caught ἐπ' αὐτοφώρῳ had nothing to do with the matter of whether the murderer delivered the blow with his own hand.
[30] Aeschin 3.9–10; Din. 1.29; [D.] 45.81. See the discussion at Harris 1994: 380–4.
[31] That public officials often tweaked plaints to make them fit with processual law is confirmed by the extraneous evidence of Isoc. 10.2, where the defendant was compelled at the *anakrisis* to add a damaging statement; on this, see Harrison 1968–71: ii.90; Griffith-Williams 2013: 213.

to notice is that the admissibility of the case against Agoratus is framed in the language of law, never in the language of politics. The trial of Agoratus illustrates the rule of law in action: the courts were there to protect and to apply the law, and though the language of vengeance is used, its contextualisation is expressly legal.

What looks superficially to be a case arising from private malice, in the rhetoric of the speech is turned into a point of law: because Agoratus has committed a crime not just against the relatives of the deceased but against the democracy, the trial is elevated to a new dimension. By that same reasoning, the rule μὴ μνησικακεῖν does not apply, because, though he is not one of the Thirty, Ten or Eleven, the principle by which members of those boards were still liable, namely that their crimes were public, applies here to Agoratus. At §3, the speaker states that the matter of punishment is both right and holy (δίκαιον καὶ ὅσιον). The verb τιμωρεῖσθαι is used once again, but it cannot here really mean 'to avenge', because it applies both to the speaker *and to the judges* (καὶ ἐμοὶ καὶ ὑμῖν ἅπασι τιμωρεῖσθαι καθ' ὅσον ἕκαστος δύναται). If it is taken to mean 'to avenge', this needs to be understood in a rather extended sense, because it is not normal in oratory for judges to avenge a murder. In a clever turn of phrase, the speaker now deflects from himself any possible riposte that he is acting from vengeful instincts, which were expressly forbidden by law. The 'vengeance' which must be inflicted is identifiable with legal 'punishment' because the crimes committed were done not against one person but against the democracy. In the next section (§4), the speaker introduces the circumstances under which the democracy was dissolved and Agoratus' role in the matter. As a *public* criminal, Agoratus is not covered by the terms of the Amnesty which, on the interpretation of Lys. 13, guarded against bringing action for private issues only. The defendant, by that reasoning, is not only the killer of the speaker's relative, which alone would have been unactionable under covenant 15, but an enemy of the people. By clever verbal trickery, the prosecution implicitly draws Agoratus into the 'exception' clause, because even though he was not one of those explicitly named as exempt from the Amnesty, the public nature of his crimes in spirit if not in letter puts him in the same bracket as the Thirty, Ten and Eleven. We may react at this point that this only shows how the law was manipulated and twisted to suit the needs of an argument. That may be so, but the inference to be drawn from that is that the point at issue was a legal one and that it took a very clever, if somewhat disingenuous, orator to model a case upon a special reading of a legal principle which was not stated overtly in the terms of the treaty, but was nevertheless implied. The wording of covenant 16, the exception and its 'exception', was that only members of the ruling oligarchy could be prosecuted. But the abstraction behind this was that the reason why an exception had to be spelled out was that the Thirty, Ten and Eleven were liable to the whole city, not just to groups within it, and it was the public character of their liability which entailed that, unlike those of private offenders, their offences remained actionable. Lys. 13 seeks to extend that principle to others, like Agoratus, who although not explicitly exempt, *implicitly* was exempt from covenant 15 because, like the Thirty, Ten and Eleven, his crimes were of a public nature.

The broader question remains how far this was a 'political' trial. A central tenet of these chapters is that litigation under the restored democracy was depoliticised and that the scrutiny of laws which resumed in 403 was geared towards enthroning the rule of law. As noted above, the opening sections of Lys. 13 would at first sight indicate a vindictive motive, but it is also important to read the Greek carefully without imported interpretations based on a preconceived understanding of how Athenian litigation worked. The opening section states:

> It behoves all of you, judges, to inflict the penalty on behalf of those men who died in good disposition towards your democracy, but it behoves me not least. For Dionysodorus was my brother-in-law and cousin. Therefore, I happen to feel the same enmity towards this fellow Agoratus here as is felt by your democracy. For this man committed such acts as a result of which he is equally hated by me as he will be punished by you justly, if god wills it. (tr. R. W. M. Lamb)[32]

The verb τιμωρεῖν is often taken to mean 'to avenge', but in a legal sense it can also mean simply 'to punish'.[33] The common way of reading this passage is to imagine that the speaker seeks to justify a vengeful and retaliatory instinct, but it is important to read it for what it actually says. There is a special reason why the speaker yokes his personal desire to see the defendant punished with the desire of the democracy for the same. The whole point is that this trial is *not* proceeding from a personal motive, or at least not from a personal motive alone. The speaker concedes that he harbours a private grudge against the defendant, as would be expected in the light of his relation to Dionysodorus,

---

[32] προσήκει μέν, ὦ ἄνδρες δικασταί, πᾶσιν ὑμῖν τιμωρεῖν ὑπὲρ τῶν ἀνδρῶν οἳ ἀπέθανον εὖνοι ὄντες τῷ πλήθει τῷ ὑμετέρῳ, προσήκει δὲ κἀμοὶ οὐχ ἥκιστα· κηδεστὴς γάρ μοι ἦν Διονυσόδωρος καὶ ἀνεψιός. τυγχάνει οὖν ἐμοὶ ἡ αὐτὴ ἔχθρα πρὸς Ἀγόρατον τουτονὶ καὶ τῷ πλήθει τῷ ὑμετέρῳ ὑπάρχουσα· ἔπραξε γὰρ οὗτος τοιαῦτα, δι' ἃ ὑπ' ἐμοῦ νυνὶ εἰκότως μισεῖται, ὑπό τε ὑμῶν, ἐὰν θεὸς θέλῃ, δικαίως τιμωρηθήσεται.

[33] See, for example, Antiphon 6.6; Lys. 25.15; Pl. *R.* 579a; *Lg.* 943d; Plu. *Art.* 14.17. Todd (2020: 308) translates the sentence to mean 'it is fitting that you should all take vengeance ... but it is particularly fitting that I should do so', but at 309 he acknowledges that the verb can mean both 'to take vengeance' and 'to punish'. On the broader range of meaning of this term in Greek as used in Athenian homicide law, see Cairns 2015.

but this is not the reason why the trial is happening. The grudge (ἔχθρα) which he holds is held *by the entire city*. The thought here is that the trial is not factional but legal. The point at issue is not a political one, involving the private attitude of one person to another, but one of law: Agoratus has committed murder, and it is therefore the *legal* duty of the judges to inflict upon him the requisite penalty such that the law prescribes. The fact that all this militates against covenant 15 of the Amnesty is, for the moment, of secondary importance; of primary importance is that the charge against Agoratus is framed in strict legal language. The appeal to justice here is crucial, because if the man in the dock pays the penalty, he will do so justly (δικαίως τιμωρηθήσεται). The same idea is taken forward in the next section: the trial must take place because this is a public, not a private, liability. The fact that it was brought by *endeixis*, rather than the more usual *dikē*, is in this connection crucial, because Agoratus by his crimes has indebted himself to the whole city, not just to one individual where vindictive action was outlawed by the promise μὴ μνησικακεῖν.

THE TRIAL OF ERATOSTHENES, LATE 403, OR POSSIBLY AFTER 401 (LYS. 12)

Shortly after the restoration of democracy, probably in the summer of 403, one of the Thirty was brought to account. Unlike Lys. 13, which was composed by Lysias for delivery by a different speaker, the speech for the prosecution of Eratosthenes (Lys. 12) was delivered by the orator himself.[34] In the course of the speech, we get a clear picture of the legal issue. The Thirty had put to death some wealthy citizens and seized their property. Two intended victims were Lysias and his brother Polemarchus, the former of whom managed to escape, while the latter was tried by the oligarchs and sentenced thereupon to death.[35] The man who carried out the arrest was one Eratosthenes, a member of the Thirty, who pleaded in his own defence that he was acting under compulsion, a plea which Lysias treated with due scorn, as the defendant had sat on the very board he claims compelled him to undertake an act against his wish. These arguments fall under the category of *epieikeia*, a form of legal argument which did not exactly disregard written law, but which applied a standard of

---

[34] For a broader discussion of the authorship of this speech and its place within the Lysianic corpus, see now Todd 2020: 1–6, 33–8. The authenticity of the speech has, with one exception (see Hecker 1848), been universally accepted.

[35] Lysias and his brother Polemarchus were both metics, though of extremely high wealth and social status (cf. Lys. *Hippotherses* fr. 170 lines 153–5; Pl. R. 127c; 328b).

justice in cases which lawgivers could not have foreseen.³⁶ Not only one of the Thirty, Eratosthenes had also taken his place alongside Critias as one of the five 'ephors' who took control of the city in the run-up to the establishment of the Thirty Tyrants. After the death of Critias and the fall of the extreme wing of the oligarchy, the rump of the Thirty withdrew to their new enclave at Eleusis, leaving behind two of their number, the defendant and Pheidon, both of whom pleaded that they were among the faction of Theramenes and that they had only ever exerted, or tried to exert, a moderating influence upon the worst of the oligarchs. In around May 403, the government of the Thirty was replaced by that of the Ten, who called upon Sparta to lend assistance against the resurgent democratic resistance at Piraeus. The rule of the Ten was very short-lived. Shortly afterwards, the City Party came to terms with the Piraeus Party, the Oaths of Reconciliation were exchanged, and democracy was once again restored.

Before the publication of the London papyrus in 1891, scholars puzzled over the issue of whether the prosecution of Eratosthenes was a public accounting (*euthynai*) or a homicide trial.³⁷ Since the Aristotelian tradition threw light on the Covenants of Amnesty, especially covenant 16, which protected those oligarchs who submitted to public account, most scholars now claim that this was a trial by *euthynai*, though perhaps it would be more precise to say that it was a *dikê phonou* (which provided the substantive charge) brought under the *euthynai* (which provided only the procedural framework through which the case could be brought). Covenants 16–18 (see Chapter 3) provided that any member of the oligarchy who wished to stand trial at Athens in the wake of the Reconciliation could do so. This is sometimes known as the 'exception to the exception', which gave legal protection to those oligarchs who agreed to an audit and were acquitted. Lys. 12 is usually placed in this historical background, as the case for the prosecution at a public trial of Eratosthenes, a member of the Thirty.³⁸ Until the discovery and publication of the *Ath. Pol.*, many scholars of the nineteenth century understood Lys. 12 to be a murder trial, akin to Lys. 13. This was because outside *Ath. Pol.* 39.6, there is no reference anywhere in ancient literature to a special process under the terms of

---

³⁶ On *epieikeia*, see Arist. *EN* 5.10.1137a–1138a, which examines *epieikeia* both as a rectifying principle for the law and as a personal virtue. For passages in the orators where the principle of *epieikeia* is applied elsewhere, see the survey and discussion of the evidence in Harris 2013: 285–91.

³⁷ For the claim that this was a homicide trial, see Frohberger 1866–71: i.16; Frohberger and Gebauer 1880: 18–19; Rauchenstein and Fuhr 1899: i.18. For the view that it was a *euthynai* trial, see Blass 1887: 541–2. For a recent survey and summary of the relevant scholarship, see Todd 2020: 33–4.

³⁸ Thus Loening 1987: 70–1.

the Amnesty which granted protection to oligarchs who had stood trial and survived.[39] The problem here is that the judges are referred to not as *ephetai* but as *dikastai*, which rules out the Areopagus as a venue for the trial.[40] Other arguments that this was a homicide trial, and not a *euthynai*, have drawn attention to the statements at §§22 and 84 that Eratosthenes came to trial of his own volition, where it might be implied that the alternative was to go into exile, but a similar turn of phrase appears at Din. 3.3, in the trial of Harpalus, and need not be taken to mean that the defendant was not brought to court by the prosecution. According to Xenophon, whose treatment of the period is notoriously lacunose, when the oligarchs were ousted they left Athens for Eleusis (X. *HG* 2.4.38), a version followed by Diodorus, dependent on Ephorus (D.S. 14.32–3),[41] and centuries later, in Justin's epitome of Trogus (Just. 5.10).[42] Most scholars have recognised, rightly, that the historians, casual and careless as they are with detail, cannot be ranged against the testimony of the *Ath. Pol.*, whose account is based on a reliable documentary tradition.[43] Recently, a case has been made for the amalgamation of two separate historical episodes at *Ath. Pol.* 39.6, one from 403, another from 401.[44] Following that argument, covenant 17 (see Chapter 3) was a genuine detail from the year of the Reconciliation, whereas covenant 16 came not from the treaty of 403 between Athens and Eleusis, but from a later treaty in 401, when Eleusis was beaten into submission and the oligarchs reabsorbed; the narrative of *Ath. Pol.* has therefore telescoped two separate historical episodes. But there is no reason to believe that a separate Treaty of Reconciliation was contracted in 401; Xenophon implies no more than that the oaths of 403 were resworn in 401.[45]

A related question is the dating of the speech. Some passages (§§35, 80, 94) refer to ongoing fighting with the enemy, which would situate the delivery of the speech somewhere in the interval between 403 and 401, when the enclave

---

[39] See, for example, Rauchenstein 1855: 599–607; Luebbert 1881: 64; *contra* Großer 1868.
[40] Thus Todd 2020: 34. On the use of ὦ ἄνδρες as the normal manner of address to homicide judges in Lys. 1, see Todd 2007: 45–6.
[41] For the *Hellenica Oxyrhynchia* as the source for Ephorus, see Krentz 1982: 131–47.
[42] Carawan (2013: 143) quotes Lys. 25.9 and Pl. *Men.* 243e–244a as evidence that there was no peace between Athens and Eleusis at this time and uses this to support his tendentious claim that the final treaty was not sworn into effect until the fall of Eleusis in 401. Yet, in citing these sources, he fails to recognise that in likelihood they refer to the events of 401 and not 403.
[43] Thus Scheibelreiter 2013.
[44] Carawan 2013: 140–70.
[45] This goes against the clear implications of And. 1.90, where the oath which enforced covenant 15 is quoted verbatim: καὶ οὐ μνησικακήσω τῶν πολιτῶν οὐδενὶ πλὴν τῶν τριάκοντα καὶ τῶν δέκα καὶ τῶν ἕνδεκα: οὐδὲ τούτων ὃς ἂν ἐθέλῃ εὐθύνας διδόναι τῆς ἀρχῆς ἧς ἦρξεν. On this as an oath which enforced an individual covenant of the Amnesty, rather than the Amnesty agreement in its totality, see Joyce 2015: 40.

at Eleusis was dissolved, and these have frequently been taken to refer directly to the rump oligarchy still stationed at Eleusis. As Todd recently has argued, however, there is no explicit mention here of Eleusis, and indeed these references do not afford a reliable *terminus ante quem*.[46] The dating is important for the issue of procedure, because if the speech was delivered before 401 it would have been delivered before a panel of oligarchic judges according to the terms laid out in the covenants, whereas if the trial took place after the dissolution of Eleusis, its venue would have been a democratic court. Especially striking in the speech is its democratic turn of phrase, which has led some to question whether the judges could have been oligarchs.[47] But it is made abundantly clear from the various appeals which Lysias makes to the adjudicating panel that it comprised democrats. At §87, he issues a warning against collaborators who 'think you good-natured and remiss, if they think they can rescue the Thirty without punishment through your democracy' (σφόδρα ἐπιλήσμονας καὶ εὐήθεις νομίζοντες ὑμᾶς εἶναι, εἰ διὰ μὲν τοῦ ὑμετέρου πλήθους ἀδεῶς ἡγοῦνται τοὺς τριάκοντα σώσειν). After the Reconciliation, everyone at least in theory was now a democrat. The old scourge of political division had been banished, and even if the judges in this trial comprised former members of the City Party, this had very little consequence. §§92–4 show that the audience was the City Party itself. Lysias goes out of his way to point out here that those whom the Thirty had wronged were the City Party, and therefore, as judges from the City Party, it was in their collective interest to punish those on trial for what had happened.[48] The appeal to the sense of injustice which his audience should feel at the injustices perpetrated against them under the Thirty puts the democratic rhetoric into sharper perspective. Of course, Lysias plays to a democratic gallery, because after the exchange of oaths democracy was restored and the ideology of democracy reified to banish any further ideological division.

The democratic language of Lys. 12 reflects not a later date when all vestiges of the old party divisions had vanished in the courts, but the fact that after 12 Boedromion 403 democracy was restored, and all memory of ideological

---

[46] Todd 2020: 35, 136–7, 216–17, 231–3.
[47] Covenant 17, the rule governing the composition of the adjudicating panels which heard the trials of oligarchs who submitted to public accounting, did not specify that the judges themselves were to show a property qualification. The awkward phrase τὰ τιμήματα παρεχομένοις should be amended to τὰ τιμήματα παρεχομένους so that it is the oligarchs who offer securities, not the judges who meet wealth criteria (see Chapter 3). Such a textual emendation gets part of the way towards resolving the quandary of the trial, whose language and phraseology is unmistakably democratic. The jurisdiction rule spelled out at covenant 17 stated that the judges were to come from the City Party, presumably as a gesture to ensure that the oligarchs who submitted to audit got a fair hearing.
[48] Carawan (2013: 155) is aware of this reference but fails to reflect sufficiently on its implications.

division officially banished. It should not matter, in context, that the tribunal which heard the audit was made of judges from the City Party. Had Lysias addressed his audience in any other way, that would have reinforced the very feeling of division which the Amnesty went out of its way to ameliorate. Of course, there were at Athens, no doubt well into the fourth century, those who continued to harbour oligarchic sympathies and privately never reconciled with the democratic victory. But the brilliance of this speech is the way it seeks to marginalise oligarchy as a force still to be reckoned with by eliminating any perception of an ongoing ideological difference between the men of the City and men of Piraeus and casting the division as between his audience (the City Party) and the oligarchs on trial. The case of Lys. 12 gives precious evidence for how the jurisdiction rule worked in the immediate wake of the Amnesty. To guarantee fair hearings, those who submitted to audit did so in the presence of those they had governed. This stood in keeping with democratic principle: why, in the ordinary democratic process, should a group of public officials be heard by anyone apart from those over whom they had formerly governed? The reason why the Thirty, Ten and Eleven were given an option of submitting to account before the City Party is not because the City Party was officially or publicly more oligarchic than anyone else, but because, legally speaking, it would have been inappropriate for the oligarchs to have been adjudicated by those over whom they had not wielded former jurisdiction. The entire set-up conforms to the democratic notion that fairness is to be measured not by the predicted sympathies of the judges, but by the matter of whether the judges were qualified to hear a trial unless it directly bore upon them. Though there was the vestige of the old City Party, it was no longer in any recognised sense 'oligarchic', and so when addressing the judges it made perfectly good sense, both legally and ideologically, for a litigator to use a democratic turn of phrase, when appealing to the trope 'your democracy'.

Like the trial of Agoratus, the prosecution of Eratosthenes turns on the legal matter of whether the defendant was guilty. It might be argued that the harangue puts Lys. 12 into a context of political feuding, whereby democrats were not really adhering to their commitment to let bygones be bygones. That would be to miss the point in a spectacular way. The trial of Eratosthenes was admissible because it adhered to the legal requirement that members of the Thirty, Ten and Eleven should submit to audit if they wished to be protected under the clauses of the Amnesty. The trial followed a legal principle from start to finish. The old theory that this was a homicide trial along the same lines of Lys. 13 is broadly untenable and has been rejected by an overwhelming majority of scholars since the discovery of the *Ath. Pol.* Knowing nothing of the 'exception to the exception' rule, Rauchenstein in the nineteenth century maintained that Eratosthenes had submitted to audit but that this trial was not the same as that audit, but a later trial after the subjection of Eleusis in 401. Though writing after the publication of the London papyrus in 1891, Cloché himself supposed that two sets of trials took place, audits in keeping with covenants 16 and 17, and homicide trials which were held subsequently against oligarchs who passed the audits.[49] The problem with Cloché's interpretation is that it needs to imagine that special exemptions were made in the clauses of the Amnesty for categories of killing, but this is untrue. Furthermore, as MacDowell has pointed out, in homicide proceedings witnesses as well as prosecutors swore. No such oath is in evidence in Lys. 12.[50] It is easiest to think that the legal process at which Lysias delivered his attack on Eratosthenes was *euthynai*, and that the trial reflected at Lys. 12 is the only historical example in the oratorical corpus of the application of the 'exception to the exception' rule outlined in the clauses of 403.

This trial adhered to the legal rule which made hearings against the Thirty, Ten and Eleven admissible. Scholars have sometimes speculated whether more than one person was on trial in Lys. 12. Though it is ostensibly aimed at the defendant Eratosthenes, Lysias in various places in the speech (§§21–2, 35–6, 79–80, 81–3) speaks of 'these men' in the plural, as if more than one man stood in the dock.[51] Cloché supposed that the war with Eleusis was ongoing at the time of the speech's delivery and that the references to 'these men' are not to men standing physically in the court, but men at Eleusis who were ready to plan to subvert democracy a second time if the outcome of the trial stood in Eratosthenes' favour. *Pace* Cloché, there is no clear evidence in Lys. 12 that a war with Eleusis was raging at the time of the trial; that was Cloché's own interpretation based on his broader claim that the terms of settlement, as outlined at *Ath. Pol.* 39, were not contracted in their most evolved form until 401, when Eleusis was brought to surrender. But Cloché was right to argue that Lysias' turn of phrase implies an abstraction, so that 'these men' does not literally point to men present in the court at the time of delivery, but stands as a bracketed phrase to refer pejoratively to all the oligarchs, whether they had taken flight or had stayed to stand trial. The prosecution states explicitly at §54 that all the oligarchs save for Eratosthenes and Pheidon had taken flight, and in the light of that statement it would be difficult to imagine more than one co-defendant in the trial. As it stands, the text implies that only two oligarchs were present, and that even if Pheidon was physically present in court, this was a hearing against Eratosthenes alone, almost certainly after the return of the democrats.

---

[49] Cloché 1915: 327–30.
[50] MacDowell 1963: 98–9.
[51] On the use of the rhetorical formulation to imply a collective condemnation of the Thirty, even though only one of their members was on trial, see Adams 1905: 77 and, more recently, Todd 2020: 124 and 134.

The working of the legal principle which allowed hearings against the Thirty to proceed is in full evidence in the opening sections of Eratosthenes' trial (Lys. 12.1–2). Lysias begins by referring to the matter of enmity (ἔχθρα), a word which appears with frequency in the opening passages. It would be superficially tempting to infer that the matter at stake was a personal feud, but close examination of the context of ἔχθρα frames it in legal terminology.[52] The point which Lysias makes from the very start is that this trial does *not* proceed from motives of private grudge. Whereas in former times prosecutors might have had to explain the reasons for harbouring enmity against the defendant (ἔδει τὴν ἔχθραν τοὺς κατηγοροῦντας ἐπιδεῖξαι), now it behoves the defendants in this trial to explain their enmity against the city (νυνὶ δὲ παρὰ τῶν φευγόντων χρὴ πυνθάνεσθαι ἥτις ἦν αὐτοῖς πρὸς τὴν πόλιν ἔχθρα). By framing the matter thus, Lysias absolves himself of all taint of personal enmity as a motive behind the prosecution. Of course, as the brother of the man whom Eratosthenes murdered, Lysias is understandably aggrieved, but that is why the prosecution goes the extra mile to clarify that the grounds upon which the trial stands is not personal, but legal. Eratosthenes is liable not just to Lysias *but to the whole city*. Like Agoratus', his crime is public and is therefore actionable through a public process. The point is just that Eratosthenes cannot retaliate in self-defence by arguing that the prosecution is acting from private motives, as might have been possible at a time when it was common for political opponents to abuse the judicial process to wage political battles. The allusion to 'former times' must here be a glance back at the sorry period of Cleon and his political successors, when indeed enmity was a motivating factor behind a lot of litigation, and the courts thereby fell into disrepute. As historical evidence for what the restored democracy sought to achieve in 403, this is vital, because it shows that from 403 a conscious effort was made to outlaw personal feuding in the courts. The trial of Eratosthenes proceeds from a legal matter: was he guilty or not of the murder of Polemarchus?

The Thirty wanted to seize the property of some wealthy citizens and metics. Among the intended victims were Lysias and his brother. Lysias escaped, but Polemarchus was arrested and killed, and their property confiscated. The man directly responsible was Eratosthenes, who ordered the arrest. Eratosthenes pleaded that there were mitigating circumstances, as he was acting through fear of the Thirty and had gone out of his way to oppose the execution of the two

---

[52] Phillips (2008: 15) defines personal enmity as a 'socially recognised state of active mutual hostility, with established norms governing its proper and expected conduct'. For a discussion of the operation of those norms elsewhere in Lysias, see Todd 2007: 336, 349 with n. 6. Yet it is also important to recognise the force of πρότερον μέν at the start of §2, where a contrast is being drawn between the operation of enmity in former time and the new norms of reconciliation where such motives of enmity are to be banished.

brothers. Lysias rebuts that plea by claiming that if Eratosthenes had been favourably disposed it is unlikely that the other members of the Thirty would have selected him for the task. Besides, the arrest was made in the broad light of day rather than at a time or place where it could not have been observed, and if the defendant had been a friend to Polemarchus as he claims, he might have warned him in advance. If the defendant could plead public services to the democracy to make any of this seem less likely, there might have been some reason to doubt what was being alleged. But Eratosthenes could point to no public benefaction to the city during the bleak months of the Thirty. There is no reason therefore to suppose that he was a 'moderate' oligarch who tried whatever he could to ameliorate the more appalling excesses of Critias. Nothing said in his defence can soften the brute fact that he was a member of the Thirty and had brought about the same level of violence and suffering as the most notorious members of that regime. We are reminded here of the plea which Agoratus made in his own defence, that he had fought for the democrats at Phyle. Unlike Agoratus, however, Eratosthenes could point to no democratic credential of the kind. The legal principle, was Eratosthenes guilty or not, could not be made clearer than at §25, where Lysias puts the matter plainly: did you arrest Polemarchus or no? Were you in the Council-chamber when the depositions were made? Did you oppose the death sentence? Did you believe that the charges laid against the victims of the Thirty were just or otherwise?[53] Eratosthenes could not deny that he had authorised the arrest, but in defence argued that he opposed the death penalty and that his guilt was therefore less.

The legal matter which follows is whether any of the defence is believable. Even if the defendant was truthful in the claim that he had opposed the death sentence, there is no reason to credit the plea that he acted under orders when instructing the arrest of the brothers. If the Thirty had wanted to test his loyalty, would they not have ordered him to arrest a citizen of high standing rather than a pair of metics? Can it be believed that the man who had opposed the death sentence would have ordered the arrests? Besides, it cannot be argued in his self-defence that Eratosthenes had acted on instructions, because as a member of the Thirty himself there was no higher authority which could have instructed him. If this had been a case of a lesser citizen collaborating with the Thirty through fear or deference to a higher power, then the arguments put in defence might have had some merit. By contrast, the arguments presented here by the defendant have no merit whatsoever,

---

[53] The participle δεδιώς seems to indicate that Eratosthenes made a plea that he was acting under direct orders from the Thirty. But Krentz (1984) argued instead that it was the Thirty who were acting through fear of a counter-revolutionary activity at the hands of Lysias and Polemarchus, and thus redates the arrest of the metics to the period after Thrasybulus' march on Phyle; *contra* Sommerstein 1984: 370; Todd 2020: 127–8.

because he was among the highest authority in the city at the time. The clearest evidence that the prosecution proceeds from a legal, and not a personal, motive is to be found in what follows at §34: if the judges were related to the defendant, that would still not have been a reason to acquit him; Eratosthenes needs to be able to prove one of two points, either that he did not carry out the arrest, or that he did authorise arrest but did so with justice on his side. As neither point can be demonstrated, the defendant must be guilty as charged and merit death in keeping with the law (§37).[54] Lysias proceeds to smear Eratosthenes further by drawing attention to his filthy history with the Four Hundred in 411 and with the events of 404 which led to the installation of the oligarchy after the naval disaster at Aegospotami. As argued in Chapter 2, the effort to discredit Theramenes in Lys. 12 is driven by a need to reduce in the perception of the judges any moral distinction between moderate and extreme oligarchs, to show that all oligarchs were fundamentally the same and any plea which Eratosthenes might produce to lessen his association with Critias could not hold up to the light of reason.

The issue, therefore, is why Eratosthenes chose to stay at Athens after the expulsion of the Thirty. Presumably, he hoped that his moderate credentials would swing the case before a partially sympathetic adjudicating panel. Here, it was crucial for Lysias to reduce any sense that a distinction between 'moderate' and 'extreme' could plausibly be maintained. This is the reason why he moves on to the period which followed the fall of the Thirty, in order to show that the oligarchy of the Ten, upon which Eratosthenes did not serve, but with which he was associated in some way through his political connection to Pheidon, who did serve on the Ten, was no better than the Thirty which preceded it. Presumably, Eratosthenes believed that by maintaining a connection with Pheidon, he could persuade the judges that he was better than the other twenty-eight members of the Thirty who took flight in May 403, and that therefore he was not guilty of the charge which had been laid against him. The job of Lysias is now to show that any attempt to ameliorate responsibility by claiming that Pheidon or the Ten can be differentiated morally from the Thirty was vain, and that by protesting a connection with those who remained in the government of the city after the Thirty departed, Eratosthenes was sullying his reputation even further. It has been alleged recently that Eratosthenes did not stay after May 403. The implication of Lys. 12.53–8 is very clear that he did, but all this has come under fire in recent years, chiefly on the grounds that the MSS of Lys. 12 are unreliable. The question is of crucial significance in the way we interpret the speech, and in order to understand how Lysias

---

[54] For a summary of modern scholarly discussion as to how the transitional passage at §§37–41 fits in with the broader structure of the speech, see Todd 2020: 140 with n. 137.

THE AMNESTY APPLIED (I)   151

connects this with the rest of his legal case, we need to follow the arguments carefully.

The passage in question is Lys. 12.53–8, which needs to be quoted in full:

[53] ἐπειδὴ δὲ εἰς τὸν Πειραιᾶ ἤλθομεν καὶ αἱ ταραχαὶ γεγενημέναι ἦσαν καὶ περὶ τῶν διαλλαγῶν οἱ λόγοι ἐγίγνοντο, πολλὰς ἑκάτεροι ἐλπίδας εἴχομεν πρὸς ἀλλήλους ἔσεσθαι, ὡς ἀμφότεροι ἔδειξαν. οἱ μὲν γὰρ ἐκ Πειραιῶς κρείττους ὄντες εἴασαν [54] αὐτοὺς ἀπελθεῖν· οἱ δὲ εἰς τὸ ἄστυ ἐλθόντες τοὺς μὲν τριάκοντα ἐξέβαλον πλὴν Φείδωνος καὶ Ἐρατοσθένους, ἄρχοντας δὲ τοὺς ἐκείνοις ἐχθίστους εἵλοντο, ἡγούμενοι δικαίως ἂν ὑπὸ τῶν αὐτῶν τούς τε τριάκοντα μισεῖσθαι καὶ τοὺς ἐν Πειραιεῖ φιλεῖσθαι. [55] τούτων τοίνυν Φείδων {ὁ τῶν τριάκοντα γενόμενος} καὶ Ἱπποκλῆς καὶ Ἐπιχάρης ὁ Λαμπτρεὺς καὶ ἕτεροι οἱ δοκοῦντες εἶναι ἐναντιώτατοι Χαρικλεῖ καὶ Κριτίᾳ καὶ τῇ ἐκείνων ἑταιρείᾳ, ἐπειδὴ αὐτοὶ εἰς τὴν ἀρχὴν κατέστησαν, πολὺ μείζω στάσιν καὶ πόλεμον ἐπὶ τοὺς ἐν Πειραιεῖ ἢ τοῖς ἐξ ἄστεως ἐποίησαν. [56] ᾧ καὶ φανερῶς ἐπεδείξαντο ὅτι οὐχ ὑπὲρ τῶν ἐν Πειραιεῖ οὐδ᾽ ὑπὲρ τῶν ἀδίκως ἀπολλυμένων ἐστασίαζον, οὐδ᾽ οἱ τεθνεῶτες αὐτοὺς ἐλύπουν οὐδ᾽ οἱ μέλλοντες ἀποθανεῖσθαι, ἀλλ᾽ οἱ μεῖζον δυνάμενοι καὶ θᾶττον πλουτοῦντες. [57] λαβόντες γὰρ τὰς ἀρχὰς καὶ τὴν πόλιν ἀμφοτέροις ἐπολέμουν, τοῖς τε τριάκοντα πάντα κακὰ εἰργασμένοις καὶ ὑμῖν πάντα κακὰ πεπονθόσι. καίτοι τοῦτο πᾶσι δῆλον ἦν, ὅτι εἰ μὲν ἐκεῖνοι δικαίως ἔφευγον, ὑμεῖς ἀδίκως, εἰ δ᾽ ὑμεῖς δικαίως, οἱ τριάκοντα ἀδίκως· οὐ γὰρ δὴ ἑτέρων ἔργων αἰτίαν λαβόντες ἐκ τῆς πόλεως ἐξέπεσον, [58] ἀλλὰ τούτων. ὥστε σφόδρα χρὴ ὀργίζεσθαι, ὅτι Φείδων αἱρεθεὶς ὑμᾶς διαλλάξαι καὶ καταγαγεῖν τῶν αὐτῶν ἔργων Ἐρατοσθένει μετεῖχε καὶ τῇ αὐτῇ γνώμῃ τοὺς μὲν κρείττους αὐτῶν δι᾽ ὑμᾶς κακῶς ποιεῖν ἕτοιμος ἦν, ὑμῖν δὲ ἀδίκως φεύγουσιν οὐκ ἠθέλησεν ἀποδοῦναι τὴν πόλιν, ἀλλ᾽ ἐλθὼν εἰς Λακεδαίμονα ἔπειθεν αὐτοὺς στρατεύεσθαι, διαβάλλων ὅτι Βοιωτῶν ἡ πόλις ἔσται, καὶ ἄλλα λέγων οἷ᾽ ᾤετο πείσειν μάλιστα.

[53] After we came to the Piraeus and the troubles had happened and negotiations were under way concerning the exchanges, each side held hopes that there would be a reconciliation between them, as each side made clear. For the Piraeus Party being strong permitted [54] them to depart; and they, coming to the town, cast out (ἐξέβαλον) the Thirty, except Pheidon and Eratosthenes, and chose leaders most hateful to them, thinking that the Thirty would be justly hated by them and the Piraeus Party loved. [55] Now among these were Pheidon {who had been one of the Thirty}, Hippocles, and Epichares of the district of Lamptra, with others who were thought to be most opposed to Charicles and Critias and

their *hetaireia*; but as soon as they in their turn were raised to power, they set up a far sharper dissension and warfare between the parties of the town and of the Piraeus, [56] and thereby revealed in all clearness that their faction was not working for the Piraeus Party nor for those who were being unjustly destroyed; and that their vexation lay, not in those who had been or were about to be put to death, but in those who had greater power or were more speedily enriched. [57] For having got hold of their offices and the city they made war on both sides, – on the Thirty who had wrought every kind of evil, and on you who had suffered it in every way. And yet one thing was clear to all men, – that if the exile of the Thirty was just, yours was unjust while if yours was just, that of the Thirty was unjust; for it was not as answerable for some other acts that they were banished from the city, but simply for these. [58] It ought therefore to be a matter for the deepest resentment that Pheidon, after being chosen to reconcile and restore you, joined in the same courses as Eratosthenes and, working on the same plan, was ready enough to injure the superior members of his party on your account, but unwilling to restore the city to you who were in unjust exile: he went to Sparta, and urged them to march out, insinuating that the city would be falling into the hands of the Boeotians, with other statements calculated to induce them. (tr. R. W. M. Lamb)

The important phrase is πλὴν Φείδωνος καὶ Ἐρατοσθένους ('except Pheidon and Eratosthenes') at §54. Taken as read, this shows that Eratosthenes stayed at Athens in 403 when the Thirty were sent into exile. The implication is that because he believed himself to have been a milder oligarch than the rest, Eratosthenes together with his political associate Pheidon took the risk of staying at Athens after the departure of the Thirty, in the hope that their plea not to have committed wrong would be heeded.[55] The MSS are clear on the point. However, to defend the theory that the contracts of 403 did not entail the 'exception to the exception' rule, it has been argued recently that the expression 'except for Eratosthenes and Pheidon' did not appear in the original speech. Words and phrases which caused nineteenth-century scholars, who knew nothing of the Aristotelian *Ath. Pol.*, justifiable anxiety and puzzlement have been excised in support of the claim. In the nineteenth century, it was held on the strength of the evidence available at that time that the arrangements of Reconciliation were not finally contracted until 401, when Eleusis was brought to terms. The allusion at Lys. 12.54 was a problem, because it must show that some of the oligarchs remained at Athens in 403 and did not

---

[55] The only other secure reference to Pheidon as a member of the Thirty is at X. *HG* 2.3.2, where he is named as number twenty-five on the list, but normally he is mentioned as one of the Ten, as at §55.

take up residence at Eleusis. Now that we have the continuous narrative of *Ath. Pol.* 39, this is a problem no longer, as we know that contractual arrangements were made in 403 at the time of the Reconciliation for oligarchs who did not choose to emigrate to submit to audit and defend themselves before democratic tribunals. The case presented by Eratosthenes in self-defence, which Lysias refutes, was that he had acted under compulsion.[56]

Pheidon became a member of the Ten who succeeded the Thirty after their departure to Eleusis, along with Hippocles and Epichares of Lamptra. The City Ten were chosen, according to Lysias, because it was initially hoped that these men would be hostile to the regime of the Thirty and that the City Party had a chance to negotiate with the Piraeus Party, which was gaining the upper hand militarily by the end of 404, once the Ten were in post. However, once those Ten got a taste of power, they resumed the lamentable record of their predecessors, in keeping with the oligarchic legacy to which they belonged (§§55–6). Lysias needs to argue this to show that the connection with Pheidon was insufficient as a plea that Eratosthenes was less guilty of the crimes of the Thirty. At the start of §55, the MSS make reference to Pheidon, 'who had been a member of the Thirty' (ὁ τῶν τριάκοντα γενόμενος), which H. Frohberger bracketed off down to τριάκοντα, on the basis that it was unnecessary within the flow of the argument. But even if the phrase is the product of editorial interpolation, the point which Lysias here makes is that the reason Pheidon and Eratosthenes remained at Athens after the expulsion of the Thirty was that of all the former oligarchs, these were the only two apart from Theramenes who had taken a decisive stand against Critias and the more extreme wing of the oligarchy. Presumably, this was the reason Eratosthenes was willing to risk his arm in remaining at Athens after 404. There is no textual justification for eradicating Eratosthenes at §54, since the MSS are consistent on the point. Uniformity among the MSS is not always a clinching reason to hold to a traditional reading, but if a new reading is offered against the uniformity of a textual tradition, there need to be external grounds to edit the text, so that a new modern interpolation or extraction is felt to be preferable to what the MSS have handed down. No such grounds present themselves. Had we not known that arrangements were made in 403 for 'moderate' oligarchs like Eratosthenes to defend themselves before a democratic court under the 'exception to the exception', we might have wished to edit the text. Yet even the nineteenth century, ignorant as it was of the provisions laid out at *Ath. Pol.* 39.6, did not make the move of extracting Eratosthenes' name from the one

---

[56] Recognising the objections which §54 presents, Carawan (2013: 154–60) argues them away by claiming that the statement that Eratosthenes and Pheidon had not taken refuge when the Thirty were expelled was never included in the original MS.

vital piece of literary testimony which places not only this trial, but indeed the application of the 'exception to the exception' rule outlined at *Ath. Pol.* 39.6, in the full light of day. The evidence is unequivocal: Eratosthenes and Pheidon stayed behind because they had opposed the extreme wing of the oligarchy while the Thirty were enthroned, and the latter was chosen on the strength of those credentials to lead the Ten. Eratosthenes chose the riskier course of action, to stay at Athens rather than emigrate, because he now had a friend and associate in power who could represent his position before a potentially hostile populace which, as Lys. 12 indicates, had suffered appallingly under the ousted regime.

The verb used at Lys. 12.54 is ἐξέβαλον, which can be understood in one of two ways. Either it can mean 'they ejected him from the panel' or it can mean 'they exiled him'. Ejection from position of power is certainly one of the ways in which the verb is attested in the orators, as at Isoc. 4.70; 5.63 and at Aeschin. 2.9, but it is also attested in the sense of exile, as at D. 21.146. Often, some other qualifying expression such as ἐκ τῆς πόλεως makes it clear that expulsion, rather than demotion from office, was meant.[57] The recent objection to the exception stated at §54 is that if Eratosthenes had stayed, it would not have been in the capacity of a private citizen living under the Ten, but as a holdover from one regime to the next, alongside Pheidon. We know from other evidence (*Ath. Pol.* 38.4) that no member of the Ten, not Pheidon or any of his colleagues, stood trial after 403. If, therefore, Eratosthenes had been a holdover rather than a private citizen demoted from position in government, as might be the implication of Lys. 12.54, he might not have been held to account subsequently on the strength of the statement at *Ath. Pol.* 38.4, that not one of the Ten ever submitted to audit. Eratosthenes did stand trial. Thus, it is argued, he could not have been one of the Ten, and so, following the argument, his name needs to be removed at the crucial point.

But, as formulated, the argument is self-refuting. If ἐξέβαλον is taken to mean 'demoted' rather than 'exiled', as is the traditional understanding, then by the logic of the argument as presented, none of the Thirty left Athens in spring 403! This is the inverse of what we are being asked by the revisionist position to believe. On the alternative reconstruction, *all* the former oligarchy, Eratosthenes included, left for Eleusis, and if that is true, it would be absurd to interpret ἐξέβαλον as if it meant 'demoted'. The least problematic way of approaching §54 is to read it as the MSS preserve it for us: the City Party, realising that the government of the Thirty was no longer tenable, drove them out, all except for Pheidon and Eratosthenes, the former of whom became a member of the Ten, the latter of whom remained as a private citizen and, in 403, stood trial for his part in the Thirty.

---

[57] Compare Lys. 1.44; 4.13; 14.36; 25.9. For a survey and discussion of its uses, see Todd 2020: 167.

In line with Frohberger's emendation of ὁ τῶν τριάκοντα at §55, it has been suggested recently that Pheidon was no longer among the Thirty at the time of their deposition from office, and that this can only make sense if we remove the phrase at §54, which begins with the adverbial πλήν.[58] If the exception of Pheidon and Eratosthenes is edited, it is argued, the fact that Pheidon was chosen to lead the Ten makes better sense, because otherwise Pheidon must have been on the board at the time of their overthrow in spring 403. To support that conjecture, speculations have arisen that Pheidon had at one time been a member of the Thirty but had lost his place at an earlier juncture, perhaps at the time when Theramenes was placed at loggerheads with Critias, and Pheidon took the former side. The text of Lys. 12 shows that Pheidon was among the Thirty at the time they were deposed, and we know of no other episode, either from Lys. 12 or from other evidence, when Pheidon fell foul of the oligarchs. On that reconstruction, by the fall of the Thirty Pheidon had already become a private citizen, so that when Eratosthenes and the remainder of the Thirty departed for Eleusis, Pheidon stepped up from retirement to become the leader of the Ten. That conjecture is bolstered by the speculation that despite the implication of §§54–61 that Pheidon was present at the trial of Eratosthenes, nothing in the text decisively indicates that he was present at the time of the trial. On that line of reasoning, the cases of Pheidon and Eratosthenes are distinct and separate from one another: Eratosthenes was driven out in April or May 403, along with the Thirty with whom he was associated, and did not return to the city until after the dissolution of the Eleusinian enclave in 401, whereupon he submitted to audit, whereas Pheidon came to power in spring 403 and was driven out a bit later, when the City Party realised that it had installed a regime as bad as the Thirty it had replaced.

The problematic passage is §57, which uses the demonstrative pronoun ἐκεῖνοι to refer to a group of fugitives, usually understood to be the Thirty. In contrast, this might be a reference not to the Thirty but to the Ten, of whom Pheidon was the leader. This is important, because the next section (§58) reveals that anger arose with Pheidon for rogue acts against the people: if ἐκεῖνοι at §57 is understood to refer to the Ten, then there are grounds to dissociate Pheidon from the Thirty.[59] In order to situate Lys. 12 in the context of 401 rather than 403, Carawan needs to distance the two cases of Pheidon and Eratosthenes historically from one another. Yet it is clear from the passage that follows that the two are closely linked. §58 implies that Pheidon 'joined

---

[58] Carawan 2013: 154–60. As Todd argues (2020: 169 n. 211), the reason the phrase ὁ τῶν τριάκοντα is bracketed off at this point is that it is otiose to have repeated what is already made clear at §54. This has no real historical bearing upon whether Pheidon was a member of the board at the time of his deposition.

[59] Todd (2020: 173) more plausibly reads ἐκεῖνοι at §57 as referring to the Thirty, not to the Ten.

with' Eratosthenes in conspiring against the interests of the people, which at face value implies that Eratosthenes was present at Athens at the time when Pheidon assumed power as leader of the Ten. This could be read to mean that Pheidon carried on in the tradition of Eratosthenes, but that is not what Lysias says. The point is that Pheidon and Eratosthenes partook of the *same* acts, meaning that whether or not Eratosthenes was among the Ten, he was still around at the time when the Ten came to power and presumably acted in close collaboration with them. The explicit linking of the two notorious criminals in these various crimes and delicts against the people is more than a mere rhetorical slur. The point Lysias makes is that even if Eratosthenes could argue that he was less extreme among the Thirty than Critias, his actions subsequent to the fall of the Thirty, when the Ten assumed government, show that he was just as bad as the worst oligarchs. Far from being the intermediary between the City Party and the democrats at Piraeus, the Ten turned out to be as ghastly as those they replaced.

On a natural reading, Lys. 12.53–8 illustrates that Eratosthenes remained at Athens after the Thirty were driven into exile and stood trial later in 403, after the democracy was restored, in accordance with the provisions set out in the 'exception to the exception' rule. The appeal to justice and reconciliation is central to the speech for the prosecution. Its closing sections put the matter succinctly: in the time of the Thirty, there was an absence of justice in the city, but now that democracy has returned, justice also has returned (Lys. 12.92–8). The trial of the defendant is about applying the principle of justice, in order to reconcile the two sides of the former civil conflict. When the Thirty were in power, there was division; now that they are gone, there is no division left. The point of all this is that by reinstating the rule of law through the courts, the democrats had created conditions not where further recrimination could happen but, on the contrary, where the possibility of recrimination and backslide into civil war could be avoided. The court was an instrument of justice, not of feuding. The allusion to the battles waged between the two parties does not violate the rule μὴ μνησικακεῖν but indeed adheres to it. The reason why we are putting Eratosthenes on trial is not because we want to reopen the conflict, but because we want the conflict to be resolved by bringing to justice those directly responsible and by ensuring thereby that those less responsible, who had been caught up in the crossfire of historical turmoil, would not suffer illegal recrimination contrary to the Amnesty settlement. Lysias appeals to the City Party as victims of the Thirty. Whether this was strictly true is of secondary importance. Within the logic of the argument, both sides of the erstwhile conflict were victims, and therefore it stands to reason that they bring to justice those who had caused them untold suffering in the period of the oligarchy. The 'us' versus 'them' is now turned on its head: if there is any division left in the city, it is between all of us (City Party and Piraeus Party) on one side versus the common enemy, the Thirty, the Ten and the Eleven, on the other. Though the language of recrimination is used, especially at §94 where Lysias calls upon the judges to join the Piraeus Party in punishing the malefactors (καὶ ὑπὲρ ὑμῶν αὐτῶν καὶ ὑπὲρ τῶν ἐκ Πειραιῶς τιμωρήσασθε), the language of vengeance perhaps ironically has a message of reconciliation buried within it, as the καὶ . . . καὶ ('both . . . and') signals a spirit of unity between the two sides of the former civil war. It would be wrong and misleading to read Lys. 12 as if it represented a return to the litigious practices of the sycophants. A careful reading of its format, structure and language has shown that, like the trial of Agoratus, it illustrates the rule of law being applied through the courts, which, as argued in Chapter 4, was the greatest achievement of the democrats when they returned from exile in 403 and restored democracy.

CHAPTER 6

The Amnesty Applied (II): The Trials of Callimachus and Socrates

The cases discussed in Chapter 5 against Agoratus and Eratosthenes illustrate the effectiveness of the Amnesty to block litigation which recalled wrongs committed under the Thirty. The first of these, the trial of Agoratus, at first sight seems to have violated the rule μὴ μνησικακεῖν which blocked frivolous litigation against those who were not among the Thirty, Ten or Eleven. Though a close conspirator and confidante of the Thirty, Agoratus had not sat on any of the boards whose members were exempted under covenant 16 (see Chapter 3). Though scholars have sought routes around this, none of the suggestions made to date pass muster. The closest suggestion to the truth that has been advanced to date is that though the Amnesty did put legal measures in place to prevent trials of this kind from happening, in the wake of the ousted oligarchy, restored citizens, despite their oaths, harboured such anger that they engaged in court litigation which was strictly illegal under the terms of the covenants. But even that is to miss a deeper point: the trial of Agoratus is evidence not of the ineffectiveness of the Reconciliation but, on the contrary, of its enormous and widespread efficacy. If the trial was inadmissible, there was nevertheless a legal grey area over whether crimes which had had such enormous significance in bringing down democracy in 404 could be relegated into same bracket of the exception made in the Amnesty clauses for the Thirty, Ten and Eleven, even if the person who committed them was not a member of any of those boards. The speech has survived in the record precisely because it exemplifies the enormous efforts litigators had to canvass in order to argue their way around the rule which specified that untried cases predating 403, whether relating to the period of oligarchy or even before, were now inadmissible. The speaker of Lys. 13 alludes to the Amnesty in anticipation that the defendant would cite it, and in that expectation presents a skewed interpretation of the

Amnesty clause μὴ μνησικακεῖν which the defence would have found easy to refute. The trial of Eratosthenes, in contrast, was admissible because the defendant had sat on the board of the Thirty. Despite the efforts of some to downdate the trial to the period after the suppression of Eleusis in 401, the natural timing of the hearing is autumn 403, when Eratosthenes, by self-profession one of the milder oligarchs, underwent audit. Like that of Agoratus, the trial of Eratosthenes was framed in legal language. Though calls to avenge the sufferings of democrats were invoked, none of this stood in violation of the rule not to bear grudges, because the motive behind the trial was not a private vendetta but a legal point of issue.

This chapter turns to two other notorious cases, those of Callimachus and Socrates. The former is important because it illustrates what could already have been inferred from the trial of Agoratus, that litigators after 403 were violating legal principle in the courts, and so further legislation was needed to discourage frivolous action. Unlike the prosecution of Agoratus, the speaker of Isoc. 18 was on the receiving end of a potential illegal lawsuit and so appealed to a law passed shortly thereafter setting out a special process of *paragraphê*, whereby a defendant in an inadmissible lawsuit could turn the tables on the opposition and prosecute for damages. What is clear from this speech is that in the aftermath of the Amnesty unlawful trials were being taken before the court, and this might induce some to infer that the efficacy of the Amnesty was weak and that angry citizens who felt aggrieved tried their best to reopen issues now closed. To argue in that way is to assume that the case of Callimachus had anything to do with the Amnesty. As argued below, in strict point of law the trial of Callimachus was about the violation not of the covenants of 403, but of the principle of *res iudicata* which underpinned the Athenian judicial system. Apparently, in the aftermath of 403 that principle was repeatedly violated. The response was further legislation making litigation less easy. The trial of Socrates is different in kind from that of Callimachus but has one important feature in common with it, which is that in a strict sense it had little bearing on the Amnesty. Of all the trials under discussion, the last is the most difficult and tenuous to analyse in any methodical way, for the simple reason that 'historical' evidence fails us. Plato's *Apology*, which at least claims to reproduce the case of the defence, is not to be read like a speech from the oratorical corpus, and as experts on the Platonic dialogues have shown, the construction of the *Apology* has a philosophical purpose and must not be treated as an exact replica of the trial. Because we do not have such a replica, we are hard-pressed to access the historical trial of Socrates or to deduce from it the application of the Amnesty. Attention is given only because it has featured in modern discussions of how the Amnesty was applied, but discussion comes with the caveat that the historical 'trial of Socrates' cannot be resurrected from the ashes of the documentation. They are paired together because they illustrate the application of the Amnesty as a moral rather than a legal principle, and in that sense are different in kind from the two trials studied in Chapter 5. With the trial of Socrates, it is tempting to believe that the real issue at stake was less a religious offence than political connections with oligarchs, yet a careful overview of the terms and principles will show that the Clauses of Amnesty bore little relevance to the issue of the trial. In short, neither of these trials, of Callimachus or Socrates, should be quoted as evidence that the Amnesty was anything less than a meaningful, lasting and tenable commitment which, though unpopular and painful among many citizens, remained legally sacrosanct and applicable in the fourth century.

THE TRIAL OF CALLIMACHUS, C. 403–400 (ISOC. 18)

In the opening to the case for the prosecution under the rule of *paragraphê*, the speaker of Isoc. 18 attests that after returning from Piraeus, the democrats realised that the Oaths and Covenants of Reconciliation were proving insufficient to prevent litigants going to court and trying to undo the terms of the Amnesty.[1] In response, Archinus proposed a law enacted by the Assembly, that if anyone should bring a lawsuit contrary to the oaths of settlement, the defendant was entitled to a special plea, which allowed him to initiate the litigation and to speak first, rather than second, and whichever of the parties lost would owe 1,000 drachmas and forfeit the right to bring any public cases in future.[2] The technical legal term for predatory litigation was συκοφάντειν.[3] The tendency was recognised in Athenian law as a perversion of the legal and judicial system, and penalties were established against it in the fourth, and presumably also the fifth, centuries to guarantee that courts were not inundated with vindictive and recriminatory cases which could only have wasted the court's time. The difficulty which Athens faced in the wake of the Reconciliation, however, was that because the rule of reclaim allowed various possibilities of interpretation, the prohibition against reopening old issues was perhaps not as straightforward as the terms of the Amnesty had entailed. Covenants 19 and 20 (Chapter 3) spelled

---

[1] On the workings of *paragraphê* as a legal process, see Paoli 1933; *contra* Wolff 1966; Harrison 1968–71: ii.106–24. For a more up-to-date summary of the relevant issues, see Harris 2013: 72–6.

[2] The dating of the law of Archinus largely depends on how we interpret the sequence of events at Lys. 17, where the plaintiff seems to describe a lengthy *iustitium*. For the dating of the law to the immediate aftermath of the Amnesty on the basis that the ordinary rules for initiating and concluding cases under the same magistrates was probably suspended at the time, see Whitehead 2002; for the downdating of the law to 401/0, see MacDowell 2008. For the nature of the penalty prescribed, see Harris 2015a.

[3] For other attestations of the term used in this sense, see Ar. *Av.* 1431; *Ach.* 828; *Ec.* 562; Lys. 22.1; D. 53.1; 55.1.

out the rule in theory: if a democrat returned and found that his goods had been confiscated by the oligarchs, he was entitled to reclaim provided they had not been sold on to a third party; if that had happened, some private arbitration was necessary so that if property was reclaimed, the third party could receive compensation.[4] This was easy in theory, but in practice it opened up problems. What would happen, for example, if the property of a democrat had been sold on to a fourth or fifth party? How would the right of reclaim have worked had property been damaged or violated? Who was to compensate aggrieved democrats if they found that their property was returned to them in a state which they found unacceptable? The practicality of reclaim was messier than its theory presented. This perhaps explains why, with the best intentions to respect the Amnesty, litigation for events prior to the Reconciliation began to spiral after 403 and why it was essential that to reduce the quantity of such litigation by means of a legal disincentive.

The process of *paragraphê* has been subject to scholarly contention. U. E. Paoli argued that when the rule was applied by one litigant against another on the grounds that the plaint was inadmissible, the matter was decided at the same trial, mainly because the surviving cases brought by *paragraphê* indicate that two legal questions, the wrongfulness of the act and the admissibility of the case, were usually discussed in the same hearing. H. J. Wolff countered that the issue at stake in *paragraphê* hearings was procedural.[5] In a recent reassessment, Harris has taken a middle line, arguing that if the defendant challenged the plaintiff by invoking the special plea and lost, there would be a separate trial to hear the merits of the case. If a plaintiff brought a case whose admissibility was not disputed by the defendant, the substantive issue and the damages were decided at a single trial. If the defendant invoked the special plea and won, that would be the end of the matter. If, however, the court rejected the plea, a separate trial would take place about the plaintiff's original suit, as seems to have been the case in the *paragraphê* brought by Meidias against Demosthenes for slander (D. 21.84).[6] The trial of Callimachus shows the rule of *paragraphê* in action. The matter before the court is whether the case was admissible in virtue of the fact that a ruling had already been given out of court over the payment of moneys. Callimachus had violated the rule of *res iudicata* by bringing action against the plaintiff over a matter which had already been settled. The task of the plaintiff was to show that the matter was now inadmissible as it had been decided in private arbitration. The issue at stake in Isoc. 18 is a technical matter of procedure and no more: by

---

[4] These covenants are reconstructed from Lys. *Against Hippotherses* lines 34–48 and Isoc. 18.20; see Chapter 3.
[5] Paoli 1933: 75–174; *contra* Wolff 1966. Paoli's view has more recently been endorsed by Carawan (2011).
[6] Thus Harris 2015a: 34; cf. also MacDowell 1990: 306–8.

seeking to overturn an earlier verdict, the defendant, that is Callimachus from the point of view of the *paragraphê*, was acting illegally, and therefore the trial was inadmissible. The effort made by the accuser is not to deny wrongdoing but to show that because the question had already been resolved, it could not be reopened. If the court ruled in his favour, that would be the end of it, but if the court ruled against, nothing in the speech indicates that damages would be decided in the same trial; the implication, rather, is that a separate trial would take place at a later point.

The principle that litigants should not reopen legal matters for which there had been prior closure was not new in 403. Before the law of *paragraphê* was introduced shortly after the Oath of Reconciliation was concluded, a special procedure known as the *diamartyria* had existed which granted the defendant in a lawsuit which had already been decided the right of appeal to the archon, who would, if evidence was sufficient to discontinue a case, throw it out of court.[7] The new rule of *paragraphê* was a development of this principle, whereby the plaintiff became the defendant and the defendant the plaintiff; the rule persisted into the late fourth century, and Demosthenes even mentions an additional law which prevented those who had been convicted under the rule of *paragraphê* from transferring their cases to the Assembly (D. 24.52–7).[8] Out-of-court settlements, or *diaitai*, were thus encouraged to reduce the body of litigation handled by the court magistrates.[9] A statute of limitations of up to five years restrained private actions.[10] As a further measure to ease pressure on the courts, litigants were expected to pay a court fee called the *prytaneia*, whose sum varied depending on the gravity of the claim, with the extra stipulation that the quantity should be paid by the litigant who lost.[11] Frivolous litigation was further discouraged by the rule that if a plaintiff did not secure one fifth of the votes, he was subject to a fine of 1,000 drachmas and the loss of the right to bring any public cases again.[12] Thus, Athenian law provided a legal machinery whereby the courts were protected from a deluge of vexatious cases which, if

---

[7] Thus Isoc. 18.11–12; see Harrison 1968–71: ii.124–5.

[8] On the vexed question of the relationship of the Assembly to the lawcourts, see Hansen 1991: 151–5; *contra* Pecorella Longo 2004: 94–103, the latter of whom makes a convincing case that the Assembly stood above the courts in the matter of sovereignty.

[9] Isoc. 18.11; D. 36.25; 37.1; 38.1. On the inauthenticity of the law on arbitrators at D.21.94, see MacDowell 1990: 317–18.

[10] D. 36.25–7; 38.17; Charles 1938; Wolff 1963; Harrison 1968–71: ii.116–20; Harris 2013: 73 n. 36.

[11] Poll. 8.38; Harrison 1968–71: ii.92–4.

[12] D. 18.266; Theophrastus *ap.* schol. 22.3 (13b Dilts); D. 53.1; [D.] 26.9; cf. Hyp. *Eux.* 34; And. 1.33; see further Harris 2006: 405–21; Wallace 2006; MacDowell 2009: 295. Most recently, Carawan (2019) has maintained on the strength of questionable references in D. 18 and other unreliable references in the biographies of Aeschines the existence of some general form of *atimia* imposed by the court in an *ad hoc* fashion, but as Harris (2019a) has shown, those references are confused and unreliable.

left unregulated, would have overwhelmed the judicial system. The problem after 403 was that because Athens had emerged from civil conflict where significant numbers of the population had lost property and where records of sale of confiscated property by the state treasury to third parties were perhaps not always easily obtainable, the courts within a short space of time would have been flooded with litigation, against which added protective measures were required in law.

The fact that a special law on *paragraphê* was passed in or shortly after 403 should not therefore worry us. The law was needed not because the Covenants of Reconciliation were taken half-heartedly, but because their practical application proved more complex than perhaps the *diallaktai* of 403 had initially anticipated.[13] The purpose of the new legislation which followed the closing of the covenants and oaths was not to shore up gaps in the Amnesty or to spell out unwritten principles in law, but to ensure that the application of those principles, which were already recognised as binding, was efficient and systematic.[14] To be sure, the covenants ruled out litigation for issues which predated the Reconciliation, but further discouragements to shady court action were required in order to ensure that the legal principle spelled out in the Treaty of Amnesty was applied in practice. The recent suggestion that the contracts of the Amnesty were not written up, and that when Athenians swore to them, they swore to a sequence of unwritten legal principles which needed to be translated into law, claims no justification in the evidence.[15] The purpose of the laws which ensued was not

---

[13] Contrast Joyce 2015: 44, where I argued that the laws which followed on from the Reconciliation Agreement were not components of that agreement, with Carawan (2013, 83–90), who includes among the covenants principles which were spelled out not by the *diallaktai* but by the lawgivers (*nomothetai*) of 403. As I argued, the laws refined, nuanced and gave a more precise application to the Covenants of Amnesty, but they are not to be confused with them.

[14] In an almost impenetrable maze of reasoning, Carawan (2013: 100–3) seems to imagine that the written format of the contracts had a less binding significance in law than their oral affirmation; this proceeds from a strange understanding of the working of contracts influenced by Millett (1991), on whose flawed methodology see Cohen (E.) 1992.

[15] See Carawan 2013: 108: 'From this perspective [viz. the orality of affirmation] we can see how the Athenians, in the decade after the Amnesty, regarded their obligation under the covenants, and perhaps we can better understand what was confusing or contentious. Their sense of what they are bound to do is fixed by their oath made aloud, not by the visual image of the text; the covenants are a sort of subtext (or "fine print"), not always in mind but nonetheless binding.' The logic behind this series of statements eludes me altogether, not least since the arguments given to downplay their written importance are unclear. If the covenants of 403 were understood as *synthêkai*, they would have had to have been written and then sworn to; on the definition of a *synthêkê* as a written contract dispensed with the intent of publication, see *IG* II² 2492–501; Kußmaul 1969: 37–55; Millett 1991: 171–8. Normally, a contract would have to be written and witnessed, but there are some examples, such as D. 56, where the lender appears to have a valid contract without witness or deposition; thus Cohen (E.) 2005: 297–301.

to 'substantiate' the covenants but to provide further legal definition as to how they were to be applied and imposed.[16] An example of how the law sought to marginalise frivolous litigation in the fourth century appears at Myrrhinous (*IG* II² 1183 lines 16–24), where provisions were passed to ensure that troublesome cases of appeal in the event that a rejected applicant went before the deme did not happen.[17] Of course, the principle that vexatious appeals should be eschewed may already have been written into the constitution of the deme and sworn to by the deme members, but some further legal measure was evidently felt to be necessary to guarantee that the application of that fundamental principle was regular and formalised. The analogy should apply to the law of Archinus: just because a law was passed after the Amnesty enforcing one of its key principles, this should not be read to mean that the Covenants of Amnesty were not written nor themselves legally binding; what is does mean, however, is that additional measures were legislated to ensure that the rule *res iudicata* was properly observed in the aftermath of Athens' most gruesome civil conflict.

The historical background to the trial of Callimachus is traceable in outline. The context is the rule not of the Thirty but of the Ten, probably in the late spring or summer of 403, not long before the return of the democrats and the exchange of the oaths. Callimachus, a member of the City Party, had lost a large sum of money to the state after it had been seized by one of the public officials under the oligarchy, a man called Patrocles, who transferred it to Pamphilus, a democrat of the Piraeus Party. When Callimachus complained, a crowd gathered, and one of the Ten, Rhinon, known also from *Ath. Pol.* 38.4, confiscated the money once a formal denunciation (*apophasis*) was made. Rhinon approached the Council and transferred the defendant's money to the treasury. When the democrats returned, Callimachus entered a plea against the oligarch Patrocles. Before the issue went to court, however, the two sides settled, whereupon the defendant brought a further suit against Lysimachus for 200 drachmas. Having been successful, he turned upon the plaintiff (from the point of view of the *paragraphê*) and accused him of complicity. Because the sum in question was so enormous, friends of the plaintiff persuaded him to settle for 200 drachmas out of court, in a process known as an arbitration on fixed terms (*diaita epi rhêtois*). Despite the fixed agreement, the defendant pursued further damages for 10,000 drachmas in the next archon year, hoping thereby that he would only

---

[16] At 2013: 109, Carawan writes: '[A]mong the provisions crucial to the Agreement and soon enacted into law was the double-edged rule, that private suits and arbitrated settlements, *dikai* and *diaitai* concluded under democracy shall be valid, and legal decisions under the Thirty are invalid. In the case of Kallimachos, Isokrates treats that rule as covenant and not yet law.' Carawan bases his view of the rule as covenant on the assumption that it is yet a covenant which the court adjudicated, but at no point in Isoc. 18 is the rule, spelled out at And. 1.87 and D. 24.26, described as a *synthêkê*.

[17] See Whitehead 1986: 119; Harris 2013: 75.

risk the court fee (*prytaneia*). Therefore, to spread the risk, the plaintiff decided to enter the special plea by the newly established process of *paragraphê* (Isoc. 18.6–12).[18] Thanks to the way the speaker links *paragraphê* to the Amnesty, it has been tempting in the past to see the trial of Callimachus as an example of how the rule of amnesty was violated. According to that interpretation, oaths were exchanged, but then litigants ignored them and began to bring actions before the court which covenant 15 of the Amnesty (see Chapter 3) expressly barred.

On closer inspection, it is unclear how any of the trial of Callimachus relates to the Amnesty. To be sure, the law of Archinus was legislated at some point after 403 probably with the messy conditions which had arisen out of the civil conflict specifically in mind, but its operation was not limited to those conditions. In this case, the reason a trial by *paragraphê* was invoked had nothing strictly to do with events which preceded the Reconciliation, as the order of events presented by the speaker shows. As §7 makes clear, the arbitration between Callimachus and the three oligarchs, Patrocles, Lysimachus and the speaker, took place after the democrats returned, and so the point at issue is the violation not of the Amnesty rule but of the rule which stated that all private arbitrations concluded when Athens was a democracy were enforceable. The reason for which *paragraphê* was invoked in the trial of Callimachus was that arbitrations concluded after the exchange of the Oaths of Reconciliation in 403 were now being undermined, not arbitrations before in the time of the oligarchy. The rule spelled out at And. 1.87 and D. 24.26 upholding judgments and arbitrations in the time of democracy applied not only to the period before the Thirty, but also (by implication) to the period after the Reconciliation in 403. And so, the fact that Callimachus had arbitrated under democracy and was now seeking to reopen a case which had been legally closed by an official democratic process is the reason why the plaintiff takes out the special plea. The admissibility of the planned litigation is held up to question not because it violated the Amnesty but, more simply, because it contravened the rule that judgments and arbitrations under democracy were valid, upholding *res iudicata*.[19]

---

[18] For the view that the case was prevented by the rule against suits for damage, see Dorjahn 1946: 27–35.

[19] Failing to reflect on any of these important implications, Carawan (2013: 94) writes: 'Isokrates frames the issue rather specifically. K's [Callimachus'] suit violates the covenants of the Reconciliation and the oaths that guarantee them in two ways: (1) he is prosecuting an accomplice whose role amounted to (at most) "informing and denouncing", and the covenants expressly barred prosecution for such complicity; moreover (2) whatever claim K could make upon our defendant [viz. plaintiff] he had settled in arbitration, and such decisions are rendered final by a rule that was embraced in the covenants and translated into law thereafter.' As argued in Chapter 4 and at Joyce 2015: 42–4, the rule spelled out at And. 1.87 and D. 24.26 was not part of the Covenants of Amnesty but the legislation which followed. Thus, the legal matter before the court in the trial of Callimachus is not strictly speaking the violation of amnesty, but the violation of the principle *res iudicata*, which was distinct and separate.

The matter of the Amnesty and its covenants is dragged into the speech of the plaintiff not because it directly affected the case at hand, but because it provides a suitable model of analogy. At §23, the speaker alludes to the cases of Thrasybulus and Anytus, heroes of the democratic victory, who had had property confiscated in the time of oligarchy and knew those responsible, but who nevertheless held back from vindictive litigation which, if allowed to proceed, would only have destabilised the city (εἰδότες δὲ τοὺς ἀπογράψαντας, ὅμως οὐ τολμῶσιν αὐτοῖς δίκας λαγχάνειν οὐδὲ μνησικακεῖν). Though the concepts δίκας λαγχάνειν and μνησικακεῖν are listed as if distinct, in the rhetorical flow of the passage they function synonymously: had democrats given in to vindictive impulses and taken the issue of reclaim to court contrary to the covenants and oaths which forbade such action, this would have amounted to μνησικακεῖν. The reference back to the moral example of Thrasybulus and Anytus is designed to illustrate to the court that Callimachus' attempt to go back on a democratic arbitration falls wildly short of that example, where so much more politically was at stake. The implication is not, however, that in its legal definition, Callimachus' action is tantamount to μνησικακεῖν. The rule about recognising the sanctity of contracts was not written into the Treaty of Reconciliation, and so any effort by a litigant to undermine or annul a contract contrary to the law could not, in a legal sense, be construed as a violation of the Amnesty, even if the Amnesty could rhetorically be referred to so as to provide a moral paradigm in rebuttal. On the strength of Isoc. 18, an extra covenant enforcing property rights at Athens has been suggested, with an imaginary rule stating that 'private obligations concluded under democracy shall be valid'.[20] Yet no such rule is spelled out in the contracts listed in the *Ath. Pol.* nor in the text of Isoc. 18.

Little has been made of the rhetorical principle observable in the orators of *auxêsis*, the rhetorical technique of building up the importance of a topic by analogy. A parallel application of the technique appears in two places in the orators, at D. 24.4 and Lyc. *Leocr.* 7. In the speech *Against Timocrates*, Demosthenes alludes to the practice of weighing upon the momentousness of the issue to make it worthy of the court's attention: 'Now it is the common practice of those who take up any piece of public business to inform you that the matter on which they happen to be making their speeches is most momentous, and worthy of your best attention. But if that claim has ever been made with propriety, I think that I am entitled to make it now.'[21] Timocrates

---

[20] Carawan 2013: 88.
[21] εἰώθασιν μὲν οὖν οἱ πολλοὶ τῶν πράττειν τι προαιρουμένων τῶν κοινῶν λέγειν ὡς ταῦθ' ὑμῖν σπουδαιότατ' ἐστὶν καὶ μάλιστ' ἄξιον προσέχειν τούτοις, ὑπὲρ ὧν ἂν αὐτοὶ τυγχάνωσι ποιούμενοι τοὺς λόγους. ἐγὼ δ', εἴπερ τινὶ τοῦτο καὶ ἄλλῳ προσηκόντως εἴρηται, νομίζω κἀμοὶ νῦν ἁρμόττειν εἰπεῖν.

stands accused of introducing an illegal measure, and to show to the court that the matter is weighty, the speaker refers back to an old feud with Androtion which, in point of law, was irrelevant to the case at trial. The reason he does so is to show that by introducing a measure that contravened the laws, the defendant was undermining the whole fabric of democracy. Similarly, Lycurgus tries to dispel the prejudice against his case that he is just pettifogging over small constitutional details. When judges vote on a charge of illegal proposals, they rectify a single error, but over the course of time the magnitude of that rectification will make itself felt. Thus, what might at the time seem like a small matter of constitutional detail may in the longer term bear enormous historical importance, which is why the survival of democracy sits in the balance if the motion of the defendant is accepted. These two parallel examples serve well to illustrate the technique employed by the speaker of Isoc. 18. The Amnesty is referred to not because the Amnesty has been violated, at least not directly, but because if one seemingly minor matter of an arbitration which had been sealed in an out-of-court settlement is reopened, the sanctity of contracts will be thrown open to the four winds, and by implication the legal fabric of the Covenants of Amnesty will be undermined, along with democracy and every painstaking measure which had been put in place to guarantee that a return to civil war and bloodshed would not occur.

The tenuous relationship of Callimachus' case to the Amnesty itself must be understood within the framework of the argument of Isoc. 18. At §24, the plaintiff draws a contrast between the noble behaviour of the democrats in forgoing their grudges, and the meanspirited conduct of Callimachus, who refused to let a matter go. The speaker makes an appeal to the pride of the audience: it would be shameful if you, who understood in your own cases that the oaths should be honoured, should now in the case of this mean wretch violate the sanctity of contracts drawn up in private; to give in to this man would be to state that contracts reached in the public sphere are now invalid, because you cannot honour the validity of those drawn up in private (τὰς μὲν ἰδίας ὁμολογίας δημοσίᾳ κυρίας ἀναγκάζετ᾽ εἶναι, τὰς δὲ τῆς πόλεως συνθήκας ἰδίᾳ τὸν βουλόμενον λύειν ἐάσετε). The point of the passage is to remind the judges of the commonality between public contracts (τὰς τῆς πόλεως συνθήκας) and private agreements (τὰς ἰδίας ὁμολογίας). In both instances, the sanctity of the principle is enforceable only if the terms of those contracts and agreements are honoured and upheld. What applies to the public sphere, by implication, applies to the private as well, and so to undermine the one is, by entailment, to undermine and nullify the other. The point is not that, by pursuing his rival, Callimachus has undermined the city's covenants (τὰς τῆς πόλεως συνθήκας), at least not directly. The point instead is that by violating an agreement of any kind, the sanctity of all contracts is imperilled. Callimachus violates the law because he refuses to abide by what has been agreed in settlement between himself and the plaintiff. If, it is argued, the validity of private arbitrations is permitted to fall by the wayside, then how can the city ever be serious about enforcing public contractual arrangements whose legal significance outweighs the case of Callimachus exponentially? The passage which, on a superficial reading, might mean that Callimachus had acted against the Amnesty in fact implies nothing of the kind. More locally, though not without significance, he had violated a law upholding the authority of a contract, and in so doing, had jeopardised the structure and framework upon which the edifice of Athenian law rests.

This conceptual relationship is made plain by what the speaker states at §§27–8:

[27] ἐνθυμεῖσθε δ' ὅτι περὶ τῶν μεγίστων ἥκετε δικάσοντες· περὶ γὰρ συνθηκῶν τὴν ψῆφον οἴσετε, ἃς οὐδὲ πώποτ' οὔθ' ὑμῖν πρὸς ἑτέρους οὔτ' ἄλλοις πρὸς ὑμᾶς ἐλυσιτέλησε παραβῆναι, τοσαύτην δ' ἔχουσι δύναμιν ὥστε τὰ πλεῖστα τοῦ βίου καὶ τοῖς Ἕλλησι καὶ τοῖς βαρβάροις διὰ συνθηκῶν εἶναι. [28] ταύταις γὰρ πιστεύοντες ὡς ἀλλήλους ἀφικνούμεθα καὶ ποριζόμεθα ὧν ἕκαστοι τυγχάνομεν δεόμενοι· μετὰ τούτων καὶ τὰ συμβόλαια τὰ πρὸς ἡμᾶς αὐτοὺς ποιούμεθα καὶ τὰς ἰδίας ἔχθρας καὶ τοὺς κοινοὺς πολέμους διαλυόμεθα· τούτῳ μόνῳ κοινῷ πάντες ἄνθρωποι διατελοῦμεν χρώμενοι. ὥσθ' ἅπασι μὲν προσήκει βοηθεῖν αὐταῖς, μάλιστα δ' ὑμῖν.

[27] I beg you, however, to bear in mind that you have come to pass judgement on matters of the highest importance; for you are going to cast your votes on the question of covenants, and covenants have never been violated to the advantage of either yourselves in relation to the other parties or of others in relation to you; and they have such binding force that almost all the daily activities of Greeks and of barbarians are governed by covenants. [28] For it is through our reliance on them that we visit one another's lands and procure those things of which we both have need; with the aid of these we make our contracts with each other and put an end to both our private animosities and our common wars. This is the only universal institution which all we of the human race constantly employ. It is, therefore, the duty of all men to uphold them, and, above all, yours. (tr. G. Norlin)

The plaintiff states at §27 that the judges are to cast a vote on the matter of covenants (περὶ γὰρ συνθηκῶν τὴν ψῆφον οἴσετε). The sanctity of contracts is of paramount importance, because if they are not respected in commerce and law, the very basis of economic and social transaction breaks down. Communication between cities and political communities is made possible as a result of the recognition that contracts are enforceable. Without respect for contracts, peaceful conditions between cities would not be possible and war would become interminable. Contracts are the one institution which all humans, Greek and barbarian alike, hold in common.[22] Now the fact that the speaker universalises the issue in the way he does suggests something basic about the contractual principle on which he is harping. By violating a matter as seemingly small as a private arbitration, by the extension of the principle all of humanity is wronged. This must not be interpreted to imply that in a legal sense, Callimachus had violated the Covenants of the Reconciliation. In a further sense, however, it means that he brings the Amnesty into disrepute.

In the scheme of the argument, it would therefore appear that Callimachus was standing in the dock because he had violated the terms of the Amnesty. Certainly, there are passages to support that interpretation. §20 makes it look as if the matter at issue is violation of an amnesty covenant: the speaker refers to a rule which protected informers and denouncers, though this is most likely an interpretation of covenant 15 (Chapter 3), as it is implied in it; the rule not to dredge up the past, by entailment, incorporates the idea that informers and denouncers were immune, which is why Loening rightly did not list this as a separate or self-contained clause.[23] Of course, the speaker includes this to bolster his case. The Amnesty forbade the pursuit of all except the Thirty, Ten and Eleven after 403, and so by threatening to bring a case against the plaintiff to trial for extorted moneys which took place by denunciation, the defendant stands in violation of the spirit of the Amnesty. Yet it is important to read this as a rhetorical buttress, not a point at issue in law. Callimachus stood in the dock, in a strict legal sense, not because he had dishonoured the clause not to dredge up the past, but because he was seeking to overturn a matter which had been settled in arbitration; the point at issue is not the clause spelled out at *Ath. Pol.* 39.6, but the law quoted at And. 1.87 and D. 24.26. From the plaintiff's point of view, the Amnesty becomes a useful reference point because he can present it as a moral exemplum. The great legislators of 403 realised that raking over the past was only going to plunge the city back into a state of civil conflict, and so laws were put in place to guarantee that the vexatious and frivolous pursuit of crimes which under the terms of the treaty had been protected from further legal prosecution was outlawed. The legal point at issue in this trial is assuredly not that the law of amnesty had been broken, but that by breaking the rule *res iudicata* on which Athens' legal system depended, the defendant had violated the spirit and example of the Amnesty.[24] The case of Callimachus is important

---

[22] For other formulations of this principle, see Pl. *R.* 359a; Arist. *Rh.* 1.15.21.1376b; D. 56 *passim*.
[23] Thus Loening 1987: 56; *contra* Dorjahn 1946: 24; Rhodes 1981: 468–9; Carawan 2013: 86, 98.
[24] The misleading idea that Callimachus stood trial for violation of an Amnesty covenant appears at Carawan 2012: 577–8 and 2013: 99; *contra* Joyce 2014: 522.

not because it exemplifies the working of the Amnesty, but because it shows how the Amnesty could be quoted as a moral paradigm. Like that of Socrates, the trial of Callimachus in a strict legal interpretation had no bearing on the Amnesty itself. Though the law of Archinus was legislated no doubt with the Amnesty in mind, its application was by no means limited to cases that arose from the Amnesty. The fact that we see it in operation in the second half of the fourth century shows that its meaning and relevance far outstretched the circumstances of 403, and its immediate aftermath. The case is valuable in that it shows how the Amnesty influenced litigation in a moral as well as in a legal sense, but the crucial point here to recognise is that litigators who cited the Amnesty did so for a variety and range of reasons, and just because the Amnesty appears as an exemplum within a court speech, that should not give grounds to assume that the case at issue was anchored in its clauses.

THE TRIAL OF SOCRATES, 399 (PL. *AP.* WITH X. *MEM.*)

In 399, Socrates was brought to trial for impiety (*asebeia*). The two main sources of evidence are the accounts of Xenophon and Plato. Though they tell events from different perspectives, they agree that Socrates was innocent of the charges levelled against him. Socrates was referred to outside the Academy; later in the fourth century, Aeschines claimed that Athenians put to death Socrates for his association with Critias, the leader of the Thirty.[25] It might be tempting to conclude from this that the trial had less to do with the real issue of impiety, and more with his oligarchic connections.[26] Some scholars have gone so far as to suggest that the political backdrop was of greater weight and consequence and argue *a fortiori* that the issue at stake in 399 was the subversion of democracy in 404.[27] To be sure, the prosecution made much of the erstwhile connections of Socrates to tarnish and defame his good character, but as with all the trials it is vital not to confuse rhetorical lambasting with the legal point at issue. Socrates may have been smeared with a connection to Critias, though what precisely this amounted to is doubtful. Vignettes from Xenophon's *Memorabilia* suggest that Socrates during the oligarchy had upbraided Critias for his mismanagement of the city's affairs and for harbouring unhealthy lusts for a youth called

---

[25] Aeschin. 1.173; X. *Mem.* 1.2.29–33; schol. Pl. *Ti.* 20a; *Chrm.* 153c; *Prt.* 316a; *Ti.* 19c; RO 88 lines 12–14. See Harris 2013: 52.
[26] Later tradition claimed that there was still a record of the indictment against Socrates in the Metroon (D.L. 2.40). For the question of its authenticity, see Schanz 1893: 13–16; Wilamowitz 1920: 47–8; Derenne 1930: 141–3.
[27] Stone 1988; Hansen 1995; Waterfield 2009; *contra* Rudhardt 1960; Mossé 1997.

Euthydemus.²⁸ Famously, Critias was 'an amateur among philosophers, and a philosopher among amateurs' (schol. Pl. *Ti.* 20a). At the same time, Critias features in Plato's later dialogues, and it would be unwise to suggest that the connection with Socrates was fabricated wholesale by his opponents.²⁹ All the same, the claim that the issue at stake in 399 was the subversion of democracy in 404 is to push the evidence well beyond its reasonable limits. There is nothing in the plaint, such as we can piece together from the very fragmentary material at our disposal, which points in that direction. To be sure, there were references at the trial to events which did take place in the time of the oligarchy, most notably the arrest and execution of Leon of Salamis (see below), but it is important to interpret those references in their appropriate setting. Socrates was put on trial not for an association with the Thirty but for his impious and deviant intellectual habits. Earlier historical references to political events, such as the trial of Leon in 404 or, two years earlier in 406, the trial and execution of the Arginusae generals, have a special place within the defence, but do not answer the plaint directly.

As far as we can discern from Plato's *Apology*, the plaint brought against the defendant was threefold: (1) introducing new gods (Pl. *Ap.* 24b–c); (2) not believing in the gods (Pl. *Ap.* 27a); and (3) corrupting the youth (Pl. *Ap.* 24c). Socrates did not contest the point that these were components of *asebeia* (impiety) but rather in his self-defence argued that he was not guilty of any of them. The definition of *asebeia* in Athenian law was open to interpretation. Elsewhere in the *Laws*, Plato lists three types: not believing in the existence of the gods, thinking that the gods do exist but have no concern for human affairs, and trying to influence the will of the gods through prayer and sacrifice (Pl. *Lg.* 885b).³⁰ Two important revisionist approaches have downplayed the legal nature of the plaint by suggesting that there were deeper motives behind the trial. I. Stone famously argued that trial needs to be set within a context of a wider discussion of the merits of democracy. According to that view, Socrates as one of Athenian democracy's most notorious critics deliberately set himself upon a collision course with the law, to show his disdain for a political system which he hated. If that is true, this was a political trial which had less to do with the substance of the plaint and more with an ongoing political feud between oligarchs and democrats. A variant of that position has been taken more recently by R. Waterfield, who claims that Socrates willed his own death to settle a seething cesspool of dispute still raging in the

---

²⁸ X. *Mem.* 1.2.29–33.
²⁹ See Pl. *Chrm.* 153c; *Prt.* 316a; *Ti.* 19c.
³⁰ On *asebeia* in Plato, see Cohen (D.) 1991: 216. For a fuller discussion of the attested trials for *asebeia* and their political context, see more recently Filonik 2013.

aftermath of the Reconciliation.³¹ On that understanding, Socrates offered himself up as a scapegoat to quell political animosity in Athens and allow the process of reconciliation to heal divisions within the city. Both of those approaches politicise the trial. It is undeniable that unsavoury associations had clung to Socrates well before 399: as early as 423, the year of the production of Aristophanes' *Clouds*, Socrates was tarnished with the shady reputation of teaching the youth how to justify beating parents, and similar prejudices appear in the *Wasps* produced a year later. Socrates had acquired a bad reputation long before the rumour of an unholy alliance with the Thirty got under way. This has led some to believe that in the late fifth century there was a 'crisis of faith', tainted with oligarchic sympathies, which led to backlash after the democratic restoration in the shape of trials launched against Socrates and Andocides, but as R. Parker has shown, this view finds scant support in the historical evidence.³² The prejudice against Socrates no doubt was there in 399, but in order to argue that the trial of Socrates was about oligarchic links requires evidence which is lacking.

More recent scholarship has now shown that, far from being a 'political trial' in the way in which this concept has conventionally been applied and understood, the trial of Socrates turned on a strict legal principle: whether he was guilty of *asebeia* (impiety), which in Athenian law was understood to be a crime. In a detailed and thought-provoking re-evaluation, C. Pelloso has argued that the older view of Socrates as a martyr to conscience, which derives ultimately from Plato, must be read and understood in its proper legal context. For thirty years, Socrates, whilst vocal in his criticisms of Athenian democracy, operated undisturbed. It was no crime to criticise democracy at Athens. To suggest that Socrates was condemned for his anti-democratic stance is to misunderstand in principle the nature of the plaint against him. The hinge question was the matter of impiety, which, if committed, would have been punishable in law.³³ To call this a 'political trial' is therefore to beg the question. The claim that the animosity against Socrates arose from his political associations, particularly Alcibiades and other notorious figures of late fifth-century Athens, is not completely out of the question. Possibly those associations, if they were current before the time of the anti-Socratic pamphleteer Polycrates (see below), may have been dredged up at the historical trial, yet it is important to bear in mind that, even if they were, they had little to bear on the legal point at issue. Many scholars have seen the Athenian legal system as having shown little interest in real justice, as if

---

³¹ Stone 1988; Waterfield 2009.
³² Parker 1996: 210–12.
³³ Pelloso 2019. Along similar lines, see also Bonazzi 2018.

justice were a subterfuge for venting personal hostilities in the courts.[34] This is to ignore the overwhelming body of evidence which shows that, as a legal and moral principle, justice was paramount in the mindset of democratic Athens, and enshrined was the principle that trials had to base themselves on the legal point at hand. To illustrate the point, every year the Athenian youth swore an Ephebic Oath, which committed it to obey the city laws (RO 88 lines 12–14). That justice was of utmost importance at Athens is reflected in tragedy; the orators themselves articulate the ideal that without justice, the fabric of democracy would be quickly undermined.[35] Though strong feelings may have been ranged against Socrates before and after the defeat of Athens in 404, it is extremely unlikely that Socrates was condemned for oligarchic associations. Moreover, the type of 'anti-democratic' theory expressed in the writings of Plato, who was taught by Socrates, was of a different ilk from that in which Critias had been schooled. Socrates taught that the best type of government was one according to which a political elite comprising philosopher kings made decisions for the city; crucially, members of the elite in Plato's ideal city are chosen on the basis not of wealth but of character (Pl. R. Books 3 and 4). This constitutes a radical departure from traditional oligarchic doctrine, which prioritised wealth and status as the most important criterion of membership in the social elite.[36] Therefore, although Socrates was known for his anti-democratic doctrines, it would be difficult to situate his trial in the backdrop of an unresolved feud between oligarchs and democrats at Athens. The type of critique of democracy in evidence in the *Republic* bears no resemblance to the specimens of oligarchic theory which drove the Old Oligarch, Critias or proponents of the Thirty.

How did Socrates rebut the charges against him? If Plato's account of the defence is to be believed, it appears that the chief grudge held against Socrates by his accusers stemmed from malice and envy.[37] Socrates had been called the wisest man in the world by Delphi because he was the only man who understood the full extent of his own ignorance. No claim had ever been laid to a divinely imparted wisdom to which no one else had access. Socrates quarrelled with artisans who thought that they were clever in all matters because they

---

[34] For an overview of the scholarship and a full refutation of those claims, see Harris 2013: 3–18, 60–98.

[35] S. *OC* 913–14; D. 24.75–6, 215–6; Aeschin. 1.179; 3.23; Isoc. 15.79. See also Hdt. 7.104.4.

[36] See the pamphlet of the Old Oligarch as a typical example of what oligarchic theory in the fifth century looked like. Critias, who is known to have written extensively on constitutions (DK 88 F 25), famously said that the best type of constitution of all was the one practised at Sparta (X. *HG* 2.3.34; DK 88 F 32–7). From what little we can gather of Critias' ideological commitments, it is difficult to establish much common bond with the Socratic tradition.

[37] On the question of the reliability of Plato's *Apology* as a historical source for the trial, and for a summary of scholarly opinion, see Colaiaco 2001: 20–1.

were highly skilled in one individual discipline. The anger incurred brought the prosecutors to lay accusations against him, Meletus representing the cause of poets, Anytus that of the artisans, and Lycon that of the orators. Socrates likened himself to a gadfly brought by 'the deity' to Athens and protested that the charges made against him were brought through grudgeful envy rather than because any of them contained any substance. Significantly, there is no evidence that Socrates was on trial for offences that took place in the period of the oligarchy. The charge of corruption turns on the matter of whether he had taught the youth not to believe in the gods. We know from independent sources that Critias was an atheist, and it is possible that many Athenians of the restored democracy blamed the fall of Athens in 404 and the terrible events which ensued on impiety which incurred the anger of heaven.[38] If so, though there was a historical subtext to the trial, the association with Critias was not a component of the charge. The trial did not therefore violate the Amnesty, because it did not bring to issue crimes before 403. But the most important component of the self-defence was the appeal to conscience. As a man of conscience, Socrates had placed himself on a collision path with the city authorities because the defence of justice at times involves standing up to those in power. The extrapolation here is that political authority is answerable to a higher principle of justice, and that justice must always be served even if that means opposing those with the power to decide life or death. If there is a political subtext to the defence, it does not frame itself in terms of allegiance to democracy or oligarchy. The point is that *any* political authority can get it wrong, and whenever authority does get it wrong it must be checked. The polarity is not between democracy and oligarchy, as we would expect if the trial were political, but between power and conscience.

Xenophon's *Memorabilia* makes out that Socrates was, in the end, a man of sound piety whose concern was the welfare of friends and family. We do not know when Xenophon wrote his memoirs, but their tone and content situates them in the context of a growing debate in the wake of the trial and execution as to whether Socrates had been a just man. The account of Socrates' life is designed to refute the allegations made by the enemies of Socrates that he had little interest in the gods or represented a subversive moral influence in the city. Only the opening chapter has anything to say about his self-defence. Against the charge of unbelief, Socrates protested that he regularly made sacrifices to the gods both at home and in public but claimed in addition to be guided by what he called 'the deity' (X. *Mem.* 1.1.2). Socrates did not reject the traditional gods of Athens nor believe that it was not important to honour them, but held that above and beyond the traditional pantheon there was a

---

[38] DK 88 F 25. For Critias' role in the Mutilation of the Herms, see And. 1.47–58.

unifying creative force which was responsible for the design of the universe (X. *Mem.* 1.1.11). Plato's *Apology*, on the other hand, presents or, at least, claims to provide the speech of self-defence made by Socrates at his trial.[39] The main prosecutor was Meletus, who called Socrates an evildoer and an obscurantist. Socrates sets out to refute the charge by pointing out that Greece has its fair share of teachers and preceptors, like Hippias of Elis and Callias son of Hipponicus, who demanded money for their teaching, yet no one thought of putting those men on trial. The 'wisdom' which his slanderers alleged against him was the type which Socrates claimed lay within the powers of human apprehension and was not imparted from some superhuman source. Socrates made the case that to speak of wisdom in this way was not to denounce the gods or to commit impiety, and he calls the Pythian priestess to bear witness. We see in the trial, at least as far as its outline is discernible, a populist rant against philosophical wisdom being initiated in the court, as if to hold human reason as a guiding light was to turn one's back on traditional religion. In rebuttal, Socrates makes every effort to argue that this is not the case, and that to put faith in the power of human reasoning is not to deny the existence of the gods, or to bring disgrace or disrepute on the demands which worship of the gods incurred.[40] Piety and reason are not polarities.

It has recently been argued that the Amnesty was not a blanket measure forbidding all types of prosecution, because it remained possible to bring Socrates to trial after 403 under the old indictment of the *graphê asebeias*.[41] This is to make two prior assumptions. The first is that the laws written near the Stoa in 403 were ones regulating criminal proceedings which left out the *graphê asebeias*. As argued in Chapter 4, the legal redaction had nothing to do with laws on criminal procedure. The second is that the legal issue in 399 pertained to events before 403. Yet nothing in the plaint, as far as it can be reconstructed from Plato's *Apology*, refers to connections with the Thirty. It is true that reference is made at Pl. *Ap.* 32 to the arrest and trial of Leon of Salamis in 404, where Socrates relates the story of how he was ordered by the Thirty to arrest Leon and have him put to death. It might be tempting to infer from this that a smear had been made in Meletus' speech of complicity with the Thirty, but more important is to observe the precise context in which Socrates alludes to the event. Like the speaker at the trial of Callimachus, who

---

[39] It should be remarked here that the use of Plato's *Apology* as a source for the actual trial is an enormously contentious issue, and it would be hazardous to assume that Plato has given a 'historical' account. For the view that the speech of self-defence as represented in the *Apology* was not an actual representation of what was said in court but was composed for a wider readership and called on readers to judge the matter for themselves, see Burnyeat 1997.
[40] On the appeal to the inner *daimonion*, see Connor 1991; Robb 1993; Marianetti 1993.
[41] Carawan 2013: 203–31, esp. 211.

alludes to the Amnesty not because it directly bore upon his case but because it provided a useful model of analogy, the reference to the time of Thirty is brought in not because anything had necessarily been alleged against Socrates to that effect, but because Socrates wants to show that he is a man of principle who has opposed both democrats and oligarchs in the past when he felt that justice compelled him. What must not be overlooked is that the reference to Leon occurs in the same section which describes Socrates' opposition to the death sentence of the Arginusae generals. The context has nothing to do with a wish to refute some oligarchic smear. The point is that, as a man of conscience, Socrates can only do what is right, even if that means standing up to political authority. It would be misleading to read any of this in the light of some festering opposition between democrats and oligarchs in 399. The point of the passage is that Socrates speaks only the truth, and if by speaking the truth he must die by execution, that would be preferable for him than to compromise conscience.

The principle of *res iudicata* stated that court verdicts reached before 403 remained in effect, but anything committed in the time of the Thirty or beforehand which had not been tried and judged was not now liable to prosecution (And. 1.87; D. 24.26). The trial of Socrates did not violate that rule. Socrates was put on trial on a legal, not political, charge.[42] Of course his track record could be brought up in court to bolster the allegation of impiety and corrupting the youth, but the chief matter was not a crime committed in the past, but the allegation of impiety now. This might have had a historical dimension, and it has been maintained that the erasure which appears on the 'wall' of stelae which the *anagrapheis* inscribed in their second term (see Chapter 4) was a response to the acts of the Thirty, who deleted the work done on the sacrificial calendar by Nicomachus during his first term.[43] But even if that speculation is true, the claim that the Thirty abolished all sacrifices would be to push the evidence far too hard. Critias was tarred with the brush of atheism at least by his critics, but the evidence is too weak to assert that the period of oligarchy was a time when Athenians turned their backs upon the gods. Socrates' trial in 399 is not an indication that the Amnesty was systematically ignored or that its protective measures were loose, and on no account can the trial of 399 be understood to stand in conflict with the principle that after 403 litigation for old crimes was forbidden. To some modern sensibilities, the idea that the trial of Socrates can only have been for a religious matter seems almost inconceivable, and it is perhaps an argument from incredulity which

---

[42] On the strictly religious nature of the plaint, see Brickhouse and Smith 1989; 1994; 2002.
[43] Fingarette 1971; Clinton 1982: 32; Carawan 2010; Shear (J. L.) 2011: 238–43. On the so-called 'sacrificial calendar', see Chapter 3.

has led several scholars and historians to seek a broader historical context for the trial, so that the real issue at stake was not religion (which was only a subterfuge) but a political connection which aligned Socrates with discredited oligarchs. To argue in such a way would be to ignore evidence that *asebeia* was conceived in Athenian law as a crime. As early as the seventh century, we can see how lawgivers laid down precepts for religious observance.[44] In the fifth and fourth centuries, failure to observe religious scruple was similarly seen as a crime against the political community ([Lys.] 6.11–12, 17), and it was this which, according to the plaint against Andocides, marked the defendant out as a *pharmakos*.[45] Respect for the gods was integral to the working of the Athenian judicial system, since perjury and suborning witnesses were regarded as components of *asebeia*.[46] The religious scandals of 415 showed beyond doubt the connection in the minds of Athenians between the political welfare of the city and respect for the gods, and so, at the trial, it might have been tempting for the prosecution, in its argument that Socrates was busy conspiring against the welfare of the city, to connect him to less savoury personalities from the past, such as Critias and Alcibiades. The trouble, quite simply, is that we lack at our disposal transcripts of the speeches brought by the three prosecutors, and it would be therefore otiose to speculate that any connection to the Thirty was ever made at the trial.

The link with the fifth century in the trial of Socrates is almost certainly the product of later fiction. We know from references in Isocrates that sometime in the 390s, the pamphleteer Polycrates introduced this fiction to make it look as if the matter for which Socrates had been tried in 399 was his connection with Alcibiades (Isoc. 11.5). According to the testimony, in an essay attacking Socrates, Polycrates had typecast Alcibiades as if as a young man he had been a student in the Socratic circle, and modern commentators have argued plausibly from this that it was Polycrates who invented the link with Alcibiades and Critias.[47] Other fragments of the orators show that Polycrates raked up this political connection as a paradigm to exemplify the nobility of democrats, such as Conon and Thrasybulus, on the one hand, against the deviant and unholy characters whom Socrates nurtured among his disciples (Lys. frr. 271–6 Carey). Isocrates himself rejected these tarnishes. As far as he was concerned, the received tradition of association between Socrates and the oligarchic agitators of 404 was nothing more than an idle rumour and speculation. Against the tradition, which may have been known to Xenophon, is ranged the story

---

[44] Thgn. 1179; Porph. *Abst.* 4.22 (on Draco of Athens).
[45] On the fate of the *pharmakos*, see Burkett 1979: 64–77; Bremer 1983.
[46] X. *Ap.* 24; *An.* 3.2.4; *Cyr.* 5.2.9–10.
[47] Brickhouse and Smith 1989: 84–5.

of how during the regime of the Thirty, Critias and Charicles had cautioned Socrates against teaching public discourse (X. *Mem.* 1.2.31–8). Socrates, on that account, put his neck out by opposing the verdict of the oligarchs, arguing that it would be absurd for them to have barred a great teacher from educating men to speak their minds. This looks much like a counter-tradition casting Socrates as a democrat, in the hurly-burly of gossip and rumour that gripped Athens in the aftermath of Socrates' trial and execution. The attempt to lump Socrates with Critias may also have drawn on a common 'atheistic' connection, because Critias was known to have praised Spartan frugality and to have held religious ritual in contempt, as did Socrates.[48] But if such parallels could be drawn, this provided flimsy material upon which to allege any political or intellectual connection between Socrates and Critias. The fact that this supposed connection is missing altogether in Plato's *Apology* should be enough to dispel the idea that at the time of the trial, erstwhile oligarchic associations came to the fore in the plaint.

In brief, modern speculations that the trial of Socrates may have revisited old grievances which stood in conflict with the Amnesty Agreement of 403 amount to a red herring. As there is no evidence that Socrates had taken any part in the oligarchy of the Thirty or had approved of any of its actions, there is little sense in the suggestion that the trial of 399 invalidated any of the commitments which Athenians swore in 403 to forget the past and move on. Whatever its rights and wrongs, there was nothing inadmissible about bringing a plaint against Socrates. The trial was wholly in keeping with law and with legal protocol, was framed with an official charge against the defendant, and decided by five hundred judges who voted by a majority to condemn Socrates. The feeling of moral outrage which this trial has generated in modern times has led to an abject confusion of issues. It may very well be that the charges against him were insubstantial and that Socrates was wrongly convicted. To argue as much is to condemn the judges of having cast an unfair and foolish vote against an innocent man, but the question of whether Socrates was guilty or not should not be confused with the issue of whether the trial was admissible. Concerning the second matter, if the representation of the trial in the *Apology* is believable, then it must appear that the trial was legal. The notorious case against Socrates is the most remembered court case in Athenian legal history and has played a significant role in distorting modern perceptions of the Athenian judicial process. The verdict against Socrates reflects not the weakness of democracy or the rule of law, but that in Athens there was not a higher standard of proof since only a simple majority was required for a guilty

---

[48] X. *Mem.* 1.3.3; Pl. *Euthphr.* 14e–15a; [Pl.] *Alc. 2* 149b; Connor 1991: 53–4.

verdict.[49] For that reason, it is essential not to base generalisations about the tenability of a judicial system upon examples where justice was not carried out. In Athens, the record must be examined in its entirety, and a compendious analysis of the court cases about which we know leads to the conclusion that the principle of justice was the cornerstone of the Athenian judicial process.

ADDENDUM (to chapter VI)

Since the appearance of the first edition, L. Rubinstein has argued from Isocrates 16 (*On the Team of Horses*) that the Reconciliation Agreement, 'which asserted the validity of all decisions made by the courts or in arbitrations while Athens had been democratically governed, provided very significant opportunities for individuals to pursue personal grievances and hostile agendas through the courts, circumventing the restrictions that were supposed to prevent precisely that' (2023: 286). Though cautious not to revive Carawan's idea of a limited amnesty, Rubinstein nevertheless believes that the Amnesty's provisions were not rigorously applied after 403. If the case against the younger Alcibiades in the 390s was a *dikê exoulês*, it was admissible because a decision of a democratic court predating 404 was being upheld. The legal difficulty was that the elder Alcibiades could not have appeared in court to face Teisias because he was in exile. Thus, if Teisias had been awarded damages in 407, this would have happened by default – his opponent, the father of the defendant, was not physically present to defend himself.

The younger Alcibiades may have taken refuge in the claim that the decision of the court had been unfair because his father could not have defended himself in exile, and further, that because the exile of the elder Alcibiades was unfair, the verdict in 407 was unfair. The first half of the speech is missing, which means that any discussion of this case rests on considerable speculation. Legally, if a democratic court had decided that moneys should be repaid by X to Y, and X then refused to repay those moneys, Y was within his legal right to demand that the verdict of the court be respected and for X to repay what was due. If this referred to an incident predating the Amnesty, this is no problem because the Amnesty, as argued above, upheld earlier judicial verdicts reached under democracy. This is further evidence of the rule of law in action after 403. The Amnesty was not violated; the principle of *res iudicata* stood.

---

[49] Thus Harris 2013: 317–19.

CHAPTER 7

The Athenian Reconciliation as the Paradigm for the Greek World in the Classical and Hellenistic Ages

Almost four centuries after the Athenian Reconciliation, the Roman orator Cicero addressed the Senate in the wake of Julius Caesar's assassination, calling for unity in Rome in a time of emergency. The state had been torn apart by political dissentions and civil wars, in consequence of which Caesar had taken on the unprecedented title of 'dictator for life' after establishing total supremacy. His overweening hubris proved too much, and on the Ides of March Caesar was murdered in the vicinity of the Theatre of Pompey. His assassins claimed to have liberated Rome from a tyrant, but the removal of a dictator paved the way for further ructions. Among the political heirs of Caesar was Mark Antony, an ambitious, scheming general who swore to avenge the dictator's death. Rome now faced a fresh crisis, how to reconcile political factions whose sworn objective was to wreak revenge. Cicero, whose sympathies resided with the conspirators, strove to bring about a concordat. In return for amnesty, the Senate pledged not to declare Caesar a tyrant, and allowed the Caesarian faction to continue as a legitimate force. In his tirade against Antony, Cicero appealed to the ancient example of the Athenians, which shone out as a paradigm of peace and reconciliation. Its purpose had been to consign to everlasting oblivion any memory of disunity and discord in the interest of restoring harmony to the city. Despite the very great bitterness which the memory of civil conflict had entailed, Athenians had been willing to put recollections of past evils to bed. It was a noble model of wisdom and foresight at a time of political crisis, when the temptation might otherwise have been to pursue internal divisions further and undermine any hope of securing a lasting peace. In imitation, Cicero even used the chosen legal phrase of the Athenians, μὴ μνησικακεῖν.[1]

---

[1] Cic. *Phil.* 1.1.1. For modern disagreement as to the reliability of Cicero's statement, see Mommsen 1899: 458; Sordi 1997; Carawan 2002; Joyce 2016.

Looking back upon the Athenian example from almost four hundred years' distance, it is tempting to wonder to what extent Cicero's view of that ancient amnesty was infused with the romanticism of hindsight. As the last two chapters showed, the more contemporary evidence of the Attic orators could arouse doubt that memories of the recent past were ever so conscientiously banished as Cicero would later believe, but what is striking is that for four centuries the Athenian example was not forgotten but held up as a paradigm. It cannot be denied that, as an educated Roman, Cicero held affinities for Athens and its cultural heritage. Oratory is not always preoccupied with historical accuracy, especially when it advances a stilted political agenda. But the possibility that Cicero romanticised should not be taken as a given. There is likelihood that he related the truth, that Athenians in 403 did, as he reminds his Roman audience, achieve something remarkable. We know of no contradictory version of events which saw the Athenian Amnesty to be anything other than what Cicero describes, and in view of this, it would be foolhardy to dismiss as a turgid fiction the praise and admiration which Cicero and others in antiquity held for Athens. The success of the Amnesty of 403 was so majestic that it went down in the historical record as the *Atheniensium vetus exemplum* and served as the archetype for other reconciliation treaties. Not all cities, of course, measured up to the example, but the encomium of Cicero is evidence enough of its lasting influence.

Athens was not alone among the Greek city states to manage reconciliation. The political history of the fifth and fourth centuries is replete with examples of cities ripped apart by internal dissension and mended subsequently. The success with which civic harmony was rebuilt varied depending on the individual city in question and the methods it employed. The historical record furnishes many examples of successful attempts at reconciliation following periods of violent and destructive discord. In most cases, the mechanisms which cities used to put an end to division made use of the law. Once the classical age came to an end and the period of history more commonly known as the Hellenistic age began, it grew more common for larger power structures to intervene in the internal affairs of cities, and increasingly we find examples of 'amnesties' which amounted to one party in a conflict being promoted to support the interest of the external power with which it held a community of interest.[2] This has led some to infer that amnesty, as we understand it in the modern world, was never part of the Greek experience, as there are examples where the reinstatement of an exiled faction did not result in lasting peace and may, in some cases, have been motivated by the selfish interests of foreign dynasts, who wielded power at arm's length by proxy rulers.[3] As soon

---

[2] Rubinstein 2013. The present chapter, based closely on Joyce 2016 (with modifications), nuances these claims.

[3] For a range of examples, see the survey in Dreher 2013. One notorious instance is the case of Dionysius of Syracuse, who used amnesty legislation purely to prop up his own power base when aspiring to tyranny (D.S. 14.9.6–8).

as the word *amnêstia*, from which we derive our 'amnesty', is attested in the Greek language in the early Hellenistic age, it is not always framed in careful legal terminology, and may have been little more than a token political gesture.[4] Still, the semantic issue of whether *amnêstia* meant 'amnesty' in the modern sense should not detain us long. The relevant question here is how Greek cities achieved reconciliation, and what sorts of parallels they might provide for the methods and processes by which Athenians in 403 reconciled their community.

This chapter focuses on the specific examples outside Athens of cities which aimed to bring together competing factions and divided interest groups in the wake of a civil conflict. The purpose is to set the Athenian example in its historical context by examining test cases from elsewhere in Greece. Though not all cities reached identical solutions, one common tendency was the bar which amnesty settlements imposed upon litigation for offences which took place in time of political crisis. As will be seen, there are some important exceptions to the rule. But in the great majority of cases, when cities sought to allay conflict, they expressly outlawed vindictive action for grievances which stemmed from the period of civil war. This would have meant that, in most instances, the beneficiaries of an amnesty would principally have been those who had found themselves on the losing side of a given conflict. It would be reductive to claim that amnesty settlements were always one-sided, and even in cases where the aim of legislation was demonstrably to create the circumstances whereby one side in a political conflict, usually the losing side, would come to no harm, on the other side there was a concomitant agreement not to resume hostilities or do anything to subvert the new order through recriminatory or hostile intent. For a broken community to become fully reconciled, it had to ensure that both sides enjoyed the fruits of peace, and that reconciliation was not a subterfuge whereby one side in a former conflict could merely subjugate the other.

First, one definitional point of clarification is needed. Because the term corresponding to our 'amnesty' does not appear in Greek political vocabulary until nearly a century after the Athenian reconciliation, some may wish to argue that the word 'amnesty' should not be used. When writing of amnesties, modern writers often conjure up images of political prisoners or refugees

---

[4] Good examples are the cases of Temnus and Clazomenae in Asia Minor (*SEG* 29.1130, esp. lines 11–22; Hermann 1979) and Miletus and Magnesia (*Milet* I 3.148) in the third century. In these instances, the term *amnêstia* entails an injunction to consign to oblivion any memory of the war between them in the interest of establishing political co-operation, but these texts do not phrase the matter in the same precise language as do earlier inscribed texts which attest the phrase μὴ μνησικακεῖν. In these examples there is no reference to restoration of exiles or ban on litigation.

being restored to rights, reinstatement of public figures in disgrace, overturning of old sentences, or a pledge of forgiveness to the participants in the *ancien régime* excepting, perhaps, those directly and personally complicit in crimes of an ousted government. Because our word bears a heavy theoretical overlay, care should be taken before superimposing any of those modern senses on the Greek world, as and where the evidence does not permit. In the case of Athens, as with most of the test examples under investigation, the term *amnêstia* was never used. And so, before over-confident assertions are made that those cities where the key phrase appears experienced 'amnesties' in the modern sense, it is vital to examine what μὴ μνησικακεῖν means in context and what can legitimately be inferred from its usage.

THE MEANING OF MH MNHΣIKAKEIN

Speaking around 380, at a time of fragmentation and disorder in Greece, the orator Isocrates recalls an oath which the Greek alliance swore after the repulse of Xerxes exactly a century earlier, to leave the temples and holy places destroyed by the Persians during their invasion of the Greek mainland in disrepair as a reminder to the Greeks of their moral duty to avenge the wrongs which they had suffered at Persian hands (Isoc. 4.106). Isocrates was a pan-Hellenist, arguing that the best way forward was to put aside local wrangling and coalesce in an anti-Persian confederation. The *Panegyricus* oration, perhaps his best-known speech, stands as a reminder to readers and listeners alike that there was a greater menace on the borders of the Greek-speaking world which needed to be taken much more seriously than it currently was. In the last decade of the Peloponnesian War and the two which followed, the Persian Empire bit by bit had clawed back the territories in western Asia which it had lost in the early years of the fifth century when beaten back by a united Greek alliance, and the King's Peace of 386 had left Persia in control of all the Greek cities along the western coast of Asia Minor. For Greeks, this had been a humiliating turn, not least since the stunning achievement of the previous century, the liberation of eastern Greeks from barbarian control, had been recklessly squandered owing to the gruesome conflict between Athens and Sparta in the last three decades of the fifth century which had drawn in Persia and had resulted in a redrawing of the geopolitical map. If the city states of mainland Greece could once and for all forgo mutual animosity, not only would that guarantee that the events of a century previous, when Persians crossed the Hellespont, could be averted, but hope might be rekindled that the painful abdication of the eastern Greeks into Persian hands might be avenged in a renewed pan-Hellenic campaign.

Like much of his oratory, Isocrates' *Panegyricus* contains a good deal of bombast, but it echoes what Herodotus reports of the conference at the Isthmus a century before, in 481, on the eve of Artemisium: if the key players like Athens and Sparta could give up the parochial issue of which of the two should stand at the political helm and instead focus on the larger matter at hand, Greece should benefit (Hdt. 8.3.1). In 494, the playwright Phrynichus had been fined 1,000 drachmas for reminding the Athenians of their failure five years earlier to rescue their kinsmen when the Ionian Revolt was crushed under the Persian heel (Hdt. 6.21). Isocrates himself understood that the Ionian question was a raw nerve even a century afterwards. Recently, it has been argued that revenge was construed by Greeks as a moral duty and that Isocrates, by raising a war cry, urged not merely the venting of grievances but the fulfilment of a moral and divine duty.[5] The problem is that the supporting evidence for vengeance in Greek morality as a duty of obligation is sparse, yet there is plenty of evidence to the contrary that eschewal of retaliation was noble. Demosthenes states that it is dangerous to be too trusting of friends and too hateful of enemies, because if indulged, those feelings can prevent reconciliation (D. 23.122). Sophocles makes similar observations, warning against overindulgence of a grudge (S. *Aj.* 678–82). Similar words of advice are attributed by ancient authors to Bias of Priene, one of the Greek sages.[6] It is true that Lysias shortly after 403 urged the Athenians to take revenge in the court on one of the notorious malefactors of the ousted oligarchy, but his exhortations stood in violation of the most important pledge of the restored democracy, not to vent grievances.[7] When Isocrates called for vengeance on Persia, the virtue of forgoing the temptation to retaliate was sidelined, but there is a more subtle objective underlying the *Panegyricus*: of course, Persia was to be punished, but to achieve that purpose the Greeks needed to put an end to their own mutual feuds. On a more careful reading, Isocrates was as much rallying the cause of mutual reconciliation among the Greeks.

The testimony of Isocrates indicates that by the time he was writing, the idea of giving up grudges was well established. Literary sources show that μὴ μνησικακεῖν could be applied in a moral sense to mean 'let bygones be bygones', or 'not rake over the past'. In *Lysistrata*, a comedy of Aristophanes produced in 411 at the time of the first oligarchic coup right after the Sicilian disaster, the commissioner (*diallaktês*) bids the women not to weep over dead sons. Lysistrata denies that women know nothing of war by reminding him that they are the ones who must see their offspring die, to which the commissioner replies μὴ μνησικακήσῃς (Ar. *Lys.* 590). Herodotus tells us that Thessalian representatives instructed the people of Phocis that they bore no grudges (οὐ μνησικακέομεν) for what had happened earlier (Hdt. 8.29.2). Some years

---

[5] Chaniotis 2013: 55–60.
[6] Arist. *Rh.* 2.13.4.1389b23–5; D.L. 1.87. For other attestations of the maxim, see Tziatzi-Papagianni 1994: 404–5.
[7] Lys. 13.2–3. For discussion of the speech, see Chapter 5.

before Thermopylae, Thessaly had invaded Phocis with ruinous consequences. Over four thousand men had been killed and their shields dedicated as trophy offerings at Abae and Delphi. Their defeat was made worse by a Phocian boast that the Thessalians were no match. Now that Thessaly had taken the side of the Persian King, the tables had turned. The Thessalians promised Phocis that, in return for monetary payment, they would ensure no harm from the invading armies (Hdt. 8.27–9). However embellished, this anecdote conveys an important feature of the promise μὴ μνησικακεῖν. Normally it brokered a deal whereby, in exchange for peace terms, the weaker side received a guarantee of protection. The example in Herodotus shows μὴ μνησικακεῖν in a moral sense. In a legal settlement, by contrast, special measures were required to ensure that *stasis* would not resurface. In some cases, they were detailed and complex, but in others, such as alliances, μὴ μνησικακεῖν was often little more than a goodwill gesture not to revert to animosity. To be sure, some attestations show that a bilateral commitment 'to forget the past' was undertaken, but others suggest that only one side took the pledge. When one-sided, it was usually the victorious faction which swore it. This was because, in political language, it was normally the winners who had 'wrongs' to forget.

Inscriptions here provide the most fruitful source of evidence. According to one view, it was a technicality which sealed pre-existing covenants of an agreement.[8] The implication is that μὴ μνησικακεῖν did not bring about a general amnesty, nor did it protect all vulnerable citizens from reprisals in the wake of the democratic victory, but was concerned instead to formalise in law a very limited set of agreements. If this is true, the principal beneficiaries of the Amnesty of 403 were not those who had taken the wrong side in a conflict. This view clashes with evidence that it was a legal clause in its own right and should be treated independently of other terms of the treaty.[9] The main beneficiaries of μὴ μνησικακεῖν were usually on the losing side of a conflict and, when the conflict ended, would otherwise have stood to lose. In inscriptions, the pledge appears among separate provisions which laid out arrangements for the restoration of exiles and other related legal matters which may have arisen. The question is whether the oath did no more than formalise the covenants listed in the decree or instead functioned as a separate free-standing provision. As in 403, the phrase ὅρκοι καὶ συνθῆκαι in inscriptions refers to an amnesty.[10] The promise μὴ μνησικακεῖν, as the inscriptional evidence further shows, was one of many oaths which disputing parties swore, and cannot stand for the entire amnesty package. Those portions of the subsequent oath which seal the Amnesty are usually distinct from μὴ μνησικακεῖν. This suggests that it had a

---

[8] Carawan 2012; 2013: 43–66.
[9] Joyce 2008; 2014; 2015.
[10] Lys. 13.88; 25.23; 28.34; [Lys.] 6.39; Isoc. 18.29; thus Joyce 2015: 26–7.

meaning that went beyond the mere formality of ratifying earlier covenants, though this is not to deny that some of its practical implications were covered in the covenants. In each example, the meaning of μὴ μνησικακεῖν varied depending on the historical circumstances under which *stasis* had arisen.

In the first years of the Peloponnesian War, Athens fell foul of her allies in Chalcidice and Bottiaea on the southern rim of Thrace. The sequence of events is related by the historian Thucydides: Athens had maintained an uneasy relationship with King Perdiccas of Macedon, whereupon in 432 hostilities erupted when Perdiccas incited his neighbours to the east to revolt from the Athenian alliance (Th. 1.57–8). The most important of the cities was Potidaea, originally a Corinthian colony but which, for geographical reasons, had fallen within Athens' orbit. On Potidaean instigation Perdiccas, a former ally of Athens, intervened in the region. The coastal cities along the two promontories of the peninsula came into alliance with Perdiccas against their former ally. This was a strategic loss for Athens, as her naval empire depended on the goodwill and cooperation of her allied cities around the coastal regions of the Aegean Sea. The loss of those allies would have been deeply felt and no doubt resulted in bitter and angry resentment. A decade later, the relationship mended when some of the cities of Bottiaea returned into alliance with Athens. Knowledge depends on an inscription,[11] which details a treaty between Athens and most of the cities of the Bottiaean peninsula.[12]

Unfortunately, not a great deal of the inscribed text is legible. The first five lines can hardly be made out, though there is a reference to suits (*dikaî*) in an unknown context. The legible portions preserve reciprocal oaths which both sides of the bargaining table were obliged to swear. On the Athenian side, a pledge was taken to defend the Bottiaeans and preserve the alliance according to what had been agreed, and to forget wrongs committed in the past (μὴ μνησικακεῖν) (lines 6–16). The Athenian oath alludes to terms of an alliance which may have been spelled out in the earlier portions of the treaty, though it is just as likely that they were laid down in another document. The Athenians pledged to defend the cities of Bottiaea, to abide by the covenants of alliance and not to rake over old coals. The third of these commitments, μὴ μνησικακεῖν, arouses greatest controversy: often but not always rendered 'to refrain from recalling past wrongs', it also means 'not to commit wrong through remembrance'. On the Bottiaean side, a promise was undertaken to have the same friends and enemies as the Athenians, not to assist the enemies

---

[11] *IG* I³ 76 = Tod 68. For the dating of this treaty to c. 422, see Tod 1946: 167 with relevant bibliography.

[12] We know that Spartolus was still unaligned with Athens by the time of Peace of Nicias in 421 (Th. 5.18.5).

of Athens and to let go of all past grievances (μὴ μνησικακεῖν) (lines 17–21). The remainder of the decree provides for its publication (lines 21–30). On one interpretation, μὴ μνησικακεῖν was a promise not to violate an agreement already reached, but was not therefore an annulment of further litigation for all past crimes.[13] In its favour, that interpretation points to the reciprocal structure of the oath, where a similar pledge is made by the Bottiaeans to Athens. Superficially, the interpretation of the oath standing as a legal formality solidifying pre-existing agreements might claim some justification.

As so little of the text survives, it is hazardous to make over-confident assertions, yet one consideration ought to warn against ready acceptance. On both sides, the oath sworn seems to have entailed three commitments: (1) to respect the alliance; (2) to come to the aid of the other in the event of external threats; and (3) to bury the past. The first two are by-clauses of the same pledge, but the third is different in that it refers not to future conditions, but to the past. At one level, there is a future point of reference here also, in that each participant promises in future to banish memory of what disturbed their friendship in the past. But unlike the first two clauses, which are both future-looking, the final pledge makes an express reference to past events. Because of the difference of emphasis, it does not follow that one term merely paraphrases the other. In this treaty, the force of μὴ μνησικακεῖν extends beyond legal formalisation of pre-existent terms. The phrase can only be meaningful if it adds an ingredient not contained in the earlier portions of the oath. The reciprocity of the oath might superficially suggest that μὴ μνησικακεῖν was a formality with no further substantive implications. This treaty, however, in notable contrast to the other two inscribed texts, implies equality between the sides, and that in this example one city is brought back into alliance with another. This is not a case of two sides of a single city broken by civil war reunited after one had been defeated. Lines 14–16 contain an Athenian commitment to honour the Bottiaeans according to the covenants and not to recall the past, which might be taken to imply that μὴ μνησικακεῖν was necessarily reciprocal in every instance of its usage. The evidence as it stands does not warrant that inference. Indeed, as in other places, it is much easier to read the phrase as a self-contained pledge which guaranteed that painful memories of past deeds should not stand in the way of the goodwill which was necessary for the treaty of alliance to prosper. The only point to be made in defence, as with another, very fragmentary, treaty involving Thasos, Paros and Neapolis (*IG* XII 5.109), is that the oath comes at the end of a series of legal measures. If the preserved texts of either inscription had been more complete, there might have been a better evidential framework. As it stands,

---

[13] Carawan 2002; 2012. For a completely different perspective, see Joyce 2008; 2014.

the evidence is extremely fragmentary and at most shows that substantive provisions of a treaty were followed by a promise of goodwill on both sides.

In 363/2, Athens engaged in a struggle with her northern neighbour Thebes, with whom she had previously been aligned. In 378 the Athenians had concluded a second naval treaty with the cities of the Aegean whose express purpose was to resist Spartan expansion.[14] Now that Sparta had receded, the league's *raison d'être* had become doubtful. We do not know that Thebes on this occasion had intervened, but its geographical proximity to the island of Ceos might well suggest that Thebes had begun to exert her influence among Athens' allies and was stirring up trouble. The decree has three principal concerns. First, Iulis was to pay an outstanding debt of three talents (lines 5–9). Secondly, the oath sworn by Chabrias to the Ceans was to be published at Iulis (lines 17–26). And thirdly, those citizens of Iulis who had organised the revolt were to go into exile (lines 27–48). The subsequent portions spell out the oaths. The Athenians on their side pledged not to harbour grievances (μὴ μνησικακεῖν) (lines 58–9). No Cean who abided by the oaths was to be exiled (lines 62–4). Any Cean who chose not to live on Ceos might live wherever he wished and enjoy his own property (lines 64–5). The Ceans, on their side, pledged to honour the Athenian alliance (lines 71–2), to make lawsuits of over 100 drachmas subject to appeal (lines 73–4), and to protect former Cean fugitives, as well as Athenians and allies, from future reprisals (lines 75–8).

In this example we see the oath in operation to secure forgiveness for Ceans who had participated in a revolt against Athens. The first fifty lines lay down the provisions to which the citizens of Iulis must adhere. Those portions allude to the past conflict between the two cities. The inscription suggests that Iulis had on at least two separate occasions revolted from the Athenian alliance and twice been reduced to submission, which resulted in an indemnity obligation. At the time of this treaty, the citizens of Iulis were in arrears, and one of the purposes of the decree was to extract payment of three talents which Iulis still owed (lines 5–9). Its main aim, however, was to stipulate the circumstances under which it was legitimate for the Athenians to carry out reprisals. This was a treaty of limitations. In circumstances where one side of a conflict had been brought to its knees, it lay in the power of the other to wreak vengeance indiscriminately. Here, the Athenians realised that yielding to vindictive instincts was not going to serve their interests, and so they decided for the sake of a new and lasting alliance to rein in desire to punish Iulis for what had happened in the war. Among other crimes, the rebellious city had exiled both Athenian representatives and

---

[14] The inscription which contains the text of the treaty which formed the Second Athenian League is *IG* II² 43 = RO 23. For general surveys and discussions, see Cargill 1981 and 1996; Horsley 1982; Mitchel 1984; Baron 2006.

the citizens of Iulis who had remained sympathetic to the Athenian alliance. When peace was restored, the pro-Athenian party was invited back. It was they whom Athens in one sense had most to fear, because they had suffered badly and desired revenge. Vindictive urges threatened the possibility of lasting peace, and so the swearing parties needed to implement legal mechanisms whereby the instinct of the victors to vent grievances were muzzled. The treaty was a trade-off, a pledge that in return for peaceful settlement, no harm would come. The citizens of Iulis were obligated under four peace conditions: to readmit the pro-Athenian faction previously in exile, to republish an old oath which the Athenian general Chabrias had sworn to the cities of Ceos, which may have been the original oath under which Athens had concluded an alliance over a decade earlier, to repay an outstanding indemnity and to exile the main ringleaders of the revolt, with the proviso that any not named among the chief conspirators had protection under terms of alliance.

The language of the decree spells out a political benefaction from the victor. Though it places Iulis under an obligation not to resume hostilities, provided terms are upheld it pledges no further danger. That much is made clear in what follows: the Athenians on their side pledge to the Ceans not to harbour grudges (μὴ μνησικακεῖν), to exile no Cean who abides by the terms, to quell subversion and to let émigrés live wherever they wish and to draw upon proceeds of their property (lines 49–68). At various points, the text makes reference to earlier oaths and covenants (for example, at lines 42–9, 75–9), and from this it could be argued that both sides swore μὴ μνησικακεῖν.[15] The Athenian oath, quoted at lines 57–61, makes a list of pledges to Ceos. It is no less than a peace offer and presupposes a bilateral agreement. But there are important caveats. The oath states: 'I shall not recall grievances (ὢ μνησικακήσω) for what is past at the hands of any Cean nor shall I kill any Cean nor shall I make an exile of anyone who abides by the oaths and covenants.' There are three principal commitments: (1) μὴ μνησικακεῖν; (2) a promise to do no violence; and (3) a promise to drive nobody into exile. The clause μὴ μνησικακεῖν, one of the various promises entailed in the oath, is not to be confused with the oath *in toto*.[16] The covenants of reconciliation would have to be observed on both sides, as lines 59–60 show, which stipulate that the Ceans also must abide by the oaths and agreements. To recognise this, however, does not entail that

---

[15] For other, more general, discussions of this complex document, see Ruschenbusch 1982; Dreher 1995: 122; Guagliumi 2003: 25–47; Cooper 2008: 31–54.

[16] Lines 57–61: τάδε συνέθεντο καὶ ὤμοσαν οἱ στρατηγοὶ οἱ Ἀθηναίων πρὸς τὰς πόλες τ[ὰ]ς ἐν Κέωι κα[ὶ] οἱ σύμμαχοι· vacat ὃ μνησικακήσω [τῶ]ν πα[ρ]εληλυθότων πρὸ[ς] Κείος οὐδ[ε]νὸς οὐδὲ ἀποκτενῶ Κ[εί]ων ὁ[δ]ένα οὐδὲ φυγάδα ποήσω τῶν ἐμμενόντων τοῖς ὅρκο[ις καὶ τ]αῖς συνθήκαις ταῖσδε, ... Notice the framing of the chiasmus in the wording of the oath: καὶ ὤμοσαν and τοῖς ὅρκο[ις καὶ τ]αῖς συνθήκαις συνέθεντο.

the pledge of μὴ μνησικακεῖν was reciprocal.[17] That part of the oath refers to Cean misbehaviour, where anything the Athenians had suffered was no longer actionable. None of this has any bearing on the other covenants.

The Ceans also swore an oath (lines 69–80), and the frequency with which the Cean oath mentions earlier covenants of reconciliation might be taken to imply that it was some sealing measure. Of course, the treaty had two sides, but μὴ μνησικακεῖν need not have featured in any of the commitments undertaken by the Ceans. Provisions are made for appeal in lawsuits involving above 100 drachmas, and returnees are to receive aid in case their interests are violated. At the end of the document, two lines survive in poor condition which list a pledge sworn by somebody, in which modern editors following Köhler restore the phrase ὢ μνησικακήσω (lines 81–2). The Ceans did not swear μὴ μνησικακεῖν, and that the phrase must be understood unilaterally.[18] The oath does recur in the edited version of the text and may have been sworn by the Ceans, but this is unlikely, as its beneficiaries were the Ceans themselves.[19] The identity of the swearing party cannot be established for certain, as a *vacat* separates the reference to the restored fugitives from the phrase ὢ μνησικακήσω. If this is a separate oath, my point stands: at least three parties are mentioned, the Athenians, the Ceans and a smaller group of former Cean exiles now restored because they had taken the Athenian side in an earlier conflict and had been driven out by the hostile party, brought to its knees. If the beneficiaries of the oath ὢ μνησικακήσω in lines 81–2 are the Ceans, as the space of the lettering would imply, it cannot be the defeated party who swears, but the restored exiles. If so, μὴ μνησικακεῖν in this treaty, as in the others, was designed principally to protect those who had most to lose.

Though these provisions were made conditional, there can be little doubt that this was a blanket remedy with the few exceptions listed. The pledge μὴ

---

[17] Carawan has misconstrued my point about the force of μὴ μνησικακεῖν being not future-looking but retrospective. The force of μὴ μνησικακεῖν is to ensure that anything done in past time is to be consigned to oblivion, not to seal the Reconciliation as such. The connection with the past is reinforced by the phrase τῶν παρεληλυθότων, a point which he overlooks in this oath and in others.

[18] Joyce 2008: 510: 'The force of μὴ μνησικακεῖν is not future looking but retrospective. It relates not to those who choose in future to respect this settlement but rather to those who, in the past, decided to support those who had violated the terms set out by Chabrias. Excepting those directly answerable for the rebellion, all are to be let off the hook. It is, in fact, a pledge of forgiveness.' Carawan quotes this verbatim as an example of what he dubs my perverse logic, as if I were denying that the Ceans were expected to swear an oath. My point was much simpler than that: the phrase μὴ μνησικακεῖν does a completely different job from the one he envisions and was not framed reciprocally.

[19] Krech 1888: 58–60. The restoration follows lines 58–60 and should not be read as a measure of reciprocity, as the beneficiaries are the same group.

μνησικακεῖν does not mean simply that pre-existing terms of a treaty were to be upheld, though that would have been expected, as the oath of the Ceans shows. Its intent was to ensure that anything the citizens of Iulis had perpetrated in the conflict would not lead to future litigation. It remains possible nevertheless that settlements for disputes below a stated threshold were permitted thereafter, since the Cean oath stipulates that lawsuits involving sums in excess of 100 drachmas were to be subject to appeal, and so within narrow limitations it may have been possible to sue for damages inflicted in the period of conflict (lines 69–79). Even larger cases may have been allowed provided the defendants were granted right of appeal. But what is evident is that the aim of the truce was to close the potential for large-scale lawsuits to reignite old grudges. In this example, we observe μὴ μνησικακεῖν functioning as a legal guarantee from one side to the other. Unlike in Bottiaea, μὴ μνησικακεῖν is not reciprocal, as it is notably absent from the Cean oath. Of course, both sides might have harboured grudges, but the crucial point is that the language of the treaty envisages wrongs endured only by one side of a struggle, in this case, naturally, by the winning side. As far as the treaty is concerned, only one of the two sides is required to forgive 'wrongs'. Evidently politicised, this reveals something significant about the understanding of limiting memory for past evils. In a legal sense, it meant that the winning side would not take advantage of its victorious position by imposing an intolerable peace. Winning the peace implied that vindictive instincts were to be restrained in the interest of renewing harmonious relations. This, no doubt, would have been a difficult objective, and so a legal formulation of the principle was necessary so that, while violent actions had now ceased, further prosecution of old hostilities in the courts was also legally limited.

In its main objective, the pledge μὴ μνησικακεῖν imposed a limit on litigious action in the courts. In this treaty, the pledge was sworn at least twice, once by the Athenians and again by pro-Athenian returnees who knew that they might otherwise have had the opportunity to vent their grudges through a welter of renewed litigation. This treaty illustrates a fundamental principle that, when conflict was ended and terms of reconciliation laid down, the success or failure of the truce lay primarily with the victor.[20] Without a guarantee to the loser that no harm would come, any truce concluded between two sides in an erstwhile conflict was bound to be fragile and liable to breakdown. The treaty between Athens and Iulis is complex, as it involved both an internal and an external reconciliation. Athens held a community of interest with those in Iulis who supported the alliance, but unlike the other examples this is a trilateral compact between two internal factions and an external agent which had backed

---

[20] Thus Joyce 2008: 509–11.

one of those factions in what had, in origin, probably been an internecine feud. The trilateral nature of this treaty is crucial to remember when considering that three separate oaths were sworn, one by the Athenians, another by the Ceans, and a third, of which only two poorly preserved lines survive, by those among the Ceans who had been exiled and were now recently restored.

At around the time that Athens drew up terms with Iulis, the phrase μὴ μνησικακεῖν is attested in a recently discovered dossier from Dicaea in northern Greece.[21] The preserved text contains seven decrees of the Dicaeopolitan assembly. The first enjoined publication of the oaths and covenants in the temple of Athena and the city agora, to which the citizens were obliged to swear within three days. Any who refused faced property confiscation, *atimia* and limitation on capacity to participate in the justice system. Perdiccas was granted permission to execute any who violated the truce or, if they chose to take refuge, to seize and retain them within his own domain. The second stipulated that outstanding homicide suits could be pursued provided they related to offences committed before the archonship of Gorgythus and took place on a specified day in the month. Any who litigated contrary to the agreed terms was liable to exile, while any who stood trials lost his rights and had his property confiscated. The third laid down that all suits for murder committed prior to the archonship of Gorgythus be adjudicated within the year of office on pain of exile for those who litigated later and loss of rights for those who authorised murder trials outside the window of time permitted. This seems to have been framed as an exception to the normal rule, which forbade litigation between the party of Demarchus and that of Xenophon. Any who violated this rule was liable to disfranchisement. The fourth granted the sons of Hieron and Epicrates and Argaeus permission to litigate in the months of Anthesterion and Lenaion and made provision for the sons of Hermippus and Epichares and Demophilus who were in transit to swear and purify according to a set procedure. The sixth was a general prohibition against litigation bar a few named persons who had to stand trial for outstanding offences. The final decree laid out the terms of the oath which all citizens swore, to abide by the ancestral constitution, to refuse admission to any outsider whose intent was to harm Dicaea, not to recall past wrongs (μὴ μνησικακεῖν) in word or deed, not to kill any exile, to show mercy to suppliants, to purify at the altars and to withdraw from illegal litigation.

Collectively, the decrees of Dicaea showcase the same principle as the reconciliation at Iulis, but the bar to litigation for deeds committed in time of civil war was more subtly nuanced. As the second and fourth decrees indicate, litigation for past offences was permitted under stated circumstances. Most

---

[21] *SEG* 57.576; Voutiras and Sismanides 2008; Gray 2013.

important was the pledge not to ban homicide litigation (lines 28–32). It is tempting to compare the exemption to Athens, where scholars have often mistakenly imagined a similar loophole created for own-hand homicide.[22] But, as Chapter 5 has argued, that assumption rests on a misreading of the terms of reconciliation in 403. More noteworthy at Dicaea is that both sides in a former conflict sought to heal their differences by agreeing not to litigate against each other, except in special cases. The onus was to spell out what those special cases were, rather than to list all the different types of litigation which were outlawed under the terms of the drafted amnesty. The aim of this treaty was to ensure that the reconciled community would not descend into civil strife again by letting old sores run. The meaning of μὴ μνησικακεῖν is exactly what we would expect: those who took the oath bound themselves not to reignite hostilities through deed or slander, and to respect the rights of those who had sworn the oaths whose interests were protected by them.

In 324, a year before Alexander's untimely death, a decree was issued to the city states of the Greek mainland to restore exiles.[23] Ostensibly the motive was to foster greater unity among the Greeks, but this was a display of imperial mastery by the leading Macedonian power. The so-called Exiles Decree marks a tipping point in Greek history when larger power blocs began to interfere in the internal affairs of individual cities and exercise their will accordingly.[24] The main purpose was to restore exiles to their homes and property. In this case, there is no sign that the exiles in question had originally fled from civil conflict. In many cases, no doubt, they had fallen foul of the law and taken refuge abroad. The historian Curtius (6.1.20) records that seven years earlier Agis of Sparta had led some Peloponnesian allies into revolt against Macedon, which was soon crushed. It could well be that those who lost their place at Tegea were those who had led the city into open revolt and had been exiled at Alexander's behest once the revolt failed. The inscribed decree restored former exiles to their right of inheritance. Though it remains unclear if all were given back sequestered property, the provisions grant all returnees a house and an adjacent plot of land, and this may have been compensation for dwellings or farmsteads destroyed or plundered. Those to whom property was restored received monetary compensation for financial losses incurred while abroad. The agreement did allow litigation within a sixty-day time limit in the event current squatters were unwilling to move, for which a tribunal was set up in the neighbouring town of Mantineia. All citizens, it seems, were bound to pay

---

[22] This mistake is made by Carawan (2013: 139–70). Against this misinterpretation, see Chapter 5.
[23] D.S. 17.109; Just. 13.5; Din. *Dem.* 81; Hyp. *Dem.* col. 18.
[24] *Syll*³ 3.306 = RO 10. For modern discussion see Lonis 1991; Worthington 1993; Maffi 1994; Carawan 2002: 7; Dössel 2003: 159–68; Dmitriev 2004; Joyce 2008: 509–10.

taxes to the temple, and for returnees who during their period of exile had been unable to make the payments, a grant was extended to pay their dues for them. The end of the text reveals a pledge not to dredge up bitter feelings (μὴ μνησικακεῖν) for anything that the former exiles might have committed in the past.[25] Here, the promise μὴ μνησικακεῖν went beyond sealing terms. In this case, the exiles, who might have been targeted victims at the hands of an angry populace, were expressly protected from the vindictive undercurrents of a citizen body which nursed hatred and resentment.[26]

Tegea bears similarities and differences with the other case studies. As in Iulis, the μὴ μνησικακεῖν is one-sided. There is no evidence in the decree that the returnees were expected to swear a reciprocal oath. Unlike in Iulis and Dicaea, the returnees were the victims of an earlier policy decision whose interests the oath of reconciliation aimed to protect. In the case of Iulis, the returnees were the victors who swore not to take vengeance on their former enemies. Here, the reverse was true. At Tegea, it was the resident population which swore to protect those who returned, not the other way around. This important difference should discourage the overuse of these examples when we seek to extrapolate general principles of what the clause μὴ μνησικακεῖν might mean. As in all cases studies so far, its express purpose was to ensure that the past not become the thorn in the side to prospects of a lasting peace arrangement, but the ways in which this objective was realised differed widely from one example to the next. The Tegean inscription does not reveal how the pledge to the returning exiles was put into practice. It is very likely that, as at Iulis and Dicaea, this involved a ban on prosecution for crimes now eradicated from the record. If the exiles in question had, as suggested here, been political victims, this would presumably also have entailed a pledge not to take criminal proceedings against them for any poor policy which they had previously advocated. Unfortunately, the text as preserved is too lacunose, but there is enough material to showcase a city state devising clear legal terms to define the position of beneficiaries.

Some decades after the death of Alexander the obscure town of Alipheira in Arcadia in the central Peloponnese reconciled following a period of internal discord. Our only surviving source is a short inscription detailing the terms and provisions (IPArk 24 = SEG 25.447). Among its clauses is relief of debt, though what this amounted to is debatable.[27] Here, civil strife appears to have

---

[25] Lines 59–60: εὐνοήσω τοῖς κατηνθηκόσι τοῖς ἔδοξε τᾶι πόλι κατυδέχεσθαι, καὶ οὐ μνασικακήσω τῶννυ οὐ δε ν[ὶ] τ[ὰ] ἂν ἀμπ[ε]ίσῃ ἀπὺ τᾶι ἀμέραι τᾶι τὸν ὅρκον ὤμοσα, οὐδὲ διακωλύσω τὰν τῶν κατηνθηκότων σωτηρίαν ... Rhodes and Osborne (2003: 531) render it thus: 'I shall not harbour grudges against any of them for what he may have [plotted].' It needs to be emphasised that the rendition is not certain.

[26] Thus Joyce 2008: 512.

[27] For discussion see Dössel 2003: 225.

arisen through a debt crisis. Unlike the other inscribed texts, this one begins with the promise not to bear grudges and moves on to the other provisions. The opening lines read: '[From the time when] Cleonymus drove out the ship and expelled the pirates and restored the city to freedom, it shall be possible for nobody to harbour grudges (μὴ μνησιχολῆσαι) against anyone for the sake of past disputes against each other, nor for anyone to bring action against anyone else if a pollution [for homicide] took place before Cleonymus drove out the ship of Aristolaus and cast out the pirates' (lines 3–8). The sense of 'not bearing grudges' is framed as a prohibition against legal action. Two kinds of litigation were forbidden, one against homicide, the other for debt. The phrase μὴ μνησιχολῆσαι is linked to debt, and even if not a *tabula rasa* in the fullest sense, there was a stipulation that any debts forgiven under the terms should be scrapped. Though the circumstances of this civil strife appear to have been different from those of Iulis, Tegea and Dicaea, a common thread runs through: if litigation continued unabated, the community would fall once again into *stasis*. The case of Alipheira reaffirms the principle observed elsewhere, that in political emergency the way to reconcile a community was to prevent litigation.

LEGACY AND PARADIGM: AMNESTY IN THE CLASSICAL AND HELLENISTIC AGES

Inscriptions collectively confirm literary sources, that the pledge μὴ μνησικακεῖν normally implied forgiveness for some set of grievances committed during *stasis* and was sworn by the winning side in a war or conflict. The purpose was to assure the losing side that if hostilities were put aside, protection was guaranteed. Whether the city states of Greece lived up to that promise or not varied from place to place, and by no means is the expression attested in every instance where an agreement was reached after *stasis*. Indeed, only in a minority of cases is it known that such a pledge was sworn. However, the finest example of its use and application, Athens in the aftermath of civil conflagration, illustrates the principle at its very best: when the pledge was sworn, it gave legal protection to partisans of the losing side from vindictive action in the courts. Other cities in Greece show different levels of success in effecting lasting reconciliation agreements. A recent survey of reconciliation agreements in the fifth and fourth centuries in Greece has put forward the case that the principle of reconciliation is not always witnessed in every amnesty agreement on record.[28] It is undoubtedly true that, in some cases, amnesties were often little better than veiled attempts by aggressive victors to bully

[28] Dreher 2013.

erstwhile foes into submission and, in some cases, protracted internal warfare even further. Care should be taken with generalisations of this kind, but it is certainly the case that not all attempts at reconciliation in the aftermath of *stasis* fulfilled its objectives. In other instances, there is better evidence that Greek cities did make genuine efforts to bring about a state of harmony after a period of internal strife or faction, and though the methods by which this was implemented varied from place to place, there is no good reason to imagine that Greeks did not understand what it meant to reconcile. On the contrary, in very many examples, it seems the principles of reconciliation were understood and applied.

In 424, Megara experienced an oligarchic coup. Those who had taken the Athenian side slipped away, while the oligarchs invited sympathisers at Pegae back into the city to establish government. Oaths were sworn not to remember past quarrels and to give the city the best advice (Th. 4.74.2). Thucydides uses the same phrase μὴ μνησικακεῖν as was used twenty-one years later at Athens. Unlike in 403, former verdicts under which exiles had been banished were annulled but there is no evidence that residents were protected from reprisals. In this example, the effect of μὴ μνησικακεῖν was to overturn older verdicts against the supporters of the oligarchy, but here we encounter the provision being used selfishly to promote the interests of a single faction, in this case the oligarchs who benefited. The trials which followed illustrate the differences with the Athenian example twenty-one years later. At Megara, once the oligarchic coup was established, the newly instated government decided to abolish the secret ballot, which meant that any voting in political trials was liable to scrutiny and manipulation by the oligarchs. The account of Thucydides does not indicate that the pledge μὴ μνησικακεῖν was backed up with any legal provision which protected citizens from unfair litigation. The crucial contrast to be noted here between Megara and Athens is that at Megara there were no legal safeguards, and so slaughter ensued, whereas at Athens there were robust provisions, which meant that society did not degenerate into civil conflict.

The next two decades illustrate amnesty in different cities used to different effects. In 411, Thucydides reports a revolt on Samos (Th. 8.73.2–6).[29] Thirty out of the three hundred ruling oligarchs were killed, whereupon a decree was issued not to bear grudges (μὴ μνησικακεῖν). Unlike Megara, this was a true measure of reconciliation which foreshadows 403. About two years after Samos, the Athenians decreed the return of exiles from Selymbria and return of confiscated property (*IG* I³ 118 = ML 87, esp. lines 8–18). The decree appears in a treaty between two states at a time when Athens was fighting a war of survival against the Peloponnesian League, Syracuse and Persia. This was a goodwill gesture and cemented interstate relations. The last years of the

---

[29] On the nature of the revolt at Samos, see Moggi 2012: 134.

fifth century yield a cluster of examples where cities, from a variety of motives, issued decrees of amnesty recalling former exiles. At the end of the fifth century, the island state of Thasos issued a decree restoring to citizen status those who had lost their rights (*IG* XII 8.262 lines 5–9).[30] Diodorus describes the circumstances under which Dionysius I established tyranny at Syracuse in 406 (D.S. 13.92.7). In a bid for power, he persuaded the Syracusan assembly to restore exiles, which, as events unfolded, turned out to be a selfish measure to bolster power and influence. In the case of Dionysius, amnesty was not used for the purpose of reconciliation. Diodorus even likens Dionysius to Peisistratus in his use of popular support to create a personal bodyguard and tighten grip on government. Unlike democracy, in the hands of an oligarch or tyrant amnesty could have the effect of dividing, not uniting, a civic community. Later in 404, the newly established tyrant of Syracuse proclaimed amnesty for 7,000 exiles (D.S. 14.9.6–8). The motives strongly resemble those at Megara in 424. Dionysius I was not interested in political reconciliation. His intent was to expand his power base with the support of those that would benefit from the amnesty.

The fourth century, no less than the fifth, indicates that amnesty arrangements could fulfil a range of objectives. In 401, the Greek-speaking city of Cyrene on the north coast of Africa swore an oath of amnesty after a bloody civil war (D.S. 14.34.6). A would-be tyrant, Ariston, had made a bid for power and put to death five hundred of the leading citizens, and banished many more. With the help of mercenaries, the exiles managed to gather enough forces and lead an assault on the city. After their victory, they decreed not to remember past evils and to live together as one united people. The story of Cyrene bears close resemblance to that of Athens, where a bloodbath might have ensued but was averted through the intelligence and foresight of a resurgent democracy. Under more dubious circumstances, the Corinthians in 392 showed comparable insight when a group of their citizens, backed by Persian money and military support from Sparta's enemies, carried out a wholesale massacre of others who were leaning towards Sparta and suing for peace (X. *HG* 4.4.2–5). At the festival of Artemis Euclea, they butchered citizens in the marketplace, especially the wealthier members of the community, and sacrilegiously turned on those who had taken refuge at the altars, especially the older men of the city. Eventually, the younger men retreated to the Acrocorinth but were invited back to the city by plea of their mothers and sisters. The rest decided not to retaliate but grant the exiles safe return with the oath that they would come to no harm. As recounted, the story is quite confused, as Xenophon does not exactly clarify who the beneficiaries were. He relates that before taking the Acrocorinth the

---

[30] See Seibert 1979: 82.

fugitives beat off an attack of the Argives. Presumably, the exiles were victims of the attack in the city, as the leaders of that murderous onslaught were allies of Argos. If so, amnesty was granted to pro-Spartan partisans at Corinth. But, according to the same narrative, the origin of the civil conflict lay with anti-Spartan groups. Xenophon's account is too vague to know precisely what took place, but this looks like a failed and desperate attempt by a divided city to unify itself in fraught times.

In the years immediately following her victory in the Corinthian War and conclusion of the King's Peace in 387/6, Sparta tightened her grip over cities within the Peloponnese who previously had been disloyal. One example was Phlius, which had exiled some of its citizens loyal to Sparta (X. *HG* 5.3.24–5). The ephors made overtures to Phlius to allow their safe return. Fearing violent repercussions, the Phliasians decreed universal amnesty. Within Phlius the exiles had friends and supporters who desired change of government. Here, amnesty was granted through the influence of a foreign power which bullied the other into submission. Some four years later, in 379, oligarchic exiles were restored at Phlius through the agency of the Spartan king Agesilaus (X. *HG* 5.3.25). Agesilaus determined that fifty men from each party should vote among themselves who should be allowed to live and who should die, and then to draw up a constitution. The case of Phlius is intriguing, because while on the one hand it shows the influence of a foreign power asserting its will by intervening in the internal affairs of a city, at the same time it indicates that the Spartans recognised the importance of due process, and were keen that procedures be put in place to guarantee fair hearings. In these years, Athens began to organise resistance. The year 378 marks the resurgence of Athenian naval power in the Aegean, but whereas the Athenians in the fifth century had exploited their influence abroad, in the fourth century they were determined not to repeat the mistakes of history. A pledge was taken not to appropriate tribute from allied members of the league for selfish expenditure and to treat all allies on an equal footing. In order to promote unity, internal divisions within the member states of the league needed to be put aside. The inscription which bears the decree mentions that the synedrion of the alliance had the authority to mediate in a civic dispute at Paros.[31] Though in the treaty no specific amnesty clause is entailed, this provides evidence in that it committed member states to internal unity.

Isocrates refers to two amnesties around 350, one at Mytilene and one at Methymna, to restore to rights those who had been exiled in the time of tyranny (Isoc. *Ep.* 8.3, 7.8). An inscription from Erythrae dating from the subsequent two decades mentions a stay on the prosecution of returning exiles

---

[31] Rhodes and Osborne 2003: 29.

(*Inscr. Erythr.* 10 lines 1–9, 18–21). In the wake of Athens' disastrous defeat to Philip in 338 BCE, the orator Hypereides moved to restore all those who had lost their citizen rights (Hyp. fr. 32 Sauppe = frr. 27 and 28 Blass). The evident motive was to increase solidarity in the event of a Macedonian invasion. At about the same time the Athenian confederacy issued a decree providing for reconciliation in the civic community of an unnamed league member (*IG* II^3 281 line 3). Both sides swore an oath to reconcile and renew their treaty with Athens. Elsewhere, in the western Peloponnese, Elis decreed that a group called *geneai* should not be banished or have property confiscated. All exiles were recalled with the assurance of immunity for all offences committed after Pyrrhon's office as *damiourgos*.[32] In all examples, the purpose seems to have been to promote unity. Though they were motivated doubtless by political exigencies, especially in the shadow of the rising power of Macedon, at the same time we should not lose sight of the commitment and insight of the Greek cities and civic communities to end internal conflict. In every documented case where amnesty was brought about by a democratic state operating on a democratic principle, we see amnesty used as an instrument of peace and reconciliation, effected by a legal mechanism.

It is sometimes held that justice and harmony are irreconcilable concepts. That view holds that whenever states tried to rebuild harmonious relationships after war and conflict, it was necessary to suspend justice. Two arguably related inscriptions from Mytilene on Lesbos would indicate otherwise. Between 340 and 330, Mytilene issued a decree recalling exiled citizens (*SEG* 36.170 = Tod 201 = RO 85B).[33] A possibly related inscription (*SEG* 36.750) is very fragmentary, but its remnants indicate that a cult of Homonoia was instituted. The twelve Olympian gods are honoured, but other personified deities are represented as well, such as Concord and Justice (lines 5–12). In order of priority, Concord has pride of place, but Justice appears right next to it. Justice, it seems, was integral to the ideology of the newly reconciled community. The text does not attest μὴ μνησικακεῖν but does indicate a bilateral commitment to honour the agreements, *synallagai* (line 30). Officials from both sides were elected to mediate in disputes and punish any who did not abide by the truce (lines 1–10, 21–2). The inscribed portions break off before spelling out the oaths by which the truce was guaranteed. What the remnants indicate is that harmony and justice were bedfellows in the reconciliation. The case of Mytilene is not unlike that of Athens after 403 BCE, which does not yield specific evidence of a cult of Homonoia, but where the verb *homonoein* is used to express an ideology of positive mutual intentions in keeping with the spirit of the amnesty (And. 1.108–9).

---

[32] Michel 1900: 1334 lines 6–8; Seibert 1979: 149–50.
[33] Heisserer and Hodot 1986; Dössel 2003: 159–68. On the relationship, see Chaniotis 2013: 66–7.

A fascinating document from Nakone in Sicily reveals a similar focus on Homonoia, but in this example legal measures are taken to enforce it through the reorganisation of the civic community (*SEG* 30.1119).[34] At Athens, though the amnesty intended to bury the hatchet, no specific clause demanding goodwill is known. At Nakone, in contrast, an attempt was made to enshrine Homonoia in law. The inscription dates anywhere from the mid-fourth to the early third century and pertains to a city on the western side of Sicily. The closest parallel comes from the East, where a decree laid out provisions for an annual festival for Athena and Homonoia to commemorate reconciliation between Margasus and Tarsus.[35] In the latter example, the cult commemorates a treaty between two cities. The case of Nakone sets out a cult of Homonoia to cement unity between two parties in a civil conflict. The factions are called upon to end fighting and to choose a list of thirty names from the other. Those names are written on ballots and chosen by lot by a member of each faction. Three men are chosen from the remainder of the citizenry to create new confraternities consisting of five members each. Further provisions are made for sacrifices to Homonoia. Significantly, the new fraternities prohibited their members to be related by blood, which was perhaps meant to break down any traditional loyalties that had led to civil conflict through family faction. The document is most unusual in that it takes to an extreme the principle that in a restored community all members should share common goals and feelings. Unlike in Athens, where feelings were allowed to smoulder, even if they were not allowed to be vented in the courts, at Nakone we encounter an attempt to control through a legal arrangement the feelings of its citizens. This was an extraordinary step, and one that was not usually canvassed, perhaps because private feelings cannot be regulated through legal means. The huge difference which Nakone presents is that amity is imposed through cult. Rather than blocking litigation, Nakone decided that the best way to prevent the fresh outbreak of hostilities was to rearrange the structure of its community. The case is very different from Athens and cities elsewhere, perhaps because the whole community had not been involved in the dispute. This marks an attempt to reconcile a portion of the citizen community by reorganising the entire citizenry. Civil concord is the aim, but the method used to achieve it is witnessed nowhere else.[36]

In the Hellenistic age, exiles could often be used as political pawns. Sometime during the early years of the reign of Alexander the Great, one of Mytilene's neighbours, Eresus, overthrew its tyrants, put them to death and

---

[34] Lupu 2005: 357–8 No. 26; Chaniotis 2010; Gray 2015: 37–41.
[35] Thériault 1996: 85–8.
[36] On the Nakone agreement in general, see Gray 2015: 37–41.

drove their families into exile.[37] The exiled families pleaded with Alexander, Philip III and Antigonus to return, but the citizens of Eresus refused because of what the city had suffered during the period of tyranny (*IG* XII 2.526 + Suppl. = *OGIS* 8). This presents a converse example where solidarity was enforced by the refusal to grant amnesty. Nevertheless, criminalisation was constricted to a small number. Diodorus records an edict of the Macedonian council in 319 to oust the oligarchies in cities controlled by Cassander and Antigonus and restore democracy. All men exiled since the time of Alexander's crossing to Asia in 334 were to be repatriated (D.S. 18.55.1–56.8). The decree was issued at the behest of the Macedonian general Polyperchon, who by that stage had acquired control of the Greek peninsula and was engaged in a dynastic squabble with his Macedonian neighbours across the sea in Asia Minor. The amnesty guaranteed restoration of property, political rights and cancellation of past verdicts. Here, we see an example where the judicial autonomy of individual states was violated to further the interests of a larger power structure. The decree does not refer to the wishes of those communities who were affected by it but was an open bid to destabilise the territory of a rival power. Over a century later, during the bitter struggle between Sparta and the Achaean League, Philopoemen forced Sparta, by that time a league member, to readmit pro-Achaean exiles (Plu. *Phil.* 16.3–6). Draconian measures followed, including the execution of Spartan citizens, the destruction of Sparta's walls, the annexation of Spartan territory to the neighbouring city of Megalopolis, the relocation of those who had been made Spartan citizens and enslavement of those who refused to comply. What passed as amnesty had the very opposite purpose from reconciliation.

Sometime in the third century, we encounter a commitment in Asia Minor between two neighbours who came into alliance after a war (*SEG* 29.1130, esp. lines 11–22). Both sides, Temnus and Clazomenae, promised to banish memory of their legal charges for all time.[38] In keeping with semantic shifts, the phrase used is not μὴ μνησικακεῖν but *amnêstia*. The oaths sworn between Temnus and Clazomenae echo the agreement between Athens and Bottiaea over a century earlier. In the same region, we encounter the use of *amnêstia* on conclusion of a war between Miletus and Magnesia on the Maeander (*Milet* I 3.148). Likewise, it enjoins that memory of the war should be banished. Later, in 246, a similar arrangement was contracted between Smyrna and Magnesia on the Sipylus not to prosecute grievances (*I.Magnesia am Sipylos* 1). These examples are of amnesties between cities, as distinct from internal parties or factions. They are not perhaps amnesties in the sense of restoring citizens to rights or barring criminal prosecutions, but a comparable

---

[37] Lott 1996; Bencivenni 2003; Dmitriev 2004.
[38] Hermann 1979.

principle is still at stake. The Hellenistic world was dominated by power blocs whose leaders were frequently called on to arbitrate between cities within their domains. Many of the treaties stop grievances (*enklêmata*). In the interest of preserving unity, individuals were expected to banish memory of the past. Alliances between cities followed the same basic principle.

Shortly after 235, the Achaean League made a treaty with the Peloponnesian town of Orchomenus (*IPArk* 16). Among its provisions was a clause forbidding court hearings for matters arising between Nearchus and the rest of Orchomenus. This Nearchus was probably the former tyrant of Orchomenus. The treaty made provision for the settlement of some Achaeans in the territory of Orchomenus (lines 11–13). Fines of 1,000 drachmas were imposed on those who ignored the moratorium. Unfortunately, not enough survives of the treaty to determine what provisions it made to reverse earlier verdicts of the tyrant. We know of no clause readmitting exiles or restoring property. As far as we can tell the effect of the measure was less to repatriate exiles who had lost their rights under the tyranny than to protect a former tyrant, perhaps to prevent a gathering of hostile military forces. Unfortunately, too little is known of the circumstances to permit anything more than conjecture as to what the motives of this amnesty were. In the early part of the second century, perhaps in the 180s, an inscription from Miletus records an *amnêstia* for legal charges (*enklêmata*), both public and private, which arose earlier in connection with war. An exception is made for *res iudicata* and public offences (*Milet* I 3.150 lines 36–9). Traditionally, this clause has been interpreted as reinforcing an existing peace treaty between two cities.[39] On that interpretation, the main thrust of the arrangement was to cement peaceful relations between two cities by preventing continued litigation. It may also have prevented litigation against internal traitors. Unlike the earlier examples from the classical period, the aim of this arrangement seems to have been very narrowly channelled. The term *amnêstia* does not entail a general proclamation of amnesty. In context, it would be difficult to render the term as 'amnesty'. The only stay it imposes upon litigation is upon cases connected with a recent war, and even here exemptions are made for those where verdicts had been delivered.

At about the same time, the historian Polybius reports that the Romans in 187/6 demanded the recall of Zeuxippus from exile (Plb. 22.4). The reluctant Boeotians protested to Rome that they could not go against their own verdicts and arbitrations. Zeuxippus had been charged and convicted *in absentia* of two offences, desecration and murder. The implication of this is that these verdicts were fabricated as a ruse to persuade the Romans not to proceed with Zeuxippus' repatriation. The ruse was successful. Pausanias reports a similar

[39] Gauthier 1972: 272–3.

demand made to the Achaeans to readmit exiles implicated in the murder of the Achaean statesman Philopoemen (Paus. 7.9.6–7). These examples together illustrate the potentially destabilising effect of amnesty. In both cases, the proposal to repatriate exiles was mediated by a foreign imperial power with a self-interested agenda. If imposed from outside, amnesty was very likely to have had a detrimental effect upon a community. In the case of Boeotia, it would have resulted in the breakdown of her alliance with Macedonia. These later examples show how 'amnesty' could mean something other than reconciliation. By the Hellenistic and Roman periods, it was used often as an instrument of faction and political suppression.

The foregoing discussion has yielded some common threads. First, the primary aim of any reconciliation agreement was to ensure that factional squabbles which had rent society apart did not resurface in the newly reconciled community. This meant that in cases where one side had got the upper hand, it was recognised that giving vent to angry feelings was potentially fatal. The only chance a city had of standing on its feet again after a period of political crisis was to consign to oblivion traces of the past which might undermine unity. Secondly, it was not enough to tell citizens to 'forgive and forget'. Vengeance for wrongs committed was a component of the Greek sense of justice, as the famous Temples Decree of the early fifth century pledging to leave unrepaired shrines destroyed by the Persians as a reminder to Greeks of their obligation to avenge the past shows.[40] Because this impulse for revenge was there, it was of paramount importance to rein in that instinct in some way. The best way to do this was by means of a bar on litigation. Without this, political infighting was most likely to start again, and so any catalyst needed to be quelled. There are two ways of looking at these reconciliation agreements. In one sense, a moratorium on litigation meant that justice needed to be suspended in the interest of establishing civic harmony. But in a broader and more far-sighted sense, limiting action in the courts was the one and only way to guarantee the long-term survival of a political system where disputes could be resolved peacefully. As Athenians recognised, if litigation for past grievances was to continue unabated, the likelihood was that this would have degenerated into conflict. This is perhaps why the example of Mytilene is so powerful in that it reminded its citizens that while in the short term, justice had to be circumvented in the interest of restoring harmony, the long-term objective was to ensure that a community could run on principles of justice rather than on a show of might. The interface between justice and harmony was probably the hardest problem for any reconciliation to deal with, but

---

[40] Isoc. 4.156. For a detailed analysis of how emotion influenced behaviour, see Chaniotis 2013: 55–60.

Solon's predictions two centuries earlier were correct: a community run on established laws and fixed legal principles, rather than on a 'might is right' ethos, was one which ultimately had the best chances of survival. The political wisdom of the Athenians in 403 proved that in the face of defeat democracy could only be regenerated if the victorious side in a civil conflict restrained its vengeful instincts and put reconciliation first.

CHAPTER 8

The Rule of Law Restored: The Legacy of the Reconciliation in the Fourth Century

The Athenian Reconciliation Agreement was the most successful of its kind ever to have been devised. For the next few centuries, it stood as the exemplum for all political negotiations which succeeded periods of crisis and conflict. Chapter 7 argued that while many city states looked to Athens as the model, not all measured up to its standard. That is not surprising, especially in cases where cities were not democratic or where foreign powers were involved. As mentioned in Chapter 4, modern scholarship has tended to see Athens in the aftermath of the Reconciliation as a less democratic replica of the fifth-century system which succumbed to the Thirty, but that tendency is mistaken. There is nothing in the ancient evidence which suggests that Athens in the wake of the amnesty was any less democratic than the fifth-century democracy which it sought to revive, and indeed the Aristotelian tradition envisages the fourth century as the most advanced stage in the democratic evolution of the city. The main point of difference is that whereas in the fifth century laws were protected by entrenchment clauses, in the fourth century they were legislated through a process known as *nomothesia*. The rule of law was not antithetical to democracy. It was a *sine qua non* without which democracy could not function. The achievement of the Reconciliation was to reinstate the rule of law after the period of the Thirty.

The question that follows is whether the democracy which followed the Reconciliation was workable and efficient. In a re-evaluation of the relationship between democracy and rule of law, a convincing case has been made that Athens of the fourth century not only was more democratic even than the late fifth, but that the functioning of democracy was guaranteed by the enshrinement of legal principle. These observations have been carried forward even more recently in the development of the concept of *nomos basileus*, which envisages the law, rather than the whim of the populace, as the guiding principle of Athenian democracy.[1] As discussed in Chapters 5 and 6, though clever litigants often presented cases in ways which sought to circumvent the legal point at issue, the fact that they had to adopt heavily rhetorical and circuitous methods of doing so indicates not that rule of law was not taken seriously, but to the contrary, that the law was supreme. Because we do not know the result of many of these trials, it would be idle to speculate how far slippery misuse of the law regularly ended in success. But even those orators whose arguments look disingenuous are conspicuous for their mishandling of legal principle as and where such malpractice is evident. As far as we can tell, the Amnesty of 403 was successful in blocking vexatious litigation relating to events which predated the Reconciliation, and the sanctified principle of *res iudicata* became a binding concept which governed the application of law in court jurisdiction subsequently. In view of this, it is therefore somewhat surprising that so many modern scholars have asserted that legal regularity was not a guiding force in Athenian litigation. Had the rule of law not been of paramount significance, it would be difficult to understand how the amnesty rule could ever have been applied and why Athens in the wake of the Amnesty chose to codify the laws (see Chapter 4). The aim of this final chapter is to assess the functioning of democracy from a more theoretical angle and to evaluate the statements and beliefs of the greatest political theorist of all, Aristotle, who is often misunderstood to have been a critic of Athens and of the democracy which belonged to his adoptive city. To be sure, Aristotle drew a distinction between what was natural and what was virtuous (see especially *Politics* Book 3), and while understanding democracy to be a natural state nevertheless regarded it less favourably than its political alternatives, which were aristocracy and kingship. Yet care must be taken before claiming that Aristotle's view of the democracy of Athens was unequivocally negative. Close re-examination of his statements will show that far from being an undifferentiated critic of democracy, Aristotle had a guarded admiration for democracy run according to legal principle. Democracy in the fourth century was not a lawless concept, and despite some misreading of the *Politics*, Aristotle assuredly did not regard lawless democracy to be democracy in its most developed and natural state.

In Chapter 4, several criteria were laid out for what constituted a society guided by the rule of law. These included the accountability of public officials, the consistency of the laws, the availability of the laws for general consultation and the application of legal principle in the lawcourts. Chapters 5 and 6

---

[1] Harris 2013. For a reconsideration of the Aristotelian understanding of the relationship between the fifth- and fourth-century incarnations of democracy at Athens, see Harris 2016. On the concept of *nomos basileus* see Pelloso 2017–18; Piovan 2017–18. See also Joyce 2022.

showed that these key features were in evidence in the four famous legal trials which ensued, those of Agoratus, Eratosthenes, Callimachus and Socrates. This last chapter addresses some theoretical objections which might be levelled against the view that the democracy of the fourth century was guided by lawful principle. Much of the misconception which has arisen in modern times stems from a casual reading of some references in Aristotle's *Politics* to lawless democracy and the concomitant assumption that Aristotle had Athens in mind. This, in turn, has caused many to conclude that in the teleological framework of Aristotle, lawless democracy was invariably the end product of an evolution which ultimately resulted in mob rule. Nothing, however, in the *Politics* states or implies this. When democracies become lawless, this is usually due to unforeseen circumstances, and in no way is lawlessness built into the political fabric of democracy. Aristotle is aware of lawless democracies in Greece, but it is remarkable how seldom he refers to Athens as an example of contemporary democracy that had degenerated into mob rule, for which a far more frequently cited case is Syracuse. Other considerations of how the rule of law operated in Athens indicate that the fourth-century courts were guided by rigorous observance of the law. This is despite the modern tendency to speak of the courts as a venting ground for personal feuds, a claim which has been generally overstated.[2] Though litigants might have attempted to use the courts as feuding battlegrounds, laws prevented this abuse from happening. The law, not vendetta, was paramount.

THE RULE OF LAW IN ACTION IN THE FOURTH CENTURY

Several features of fourth-century litigation indicate that Athenians understood the rule of law in terms which would make sense in modern legal systems. The first and most important was the principle of *res iudicata*, which guaranteed that once a court had delivered a verdict, that legal decision was binding and could not be subverted (D. 20.147; 38.16; 40.39–43; Antiphon 5.87; 6.3). In the fourth century, this principle was upheld by the newly created process of *paragraphê*, which displaced the *diamartyria* which had existed in the century previous (see Chapter 6). The laws of Athens recognised that out-of-court settlements (*diaitai*) were legally binding (Isoc. 18.11; D. 36.25; 37.1; 38.1).[3] A statute of limitations required litigants to bring actions within a five-year period after the offence (D. 36.25–7; 38.7). It has been argued from Lys. 13.83

---

[2] See, for example, Cohen (D.) 1995; Phillips 2008.
[3] Against the authenticity of the law on arbitrators at D. 21.94, see MacDowell 1990: 317–18 and Harris 2013: 73.

that a similar statute of limitations applied also in homicide cases, but important to note is that the case against Agoratus after 403 was a public trial brought by *endeixis*, and there is little good reason to doubt or deny that private actions for homicide had similar legal limitations imposed upon them.[4] Frivolous litigation was discouraged in private cases by the imposition of a fine known as the *prytaneia* (Poll. 8.38). In public cases, if a prosecutor failed to gain at least one fifth of the votes, he lost his right to prosecute at any point in the future and was subjected to a fine of 1,000 drachmas.[5] Litigants who lost private suits were subject to the penalty of the *epôbelia* (Poll. 8.47–8; Isoc. 18.11–12; D. 27.67; 45.6; [D.] 47.64), imposed if the litigant failed to secure one fifth of the votes.[6] If a litigant in a case concerning citizenship appealed from the deme to the *polis* and lost at the appeal stage, he was sold into slavery (*Ath. Pol.* 42.1; Isoc. 12 *hypoth.*). Though unseemly by modern standards, the harshness of this last provision shows that every measure was taken to provide against frivolous litigation. This did not mean, of course, that Athenians could not act from personal motives, but the fact that the laws laid out such stern provisions against such litigation indicates that Athenians recognised the potential for the misuse of the courts and took special measures to stem the tide.

Revisionist discussions of *nomothesia* have shown that the rule of law in Athens in the fourth century was seen not as a counterpoise to democracy, but the guarantor of democratic principle. Whilst in the past it was fashionable to speak of fourth-century democracy as a 'more conservative' form of democracy than what existed in the fifth century, as argued in Chapter 4 that approach is mistaken. When Athens decided after 403 to institute a new process known as *nomothesia*, the process was fully democratic and consistent with democratic principle. From an early stage, it had been understood that the Assembly was empowered to enact laws, that is, legal statutes which had a permanent status and meaning (*Ath. Pol.* 22.1, 5; 26.2, 4; 47.1). To deal with the problem of internal contradiction, a special process called *graphê paranomôn* had been set up before 404 (And. 1.17, 22). In the fifth century, this allowed any one of the citizens in the Assembly to indict a bill as being contrary to the laws either during the discussion of the proposal or after its ratification (X. *HG* 1.7.12–14; D. 22.5, 9–10). The case was then adjudicated by a panel whose numbers ranged anywhere from 500 to 6,000 citizens (And. 1.17). From 403, a special board of *nomothetai* was instituted at Athens to enact laws (*nomoi*), distinct from decrees (*psêphismata*) (And. 1.81–9). The sources for *nomothesia*

---

[4] *Pace* Harris 2013: 73 n. 36.
[5] For a discussion of the evidence, see Harris 2006: 405–21.
[6] Thus Harrison 1968–71: ii.185. For further discussion as to whether the *epôbolia* was enforced by a general statute, see MacDowell 2008: 94; *contra* Wallace 2008: 97. That this was applied also at the level of the deme is clear from *IG* II²1183 lines 16–24, with Whitehead 1986: 119.

are D. 24.20 and Aeschin. 3.38–40, as well as some inscribed materials.[7] The new process of *nomothesia* resulted in a clear and comprehensive statement of the valid laws (*nomoi*) of Athens, though the list of laws was continually updated throughout the fourth century, and because of this continual updating it would be unduly misleading to term the list a 'code of laws', as was once fashionable (see Chapter 4).[8] The new process of *nomothesia* in the fourth century did not clamp democratic principle but refined processes which had existed previously.

New approaches to the complex problem of lawgiving at Athens have yielded the following reconstruction: (1) a *probouleuma* was approved by the Council to introduce a vote to the Assembly; (2) following that, a vote was taken in the Assembly, at any point in the year, as to whether new laws could be introduced (D. 24.25; *IG* II^2 333; *IG* II^3 320; *IG* II^2 140); (3) all new proposals were posted before the Eponymous Heroes (D. 20.94; 24.25); (4) the proposals were read out at each meeting of the Assembly so that its members could make up their minds (D. 20.94); (5) in the third meeting after the preliminary vote, the Assembly passed a decree of appointment of *nomothetai* (D. 20.92; 24.25); (6) opposing laws would be repealed (D. 20.93; 24.32, 34–5); (7) experts were appointed to defend the laws before the Assembly (D. 20.146; 24.36); (8) if a proposer had introduced a new law contrary to the existing ones, he was liable to the process *graphê nomon mê epitêdeion theinai* (D. 24.32). What is essential to note is that the *nomothetai* were not in any institutional way distinct from the Assembly but were appointed by the Assembly for the sake of creating laws. Aeschin. 3.38–40 and D. 20.93–4 show further that the laws were voted on by the *dêmos* sitting in a nomothetic capacity and that traditional scholarly distinctions between the Assembly and the *nomothetai* should be removed.[9] A little-known lexicographic entry makes the connection even clearer (*Lex. Seg.* N 282 s.v. νομοθέται), which states: καὶ οἱ τοὺς νόμους εἰσηγούμενοι νομοθέται καλοῦνται, καὶ ἐκκλησία τις Ἀθήνῃσι νομοθέται καλεῖται, οἳ τοὺς εἰσφερομένους ἐδοκίμαζον νόμους, καὶ δι' ὧν οἱ ἀσύμφοροι ἐλύοντο ('Those who enacted the laws are called *nomothetai*, and the Assembly

---

[7] For differences in approach to these sources, see MacDowell 1975: 62–7; Rhodes 1984; Piérart 2000: 229–56; Canevaro 2013a; Harris 2013: 225–33; Canevaro and Esu 2018: 106–45. Canevaro shows that the document inserted into D. 24.20–3 is a forgery and cannot therefore be relied upon to sketch out an understanding of how the process worked.

[8] For differences of view on how to interpret And. 1.81–2, see Carawan 2012; *contra* Joyce 2014, where I showed that the laws under scrutiny after 403 were the entire body of valid law at Athens, not a subset of laws related to the Amnesty.

[9] Harris 2013: 225–33. Harris's observations add to the observations of Piérart 2000: 229–50, who was the first to approach Aeschin. 3.38–40 correctly. Harris then added D. 20.93–4 as further proof. For parallel procedures in private associations, see Joyce 2021: 152–7.

at Athens is called *nomothetai*, who vetted the laws introduced, and through whom inexpedient ones were removed'). The identity of the *nomothetai* at D. 24.25 can be established from Aeschin. 3.38–40, which required that every year the *thesmothetai* reconcile the laws after scrutiny, whereupon irregularities were to be posted at the ten Eponymous Heroes, after which the *prytaneis* held an assembly ἐπιγράψαντας νομοθέτας and the people by show of hands vote. What this shows is that the laws were voted by the *dêmos*. *Nomothesia* was in the most important sense a democratic process in its internal operation.

This has crucial implications for the way we read the prescripts to laws and decrees. There are ten extant fourth-century laws (*nomoi*) from Athens preserved on stone, all of which conform to the same prescript formula (ἔδοξε/δεδόχθαι τοῖς νομοθέταις).[10] In contrast, the normal way of introducing a decree in the fifth and fourth centuries was by the standard formula ἔδοξε/δεδόχθαι τῷ δήμῳ/τῇ βουλῇ. At face value, this might indicate a constitutional distinction between the *nomothetai* and the Assembly. But it is crucial here not to judge by appearances. As Canevaro states,

> The new legislative procedures gave the *dêmos* the power to enact new laws whenever necessary and appropriate throughout the fourth century. At the same time, the new procedures helped to preserve the consistency of the laws of the city and to protect them against hasty and ill-considered legal changes. They provided clear rules of change and procedures for judicial review of new laws, at the same time banning retroactive legislation and securing a degree of stability for the legal system.[11]

The power lay with the *dêmos* to create and enact laws. When the prescripts mention *nomothetai*, without an explicit stated reference to the Council or People, this should not be taken to mean that the *nomothetai* were constitutionally distinct from, or above, the *dêmos*. Scholars have often worried about the absence of mention of the *nomothetai* in the account of the *Ath. Pol.*, but that is only a problem if the *nomothetai* constituted an organ of government distinct from, or above, the Assembly.[12] More recent studies have shown, however, that the author of the *Ath. Pol.* had no pressing need to write separately about *nomothesia*, because it fell under the bracket of the authority of the Council

---

[10] SEG 26.72; IG II² 140, 244; IG II³ 320, 445, 447; IEleusis 138; SEG 52.104. Three more inscriptions appear at first glance not to respect this distinction, but in fact conform to it (IG II³ 327, 355, 452).

[11] Canevaro 2016.

[12] For modern discussions as to why the author of the *Ath. Pol.* said nothing about the lawgivers, see Ingravalle 1989; Wallace 1993; Bertelli 1993: 61; Bravo 1994: 237–8; Poddighe 2014: 123–5.

and Assembly to which chapters 43.2–49 are devoted.[13] This keeps with what Aristotle says about law-making belonging to the deliberative competences of the councils and assemblies of the Greek city states (Arist. *Pol.* 4.14.1298a3–5).

Though *nomothesia* was an innovation of the restored democracy in 403, the conceptual distinction between a decree and a law was much older. As early as the mid-seventh century, the Greek city states understood a 'law', variously termed *thesmos*, *graphos*, *rhêtra* or *nomos*, as a legal enactment which dealt with a permanent or universal legal matter, such as homicide, theft or rape, as distinct from an *ad hoc* decision. Legendary lawgivers (*nomothetai*) are attested from around 650, such as Zaleucus of Locri and Draco of Athens (Arist. *Pol.* 2.27.1274a). Even before the first written laws, the Homeric poems make it clear that early society was governed by unwritten norms which many of the later written laws will have enshrined in written medium (Hom. *Il.* 9.632–6; 19.497–508).[14] The earliest known laws aimed at preventing tyranny and distributing powers among property classes (*Ath. Pol.* 7.3–4) and among elected magistrates who, unlike tyrants, occupied specified terms of office.[15] The laws of Solon, carried in 594/3, included laws on neutrality, speaking ill of the dead, bequests, funerals, dowries and sacrifices (Plu. *Sol.* 20–4).[16] In the case of the Solonian laws, special entrenchment clauses were inserted to ensure that the Athenians would continue to abide by their terms (*Ath. Pol.* 7.2; Plu. *Sol.* 25).[17] From the archaic period onward, Greek civic institutions recognised that laws, however termed, were different from *ad hoc* legal decisions, even if the processual arrangements through which that substantive distinction could be expressed were relatively late coming. This was no less true of religious and private bodies than it was of state institutions, as the enactment phrases of private cultic bodies in and outside Athens abundantly attest.[18]

This all shows that the concept of the rule of law was not new in the fourth century, even if methods by which the rule of law was enforced were refined and updated. The Athenian Reconciliation of 403 was the benchmark of amnesty agreements in the ancient world and, today, shines out as

---

[13] See Canevaro and Esu 2018: 130–1.
[14] For similar views, see Rhodes and Leão 2015: 6.
[15] For examples of this from Chios and elsewhere in the archaic Greek world, see Koerner 1993: Nos. 39, 74, 77, 87, 90, 121. For the view that archaic laws were designed to banish tyranny, with extensive examples, see also Harris 2006: 3–39.
[16] It would, however, be mistaken to speak of 'law codes'; for a general discussion of this problem, see Hölkeskamp 1999: 263–4.
[17] Lewis 1997: 136–49.
[18] For a comprehensive list of these enactment phrases, see the appendix to Harris 2015c. On the intrinsic role of religious and cultic bodies within the fabric of Athenian democracy throughout the classical age, see Joyce 2019. For a detailed overview and analysis of how democratic language is in evidence in the enactments of the phratry of the Demotionidae, see Joyce 2021.

the historical exemplum of all amnesties. Its lasting benefaction was to banish civil conflict and to restore the rule of law. Its most salient hallmarks were: (1) to make inadmissible litigation for untried offences which predated 12 Boedromion 403; (2) to reinstate the courts as a forum for legal justice, rather than political feuding; (3) to remove the political division, which the tragic, blood-drenched interlude of the Thirty had created, between 'democrat' and 'oligarch' among the citizenry; (4) to guarantee that old vendettas which might have destabilised the newly united citizen body would not tip the citizenry back into a state of civil war. Its success is borne out by the fact that though resentments continued to bubble away, Athens did not relapse into civil conflict. Several centuries later, Cicero was therefore right to call it the *Atheniensium vetus exemplum*. It is easy to dismiss the period as romanticised fiction, generated at a time when Athens grappled with the harsh realities of the loss of empire and its humiliating defeat to foreign powers on whom, politically as well as culturally, it looked down. There can be little doubt that the Reconciliation was a bitter pill to swallow, especially for those who had lost everything they once possessed under the now banished oligarchy. Here, attention is due to the absence of any formal decree which regulated emotion. The trials which followed on from the Amnesty indicate beyond reasonable doubt that resentment was deep and poignant. Some cities, like Nakone in Sicily, after periods of civil strife, sought to remedy division by legislating into existence institutional methods whereby citizens could relinquish former feuds and grudges. Athens, notably, avoided that model. A key ingredient of democracy, both ancient and modern, is the recognition that citizens should be free to think and feel as they please. The fact that Athens, at the height of its democracy in the fifth century, permitted the existence of political clubs and societies whose members may have frowned upon democratic institutions furnishes incontrovertible evidence that the liberty to think and express heterodox opinions was a key component of what it meant, in ancient times, to live under a democratic regime. It should come as no surprise, therefore, to discover that, after the Reconciliation, resentful voices still made themselves heard. This, ironically, signals not its failure, but its success.

CONCLUSIONS

This study has traced the evolution of the Reconciliation Agreement, from its historical origins in the aftermath of the defeat of the Thirty and Ten to its legal implementation in the years that followed. The Reconciliation cannot be understood outside the framework of the rule of law. As the Covenants of Amnesty show, its terms and conditions were legally constructed. This was no abstract, or legally disembodied, decree to abandon civic discord, as some have claimed, but a legally engineered roadmap to peace, which ensured that subsequent litigious action should be subject to a universal statute of limitations. This needs to be understood more broadly in the context of the events which led to Athens' defeat in 404. In the last decades of the fifth century, chiefly under the pernicious influence of Cleon, the courts were usurped by politicians for subversive political ends. This was a disastrous development, which led to the undermining of Athens' most sacred political institution, democracy. When the oligarchs established power in autumn 404, they seized the opportunity to subvert the most important pillar of democracy, which was the rule of law. The ascendency of the Thirty is to be explained not along the old Marxist model of 'class struggle', which fails to account for the vast support which the democracy had among the richest and most powerful among the citizens, but by the fact that the fabric of democracy, enshrined in the lawcourts, had been institutionally discredited. This resulted in the rise of the authority of magistrate, which, under the Thirty, was unlimited and unaccountable. The ghastly consequences of that unaccountability revealed itself in no uncertain terms in the events which ensued, and when the oligarchs were overthrown in a matter of months, the matter of paramount concern was to re-establish democracy on the back of its most ancient guarantor, the rule of law. The institutional application of legal mechanisms is key to understanding why democracy, together with the principles of justice and fairness on which it was grounded, could be resurrected in 403. As Aristotle recognised, the rule of law is essential if democracy is to function. Democracies which do not observe the rule of law swiftly degenerate into their worst and most hateful antithesis, tyranny. In a modern world where the survival of democracy, in some places, is looking increasingly fragile and uncertain, this is an important lesson. Democracy and the rule of law are inextricably intertwined. When the rule of law breaks down, democracy comes under threat, as it did at Athens in those last desperate days when defeat to Sparta and her allies was looking ever imminent. The rule of law is upheld when the courts are free to apply the law according to legal principle and justice. For all its imperfections, the justice system of Athens demonstrates that the courts upheld the rule of law.

The foregoing chapters have examined the terms of the Reconciliation, the scrutiny of laws to which it led, and six legal cases which came to light in the years shortly afterwards. It has argued that the cases in question are not 'political' trials, which is to misunderstand the nature of legal justice at Athens, but litigations which observed legal and constitutional principle. Perhaps the most notorious, the trial of Socrates in 399, which led to a scandalous judicial verdict, though it has gone down in history as a gross miscarriage of justice, nevertheless observed legality in essence. There is not a single trial on record which violated the terms of the Amnesty. It is true that the trial of Agoratus (c. 403–399) came close to doing so, but even here, the issue of how strictly according to the wording of its covenants the Amnesty could be applied was carefully and methodically worked out by the prosecution. The Covenants could not be casually ignored. It remained for prosecutors, in legal grey areas, to show that the case was admissible under the terms of the Amnesty, provided a legal case could be made that the defendant was not protected. In the case of Agoratus, this was questionable, but the fact that the trial came to light cannot be cited as proof that the Amnesty was taken half-heartedly. The legal bars against admissibility were sturdy and, to argue for admissibility, careful argumentative steps were required to show that the defendant could not counter with a special plea. We do not, sadly, have a transcript of the defence, and so it would be fruitless to speculate how Agoratus might have replied on legal grounds to the charge levelled against him. Almost certainly, the terms of the Amnesty would have been cited to show that, whether a sound case could be made for murder, he could not stand accountable, as the offence predated 12 Boedromion. Equally, the Reconciliation Agreement upheld the sacred principle of *res iudicata*. As the case of Andocides shows, though the orator deployed every trick in the book to argue for a clean slate, if he had been convicted in 415 for his part in the religious scandals of that year, the verdict of the court stood, provided the court (or panel of arbitrators) had been democratic. Examination of the rhetorical tactics used by both prosecution and defence has shown that though orators did use slippery methods to wind their way around legal principle, the sovereignty of the law stood. To put it slightly differently, it was precisely because orators were clever, and often disingenuous, that the law was firm.

The application of amnesty agreements in antiquity did not always follow the Athenian example. Examination of the numerous attempts to reconcile divided citizenries elsewhere in Greece in the classical and Hellenistic ages has shown that whilst some were successful, others were not. Those that were successful adhered to the principle of law and legal mechanism. The fact that Greece knew many failed attempts to reconcile citizen bodies torn asunder by civic faction does not mean that Greece lacked a modern understanding of 'amnesty'. As in modern times, amnesty agreements varied hugely in type and efficacy. Some had lasting effect, whereas others failed because they were imposed by larger power structures which operated by force, or because they were contracted according to partisan principles which ignored the important recognition that civic society can only cohere if centrifugal partisan impulses are sufficiently restrained. The best way to restrain those impulses is through institutional mechanisms which observe the rule of law. Much has been made of the 'lawlessness' of Athenian democracy in the fourth century, as if the law was only something to which Athenians paid token lip service. The causes of that modern caricature are multifarious. Among some, it has arisen through a misreading of the text of Aristotle's *Politics*, which, on closer reading, shows that Aristotle did not condemn mature democracy but indeed endorsed it, provided it observed legal principle. Among others, there has been a seductive tendency to assume that because ancient democracy failed in ways which modern democracies would regard as essential for a society or community to be called democratic, such as universal suffrage, bills of human rights, abolition of slavery, gender and racial equality and the like, it was not therefore 'democratic' in anything but name. This study has argued otherwise. To be a citizen at Athens, exercising full political rights, it was required to be male, adult, Athenian by blood line and legally free. This narrow definition excluded women, resident aliens (metics), slaves and those who could not show Athenian parentage on both sides. By any modern democratic standard, the Athenian paradigm is sorely inadequate. Yet it is mistaken in principle to apply modern standards, because modern standards cannot obtain for the ancient world. The question needs to be how, and to what extent, Athens rated as a society which upheld justice and the rule of law as compared to other societies of its day. Here, there can be little doubt that its paradigm far exceeded that of any rival contemporary society. The Reconciliation Agreement of 403 proves the working of Athenian democracy and of all the high-minded principles of freedom and justice for which it stood.

To give the discussion finality, it is worth summarising my principal conclusions, and then dealing with theoretical objections which may arise. This study has made ten key claims:

1. The *stasis* of 404/3 at Athens was less about 'class struggle' and more about the accountability of magistrates and the rule of law. This was fuelled by an abuse of the lawcourts under Cleon and his successors, which had resulted in the authority of the courts being undermined.
2. The suspension of democracy in 404 resulted from two separate but mutually reinforcing factors, which were the changes in Spartan policy from liberator to enslaver and the loss of credibility at Athens of the lawcourts as an instrument of legality.
3. The ascent of the Thirty depended on the suspension of the rule of law, which meant that to rule without accountability, the Thirty needed to suspend ordinary legal processes which made magistrates accountable and rule according to their own whim.
4. The Thirty fell from power because they lost the support of Sparta, which realised that the regime hatched by Lysander was untenable and that the best way to draw Athens into a Spartan-led alliance was to restore Athens to its ancestral democracy.
5. The Reconciliation Agreement of 403 was, above all, the restoration of democracy. It is impossible to understand the Reconciliation divorced from political principle.

6. The democrats faced an important challenge, which was to banish civil strife and ensure that the spectre of civil war would not resurface. This was accomplished through legal instruments.
7. The most important effect of the Reconciliation was to impose a statute of limitations, whereby any untried offence committed prior to 12 Boedromion 403 was inadmissible in the courts. At the same time, the Reconciliation upheld the principle of *res iudicata*.
8. The scrutiny of laws which followed continued a process begun in 410, after the fall of the first oligarchy. Its aim was to ensure that the laws of Athens were consistent.
9. The legal trials which followed on from the Reconciliation turned on a legal, not a political, principle, and adhered to the terms of the Reconciliation.
10. The Reconciliation was the legal bedrock of the restoration of the rule of law and democracy in the fourth century. Its success is borne out in the observable fact that democracy survived until the Macedonian suppression almost a century later.

There are, of course, some theoretical objections, and it is important to address one or two misconceptions which have arisen in recent times as to the lawlessness of democratic Athens. Aristotle, the greatest political theorist of Greece, is often characterised as a critic of Athens.[19] It is a commonplace that Aristotle belongs to a polemical tradition which saw the fourth-century democracy of Athens as perverse and corrupted, and which advocated an alternative system of government whereby the sovereignty of the 'mass' was to be curtailed by other checks and balances, such as a power of the Areopagus Council and the rule of law.[20] Like many scholars, Ober holds that Aristotle wrote against the backdrop of a contemporary ideological debate surrounding the ancestral constitution in which the rights and wrongs of the fourth-century *status quo* was contested among those who advocated 'extreme democracy' and others who proposed a less democratic dispensation. This connects Aristotle's theoretical treatise to an earlier tradition of ideological debate extending back to the Old Oligarch in the fifth century and continued in various literary guises

---

[19] For modern translations of and commentaries upon Aristotle's *Politics*, see Schütrumpf 1991; Keyt and Miller 1991; Schütrumpf and Gehrke 1996; Simpson 1997; Keyt 1999; Lintott 2018.

[20] Ober 1998: 290–351. Ober's arguments develop those of his earlier monograph; see Ober 1989. Those views were followed by Brunt 1993: 349 n. 16: '[Aristotle] has in mind the possibility that the model city might be established in a non-Greek land in which the existing barbarian population would be reduced to serfdom, like the Mariandyni of Heraclea Pontica.' Most recently, the claim that Aristotle advocated a type of 'hoplite democracy' which was democracy in name only has been advanced by Lintott (2018), who makes much of Aristotle's advocacy of the *politeia* which he understands to be a form of mixed constitution.

by Aristophanes, Thucydides, Xenophon, Plato and Isocrates. The received assumption is that democracy's critics harked back to a time when Athens was less democratic than it had since become and sought to justify their alternative political proposals by reference to the more oligarchic governments of the past.[21] By the same paradigm, as an educated man Aristotle disliked popular rule because it empowered those less educated, and like other literati, viewed democracy as an undesirable phenomenon wherein those best suited to rule, viz. the rich, were ruled over by an uneducated illiterate mass.[22]

Such an approach needs to address two fundamental objections. The first is: if educated people in antiquity were disposed to dislike democracy, why do modern counterparts not also speak more disapprovingly than they do about Athens and her boasted political system? To be educated or enlightened should not engender dislike of democratic government, even in societies where education traditionally has been the preserve of the wealthy and privileged. The second, more historically grounded, objection is that the Athenian democracy not only emerged from a feud between rival nobles but throughout the fifth and fourth centuries, as far as is discernible, was supported by moneyed families with political connections and private resources of wealth.[23] This is demonstrable from the abundant references in the sources to men of property who occupied high political positions and profiles in democratic Athens,[24] and

---

[21] A recent exposition of the doctrine is in Rhodes 2011: 13–30. For other similar claims that the *patrios politeia* was a political watchword in the fifth and fourth centuries, see Jacoby 1949; Hignett 1952; Fuks 1953; Ruschenbusch 1958; Aalders 1968; Finley 1971; Ruschenbusch 1981. Wallace 1989; Bruyn 1995; Shear (J. L.) 2011. This is not the place to cross-examine the senses in which *patrios politeia* as a concept was used at Athens in the fifth and fourth centuries, but the claim that the virtues of democracy were actively contested by Athenian politicians in the fourth century has been generally overstated.

[22] The dichotomy of 'mass' versus 'elite is central to much of Ober's thinking about ancient Athenian democracy and gives itself as a title to an earlier monograph; see Ober 1989. It is true that democracy's critics in antiquity adhered to similar dichotomies and even described the democracy of Athens as 'the rule of the mass'. But equally important to recognise is that this is not how Athenian democracy saw or understood itself; thus Hansen 1991: 64–85; Harris 2013: 60–98.

[23] On the dynastic feud between Cleisthenes and Isagoras at the end of the sixth century, see Hdt. 5.66–73; *Ath. Pol.* 20, both of which accounts make it clear that Athenian democracy was the result not of popular uprising but of dynastic struggle, during which the idea of democracy fermented. Ober, in contrast, champions the view that democracy was all about the assertion of the popular mass over the aristocratic elites which began with a popular revolution in the time of Cleisthenes, yet his understanding appears to proceed from a preconceived theoretical approach and bypasses the evidence which tends to undermine it; see Ober 1996.

[24] Examples of wealthy and prominent men operating in Athenian politics at the height of the democracy are Pericles, Pyrilampes, Thucydides son of Milesias, Callias and Andocides. For the evidence of the wealth and connections of the families of these men, see Davies 1971: 27–32, 230–7, 254–70, 322–35.

can be inferred from the fact that at the time of the oligarchic junta of 404/3, many of the oligarchy's victims were wealthy and no doubt educated people, such as Leon of Salamis,[25] Niceratus son of Nicias the general who died during the Sicilian campaign,[26] and Lycurgus son of Lycomedes, whose estate worth fourteen talents was confiscated by the Thirty.[27] If one was wealthy, one could easily hold a stake in democracy. Conversely, if one was poor, one could just as likely support a government which was non- or anti-democratic. What is clear in the last decade of the fifth century is that a number of citizens who had been active participants in democracy prior to the interlude of the Four Hundred in 411 played a role in the oligarchic regimes when those were in ascendency, such as Chremon,[28] Charicles[29] and Eratosthenes.[30] To divide the citizenry down schematic lines of rich versus poor, the former supporting oligarchy, the latter democracy, is to ignore an abundance of independent and incidental evidence which discourages sweeping generalisations of this kind.

But surely democracy was the rule of the poor over the rich: is it not natural, therefore, that those from rich and wealthy families resented democracies which empowered citizens of lesser birth, wealth and status? Such a characterisation is problematised by the fact that in the language of its fourth-century practitioners, democracy was never understood as 'rule of the poor' and, indeed, was only ever presented as such in the vocabulary of its staunchest critics, most notably in the political rantings of the Old Oligarch.[31] Democracy, in a legal and constitutional sense, was the rule of the whole of the people regardless of social rank, wealth or status, not the rule of one portion of the populace over another.[32] Older scholarship used to claim that from the mid-fifth century, when the Athenian democracy became 'radicalised', the stranglehold of the nobility in politics was shaken off and government opened up to the poor.[33] The problem with that assertion is that 'radical democracy' needs to be appropriately defined. Our main source for the mid-century reforms is *Ath. Pol.* 25, fraught as it is with confusion,

---

[25] For Leon of Salamis, see X. *HG* 2.3.39.
[26] For Nicoratus son of Nicias, see X. *HG* 2.3.39; D.S. 14.5.5; Lys. 18.6; 19.47; Plu. *Mor.* 998b.
[27] For Lycurgus son of Lycomedes, see Plu. *Mor.* 998b.
[28] On Chremon, see Lys. 30.14.
[29] On Charicles, see Davies 1971: 502.
[30] On Eratosthenes, see Lys. 12.42.
[31] [X.] *Ath. Pol.* 1.6–8. For general discussions of this disputed text, see Donlan 1970: 381–95; Raaflaub 1983: 524; Petrey 1988: 43–6; Ober 1989: 4; 1998: 14–51.
[32] This fundamental point is rightly emphasised by Hansen 1991: 64–85, and by Harris 2013: 60–98.
[33] For the received view that the reforms of 462/1 mark the beginning of 'radical democracy' at Athens, see *inter alios* Hignett 1952: 217–18; Ste Croix 1972: 179; Cole 1974: 369–85; Wallace 1974: 259–69; Audring 1977: 234–8.

anachronism and falsehood.[34] Independent evidence shows that in the period after the so-called reforms, wealthy families were no less advantaged than they had been previously. In his commentary, Rhodes admits: '[W]e have no reason to suppose that the men elected were either more or less experienced in the earlier period than in the later [viz. after 462/1]'.[35] As C. Mann points out, the fact that in the years following no less than six prominent families continued to hold positions of responsibility in democratic Athens ought to rein in the assumption that democracy automatically limited the power of the rich.[36] Even though Cimon was ostracised at this time, perhaps in the same year that Ephialtes carried his reforms into effect, epigraphic and literary evidence shows that his son, Lacedaemonius, was active as general in 433/2.[37] Equally important to note is that before 462/1 we know of at least two influential politicians, Aristides and Themistocles, who came from undistinguished backgrounds.[38] As Harris argues, there was no shift in politics between the end of the Persian and start of the Peloponnesian Wars.[39] Outside the vocabulary of its critics, democracy was not antithetical to the rich but may have provided a forum in which the influence of the leading families could be felt.[40]

Aristotle at various points engages with aspects of Athenian constitution and history. In *Politics* 2 he mentions Solon in connection with economic equality (1266b15–20). Later in Book 2 he expresses the view that unlike the majority of lawgivers in Greece who left only laws, Solon like Lycurgus at Sparta left a constitution (1273b30–1274a22).[41] Elsewhere, in Book 5, he refers to the oligarchic revolution of 411 as an example of how the Four Hundred who suppressed democracy operated by use of fraud (1304b12–15).[42] Yet

---

[34] For a convincing demonstration that this portion of the *Ath. Pol.* cannot be given historical credence and must be rejected as completely worthless, see now Harris 2019a: 389–416.

[35] Rhodes 1981: 328. Rhodes fails, however, to draw the necessary inference that if this was a 'radical democracy' (whatever we are to understand by that) from the time of Ephialtes, radical democracy was neither opposed by, nor did it curtail, the power and influence of the leading families.

[36] Mann 2007: 98–123.

[37] Th. 1.45.2; *IG* I³ 364 lines 8–9.

[38] See Davies 1971: 48–53, 211–20.

[39] Harris 2016: 308–13; see also Mann 2007: 124–42.

[40] Rhodes 1981: 287, mainly in an effort to rescue the historical credibility of the middle portions of the *Ath. Pol.*, clings on to the idea of an 'Areopagite ascendency' in the period following the end of the Persian Wars and leading up to the reforms of Ephialtes, yet fails to find a satisfactory explanation of what that so-called ascendency amounted to, or to account for the near complete silence of more contemporary sources. On this, see further Harris 2019a: 400–4.

[41] The claims of Ruschenbusch (1958) that Solon did not authorise a constitution run up against the opinion of Aristotle to the contrary.

[42] On the historicity of this claim, see Rhodes 1981: 362–410; Andrewes 1981: 184–256; Osborne 2003: 258–61; Shear (J. L.) 2011: 19–69.

though Aristotle has occasion to mention Athens in passing in these and in other places in the course of the *Politics*, he is remarkably reserved about making any kind of value judgement about the Athenian democracy. It is noteworthy in this context that the city upon which Aristotle comments the most explicitly is not Athens but Sparta, and when Aristotle focuses on democracy in Books 5 and 6, the city to which he alludes the greatest number of times is not Athens, but Syracuse. A. W. Lintott argues that the analysis of democracy and its deviant forms in Book 6 represents an implicit commentary upon the Athenian democracy of his day, but this is far from agreed universally in modern scholarship.[43] There are two risks in adopting an Athenocentric model, the first of which is to assume that Aristotle's critique of pay for jury service at 1317b35–8 should be limited to Athens, the second of which is to overlook the fact that Athens was ruled by law, and that the main criticism which Aristotle had to make of 'corrupt' democracy was that it was lawless, which, as Lintott notes, should perhaps have applied to more to the fifth century than to the fourth.[44] The fact that fourth-century Athens was lawful constitutes the strongest objection to the view that, when lambasting lawless democracy, Aristotle had Athens specifically in mind. There is a further problem with the view of fourth-century Athenian democracy as 'ultimate' democracy based on a teleological view of constitutional evolution at *Ath. Pol.* 41. Little in the *Politics* warrants the view that the most corrupt type of democracy is 'final' or 'ultimate' or 'most developed' in a deterministic sense.[45] Though the *Ath. Pol.* understands fourth-century democracy at Athens to be the final stage in a lengthy process of historical evolution, this does not afford enough grounds to

---

[43] Lintott 2018: 31: 'Although Aristotle is hostile to the "extreme" democracy characteristic of Athens from the reforms of Ephialtes and Pericles in the 450s onwards, a major principle of democracy, that of "ruling and being ruled in turn" ... responds to his belief that all citizens should participate in government.' Against the view that Aristotle's critique of aberrant forms of democracy had Athens specifically in mind, see Robinson 2011: 220–2.

[44] Cammack 2019a. On the widespread practice of pay for dikastic service among Greek democracies, see Ste Croix 1981: 602–3. Lintott (2018: 176) in his commentary on this portion of the *Politics* does mention the case of Iasos but otherwise restricts the discussion to Athens, even though we know of examples elsewhere in Greece, such as Boeotia (*Hell. Oxy.* 19.4 Chambers) and Rhodes (Arist. *Pol.* 5.5.1304b27–31) where jury pay sparked a revolution (discussed at Lintott 2018: 97).

[45] The term *teleutaios*, as used by Aristotle in the *Politics*, does not equate to *teleios*, which is what we would expect if he had meant 'final' in a teleological or historical sense. If read with due care, there is little in the *Politics* to support the view that Aristotle thought of lawless democracy as the ineluctable consequence of its lawful counterpart. In context, the 'last' democracy means 'the last, or fourth, mentioned on the list', not 'the last' in the sense of ultimate or inevitable.

measure up the Athenian democracy of the fourth century with the 'last type' of democracy discussed in the *Politics*.[46]

Elsewhere in Book 5, Aristotle likens the attitudes of those living in certain types of democracy to the rule of law as if it equates to slavery (5.9.1310a25–36):

> ἐν δὲ ταῖς δημοκρατίαις ταῖς μάλιστα εἶναι δοκούσαις δημοκρατικαῖς τοὐναντίον τοῦ συμφέροντος καθέστηκεν, αἴτιον δὲ τούτου ὅτι κακῶς ὁρίζονται τὸ ἐλεύθερον. δύο γάρ ἐστιν οἷς ἡ δημοκρατία δοκεῖ ὡρίσθαι, τῷ τὸ πλεῖον εἶναι κύριον καὶ τῇ ἐλευθερίᾳ: τὸ μὲν γὰρ δίκαιον ἴσον δοκεῖ εἶναι, ἴσον δ' ὅ τι ἂν δόξῃ τῷ πλήθει, τοῦτ' εἶναι κύριον, ἐλεύθερον δὲ καὶ ἴσον τὸ ὅ τι ἂν βούληταί τις ποιεῖν: ὥστε ζῇ ἐν ταῖς τοιαύταις δημοκρατίαις ἕκαστος ὡς βούλεται, καὶ εἰς ὃ χρῄζων, ὡς φησὶν Εὐριπίδης: τοῦτο δ' ἐστὶ φαῦλον: οὐ γὰρ δεῖ οἴεσθαι δουλείαν εἶναι τὸ ζῆν πρὸς τὴν πολιτείαν, ἀλλὰ σωτηρίαν.

Lintott translates the passage as follows:

> By contrast, in democracies which are generally held to be the most democratic the established practice is the opposite of what is in the interest of the system, and the reason for this is their flawed definition of freedom. For there are two criteria which are supposed to define democracy – the sovereignty of the majority and freedom. For equality is held to be just, and it is a matter of equality that whatever the masses decide should prevail, while it is a matter of freedom that anyone does whatever he wishes. The result is that in such democracies everyone lives as he wants and, in Euripides' words, 'for what he yearns'. This is bad. For one should not think it subservience to live in accordance with the political system but self-preservation.[47]

The passage quoted is often thought to imply that, in Aristotle's mind, extreme democracies engendered the dangerous habit of citizens doing as they pleased and disrespecting the laws. In his commentary on these lines, Lintott writes: 'Living as one wishes is something of an opponent's caricature of the nature of extreme democracy, found also in Plato (*Resp.* 8.557b, 560c, 9.572e) and Isocrates (7 *Areop.* 20; 12 *Panath.* 131).' More recently still, J. Filonik, following D. Keyt's rendition of these lines, comments that 'Aristotle attempts

---

[46] The exact date of the *Politics* is not known for certain, though a *terminus ante quem* is given by a reference to the conflict 'now' between the members of the court of Dionysius of Syracuse (5.10.1312b10–11), which suggests a date prior to Timoleon's liberation of Syracuse in 344. For further discussion, see Weil 1960: 202; Lintott 2018: 7.
[47] Lintott 2018: 76–7.

to impute to the democrats the belief that living according to a certain principle, especially one pertaining to the state laws, is worthy of a slave, rather than the free', and sets Aristotle's remarks in a tradition of anti-democratic polemic.[48] Yet modern English translations have a seductive habit of glossing over the force of ταῖς μάλιστα εἶναι δοκούσαις δημοκρατικαῖς at the start of the lemma. Both Keyt and Lintott have this as signifying 'democracies **held to be** especially democratic', without recognising the point which Aristotle makes, that systems of government which ignore rule of law only *seem* to be very democratic. Though perhaps a subtle distinction, the point is crucial, because it shows that Aristotle does not take up the mantle of those who liken extreme democracy to lawless behaviour. As Filonik shows, what is conspicuously absent in democratic ideology is the idea that anyone may do as he pleases, and there are references in the orators where doing as one likes is evidently regarded as ignoble and tyrannical.[49] Thus, the condemnation of licentious behaviour seen in Aristotle is much of a piece with democratic, rather than anti-democratic, thinking. This passage links up with other texts of a broadly pro-democratic persuasion which say similar things, but the objection to lawless behaviour cuts across an ideological line. The fact that Aristotle says something so familiar and recognisable at Athens should discourage the view that Aristotle was writing within an anti-Athenian milieu.

Some readers may object to the claim that the legal cases under examination illustrate the rule of law in action. Andocides' self-defence is, to say the least, disingenuous in many key places, and there is little doubt that he alludes to the Reconciliation in ways which misrepresent its objectives. We do not know the outcome of the trial. The fact that Andocides was in the political fray in the 390s may be taken to indicate that he was acquitted, but the evidence is just too weak to make assertions one way or the other. However we read it, the trial signals that there were clever orators in Athens who knew how to distort legal issues in their own interest. To recognise this is to recognise a common feature of most societies where the rule of law is a reality. Skilful manipulation of legal issues is evidence that the law was taken extremely seriously, not that its force was disregarded or trivialised. We cannot know from the evidence which survives how the trial of Socrates in 399 proceeded, but even if his accusers tried to tarnish his reputation by dredging up an ancient connection with Critias, this was tangential to the issue at hand. What can be inferred about the plaint against him seems to suggest that the conviction turned on the legal, not the political matter at stake. Similarly, the prosecution

---

[48] Filonik 2019: 3. See also Trott 2017: 115–35.
[49] Lys. 7.27; 25.17, 32–3; D. 24.47; 42.2, 9; [D.] 25.20–6; 44.63; cf. X. *HG* 2.3.23. For other modern discussions of the relationship between freedom and democracy in Athens and of the evidence cited above, see Hansen 1991: 75 with n. 200; Balot 2006: 59; Liddel 2007: 21; Wallace 2009: 59.

of Callimachus alludes to the Reconciliation, but this does not substantially affect the legal issue. The most puzzling of the trials is that of Agoratus, where there is evidence that the key clause of the Reconciliation was interpreted in a special way. In a technical sense, the trial may have been inadmissible because Agoratus was not one of the Thirty or Ten, but the covenants prohibited actions over private matters. Given the enormity of the crime alleged against Agoratus, which was not only against an innocent citizen but against the entire citizen body, it was argued that the case fell into a legal grey area where the rule of exception applied. This shows that the law, however black and white in appearance, admitted of shades of nuance and subtlety which needed to be applied and handled with legal skilfulness and dexterity.

The Athenian Reconciliation was the paradigm of amnesty agreements in the ancient world and remains today a model and a benchmark of reconciliation. Democracy and the rule of law are bedfellows. To establish a lasting reconciliation, the rule of law must be paramount. Once the rule of law had been re-enshrined in consequence of the Amnesty, the court procedure of the restored democracy indicates abundantly in the century that followed that the rule of law, rather than politically normalised motives, was the guiding principle of the judicial system at Athens. Demosthenes' dispute with his guardians illustrates the sovereignty of the court's judgment in the fourth century.[50] To make the case from a converse perspective, the long and bitter conflict in the second half of the fourth century between Demosthenes and his great rival, Aeschines, produced remarkably little court litigation.[51] The only case which came to court was in 343, when Demosthenes prosecuted Aeschines. It is true that political associates were drawn into the fray, but notable is the absence of evidence that family members were drawn into the matter. Aeschines famously objected to the arrest of Antiphon by Demosthenes, who accused him of spying, but the objection seems to have proceeded from a legal point, rather than from a matter of political allegiance (D. 18.132–3). Similarly, the objections which Aeschines ranged against the torture of Anaxinus of Oreus were legal ones, which took no cognizance of political relationship (Aeschin. 3.223–5; D. 18.137). The evidence of the fourth century shows that penalties for frivolous action in the courts were considerable. If a prosecutor failed to obtain one fifth of the votes of the judges, typically they disappeared altogether from political life. This is clear from the cases of Tisis of Agryle (Hyp. *Eux.* 34), Euctemon (D. 21.103) and Lycinus (Aeschin. 2.14; 3.32). Some objectors would point here to notoriously litigious Athenians, such as Apollodorus, the son of Pasion, and Mantitheus, but it is important to gain a proper perspective on those test

---

[50] Harris 2013: 81.
[51] Harris 1995: 141–2, 173–4; 2013: 85–7; *contra* Christ 2005: 146.

cases. Not a single known case brought by the former in the years from 370 to 340 invoked family relationships or political allegiances.[52] In the case of the latter, the principle *res iudicata* was rigorously observed and upheld, since Mantitheus never challenged the decision of the court once it had been delivered, and it is also worth noting that the events which came to the attention of the court took place over a span of well over a decade, from 362 to 347.[53] Though litigation was a regular feature of Athenian life in the fourth century, there is remarkably little evidence to connect any of this to what might be described as political feuding or infighting.

Perhaps most important is the Judicial Oath, which framed the basis upon which all legal decisions in democratic Athens were taken. No inscribed copy of this oath survives, but its terms can be reconstructed from a range of oratorical references in the fourth century. The Oath had four principal components: (1) to vote in accordance with the laws and decrees (Aeschin. 3.6; Antiphon 5.8; D. 20.118); (2) to listen to both sides of the case equally and fairly (Aeschin. 2.1; D. 18.2; Isoc. 15.21); (3) to judge according to a principle of justice in cases where there were no established written laws according to which a judgment might be laid (D. 23.96; 57.63); and (4) to undertake to cast judgment in accordance with the merits of the case, and in accordance with no other intervening consideration or principle (Aeschin. 1.154; D. 45.50).[54] The clauses of the Judicial Oath, as far as they can be reconstructed from the evidence which survives, tie in with principles which the Reconciliation of 403 reified. From 12 Boedromion 403, it was disallowed to bring action in the courts for any offence blocked by the clauses of the Amnesty. Judges had to swear that they would adjudicate in accordance with the laws. The law, from 403, stipulated that if an untried offence had taken place prior to 12 Boedromion, it was now inadmissible in the court. If ever there was a period of Athenian history when the local population was divided among itself, it was during the interval of the oligarchy in 404/3 and in the period which immediately followed. By enshrining the principle that only cases admissible in law could be tried, the commissioners of 403 created the legal template upon which the Judicial Oath in the fourth century could be modelled. With the Reconciliation came the recognition that the law was paramount and the courts, as instruments through which the law was enforced, were sovereign. This noble principle was the defining hallmark of the restored democracy of Athens in the period after 403.

---

[52] Harris 2013: 87–93.
[53] Harris 2013: 93–6.
[54] The list of references to the Judicial Oath in the Attic orators is huge. For a compendious collection and survey, see Harris 2013: 353–6.

This study has shown that the rule of law was the galvanising conceptual principle behind the Athenian Reconciliation of 403. Had the commissioners of that year not built a lasting reconciliation upon a legal principle, the history of Athens in the years that followed would have turned out very differently. Some of the test cases studied in Chapter 7 illustrate that, in the absence of a legal remedy, very often the only solution to civil conflict was tyranny or prolonged factionalism, as the example of Syracuse in the early fourth century under Dionysius I proves. Athens did not go down that route, because the architects of the restored democracy had the political wisdom to see that, unless they devised a system wherein the centrifugal forces which might otherwise have torn society apart could be restrained legally, the only way perhaps to stabilise civil conflict might have been the renewed military presence of a foreign garrison. Many modern interpreters have downplayed the moral and political principle behind the Amnesty. This study has argued, in contrast, that a purely utilitarian analysis of the methods by which Athenians reconciled is inadequate in effort to explain why and how the Athenian body politic managed to reconcile. Athens shone out as the exemplum by which all amnesty measures in the ancient world were measured. Its reputation in antiquity was justly deserved. When Cicero over three and a half centuries later praised the *Atheniensium vetus exemplum*, he did so for good reason. The test case of Athens was the benchmark of all ancient amnesty agreements, and its political and moral legacy continues to be felt today.

Bibliography

Aalders 1968: Aalders, G. J. D., *Die Theorie der gemischten Verfassung im Altertum*. Amsterdam.
Adams 1905: Adams, C. D., *Lysias, Selected Speeches, Edited with Introduction, Notes and Appendices*. New York (repr. 1989).
Adeleye 1974: Adeleye, G., 'Critias: member of the Four Hundred?', *TAPhA* 104: 1–9.
Albini 1955: Albini, U., *Lisia, i discorsi: testo critico, introduzione, traduzione e note*. Florence.
Allen 2000: Allen, D., *The World of Prometheus: The Politics of Punishing in Democratic Athens*. Princeton.
Anderson (G.) 2003: Anderson, G., *The Athenian Experiment: Building an Imagined Political Community in Ancient Attica, 508–490 BC*. Ann Arbor.
Ando, C. and Rüpke, J. 2015: Ando, C. and Rüpke, J., *Public and Private in Ancient Mediterranean Law and Religion*. Religionsgeschichtliche Versuche und Vorarbeiten 65. Berlin, Munich, Boston.
Andrewes 1970: Andrewes, A., 'Lysias and the Theramenes Papyrus', *ZPE* 6: 35–8.
Andrewes 1981: Andrewes, A., *Greek Society*. Harmondsworth.
Audring 1977: Audring, G., 'Ephialtes Stürtz den Areopag', *Altertum* 23: 234–8.
Avery 1963: Avery, H. C., 'Critias and the Four Hundred', *CPh* 58.3: 165–7.
Balot 2006: Balot, R. K., *Greek Political Thought*. Malden, MA.
Balot 2009: Balot, R. K. (ed.), *A Companion to Greek and Roman Political Thought*. Malden, MA.
Barbato 2020: Barbato, M., *The Ideology of Democratic Athens: Institutions, Orators, and the Mythical Past*. Edinburgh.
Baron 2006: Baron, C. A., 'The Aristoteles decree and the expansion of the Second Athenian League', *Hesperia* 75: 379–95.
Bearzot 1997: Bearzot, C., *Lisia e la tradizione su Teramene: commento storico alle orazioni XII e XIII del corpus lysiacum*. Milan.
Bearzot et al. 2018: Bearzot, C., Canevaro, M., Gargiulo, T. and Poddighe, E. (eds.) *Athenaion Politeiai tra storia, politica e sociologia: Aristotele e pseudo-Senofonte*. Milan.
Bekker-Nielsen and Hannestad 2001: Bekker-Nielsen, T. and Hannestad, L. (eds.), *War as a Cultural and Social Force: Essays on Warfare in Antiquity*. Copenhagen.
Beloch 1922: Beloch, K. J., *Griechische Geschichte*, vol. 3. Berlin and Leipzig.

Bencivenni 2003: Bencivenni, A., *Progetti di riforme costituzionali nelle epigrafi greche dei secoli IV–II a.C.* Bologna.
Bertelli 1993: Bertelli, L., 'La "costituzione di Atene" era una democrazia?', in Cresci and Piccirilli 1993: 53–98.
Bertelli 2018: Bertelli, L., 'The *Athenaion Politeia* and Aristotle's political theory', in Bearzot et al. 2018: 71–86.
Bingham 2010: Bingham, T., *The Rule of Law*. London.
Blass 1887: Blass, F., *Die attische Beredsamkeit*, 2nd ed., 3 vols. (1887–1898) Leipzig.
Blaug and Schwarzmantel 2001: Blaug, R. and Schwarzmantel, J. (eds.), *Democracy: A Reader*. Edinburgh (repr. 2016).
Blundell 1989: Blundell, M. W., *Helping Friends and Harming Enemies*. Cambridge.
Boffo and Faraguna 2021: Boffo, L. and Faraguna, M., *Le poleis e i loro archivi. Studi su pratiche documentarie, istituzioni e società nell'antichità greca*. Trieste.
Bonazzi 2018: Bonazzi, M., *Processo a Socrate*. Rome.
Bonner 1924: Bonner, R. J., 'Note on Aristotle *Constitution of Athens* XXXIX.5', *CPh* 19: 175–6.
Börm 2019: Börm, H., *Mordender Mitbürger: Stasis und Bürgerkrieg in griechischen Poleis des Hellenismus*. Historia Einzelschriften 258. Stuttgart.
Bowersock 1967: Bowersock, G. W., 'Pseudo-Xenophon', *HSCPh* 71: 33–55.
Bravo 1994: Bravo, B., 'Le prime reazioni (1891–1898) al racconto dell'*Athenaion Politeia* su Atene arcaica e in particolare sulle riforme di Clistene', in Maddoli 1994: 217–39.
Bremer 1983: Bremer, J. M., 'Scapegoat rituals in ancient Greece', *HSCPh* 87: 299–320.
Brenne 2001: Brenne, S., *Ostrakismos und Prominenz in Athen*. Vienna.
Brickhouse and Smith 1989: Brickhouse, T. C. and Smith, N. D., *Socrates on Trial*. Princeton.
Brickhouse and Smith 1994: Brickhouse, T. C. and Smith, N. D., *Plato's Socrates*. Oxford.
Brickhouse and Smith 2002: Brickhouse, T. C. and Smith, N. D. (eds.), *The Trial and Execution of Socrates: Sources and Controversies*. Oxford.
Brock 1991: Brock, R., 'The emergence of democratic ideology', *Historia* 40: 160–9.
Brock 2009: Brock, R., 'Did the Athenian empire promote democracy?', in Ma et al. 2009: 149–66.
Brosius and Hüsken 2010: Brosius, C. and Hüsken, U. (eds.), *Ritual Matters: Dynamic Dimensions in Practice*. London, New York, New Delhi.
Brunt 1993: Brunt, P. A., *Studies in Greek History and Thought*. Oxford.
Bruyn 1995: Bruyn, O. de, *La compétence de l'Aréopage en matière de procès publics: des origines de la polis athénienne à la conquête romaine de la Grèce (vers 700–146 avant J.-C.)*. Stuttgart.
Bryce 1889: Bryce, J., *The American Commonwealth*, vol. 1. Indianapolis.
Bultrighini 2005: Bultrighini, U. (ed.), *Democrazia e antidemocrazia nel mondo greco: atti del convegno internazionale di studi, Chieti 9–11 aprile 2003*. Alessandria.
Burkett 1979: Burkett, W., *Structure and History in Greek Mythology and Ritual*. Berkeley.
Burnyeat 1997: Burnyeat, M. F., 'The impiety of Socrates', *AncPhil* 17: 1–12.
Cairns 2011: Cairns, D., 'Review article, D. Konstan, *Before Forgiveness*', *AHB Online Reviews*: 103–13.
Cairns 2015: Cairns, D., 'Revenge, punishment, and justice in Athenian homicide law', *Journal of Value Inquiry* 49: 645–65.
Cairns et al. 2022: Cairns, D., Canevaro, M. and Mantzouranis, K., 'Recognition and redistribution in Aristotle's account of *stasis*', *Polis* 39: 1–34.

Cammack 2019a: Cammack, D., 'Aristotle, Athens, and beyond', *CR* 69.1: 63–5.
Cammack 2019b: Cammack, D., 'Liberal ends, democratic means? A response to Josiah Ober's *Demopolis*', *Polis* 36: 516–23.
Canevaro 2013a: Canevaro, M., '*Nomothesia* in Classical Athens: What sources should we believe?', *CQ* 63: 1–22.
Canevaro 2013b: Canevaro, M., *The Documents in the Attic Orators: Laws and Decrees in the Public Speeches of the Demosthenic Corpus*. Oxford.
Canevaro 2015: Canevaro, M., 'Making and changing laws in ancient Athens', in Harris and Canevaro 2015: pages online. https://doi.org/10.1093/oxfordhb/9780199599257.013.4.
Canevaro 2016: Canevaro, M., 'Legislation (*nomothesia*)', *OCD4*. https://doi.org/10.1093/acrefore/9780199381135.013.8020.
Canevaro 2017: Canevaro, M., 'The rule of law as a measure of political legitimacy in the Greek city states', *Hague Journal on the Rule of Law* 9: 211–36.
Canevaro 2018: Canevaro, M., 'The authenticity of the document at Dem. 24.20–3, the procedures of *nomothesia* and the so-called ἐπιχειροτονία τῶν νόμων', *Klio* 100: 70–124.
Canevaro and Esu 2018: Canevaro, M. and Esu, A., 'Extreme democracy and mixed constitution in theory and in practice: *Nomophylakia* and fourth-century *nomothesia* in the Aristotelian *Athenaion Politeia*', in Bearzot et al. 2018: 106–45.
Canevaro and Harris 2012: Canevaro, M. and Harris, E. M., 'The documents in Andocides' *On the Mysteries*', *CQ* 62: 98–129.
Canevaro and Harris 2016–17: Canevaro, M. and Harris, E. M., 'The authenticity of the documents at Andocides' *On the Mysteries* 77–79 and 83–84', *Dike* 19/20: 9–49.
Carawan 1998: Carawan, E., *Rhetoric and the Law of Draco*. Oxford.
Carawan 2002: Carawan, E., 'The Athenian Amnesty and scrutiny of the laws', *JHS* 122: 1–23.
Carawan 2008: Carawan, E., 'Pericles the Younger and the citizenship law', *CJ* 103: 383–406.
Carawan 2010: Carawan, E., 'The case against Nicomachos', *TAPhA* 140: 71–95.
Carawan 2011: Carawan, E., '*Paragraphê* and the merits', *GRBS* 51: 254–95.
Carawan 2012: Carawan, E., 'The meaning of *mê mnêsikakein*', *CQ* 62: 567–81.
Carawan 2013: Carawan, E., *The Athenian Amnesty and Reconstructing the Law*. Oxford.
Carawan 2016: Carawan, E., 'Documents in the case: Demosthenes 23–24', *TAPhA* 146: 37–60.
Carawan 2017: Carawan, E., 'Decrees in Andocides' *On the Mysteries* and "latent fragments" from Craterus', *CQ* 67: 400–21.
Carawan 2019: Carawan, E., 'How the "crown case" came to trial and why', *GRBS* 59: 109–33.
Carawan 2020: Carawan, E., *Control of the Laws in the Ancient Democracy at Athens*. Baltimore.
Cargill 1981: Cargill, J., *The Second Athenian League: Empire of Free Alliance?* Berkeley, Los Angeles, London.
Cargill 1996: Cargill, J., 'The decree of Aristoteles: Some epigraphical details', *AncW* 27: 1–12.
Carter 2007: Carter, D. M., *The Politics of Greek Tragedy*. Liverpool.
Cartledge 2001: Cartledge, P. A., *Spartan Reflections*. London.
Carugati 2019: Carugati, F., *Creating a Constitution: Law, Democracy and Growth in Ancient Athens*. Princeton.
Cawkwell 1995: Cawkwell, G., 'Early Greek tyranny and the people', *CQ* 45: 73–85.
Cawkwell 1997: Cawkwell, G., *Thucydides and the Peloponnesian War*. London.
Chaniotis 2010: Chaniotis, A., 'Dynamic of emotions and dynamic of rituals: Do emotions change ritual norms?', in Brosius and Hüsken 2010: 208–33.
Chaniotis 2013: Chaniotis, A., 'Normen stärker als Emotionen? Der kulturhistorische Kontext der griechischen Amnestie', in Harter-Uibopuu and Mitthof 2013: 47–70.
Charles 1938: Charles, J. F., *Statutes of Limitations at Athens*. Chicago.
Christ 1998: Christ, M. R., *The Litigious Athenian*. Baltimore and London.

Christ 2005: Christ, M. R., 'Response to Edward Harris', in Wallace, R. W. and Gagarin, M. (eds.), *Symposium 2001: Akten der Gesellschaft für griechische und hellenistische Rechtgeschichte.* Vienna: 143–6.
Clinton 1982: Clinton, K., 'The nature of the late fifth-century revision of the Athenian law-code', in *Studies in Attic Epigraphy, History and Topography Presented to Eugene Vanderpool.* Hesperia Suppl. 19. Princeton.
Cloché 1915: Cloché, P., *La restauration démocratique à Athènes en 403 avant J.-C.* Paris.
Cohen (D.) 1991: Cohen, D., *Law, Sexuality and Community: The Enforcement of Morals in Classical Athens.* Cambridge.
Cohen (D.) 1995: Cohen, D., *Law, Violence, and Community in Classical Athens.* Cambridge.
Cohen (E.) 1992: Cohen, E., 'Review of P. Millett, *Lending and Borrowing in Ancient Athens*', *BMCR* 1992.04.10
Cohen (E.) 2005: Cohen, E., 'Commercial law', in Gagarin and Cohen 2005: 290–302.
Colaiaco 2001: Coilaiaco, J. A., *Socrates against Athens: Philosophy on Trial.* New York and London.
Cole 1974: Cole, J. R., 'Cimon's dismissal, Ephialtes' revolution and the Peloponnesian Wars', *GRBS* 15: 369–85.
Connor 1971: Connor, W. R., *The New Politicians of Fifth-Century Athens.* Princeton.
Connor 1991: Connor, W. R., 'The other 399: Religion and the trial of Socrates', in Flower and Toher 1991: 49–56.
Consolo Langer 2005: Consolo Langer, S., 'Democrazia e antidemocrazia a Siracusa: *isotes e ges anadasmos* nelle lotte sociali del IV secolo', in Bultrighini 2005: 235–50.
Constant 1819: Constant, B., 'The Liberty of Ancients compared to that of Moderns', *Essay Presented to the Royal Athenaeum of Paris.* Paris.
Cooper 2008: Cooper, C. (ed.), *Epigraphy and the Greek Historian.* Toronto.
Cresci and Piccirilli 1993: Cresci, L. R. and Piccirilli, L. (eds.) 1993: *L'Athenaion Politeia di Aristotele.* Genoa.
Dalmeyda 1930: Dalmeyda, D., *Andocide.* Paris.
Davies 1971: Davies, J. K., *Athenian Propertied Families, 600–300 B.C.* Oxford.
Davies 1996: Davies, J. K., 'Deconstructing Gortyn: When is a code not a code?', in Foxhall and Lewis 1996: 33–56.
Davis 2011: Davis, G., '*Axones* and *kurbeis*: A new answer to an old problem', *Historia* 60: 1–35.
Derenne 1930: Derenne, E., *Les procès d'impiété intentés aux philosophes à Athènes au Vme et au IVme siècle avant J.-C.* Liège and Paris.
Dicey 1885: Dicey, A. V., *An Introduction to the Study of the Law of the Constitution.* London.
Dillery 1995: Dillery, J., *Xenophon and the History of His Times.* London and New York.
Dmitriev 2004: Dmitriev, S., 'Alexander's Exiles Decree', *Klio* 86: 248–381.
Dmitriev 2015: Dmitriev, S., 'Athenian *atimia* and legislation against tyranny and subversion', *CQ* 65: 35–50.
Dobree 1831: Dobree, P. P., *Adversaria,* vol. 1: 192–262. Cambridge.
Donlan 1970: Donlan, W., 'Changes and shifts in the meaning of *demos* in the literature of the archaic period', *PP* 135: 381–95.
Dorjahn 1946: Dorjahn, A., *Political forgiveness in Old Athens: The amnesty of 403 B.C.* Evanston.
Dössel 2003: Dössel, A., *Die Belegung innerstaatlicher Konflikte in den griechischen Poleis vom 5.–3. Jahrhundert v. Chr.* Frankfurt.
Dover 1974: Dover, K. J., *Greek Popular Morality.* Oxford.
Dow 1959: Dow, S., 'The law codes of Athens', *Proceedings of the Massachusetts Historical Society* 71: 2–36.
Dow 1960: Dow, S., 'The Athenian sacred calendars', *BCH* 92: 58–73.
Dow 1961: Dow, S., 'The laws inscribed with Nichomakhos' law code', *Hesperia* 30: 58–73.

Dreher 1995: Dreher, M., *Hegemon und Symmachoi: Untersuchungen zum Zweiten Athenischen Seebund*. Berlin and New York.
Dreher 2013: Dreher, M., 'Die Herausbildung eines politischen Instruments: die Amnestie bis zum Ende der klassischen Zeit', in Harter-Uidopuu and Mitthof 2013: 127–61.
Drews 1972: Drews, R., 'The first tyrants of Greece', *Historia* 21: 129–44.
Esu 2021: Esu, A., 'Review of Carawan, *Control of the Laws in the Ancient Democracy at Athens*', *BMCR* 2021, 12.33.
Fabiani 2021: Fabiani, R., 'Review of Henning Börm (2019)', *Klio* 103: 320–6.
Faraguna 2015: Faraguna, M., 'Archives, documents and legal practices in the Greek poleis', in Harris and Canevaro 2015: pages online. https://doi.org/10.1093/oxfordhb/9780199599257.013.14.
Faraguna 2021: Faraguna, M., 'Magistrates' accountability and epigraphic documents: The case of accounts and inventories', in K. Harter-Uibopuu, W. Riess (eds.), *Symposion 2019: Vorträge zur griechischen und hellenistischen Rechtsgeschichte (Hamburg, 26–28 August 2019)*, 228–53. Vienna.
Filonik 2013: Filonik, J., 'Athenian impiety trials: A re-appraisal', *Dike* 16: 11–96.
Filonik 2019: Filonik, J., '"Living as one wishes" in Athens: The (anti-)democratic polemics', *CPh* 114: 1–24.
Fine 1983: Fine, J. V. A., *The Ancient Greeks: A Critical History*. Cambridge, MA.
Fingarette 1971: Fingarette, A., 'A new look at the wall of Nikomakhos', *Hesperia* 40: 330–5.
Finley 1971: Finley, M. I., 'The ancestral constitution', reprinted in *The Use and Abuse of History* (1975): 34–59. New York.
Finley 1973: Finley, M. I., *The Ancient Economy*. Berkeley and Los Angeles.
Fisher 1998: Fisher, N. R. E., 'Violence, masculinity and the law in Classical Athens', in Foxhall and Salmon 1998: 68–97.
Fisher and Wees 2015: Fisher, N. and Wees, H. van (eds.), *'Aristocracy' in Antiquity: Re-defining Greek and Roman Elites*. Swansea.
Flower and Toher 1991: Flower, M. A. and Toher, M. (eds.), *Georgica: Greek Studies in Honour of George Cawkwell*. London.
Forsdyke 2005: Forsdyke, S., *Exile, Ostracism and Democracy: The Politics of Expulsion in Ancient Greece*. Princeton.
Forsdyke et al. 2017: Forsdyke, S., Foster, E. and Balot, R. (eds.), *The Oxford Handbook of Thucydides*. Oxford.
Foxhall and Lewis 1996: Foxhall, L. and Lewis, A. D. E. (eds.), *Greek Law in Its Political Setting: Justification Not Justice*. New York and Oxford.
Foxhall and Salmon 1998: Foxhall, L. and Salmon, J. (eds.), *When Men Were Men: Masculinity, Power, and Identity in Classical Antiquity*. London.
Frohberger 1866–71: Frohberger, H., *Ausgewählte Reden des Lysias*. Leipzig.
Frohberger and Gebauer 1880: Frohberger, H. and Gebauer, G., *Ausgewählte Reden des Lysias, für den Schulgebrauch erklärt*, vol. 2. Leipzig.
Frohberger and Thalheim 1892–5: Frohberger, H. and Thalheim, T., *Ausgewählte Reden des Lysias, für den Schulgebrauch erklärt*, vol. 3. Leipzig.
Fuks 1953: Fuks, A., *The Ancestral Constitution: Four Studies in Athenian Party Politics at the End of the Fifth Century B.C.* London.
Fuller 1964: Fuller, L. L., *The Morality of Law*. New Haven.
Furley 1996: Furley, W. D., *Andokides and the Herms: A Study of Crisis in Fifth-Century Athenian Religion*. London.
Gagarin and Cohen 2005: Gagarin, M. and Cohen, D. (eds.), *The Cambridge Companion to Ancient Greek Law*. Cambridge.

Gagliardi and Pepe 2019: Gagliardi, L., and Pepe, L., (eds.), *Dike. Essays in Honor of Alberto Maffi*. Milan.
Gauthier 1972: Gauthier, P., *Symbola: les étrangers et la justice dans les cités grecques*. Nancy.
Gawlinksi 2007: Gawlinski, L., 'The Athenian calendar of sacrifices: A new fragment from the Athenian agora', *Hesperia* 76: 37–55.
Gerhke 1985: Gehrke, H.-J., *Stasis: Untersuchungen zu den inneren Kriegen in den griechischen Staaten des 5. und 4. Jahrhunderts v. Chr.* Munich.
Gerhke 1994: Gehrke, H.-J., *Rechtskodifizierung und soziale Normen*. Tübingen.
Gernet and Bizos 1999 [1926]: Gernet, L. and Bizos, M., *Lysias: Discours*, 2 vols. Paris.
Gomme 1962a: Gomme, A., 'The Old Oligarch', in Gomme 1962b: 38–69.
Gomme 1962b: Gomme, A., *More Essays in Greek History and Literature*. Oxford.
Goodell 1893: Goodell, T. D., 'An Athenian parallel to a function of our Supreme Court', *Yale Review* 2: 64–73.
Goukowski and Brixhe 1991: Goukowski, P. and Brixhe, P. (eds.), *Hellenika Symmikta*. Nancy.
Grau 1972: Grau, P., *Prooemiengestaltung bei Lysias*. Bonn.
Gray 2013: Gray, B., 'Justice or harmony? Reconciliation after stasis in Dikaia and the fourth century B.C. polis', *REA* 115: 369–401.
Gray 2015: Gray, B., *Stasis and Stability: Exile, the Polis, and Political Thought, c. 404–146 B.C.* Oxford.
Green 1991: Green, P., 'Re-booking the flute girls: A fresh look at the chronological evidence for the fall of Athens and the ὀκταμήνος ἀρχή of the Thirty', *AHB* 5.1: 1–16.
Griffith-Williams 2013: Griffith-Williams, B., *A Commentary on Selected Speeches of Isaios*. Mnemosyne Supplement 364. Leiden and Boston.
Großer 1868: Großer, R., *Die Amnestie des Jahres 403 v. Chr.* Minden.
Grote 1846–56: Grote, G., *History of Greece*, 12 vols. London.
Guagliumi 2003: Guagliumi, B., 'Il racconto di una stasis nel decreto ateniese per Iulis (*IG* II² 111)', *Quaderni del Dipartimento di filologia e tradizione classica*, Bologna, n.s. 2: 25–47.
Guía and Gallego 2010: Guía, M. V. and Gallego, J., 'Athenian *zeugitai* and the Solonian census classes: New reflections and perspectives', *Historia* 59: 257–81.
Hall 1990: Hall, L. G. H., 'Ephialtes, the Areopagus and the Thirty', *CQ* 40: 319–28.
Hamel 2012: Hamel, D., *The Mutilation of the Herms: Unpacking an Ancient Mystery*. North Haven, CT.
Hamilton 1970: Hamilton, C. D., *Sparta's Bitter Victories*. Ithaca, NY.
Hansen 1974: Hansen, M. H., *The Sovereignty of the People's Court in Athens in the Fourth Century B.C. and the Public Action and Unconstitutional Proposals*. Odense.
Hansen 1975: Hansen, M. H., *Eisangelia: The Sovereignty of the People's Court in Athens in the Fourth Century B.C. and the Impeachment of Generals and Politicians*. Odense.
Hansen 1976: Hansen, M. H., *Apagoge, Endeixis and Ephegesis against Kakourgoi, Atimoi and Pheugontes*. Odense.
Hansen 1979: Hansen, M. H., 'Did the Athenian *Ecclesia* legislate after 403/2?', *GRBS* 20.1: 27–53. Reprinted in Hansen 1983: 179–205.
Hansen 1983: Hansen, M. H., *The Athenian Ecclesia*. Copenhagen.
Hansen 1986: Hansen, M. H., *Demography and Democracy: The Number of Athenian Citizens in the Fourth Century B.C.* Herning.
Hansen 1991: Hansen, M. H., *The Athenian Democracy in the Age of Demosthenes: Structure, Principles, and Ideology*. Oxford.
Hansen 1995: Hansen, M. H., *The Trial of Socrates: From the Athenian Point of View*. Copenhagen.

Hansen 2005: Hansen, M.H., *The Tradition of Ancient Greek Democracy and its Importance for Modern Democracy: Direct Democracy, Ancient and Modern*. Copenhagen.
Hansen 2014: Hansen, M. H., 'Political parties in democratic Athens?', *GRBS* 54: 379–403.
Hansen 2015: Hansen, M. H., 'Is Patrokleides' decree (Andoc. 1.83–84) a genuine document?', *GRBS* 55.4: 884–901.
Hansen 2016: Hansen, M. H., 'Is Teisamenos' decree (Andoc. 1.83–84) a genuine document?' *GRBS* 56: 34–48.
Harding 1974: Harding, P. E., 'Androtion's view of Solon's Seisachtheia', *Phoenix* 28: 282–9.
Harris 1990: Harris, E. M., 'The constitution of the Five Thousand', *HSCPh* 93: 243–80.
Harris 1992: Harris, E. M., 'Pericles' praise of Athenian democracy: Thucydides 2.37.1', *HSCPh* 94: 157–67.
Harris 1994: Harris, E. M., '"In the act" or "red-handed"? *Apagoge* to the Eleven and Furtum Manifestum', in G. Thür (ed.), *Symposion 1993: Vorträge zur griechischen und hellenistischen Rechtsgeschichte*: 169–84. Cologne.
Harris 1995: Harris, E. M., *Aeschines and Athenian Politics*. New York.
Harris 1997: Harris, E. M., 'A new solution to the riddle of the Seisachtheia', in L. G. Mitchell and P. J. Rhodes (eds), *The Development of the Polis in Archaic Greece*: 103–12. London.
Harris 2000: Harris, E. M., 'The authenticity of Andokides' *De pace*: A subversive essay', in P. Flensted-Jensen, T. H. Nielsen and L. Rubinstein (eds.), *Polis and Politics: Studies in Ancient Greek History Presented to Mogens Herman Hansen on His Sixtieth Birthday*: 479–506. Copenhagen, 2000.
Harris 2002: Harris, E. M., 'Did Solon abolish debt-bondage?' *CQ* 52.2: 415–30.
Harris 2005a: Harris, E. M., 'Feuding or the rule of law? The nature of litigation in classical Athens: An essay in legal sociology', in *Symposion 2001: Vorträge zur griechischen und hellenistischen Rechtsgeschichte (Evanston, Illinois, 5–8 September 2001) = Papers on Greek and Hellenistic Legal History (Evanston, Illinois, September 5–8, 2001)*: 125–42. Vienna.
Harris 2005b: Harris, E. M., 'Was all criticism of Athenian democracy anti-democratic?', in Bultrighini 2005: 11–24.
Harris 2006: Harris, E. M., *Democracy and the Rule of Law in Classical Athens: Essays on Law, Society, and Politics*. Cambridge.
Harris 2013: Harris, E. M., *The Rule of Law in Action in Democratic Athens*. Oxford.
Harris 2013–14: Harris, E. M., 'The document at Andocides 1.96–98', *Tekmeria* 12: 121–53.
Harris 2015a: Harris, E. M., 'The role of pollution in Athenian homicide law', in Ando and Rüpke 2015: 11–35.
Harris 2015b: Harris, E. M., 'Suits for homicide at *Ath. Pol.* 39.5', appendix to Joyce 2015: 45–9.
Harris 2015c: Harris, E. M., 'Toward a typology of Greek regulations about religious matters: A legal approach', *Kernos* 28: 52–85.
Harris 2016: Harris, E. M., 'From democracy to the rule of law? Constitutional change in Athens in the fifth and fourth centuries BCE', in Tiersche 2016: 73–87.
Harris 2017: Harris, E. M., 'Applying the law about the award of crowns to magistrates (Aeschin. 3.9–31): Epigraphic evidence for the legal arguments at the trial of Ctesiphon', *ZPE* 202: 105–17.
Harris 2019a: Harris, E. M., 'Aeschylus' *Eumenides*: The rule of the Areopagus, the rule of law and political discourse in Greek tragedy', in Markantonatos and Volonaki 2019: 389–419.
Harris 2019b: Harris, E. M., 'Review of M. Simonton (2018)', *JHS* 129: 256–7.

Harris 2021: Harris, E. M., 'The work of Craterus and the documents in the "Lives of the Ten Orators"', *Klio* 103: 463–504.
Harris 2022: Harris, E. M., 'Review of F. Carugati (2019)', *Polis* 39: 203–12.
Harris and Canevaro 2015: Harris, E. M. and Canevaro, M. (eds.), *The Oxford Handbook of Ancient Greek Law*. Oxford. https://doi.org/10.1093/oxfordhb/9780199599257.001.0001.
Harris and Rubinstein 2004: Harris, E. M. and Rubinstein, L. (eds.), *The Law and the Courts in Ancient Greece*. London.
Harrison 1968–71: Harrison, A. R. W., *The Law of Athens*, 2 vols. Oxford.
Harter-Uibopuu and Mitthof 2013: Harter-Uibopuu, K. and Mitthof, F. (eds.), *Vergeben und Vergessen? Amnestie in der Antike: Wiener Kolloquien zur Antiken Rechtsgeschichte I*. Vienna.
Hecker 1848: Hecker, A., *De Oratione in Eratosthenem trigintavirum Lysiae falso tributa*. Leiden.
Heisserer and Hodot 1986: Heisserer, A. J. and Hodot, R., 'The Mytilenean decree on concord', *ZPE* 63: 120–8.
Henderson 2007: Henderson, J., 'Drama and democracy', in Samons 2007: 179–95.
Herman 2000: Herman, G., 'Athenian beliefs about revenge: Problems and methods', *PCPhS* 46: 7–28.
Herman 2006: Herman, G., *Morality and Behaviour in Democratic Athens: A Social History*. Cambridge.
Hermann 1979: Hermann, P. H. G., 'Die Stadt Temnos und ihre auswärtigen Beziehungen in hellenistischer Zeit', *MDAI(I)* 29: 239–71.
Hignett 1952: Hignett, C., *A History of the Athenian Constitution*. Oxford.
Hodkinson and Powell 1999: Hodkinson, S. and Powell, A. (eds.), *Sparta: New Perspectives*. Swansea.
Hölkeskamp 1999: Hölkeskamp, K.-J., *Schiedsrichter, Gesetzgeber und Gesetzgebung im archaischen Griechenland*. Stuttgart.
Hornblower 1991: Hornblower, S., *A Commentary on Thucydides*, vol. 1. Oxford.
Horsley 1982: Horsley, G. H. R., 'The second Athenian confederacy', in *Hellenika: Essays in Greek Politics and History*: 131–50. North Ryde.
Hume 1742: Hume, D., 'Of some remarkable customs', in *Essays and Treatises on Several Subjects*, vol. 1, *Essays, Moral, Political, and Literary*: 361–9. Edinburgh.
Humble 1999: Humble, N., '*Sophrosyne* and the Spartans in Xenophon', in Hodkinson and Powell 1999: 339–54.
Ingravalle 1989: Ingravalle, F., 'Conflitti e trasformazioni costituzionali nella *Constituzione degli Ateniesi* di Aristotele', *Filosofia Politica* 3: 327–52.
Jacoby 1949: Jacoby, F., *Atthis: The Local Chronicles of Ancient Athens*. Oxford.
Jordović 2014: I. Jordović, 'The origins of Philolaconism: Democracy and aristocratic identity in fifth-century BC Athens', *C&M* 65: 127–50.
Joyce 2008: Joyce, C. J., 'The Athenian amnesty and scrutiny of 403', *CQ* 58: 507–18.
Joyce 2014: Joyce, C. J., 'Μὴ μνησικακεῖν and "all the laws" (Andocides *On the Mysteries* 81–2): A reply to E. Carawan', *Antichthon* 48: 37–54.
Joyce 2015: Joyce, C. J., 'Oaths (ὅρκοι), covenants (συνθῆκαι) and laws (νόμοι) in the Athenian Reconciliation Agreement of 403 BC', *Antichthon* 49: 24–49.
Joyce 2016: Joyce, C. J., 'The Athenian Reconciliation Agreement of 403 BCE and its legacy for the Greek city-states in the classical and Hellenistic ages', in Harris and Canevaro 2015: pages online. https://doi.org/10.1093/oxfordhb/9780199599257.013.26.
Joyce 2018: Joyce, C. J., '*Atimia* and outlawry in archaic and classical Greece', *Polis* 35: 33–60.
Joyce 2019: Joyce, C. J., 'Citizenship or inheritance? The phratry in classical Athens', *Polis* 36: 466–78.
Joyce 2021: Joyce, C. J., 'The Demotionidai inscription', *Rivista di Diritto Ellenico* 11: 121–79.

Joyce 2021/2: Joyce, C. J., 'The Solonian amnesty law (Plu. *Sol.* 19.3–4) and the Athenian law on homicide', *CJ* 117: 127–56.
Joyce 2022: Joyce C.J., 'A positive doctrine of tyranny? The rule of law vs. rule of a tyrant in archaic and classical Greece', *Antichthon* 56, at press.
Kagan 2013: Kagan, D., *A New History of the Peloponnesian War*. Ithaca, NY.
Kaibel 1893: Kaibel, G., *Hermes 1893. Zeitschrift für Classische Philologie* 28. Berlin.
Kahrstedt 1937–8: Kahrstedt, U., 'Untersuchungen zu athenischen Behörden', *Klio* 30: 10–33.
Kenyon 1892: Kenyon, F. G., *Aristotle on the Constitution of Athens*. London.
Keyt 1999: Keyt, D. (tr.), *Aristotle: Politics Books V and VI*. Oxford.
Keyt and Miller 1991: Keyt, D. and Miller, F. D. (eds.), *A Companion to Aristotle's Politics*. Oxford.
Koerner 1993: Koerner, R., *Inschriftliche Gesetzestexte der frühen grieschichen Polis: aus dem Nachlaß herausgegeben von K. Hallof*. Cologne, Weimar, Vienna.
Konstan 2010: Konstan, D., *Before Forgiveness: The Origins of a Moral Idea*. Cambridge.
Krech 1888: Krech, P., *De Crateri Ψηφισμάτων συναγωγή*. Greifswald.
Krentz 1982: Krentz, P., *The Thirty at Athens*. Ithaca, NY.
Krentz 1984: Krentz, P., 'Was Eratosthenes responsible for the death of Polemarchus?', *PP* 39: 23–32.
Kron 2011: Kron. J. G., 'The distribution of wealth at Athens in comparative perspective', *ZPE* 179: 129–38.
Kühn (G.) 1985: Kühn, G., 'Untersuchungen zur Funktion der Säulenhalle III: die Stoa Basileios in Athen', *JDAI* 100: 200–26.
Kühn (J.-H.) 1967: Kühn, J.-H., 'Die Amnestie von 403 v. Chr. im Reflex der 18. Isokrates-Rede', *WS* 1: 31–73.
Kußmaul 1969: Kußmaul, P., *Synthekai: Beiträge zur Geschichte des attischen Obligationrechtes*. Diss. Basel.
La'da 2013: La'da, C., 'Amnesty in Hellenistic Egypt: A survey of the sources', in Harter-Uidopuu and Mitthof 2013: 163–209.
Ladek 1891: Ladek, F., 'Über die Echtheit zweier auf Demosthenes und Demochares bezüglichen Urkunden in Pseudo-Plutarch', *WS* 13: 63–128.
Lambert 2002: Lambert, S. D., 'The sacrificial calendar of Athens', *ABSA* 97: 353–99.
Lanni 2010: Lanni, A., 'Transitional justice in ancient Athens: A case study', *University of Pennsylvania Journal of International Law* 32: 551–94.
Lanni 2016: Lanni, A., *Law and Order in the Courts of Classical Athens*. Cambridge.
Lasagni 2018: Lasagni, C., '"For anyone who wishes to read up close . . ." A few thoughts revolving around the formula ΣΚΟΠΕΙΝ ΤΩΙ ΒΟΥΛΟΜΕΝΩΙ in Attic inscriptions,' *RFIC* 146: 334–80.
Legon 1968: Legon, R. P., 'Megara and Mytilene', *Phoenix* 22: 145–58.
Legon 1972: Legon, R. P., 'Samos in the Delian League', *Historia* 21: 145–58.
Lehmann 1972: Lehmann, G. A., 'Die revolutionäre Machtergreifung der "Dreißig" und die staatliche Teilung Attikas (404–401/0 v. Chr.)', in Stiehl and Lehmann 1972: 201–33.
Levi 1967–8: Levi, D., 'Gli scavi di Iasos', *ASAthene* 45–6: 537–90.
Lévy 2000: Lévy, E. (ed.), *La codification des lois dans l'antiquité*. Paris.
Lévy 2005: Lévy, E., 'Isonomia', in Bultrighini 2005: 11–23.
Lewis 1997: Lewis, D. M., 'The federal constitution of Keos', *ABSA* 57 (1962): 1–4, republished in P.J. Rhodes (ed.), *Selected Papers in Greek and Near Eastern History*: 22–8. Cambridge.
Lewis 2018: Lewis, D.M., *Greek Slave Systems in their Ancient Mediterranean Context, c. 800–146 BC*. Oxford.

Liddel 2003: Liddel, P. P., 'The places of publication of Athenian state decrees from the 5th century to the 3rd century AD', *ZPE* 143: 79–93.
Liddel 2007: Liddel, P. P., *Civic Obligation and Individual Liberties in Ancient Athens*. Oxford.
Liddel 2009: Liddel, P. P., 'Democracy ancient and modern', in Balot 2009: 131–48.
Liddel 2020: Liddel, P. P., *Decrees of Fourth-Century Athens (403/2–322/1 BC)*, 2 vols. Cambridge.
Lintott 1982: Lintott, A. W., *Violence, Civil Strife and Revolution in the Classical City, 750–330 BC*. Baltimore.
Lintott 2018: Lintott, A. W., *Aristotle's Political Philosophy in Its Historical Context: A New Translation and Commentary on Politics Books 5 and 6*. New York.
Lipsius 1905–15: Lipsius, J.-H., *Das attische Recht und Rechtsverfahren*. 3 vols. in 4. Leipzig.
Loening 1987: Loening, T. C., *The Reconciliation Agreement of 403/2 B.C. in Athens*. Hermes Einzelschriften 53. Stuttgart.
Loeper 1896: Loeper, R., 'Tridzatj Tiranov', *Zhurnal Ministerstva narodnogo prosveshcheniya* 305: 90–101.
Loftus 2000: Loftus, A., 'A new fragment of the Theramenes papyrus (P. Mich. 5796b)', *ZPE* 133: 11–20.
Lonis 1991: Lonis, R., 'La réintégration des exilés politiques en Grèce: le problème des biens', in Goukowski and Brixhe 1991: 91–109.
Loraux 1986: Loraux, N., *The Invention of Athens: The Funeral Oration in the Classical City* (tr. A. Sheridan). Cambridge, MA.
Loraux 1997: Loraux, N., *The Divided City: On Memory and Forgetting in Ancient Athens* (tr. C. Pache and J. Fort). Paris.
Lott 1996: Lott, J. B., 'Philip II, Alexander, and the two tyrannies at Eresos of *IG* XII.2.526, 26', *Phoenix* 50: 26–40.
Luebbert 1881: Luebbert, J., *De Amnestia Anno CCCCIII a Chr. n. ab Atheniensibus decreta*. Kiel.
Lupu 2005: Lupu, E., *Greek Sacred Law: A Collection of New Documents*. Leiden and Boston.
Ma et al. 2009: Ma, J., Papazarkadas, N. and Parker, R. (eds.), *Interpreting the Athenian Empire: New Essays*. London.
McCormick 2019: McCormick, J. P., 'On Josiah Ober's *Demopolis*: Basic democracy, economic inequality, and political punishment', *Polis* 36: 535–42.
McCoy 1975: McCoy, W. J., 'Aristotle's *Athenaion Politeia* and the establishment of the Thirty Tyrants', *YCIS* 24: 131–45.
MacDowell 1962: MacDowell, D. M., *Andokides: On the Mysteries*. Oxford.
MacDowell 1963: MacDowell, D. M., *Athenian Homicide Law in the Age of the Orators*. Manchester.
MacDowell 1975: MacDowell, D. M., 'Law-making in the fourth century B.C.', *JHS* 95: 62–74.
MacDowell 1978: MacDowell, D. M., *The Law in Classical Athens*. London.
MacDowell 1990: *Demosthenes: Against Meidias*. Oxford.
MacDowell 2008: MacDowell, D. M., 'The Athenian penalty of *epobelia*', in Harris, E.M. and Thür, G. (eds.), *Symposion 2007. Akten der Gesellschaft für griechische und hellenistische Rechtsgeschichte*, 87–94. Vienna.
MacDowell 2009. MacDowell, D. M., *Demosthenes the Orator*. Oxford.
McGlew 1993: McGlew, J. F., *Tyranny and Political Culture in Ancient Greece*. Ithaca, NY.
Maddoli 1994: Maddoli, G. (ed.), *L'Athenaion politeia di Aristotele I*. Perugia.
Maffi 1994: Maffi, A., 'Regole matrimoniali e successorie nell'iscrizioni di Tegea sul rientro degli esuli', in Gehrke 1994: 5–31.

Maidment 1941: Maidment, K. J., *Minor Attic Orators*, vol. 1, *Antiphon, Andocides. With an English Translation*. London.
Mann 2007: Mann, C., *Die Demagogen und das Volk: zur politischen Kommunikation im Athen des 5. Jahrhunderts v. Chr. Klio* Suppl. n.s. 13. Berlin.
Mansbridge 2019: Mansbridge, J., 'Is *Democracy before Liberalism* a justification for democracy *without* liberalism?' *Polis* 36: 524–34.
March and Olsen 1989: March, J. G., and Olsen, J. P., *Rediscovering Institutions: The Organizational Basis of Politics*. New York.
Marianetti 1993: Marianetti, M. C., 'Socratic mystery-parody and the issue of *asebeia* in Aristophanes' *Clouds*', *SO* 68: 5–31.
Markantonatos and Volonaki 2019: Markantonatos, A. and Volonaki, E. (eds.), *Poet and Orator: A Symbiotic Relationship in Democratic Athens*. Berlin.
Marr 1971: Marr, J. L., 'Andocides' part in the Mysteries and Hermae affairs 415 B.C.' *CQ* 2: 326–38.
Meiggs 1972: Meiggs, R., *The Athenian Empire*. Oxford.
Merkelbach and Youtie 1968: Merkelbach, R. and Youtie, H. C., 'Ein Michigan-Papyrus über Theramenes', *ZPE* 2: 161–9.
Mess 1911: Mess, A. von, 'Aristoteles ΑΘΗΝΑΙΩΝ ΠΟΛΙΤΕΙΑ und die politische Schriftsstellerei Athens', *RhM* 66: 356–92.
Meyer 2008: Meyer, E. A., 'Thucydides on Harmodius and Aristogeiton, tyranny, and history', *CQ* 58: 13–34.
Meyer 2016: Meyer, E. A., 'Posts, kurbeis, metopes: The origins of the Athenian "documentary" stele', *Hesperia* 85: 323–83.
Michel 1900: Michel, C., *Receuil d'inscriptions grecques*. Brussels.
Miller 2019: Miller, B., 'The importance of *Demopolis* for today's political science', *Polis* 36: 511–15.
Millett 1991: Millett, P., *Lending and Borrowing in Ancient Athens*. Cambridge.
Mitchel 1984: Mitchel, F. W., 'The assessment of the allies in the Second Athenian League', *EMC* 3: 23–37.
Mitchell 2013: Mitchell, L. G., *The Heroic Rulers of Archaic and Classical Greece*. London, New Delhi, New York, Sydney.
Mitchell 2019: Mitchell, L. G., 'Political thinking on kingship in democratic Athens', *Polis* 36: 442–65.
Mitford 1829: Mitford, W., *The History of Greece*, vol. 6. London.
Moggi 2012: Moggi, M., 'Strategie e forme della reconciliazione: Μὴ μνησικακεῖν', in S. Cataldi, E. Bianco and C. Cuniberti (eds.), *Salvare le poleis, construire la Concordia, progettare la pace: atti del Convegno internazionale di storia Greca*. Alessandria.
Mommsen 1899: Mommsen, T., *Römisches Strafrecht*. Leipzig.
Monoson 2000: Monoson, S. S., *Plato's Democratic Entanglements: Athenian Democracy and the Practice of Politics*. Princeton.
Morgan 2003: Morgan, K. A. (ed.), *Popular Tyranny: Sovereignty and Its Discontents in Ancient Greece*. Austin.
Mossé 1997: Mossé, C., 'L'amnistie de 403: une illusion politique?', in Sordi 1997: 53–8.
Németh 2006: Németh, G., *Kritias und die Dreißig Tyrannen: Untersuchungen zur Politik und Prosopographie der Führungselite in Athen 404/403 v. Chr.* Stuttgart.
Nippel 1997: Nippel, W., 'Bürgerkrieg und Amnestie: Athen 411–403', in Smith and Margalit 1997: 103–19.
Ober 1989: Ober, J., *Mass and Elite in Democratic Athens: Rhetoric, Ideology, and the Power of the People*. Princeton.

Ober 1996: Ober, J., *The Athenian Revolution: Essays on Ancient Greek Democracy and Political Theory*. Princeton.
Ober 1998: Ober, J., *Political Dissent in Democratic Athens: Intellectual Criticism of Popular Rule*. Princeton and Oxford.
Ober 2017: Ober, J., *Demopolis: Democracy before Liberalism in Theory and Practice*. Cambridge.
Ober 2019: Ober, J., 'A response to the comments of Mansbridge, Cammack, McCormick, and Urbinati on *Demopolis: Democracy before Liberalism in Theory and Practice*', *Polis* 36: 555–64.
Ober and Hedrick 1996: Ober, J. and Hedrick, C., *Demokratia: A Conversation on Democracies, Ancient and Modern*. Princeton.
Oost 1972: Oost, S. I., 'Cypselus the Bacchiad', *CPh* 67: 10–30.
Osborne 2003: Osborne, R., 'Changing the discourse', in Morgan 2003: 251–72. Austin, TX.
Osborne 2004: Osborne, R., *Greek History*. London and New York.
Ostwald 1986: Ostwald, M., *From Popular Sovereignty to the Sovereignty of Law: Law, Society and Politics in Fifth-Century Athens*. Berkeley.
Ostwald 1993: Ostwald, M., 'Stasis and autonomia in Samos: A comment on an ideological fallacy', Scripta *Classica Israelica* 12: 51–66.
Paoli 1930: Paoli, U. E., *Studi di diritto attico*. Florence.
Paoli 1933: Paoli, U. E., *Studi sul processo attico*. Padua.
Parker 1996: Parker, R., *Athenian Religion: A History*. Oxford.
Patterson 1981: Patterson, C., *Pericles' Citizenship Law*. Salem.
Pecorella Longo 2004: Pecorella Longo, C., 'Il condono della pena in Atene in età classica', *Dike* 7: 85–111.
Pelloso 2017–18: Pelloso, C., '*Nomos basileus* e potere giudicante nell' Atene de IV secolo a.C.', in Pelloso and Cobetto Ghiggia 2017–18: 9–36.
Pelloso 2019: Pelloso, C., *Socrate: la democrazia contro il libero pensiero*. Milan.
Pelloso and Cobetto Ghiggia 2017–18: Pelloso, C., and Cobetto Ghiggia, P. (eds.), '*Nomos Basileus*': *la regalità del diritto in Grecia antica*. Milan and Alessandria.
Peseley 1989: Peseley, G. E., 'The origins and value of the Theramenes papyrus', *AHB* 3: 29–35.
Petrey 1988: Petrey, S., *Realism and Revolution: Balzac, Stendahl, Zola and the Performances of History*. Ithaca, NY.
Phillips 2008: Phillips, D. D., *Avengers of Blood: Homicide in Athenian Law and Custom from Draco to Demosthenes* (Historia Einzelschriften 202). Stuttgart.
Piérart 2000: Piérart, M., 'Qui étaient les nomothètes à Athènes à l'époque de Démosthène?', in Lévy 2000: 229–56.
Piovan 2017–18: Piovan, D., '*Nomos Basileus* o *demos basileus*? Sulla democrazia ateniese di V e IV secolo a.C.', in Pelloso and Cobetto Ghiggia 2017–18: 141–54.
Poddighe 2014: Poddighe, E., *Aristotele, Atene e la metamorfosi dell'idea democratica*. Rome.
Porter 2019: Porter, J. D., 'Slavery and Athens' economic efflorescence', *Mare Nostrum* 10: 25–50.
Press 1993: Press, G. A. (ed.), *Plato's Dialogues: New Studies and Interpretations*. Lanham, MD.
Price 2001: Price, J. J., *Thucydides and Internal War*. Cambridge.
Raaflaub 1983: Raaflaub, K., 'Democracy, oligarchy, and the concept of the "free citizen" in late fifth-century Athens', *Political Theory* 11: 517–44.
Raaflaub 1996: Raaflaub, K., 'Equalities and inequalities in Athenian democracy' in Ober and Hedrick 1996, 139–74.

Rauchenstein 1855: Rauchenstein, R., 'Über das Ende der Dreissig in Athen und einige damit zusammenhängende Fragen', *Philologus* 10: 591–607.
Rauchenstein and Fuhr 1899: Rauchenstein, R. and Fuhr, K., *Ausgewählte Reden des Lysias*, 2 vols. Berlin.
Rawls 1971: Rawls, J., *A Theory of Justice*. Cambridge, MA.
Rawls 2001: Rawls, J., *Justice as Fairness: A Re-statement*. Cambridge, MA.
Raz 1977: Raz, J., 'The rule of law and its virtue', *The Law Quarterly Review* 93: 195–211.
Reinach 1891: Reinach, S., *Chroniques d'Orient: documents sur les fouilles et découvertes dans l'Orient hellénique de 1883 à 1890*. Paris.
Rhodes 1980: Rhodes, P. J., 'Athenian democracy after 403 B.C.', *CJ* 75: 305–23.
Rhodes 1981: Rhodes, P. J., *A Commentary on the Aristotelian Athenaion Politeia*. Oxford.
Rhodes 1984: Rhodes, P. J., '*Nomothesia* in fourth-century Athens', *CQ* 35: 55–60.
Rhodes 1987: Rhodes, P. J., '*Nomothesia* in classical Athens', *L'educazione giuridica* 5.2: 5–26.
Rhodes 1988: Rhodes, P. J. (ed. and tr.), *Thucydides: History II*. Warminster.
Rhodes 1991: Rhodes, P. J., 'The Athenian code of laws, 410–399 B.C.' *JHS* 111: 87–100.
Rhodes 1994: Rhodes, P. J., 'The ostracism of Hyperbolus', in R. Osborne and S. Hornblower (eds.), *Ritual, Finance and Politics: Athenian Democratic Accounts Presented to David Lewis*: 85–98. Oxford.
Rhodes 1995: Rhodes, P. J., 'Judicial procedures in fourth-century Athens', in W. Eder (ed.), *Die athenische Demokratie im 4. Jahrhundert v. Chr.: Vollendung oder Verfall einer Verfassungsform?* Stuttgart.
Rhodes 2003: Rhodes, P. J., 'Nothing to do with democracy: Athenian drama and the *polis*', *JHS* 123: 104–19.
Rhodes 2011: Rhodes, P. J., 'Appeals to the past in Classical Athens', in G. Herman (ed.), *Stability and Crisis in the Athenian Democracy*. Historia Einzelschriften 220: 13–30. Stuttgart.
Rhodes and Leão 2015: Rhodes, P. J. and Leão, D., *The Laws of Solon: A New Edition with Introduction, Translation and Commentary*. London and New York.
Rizzo and Vox 1978: Rizzo, R. and Vox, O., 'διαβολή', *QS* 8: 307–21.
Robb 1993: Robb, K., '*Asebeia* and *Sunousia*: The issues behind the indictment of Socrates', in Press 1993: 77–106.
Roberts 1996: Roberts, J., 'Athenian equality: A constant surrounded by flux', in Ober and Hedrick 1996: 139–74.
Robertson 1990: Robertson, N., 'The laws of Athens, 410–399 BC: The evidence for review and publication', *JHS* 110: 43–75.
Robinson 2011: Robinson, E. W., *Democracy before Athens*. Cambridge.
Rocchi 2022: Rocchi, L., '*Atimia*: dishonour, disfranchisement, and civic disability in archaic and classical Athens' (Ph.D. thesis). Edinburgh.
Rose 2012: Rose, P. W., *The Class Struggle in Archaic Greece*. Cambridge.
Rosivach 1987: Rosivach, V., 'Execution by stoning in Athens', *ClAnt* 6: 232–48.
Rubinstein 2000: Rubinstein, L., *Litigation and Cooperation: Supporting Speakers in the Courts of Classical Athens*. Stuttgart.
Rubinstein 2013: Rubinstein, L., 'Forgive and forget? Amnesty in the Hellenistic period', in Harter-Uibopuu and Mitthof 2013: 127–62.
Rubinstein 2018: Rubinstein, L., 'The Athenian Amnesty of 403/2 and the "forgotten" amnesty of 405/4', in W. Riess (ed.), *Colloquia Attica: Neuere Forschungen zur Archaik, zum athenischen Recht und zur Magie*, 123–144. Stuttgart.

Rubinstein 2023: Rubinstein, L., 'Friendship betrayed: Isocrates 16 and the Athenian Reconciliation of 403/2 BCE', in E. Volonaki, A. Efstathiou, J. Filonik, and C. Kremmydas (eds.), *Friendship in Ancient Greek Thought and Literature: Essays in Honour of Chris Carey and Michael J. Edwards*. Mnemosyne Supplement 474, 282–305. Leiden.

Rudhardt 1960: Rudhart, J., 'La définition du délit d'impiété d'après la législation attique', *MH* 17: 87–105.

Ruschenbusch 1956: Ruschenbusch, E., 'Der sogenannte "Gesetzcode" vom Jahre 410 v. Chr.', *Historia* 5: 123–8.

Ruschenbusch 1958: Ruschenbusch, E., 'ΠΑΤΡΙΟΣ ΠΟΛΙΤΕΙΑ: Theseus, Drakon, Solon und Kleisthenes in Publizistik und Geschichts-schreibung des 5. und 4. Jahrhunderts v. Chr.', *Historia* 7: 398–424.

Ruschenbusch 1966: Ruschenbusch, E., *ΣΟΛΩΝΟΣ ΝΟΜΟΙ: die Fragmente des solonischen Gesetzwerkes mit einer Text- und Überlieferungsgeschichte*. Wiesbaden.

Ruschenbusch 1982: Ruschenbusch, E., 'Eine Bürgerliste von Iulis und Koresia auf Keos', *ZPE* 48: 175–88.

Rusten 1989: J. S. (ed.), *Thucydides: The Peloponnesian War Book II*. Cambridge.

Sakurai 1995: Sakurai, M., 'A new reading in *POxy* 13.1606', *ZPE* 109: 177–80.

Salmon 1969: Salmon, P., 'L'établissement des Trente à Athènes', *AC* 38: 497–500.

Samons 2004: Samons, L. J., *What's Wrong with Democracy? From Athenian Practice to American Worship*. London and Berkeley.

Samons 2007: Samons, L. J. (ed.), *The Cambridge Companion to the Age of Pericles*. Cambridge.

Scafuro 2006: Scafuro, A. C., 'Identifying Solonian laws', in J. H. Blok and A. P. M. H. Lardinois (eds.), *Solon of Athens: New Historical and Philological Approaches*: 175–96. Leiden and Boston.

Scafuro 2012: Scafuro, A. C., 'The legal horizon of Euripides' Ion: A response to Delfim Leão', in B. Legras and G. Thür (eds.), *Symposion 2011: Vorträge zur griechischen und hellenistischen Rechtsgeschichte*. Cologne, Weimar, Vienna: 153–64.

Schanz 1893: Schanz, M., *Sammlung ausgewählter Dialoge Platos mit deutschem Kommentar*, vol. 3, *Apologia*. Leipzig.

Scheibelreiter 2013: Scheibelreiter, P., '*Atheniensium vetus exemplum*: zum Paradigma einer antiken Amnestie', in Harter-Uibopuu and Mitthof 2013: 95–126.

Schöll 1886: Schöll, R., 'Über attische Gesetzgebung', *SBMünchen*, 83–139.

Schütrumpf 1991: Schütrumpf, E., *Aristoteles Politik Buch I. übersetzt und erläutert in Aristoteles Werke in deutscher Übersetzung*, vol. 9, Part I. Berlin and Darmstadt.

Schütrumpf and Gehrke 1996: Schütrumpf, E. and Gehrke, H. J., *Aristoteles Politik Buch IV–VI. übersetzt und erläutert in Aristoteles Werke in Deutscher Übersetzung*, vol. 9, Part III. Berlin and Darmstadt.

Sealey 1960: Sealey, R., 'Regionalism in Archaic Athens', *Historia* 9: 155–80.

Sealey 1973: Sealey, R., 'The origins of *demokratia*', *California Studies in Classical Antiquity* 6: 253–95.

Sealey 1982: Sealey, R., 'On the Athenian conception of law', *CJ* 77: 289–302.

Seibert 1979: Seibert, J., *Die politischen Flüchtlinge und Verbannten in der griechischen Geschichte*. Darmstadt.

Shear (J. L.) 2011: Shear, J. L., *Polis and Revolution: Responding to Oligarchy in Classical Athens*. Cambridge.

Shear (T. L.) 1970: Shear, T. L., 'The monument of the Eponymous Heroes in the Athenian Agora', *Hesperia* 39: 145–222.

Shear (T. L.) 1971: Shear, T. L., 'The Athenian Agora: Excavations of 1970', *Hesperia* 40: 241–79.

Sickinger 1999: Sickinger, J. P., *Public Records and Archives in Classical Athens*. Chapel Hill.

Sickinger 2004: Sickinger, J. P., 'The laws of Athens: Publication, preservation and consultation', in Harris and Rubinstein 2004: 99–112.
Siewert 2002: Siewert, P., et al. (eds.), *Ostrakismos-Testimonien I*. Stuttgart.
Simonton 2018: Simonton, M., *Classical Greek Oligarchy: A Political History*. Princeton.
Simpson 1997: Simpson, P. L. P., *The Politics of Aristotle: Translated with Introduction, Analysis and Notes*. Chapel Hill and London.
Sinclair 1988: Sinclair, R. K., *Democracy and Participation in Athens*. Cambridge.
Smith and Margalit 1997: Smith, G., and Margalit, A. (eds.), *Amnestie oder die Politik der Erinnerung in der Demokratie*. Frankfurt am Main.
Sommerstein 1984: Sommerstein, A. H., 'The murder of Polemarchos', *PP* 39: 370–2.
Sommerstein 2014: Sommerstein, A. H., 'The authenticity of the Demophantus decree', *CQ* 61.1: 49–57.
Sordi 1997: Sordi, M. (ed.), *Amnistia: perdono e vendetta nel mondo antico*. Contributo dell' Instituto di storia antica 23. Milan.
Stahl 1891: Stahl, J. M., 'Über athenische Amnestie Beschlüsse', *RhM* 46: 250–86.
Ste Croix 1972: Ste Croix, G. E. M., *The origins of the Peloponnesian War*. London.
Ste Croix 1981: Ste Croix, G. E. M., *The Class Struggle in the Ancient Greek World*. London.
Stevens 1882: Stevens, W. A., *Select Orations of Lysias, with Introductions and Explanatory Notes*, 2nd ed. Chicago.
Stiehl and Lehmann 1972: Stiehl, R. and Lehmann, G. A., *Antike und Universalgeschischte: Festschrift Hans Erich Stier*. Münster.
Stone 1988: Stone, I. G., *The Trial of Socrates*. Boston.
Strauss 1986: Strauss, B. S., *Athens after the Peloponnesian War: Class, Faction and Policy 403–386 B.C.* London and Sidney.
Stroud 1979: Stroud, R. S., *The Axones and Kyrbeis of Drakon and Solon*. Berkeley.
Thériault 1996: Thériault, G., *Le culte d'Homonoia dans les cités grecques*. Lyon.
Thomas 1989: Thomas, R., *Oral Tradition and Written Record*. Cambridge.
Thompson 1973: Thompson, W. E., 'Observations on Spartan politics', *Rivista storica dell' antichità* 3: 47–58.
Tiersche 2016: Tiersche, C. (ed.), *Die athenische Demokratie im 4. Jahrhundert: zwischen Modernisierung und Tradition*. Stuttgart.
Tocqueville 1835–40: Tocqueville, A. de, *Democracy in America* (tr. H. Reeve). London.
Tod 1946: Tod, M. N., *A Selection of Greek Historical Inscriptions*. Oxford.
Todd 1993: Todd, S. C., *The Shape of Athenian Law*. Oxford.
Todd 1996: Todd, S. C., 'Lysias against Nikomachos: The fate of an expert in Athenian Law', in Foxhall and Lewis 1996: 101–32.
Todd 2007: Todd, S. C., *A Commentary on Lysias, Speeches 1–11*. Oxford.
Todd 2020: Todd, S. C., *A Commentary on Lysias, Speeches 12–16*. Oxford.
Trott 2017: Trott, A. M., '"Not slavery, but salvation": Aristotle on constitution and government', *Polis* 34: 115–35.
Tziatzi-Papagianni 1994: Tziatzi-Papagianni, M., *Die Sprüche der sieben Weisen: zwei byzantinische Sammlungen. Einleitung, Text, Testimonien und Kommentar*. Stuttgart and Leipzig.
Urbinati 2019: Urbinati, N., 'The ambiguities of liberal-democracy'. *Polis* 34: 543–54.
Usher 1968: Usher, S., 'Xenophon, Critias and Theramenes', *JHS* 88: 128–35.
Verlinksi 2017: Verlinski, A., 'Draco's constitution in the *Athenaion Politeia* 4: Is it an interpolation or an author's late addition?', *Hyperboreus* 23: 142–71.
Volonaki 2001: Volonaki, E., 'The re-publication of the Athenian laws in the last decade of the fifth century B.C.', *Dike* 4: 137–167.

Voutiras 2001: Voutiras, E., 'La réconciliation des Dikaiopolites: une nouvelle inscription de Dikaia de Thrace, colonie d'Érétrie', *CRAI* 52: 781–92.
Voutiras and Sismanides 2008: Voutiras, E., and Sismanidis, K., 'Δικαιοπολιτῶν Συναλλαγαί', *Ancient Macedonia* 7: 253–74.
Wallace 1974: Wallace, R. W., 'Ephialtes and the Areopagos', *GRBS* 15: 259–69.
Wallace 1989: Wallace, R. W., *The Areopagos Council, to 307 B.C.* Baltimore and London.
Wallace 1993: Wallace, R. W., 'La *Politeia* aristotelica e l'*Athenaion Politeia*', in Cresci and Piccirilli 1993: 25–52.
Wallace 2006: Wallace, R. W., 'Withdrawing *graphai* in ancient Athens: A case study in "sycophancy" and legal idiosyncracies', in M.-A Rupprecht (ed.), *Symposion 2003. Vorträge zur griechischen und hellenistischen Rechtsgeschichte*, 57–66. Cologne and Vienna.
Wallace 2008: Wallace, R. W., 'Response to Douglas MacDowell', in E.M. Harris and G. Thür eds.), *Symposion 2007. Akten der Gesellschaft für griechische und hellenistische Rechtsgeschichte*, 95–8. Vienna.
Wallace 2009: Wallace, R. W., 'Personal freedom in Greek democracies, republican Rome, and modern liberal states', in Balot 2009: 164–77.
Wallach 2001: Wallach, J. R., *The Platonic Political Art: A Study of Critical Reason and Democracy*. University Park, PA.
Waterfield 2009: Waterfield, R., *Why Socrates Died*. London.
Wees 2001: Wees, H. van, 'The myth of the middle-class army', in Bekker-Nielsen and Hannestad 2001: 45–71.
Weil 1960: Weil, R., *Aristote et l'histoire: essai sur la "Politique"*. Paris.
Whitehead 1980: Whitehead, D., 'The tribes of the Thirty Tyrants: A note', *JHS* 100: 208–13.
Whitehead 1982–3: Whitehead, D., 'Sparta and the Thirty Tyrants', *AncSoc* 12–14: 105–30.
Whitehead 1986: Whitehead, D., *The Demes of Attica 508/7 to ca. 250 B.C.: A Political and Social Study*. Princeton.
Whitehead 2000: Whitehead, D., *Hypereides: The Forensic Speeches. Introduction, Translation, and Commentary*. Oxford.
Whitehead 2002: Whitehead, D., 'Athenian laws and lawsuits in the late fifth century BC', *MH* 59: 71–96.
Wilamowitz 1893: Wilamowitz-Moellendorff (von), U., *Aristoteles und Athen*, 2 vols. Berlin.
Wilamowitz 1920: Wilamowitz-Moellendorff (von), U., *Platon II: Beilagen und Textkritik*. Berlin.
Wolff 1963: Wolff, H.-J., 'Verjährung von Ansprüchen nach attischem Recht', in *Eranion in Honorem G. S. Mariadakis*, vol. 1, *Historia Iuris*: 87–109. Athens.
Wolff 1966: Wolff, H.-J., *Die attische Paragraphe: ein Betrag zum Problem der Auflockerung archaischer Prozessformen*. Weimar.
Wolff 1970: Wolff, H.-J., *Normenkontrolle und Gesetzbegriff in der attischen Demokratie*. Heidelberg.
Wolpert 2002: Wolpert, A., *Remembering Defeat: Civil War and Civic Memory in Ancient Athens*. Baltimore and London.
Wolpert 2017: Wolpert, A., 'Thucydides on the Four Hundred and the fall of Athens', in Forsdyke et al. 2017: pages online.
Worthington 1993: Worthington, I., 'The date of the Tegea decree: A response to the *diagramma* of Alexander III or Polyperchon?', *AHB* 7: 59–64.
Yarlan 1965: Yarlan, G., 'Études d'histoire militaire et diplomatique I', *BCH* 89: 332–48.
Youni 2001: Youni, M.S. The different categories of unpunished killing and the term *atimos* in ancient Greek law', in Cantarella, E. and Thür, G. (eds.), *Symposion 1997. Vorträge zur griechischen und hellenistischen Rechtsgeschichte*, 117–137: Vienna.

Youni 2019: Youni, M.S., '*Atimia* in Classical Athens: What the sources say', in Gagliardi and Pepe 2019, 361–78.
Yunis 1970: Yunis, H., 'Law, politics, and the *graphe paranomon* in fourth-century Athens', *GRBS* 29: 361–82.
Yunis 1996: Yunis, H., *Taming Democracy: Models of Political Rhetoric in Classical Athens*. Ithaca, NY and London.
Zaccarini 2018: Zaccarini, M., 'The fate of the lawgiver: The invention of the reforms of Ephialtes and the *patrios politeia*', *Historia* 67: 495–512.

Index Locorum

I: Greek Authors

Aeschines
1.5: 14
1.18–27: 58 n.86
1.39: 121
1.126: 44 n.17
1.152: 44 n.17
1.154: 224
1.173: 170 n.25
1.179: 11 n.25, 173 n.35
2.1: 224
2.9: 154
2.10: 44 n.17
2.11: 44 n.17
2.14: 223
2.145: 44 n.17
2.147–8: 62 n.100
3.6: 11 n.25, 224
3.11: 26
3.12–27: 3 n.2, 93
3.17–22: 26
3.32: 223
3.223–5: 223
3.31: 26
3.38–40: 95, 209 with n.9, 210
3.223: 44 n.17
3.235: 54 n.58

Aeschylus
Ag. 1613–14: 134
Eum. 701–2: 56 n.77

Andocides
1: 5, 24, 25, 27, 28, 69, 73, 97, 98, 112
1.11–14: 112

1.15: 112
1.17: 112, 208
1.22: 208
1.33: 58 n. 88, 162 n.12
1.35: 112
1.40–1: 113
1.42: 113
1.43–7: 113
1.47: 112 n.54
1.47–68: 48, 174 n.38
1.51: 113
1.61–8: 113
1.71: 110
1.72–105: 113
1.73–6: 110
1.73: 58 n.87
1.77–9: 25
1.81: 70, 109 n.46, 114
1.81–2: 96, 209 n.8
1.81–7: 108
1.81–9: 208
1.81–90: 72, 74 n.15
1.82: 72, 95, 99, 113, 120, 121, 123
1.82–5: 72
1.83–4: 25, 103, 117, 120
1.84: 103
1.85: 94, 104, 117, 123, 124
1.85–9: 72, 124
1.87: 3 n.4, 90, 93, 94, 164 n.16, 65 with n.19; 169, 176
1.88: 114 n.62
1.89: 121, 123
1.90: 42 n.10, 70 n.4, 71, 72, 75, 77, 83 n.47, 70, 84 with n.51, 144 n.45

1.94: 55 n.69, 131, 134
1.95: 64
1.96–8: 25
1.107–8: 73
1.108–9: 116, 199
1.132: 25
1.141: 25
2.13–15: 112

Androtion of Athens (Atthidographer)
FGrHist 324 F 8: 44

Antiphon
1: 134
5: 134
5.8: 224
5.9: 133
5.87: 207
6: 134
6.3: 207
6.6: 141 n.33

Aristophanes
Av. 1431: 160 n.3
Ach. 82: 160 n.3
Ec. 562: 160 n.3
Lys. 590: 184
Nub. 172
Vesp. 894–1008: 44

Aristotle
EN. 3.8.2.1117a7: 128 n.5
EN. 5.5.5.1126a8–9: 128 n.5
EN. 5.10. 1137a–1138a: 143 n.36

INDEX LOCORUM 245

EN. 5.10.1138a1–3: 128 n.7
Pol. 2.27.1274a: 211
Pol. 4.14.1298a3–5: 211
Pol. 4.14.1298a28–35: 91
Pol. 5.31.1319b1–3: 91
Pol. 5.5.1304b27–31: 220 n.44
Pol. 6.31.1318b30–2: 85 n.64
Rh. 1.9.20.1367a24–5: 128 n.5
Rh. 1.11.3.1370b13: 128 n.3
Rh. 1.13.18.1374b: 128 n.2
Rh. 1.15.21.1376b: 169 n.22
Rh. 2.4.12.1381b: 128 n.7
Rh. 2.4.17–18.1381b: 128 n.7

pseudo–Aristotle
Ath. Pol. 4.2: 85 n.64
Ath. Pol. 7.2: 211
Ath. Pol. 7.3–4: 211
Ath. Pol. 20: 217 n.23
Ath. Pol. 22.1: 208
Ath. Pol. 22.5: 208
Ath. Pol. 25: 218
Ath. Pol. 26.2: 208
Ath. Pol. 30.2–5: 52
Ath. Pol. 34: 46 n.38
Ath. Pol. 34.3: 20 n.61, 48 n.38, 50 n.45, 52
Ath. Pol. 35: 51 n.46
Ath. Pol. 35.1: 64 n.115, 101
Ath. Pol. 35.2: 56 n.72, 57 n.79
Ath. Pol. 38.1: 64 n. 114
Ath. Pol. 39: 5, 7, 8, 22, 22 n.68, 39, 69, 71, 74, 75, 138, 147, 153
Ath. Pol. 39.1–5: 81
Ath. Pol. 39.1: 74 n.13, 76
Ath. Pol. 39.2: 76
Ath. Pol. 39.2: 77
Ath. Pol. 39.3: 76, 77, 79.n.33
Ath. Pol. 39.4: 77
Ath. Pol. 39.5: 22 n.69, 74 n.15, 76, 77, 80, 135
Ath. Pol. 39.6: 72, 74, 76, 77, 85 n.63, 87, 144, 153, 154, 169
Ath. Pol. 41: 90 n.1, 220
Ath. Pol. 41.3: 95
Ath. Pol. 42.1: 208
Ath. Pol. 43.2–49: 95
Ath. Pol. 47.1: 208
Ath. Pol. 48.4–5: 3 n.2, 93
Ath. Pol. 52.1: 84.55
Rh. Al. 2.21.1424b15–16: 93 n.8

Cratippus
FGrHist 64 T 2: 62 n.102

Critias of Athens
DK 88 F 25: 48 n.33, 173 n.36, 174 n.38
DK 88 F 32–7: 48 n. 34, 173 n. 36

Demosthenes
7.41: 77 n.26
15.22: 63 n. 106
18: 162 n.12
18.2: 224
18.7: 44 n.17
18.11: 44 n.17
18.12: 128
18.15: 128
18.137: 223
18.225: 44 n.17
18.111–18: 26
18.120–2: 16, 26
18.132–3: 223
18.266: 162 n.12
20.11–12: 87 n.70
20.41–5: 27
20.92: 209
20.93: 93, 209
20.93–4: 209 with n. 9
20.94: 93, 209
20.146: 209
20.147: 207
20.118: 224
20.149: 87 n.71, 93
20.158: 47
21: 126
21.32: 58 n.86
21.67: 93
21.84: 161
21.87: 58 n.86
21.94: 207 n.3
21.103: 223
21.146: 154
21.188: 93
22.5: 208
22.9–10: 208
23.24: 93
23.25–7: 207
23.30: 58 n.86
23.37–8: 26
23.38: 93
23.45: 93
23.55: 25
23.60: 93
23.60–1: 26
23.63–81: 134
23.96: 224
23.122: 184
23.204–5: 44 n.19
24.4: 166
24.20: 208
24.20–3: 95
24.25: 209, 210
24.26: 118, 164 n.16, 165 with n. 19, 169, 176
24.32: 209
24.34–5: 209
24.42: 99
24.43: 3 n.4, 94
24.45: 208

24.47: 22 n.49
24.52–7: 162
24.56: 115 n.64
24.75–6: 173 n.35
24. 116: 93 n.7
24. 159: 93 n.7
24. 188: 93 n.7
24.215–6: 11 n.25, 173 n.35
24.134: 62 n.103
24.135: 62 n.102
24.200: 58 n.87
25.75: 58 n.88
27: 126
27.67: 208
29: 126
30: 126
36: 126
36.25: 162 n.9
36.25–7: 162 n.10
37.1: 162 n.9, 208
38.1: 162 n.9, 208
38.7: 207
37.8: 207
38.1: 207
38.16: 207
39: 126
40: 126
40.39–43: 207
42.9: 222
42.9: 222
43.51: 118
45.6: 208
45.50: 224
46.12–13
47.71: 123
53.1: 162 n.12
56: 169 n.22
56: 163 n.15
57.30: 118
57.63: 224

pseudo-Demosthenes
25.20–6: 222 n.49
26.9: 162 n.12
53: 126 n.1
45.81: 139 n.30
47.64: 208
59.5: 44 n.17
59.7: 58 n.97
59.102: 77 n.26

Dinarchus
1.25: 63 nn. 105 and 106
1.29: 139 n.30
3.3: 144

Diodorus Siculus
12.45.4: 44
13.52–3: 46
13.92.7: 197
14.3.5–7: 48 n.38, 49 n.40

14.4.2: 54 n. 59
14.4.3–4: 63 n.110, 64 n.112
14.4.4–5: 59 n.92
14.5.5: 55 n.67, 218 n.26
14.5.6: 56
14.6.1: 63 n. 105
14.6.2: 63 n. 106
14.6.2–3: 62 n.100
14.9.6–8: 181 n.3, 197
14.11.1–4: 218 n.25
14.32–3: 114
14.32.2–3: 63 n. 104
14.32.4: 50 nn. 84 and 91, 63 n.108
14.32.5–6: 79 n.32
14.32.6: 64 n.113
14.32.6–33.1: 64 n. 114
14.33.2–4: 64 n.113
14.33.5: 64 n.118
14.33.5–6: 84 n.54
14.36.6: 197
14.38.2: 60 n.96
17.109: 193 n.23
18. 64.3–5: 201
18.66.2: 201

Diogenes Laertius
1.87: 184
2.41: 170 n.26
7.5: 54 n.58

Eupolis
8.6D: 19.n58
Com. Adesp. 22.31D: 19.58

Euripides
Hipp. 1148–50: 134
Supp. 404–7: 14
Suppl. 433–4: 93.8
Supp. 433–41: 14
Tr. 74: 94 n.15

Herodotus
1.14: 94 n.15
1.59–60: 19 n.56
2.54: 94 n.15
3.80–3: 12
5.66–73: 217 n.23
5.90–1: 43
5.92: 19 n. 56
6.21: 184
6.72: 139
7.104.4: 173 n.35
8.3.1: 184
8.27–9: 185
8.29.2: 184
8.79.1: 44 n.19

Homer
Il. 9.632–6: 211
Il. 19.497–508: 211

Hyperides
Dem. col. 18: 193 n.23
Eux. col. 31: 56 n.86
Eux. col. 34: 162 n.12, 223
fr. 32 Sauppe = frr. 27 and 28 Blass: 199
Lyc. col. 16: 56 n.86

Isocrates
4: 89, 184
4.70: 154
4.89: 19 n.58
4.106: 183
4.131: 221
5.67: 154
6.47: 121
7.20: 221
7.67: 54 n.58, 74 n.16
7.58: 87 n. 70
10.2: 139 n.31
18: 22, 27, 28, 70 n. 6, 159, 160, 161, 164, 166, 167
18.1–4: 88 n.76
18.2: 70.6
18.6: 64 n.116
18.6–12: 165
18.7: 165
18.11: 162 n.9
18.11–12: 162 n.7
18.20: 88, 89, 161 n.4
18.23: 166
18.24: 167
18.27: 168
18.27–8: 168
18.29: 74 n.14
18.49: 64 n.119
20.11: 54 n.58
Ep. 7.8: 198
Ep. 8.3: 198

Lexica
Lex. Seg. N. 282 s.v. νομοθέται: 209

Lycurgus,
Leocr. 126 n.1
Leocr. 112: 134

Lysias
1.30–5: 26
1.44: 154 n.57
1: 144 n.40
2.19: 11 n.25
4.13: 154 n.57
6.45: 88 n.74
7.27: 222 n.49
12: 86, 132, 142, 143, 145, 146, 147, 150, 154, 155, 157
12.1–2: 148
12.2: 148 n.52
12.5: 55 n.63
12.6: 56 n.71

12.17: 62 n.100
12.21–2: 147
12.22: 144
12.34: 150
12.35: 144
12.35–6: 147
12.37–41: 150 n.54
12.42: 48, 137 n.27
12.43–6: 20 n.61
12.44: 129 n.10
12.48: 88 n.74
12: 50, 58 n.90
12.52: 63 n.108, 79 n.32
12.53: 70
12.53–8: 150, 151, 156
12.54: 152, 153 with n.56, 154
12.54–61: 155
12.55: 19 n.58, 64 n.116, 154 n.55, 153, 154
12.55–6: 153
12.57: 155
12.58: 155
12.58–60: 84 n.54
12.59: 87 n.70
12.59–60: 64 n.118
12.68: 129 n.10
12.71: 48
12.76: 54
12.71–6: 48 n.38
12.79–80: 147
12.80: 144
12.81–3: 147
12.84: 144
12.85–6: 129 n.10
12.87: 145
12.92–4: 145
12.92–6: 156
12.92–8: 156
12.94: 63 n.111, 144
12.95: 63 n.105
13: 54 n.60, 58 n.90, 129, 132, 135, 138, 140, 141, 142, 143, 146, 158
13.1–61: 88 n.74
13.2–3: 184 n.7
13.4: 140
13.7–8: 132
13.23–41: 55 n.62
13.44: 63 n.108
13.44–6: 79 n.32
13.50: 55 n.61
13.70: 136
13.78: 62 n.103
13.83: 207
13.84: 138
13.85: 139
13.88: 74 n.14, 136, 137, 185 n.10
13.88–90: 137
13.90: 136
14.36: 154 n.57
17: 160 n.2
18.6: 55 n.67, 218 n.26

INDEX LOCORUM 247

18.10: 65, 66 n.121
19.47: 218 n.26
21.19: 45 n.21
22.1: 160 n.3
25.9: 144 n.42, 154 n.57
25.15: 141 n.33
25.17: 222 n.49
25.19: 54 n.59
25.22: 58 n.84, 63, 68
25.23: 185 n.10
25.32–3: 222 n.49
28.34: 74 n.14, 185 n.10
30: 34, 97, 98, 104, 105, 106, 118 n.74, 124
30.2: 99
30.2–5: 121
30.3: 99, 127
30.4–5: 100
30.7–8: 101, 102 n.32
30.8–9: 102
30.9: 102
30.10–13: 132
30.11–14: 100
30.14: 137, 218 n.28
30.17: 104, 106
30.19: 104
30.21: 123
30.22: 87 n.71
frgs 271–6 Carey: 177
Against Hippotherses 34–48: 77, 161 n.4
Against Hippotherses 153–5: 142 n.35

pseudo–Lysias
6.39: 74 n.14
6.11–12: 177
6.17: 177
6.39: 185 n.10

Nicolaus of Damascus
FGrHist 90 F 57: 19 n.56

Pausanias
1.2.2: 46 n.29
7.9–6–7: 203

Plato
Ap. 24bc: 171
Ap. 24c: 171
Ap. 27a: 171
Ap. 32: 175
Ap. 32b: 45
Chrm. 163c: 171 n.29
Euthyphr. 14e–15a: 177 n.48
Grg. 516d: 44 n.19
Lg. 843d: 141 n.33
Lg. 855b: 171
Men. 243e–244a: 144 n.42
Prt. 316a: 171 n.29
R. 3: 173
R. 4: 173
R. 359a: 169 n.22

R. 365d: 19 n.58
R. 520a: 94 n.15
R. 527c: 142 n.35
R. 328b: 142
R. 528a: 94.15
R. 557a–d: 14
R. 562a–d: 14
R. 579a: 141 n.33
Ti. 19c: 171 n.29
Ti. 20a: 47 n.32, 171
Ti. 32cd: 55

pseudo–Plato
Alc.2. 149b: 178 n.48

Plutarch
Alc. 7–9: 55 n.66
Alc. 21: 25
Alc. 28.2: 46 n.27
Alc. 36.7–37.3: 46 n.27
Alc. 37–9: 218 n.25
Arist. 2: 19 n.58
Arist. 26.3: 44
Art. 14.17: 141 n.33; 141 n.33
Cim. 17: 19 n.58
Lys. 1: 46. n.27
Lys. 15: 48 n.38
Lys. 15.1: 51
Lys. 15.5: 46.29
Lys. 19.4: 65
Lys. 21.2: 87 n.70, 64 n.118
Lys. 21.3–4: 66 n.121
Lys. 27.2: 62 n.100, 63 n.105, 66 n.122
Lys. 27.2–4: 63 n.106
Mor. 349 F: 79
Mor. 833: 55 n.65
Mor. 835F: 87 n.71
Mor. 841ab: 55 n.68
Mor. 843d: 55 n.70
Mor. 845d: 62 n.101
Mor. 349f: 79
Mor. 349f1–3: 51
Mor. 852a: 55 n.70
Mor. 858: 43
Mor. 998a: 55 n.67; 218 nn.26 and 27
Nic. 6.1: 44
Phil. 16.3–6: 201
Pel. 6.3: 63 n.106
Pel. 30. 9–13: 60 n.97
Per. 11–14: 20 n.60
Per. 13: 19
Per. 32.3–4: 44
Per. 35.2
Sol. 19.3–4: 82 n.45, 125.
Sol. 20–4: 211
Sol. 25: 211
Them. 21.5: 44 n.19

Pollux
8.38: 162 n.11, 208
8.47–8: 208

Polybius
22.4: 202

Scholia
schol. Aeschin. 1.39: 54 n.58, 115
schol. D. 22.3 (13b Dilts): 162 n.12
schol. Pl. *Ti.* 20a: 47, 170 n.25, 171
schol. Pl. *Tht.* 173d: 19 n.58

Sophocles
Aj. 678–82: 184
OC 1628: 94 n.15

Theophrastus
ap. schol. D. 22.3: 162 n.12

Thucydides
1.45.2: 219 n.37
1.57–8: 186
1.115.3: 40 n.3
1.135.2–3: 44 n.19
2.35–43: 41 n.7
2.37: 11 n. 25, 14
2.37.1: 14 n. 33, 93 n.8
2.65: 42 n. 12
2.65.3: 44
2.65.10: 44
3.18: 44
3.25–6: 44
3.36–49: 10
3.37.3–4: 16
3.38.2 45 n.21
3.42.3: 45 n.21
3.43.1: 45 n.21
3.49–50: 46
3.82: 18, 19 n.58
3.82.2: 18
3.82.8: 59
3.82–3: 40 n.2
4.21: 42 n.14
4.65.4: 44
4.74.2: 196
5.18.5: 186 n.12
5.26.5: 59
6.27: 111
6.28: 111
6.39.1: 16
6.56–9: 112 n. 52
8.1–2: 46 n. 24
8.17.4: 46 n.24
8.29: 46 n.24
8.30: 130 n.11
8.72.2–6: 196
8.97: 85 n.64
8.97.2: 94, 95

Xenophon
An. 3.2.4: 177 n.46
An. 7.7.57: 59
Ap. 24: 177 n.46
Cyr. 5.2.9–10: 177 n.46

HG 1.1.14: 46 n.27
HG 1.1.23: 46 n.27
HG. 1.3.19: 60
HG 1.6.27–7.35: 10
HG 1.7.1–34: 45, 60
HG 1.7.12–14: 208
HG 2.2.1–2: 49 n.41
HG 2.2.16: 50
HG 2.2.19–20: 49 n.42
HG 2.2.20: 48 n.38
HG 2.2.21: 48 n.36
HG 2.3.11: 45, 73 n.12
HG 2.3.12: 54 n.59, 61
HG 2.3.13: 58
HG 2.3.15: 59
HG 2.3.19: 57 n.80
HG 2.3.2: 45, 46 n.2, 48 n.38, 152 n.55
HG 2.3.21: 59
HG 2.3.21–2: 56 n.71
HG 2.3.23: 222 n.49
HG. 2.3.34: 48 n.34, 173 n.36
HG 2.3.35–47: 59
HG 2.3.39: 55 n.69, 218 n.26
HG 2.3.40: 55 n.65
HG 2.3.51: 56 n.75
HG 2.3.55–6: 84 n.56
HG 2.4.1: 58 n.84, 62 n.100
HG 2.4.2: 62 n.101
HG 2.4.2–3: 63 n.104
HG 2.4.8–10: 63 n.108, 79 n.32
HG 2.4.10–22: 64 n.114
HG 2.4.11–19: 64 n. 114
HG 2.4.20–2: 78
HG 2.4.23: 64 n.115
HG 2.4.26: 64
HG 2.4.28: 64 n.118, 87 n.70
HG 2.4.29–30: 66 n.122
HG 2.4.30: 43, 65
HG 2.4.31: 65
HG 2.4.32–3: 65
HG 2.4.33: 65
HG 2.4.35–8: 66
HG 2.4.38: 66 nn.121 and 123, 67 nn.1 and 2, 70, 71, 72, 76, 77, 84 n.51, 144
HG 2.4.38–9: 74 n.13
HG 2.4.43: 71, 74 n.16, 102
HG 3.2.1: 60 n.96
HG 3.5.8–10: 66 n.122
HG 4.1.35: 77 n.51
HG 4.4.2–5: 197
HG 5.3.24–5: 198
HG 5.3.25: 198
HG 7.1.35: 60 n.97
Lac. 14: 21 n.63
Mem. 1.1.2: 174
Mem. 1.1.11: 175
Mem. 1.2.29–33: 47 n.32, 170 n.25, 171 n.28
Mem. 1.2.31: 56 n.76
Mem. 1.2.31–8: 178
Mem. 1.3.3: 178 n.48

pseudo-Xenophon
Ath. Pol. 40 n.5, 55 n.64
Ath. Pol. 1.6–8: 40 n.6, 218 n.31

II: Latin Authors

Cicero
Phil. 1.1.1: 4, 180 n.1

Curtius
6.1.20: 193

Justin
5.8.11: 63 n.110, 64 n.112
5.8.12–14: 218 n.25
5.9.2: 59 n.92
5.9.4: 62 n.100, 63 n.105
5.9.4–5: 63 n.106
5.9.10: 63 n.104
5.9.12: 58 nn. 84 and 91
5.9.13: 63 n.109
5.9.14–10.3: 64 n.114
5.10: 144
5.10.5: 84 n.54
5.10.7: 66 n.121
5.10.11: 74 n.16, 74 n.16
5.10.12–13: 66 n.122
13.5: 193 n.23

Nepos
2.1: 62 n.101
2.5–7: 64 n.114
3.1: 64 n.115, 66 n.121, 84 nn. 51 and 54
3.2: 74 n.15
7.10: 218 n.25

Orosius
2.17.5: 63 n.110, 64 n.112
2.17.6: 218 n.25
2.17.7: 59 n.92
2.17.8: 62 n.100, 63 n.105
2.17.10: 63 n.104
2.17.11: 63 n.109
2.17.11–12: 64 n.114
2.17.15: 74 n.16

III: Inscriptions

Agora Excavations inv. no. I 7495 (unpublished): 210 n.10
IC IV 72: 97
IEleusis 138: 210 n.10
IG XII 5.109

IG XII 8. 262 lines 5–9: 197
IG XII + suppl. (= OGIS 8): 201
IG I³ 6: 78
IG I³ 18 (= ML 87), esp. lines 8–18: 196
IG I³ 21: 85 n.64
IG I³ 25: 27
IG I³ 40 lines 4–16: 112
IG I³ 40 lines 21–32: 112
IG I³ 61: 122
IG I³ 71: 122
IG I³ 76 (=Tod 68): 186
IG I³ 76 (=Tod 68) lines 6–16: 186
IG I³ 76 (=Tod 68) lines 14–16: 187
IG I³ 76 (=Tod 68) lines 17–21: 187
IG I³ 76 (=Tod 68) lines 21–30: 187
IG I³ 93: 122
IG I³ 102 (= Tod 86): 130
IG I³ 104 (= ML 86): 82, 99, 112, 123
IG I³ 104 (= ML 86) lines 1–9: 75 n.21
IG I³ 104 (= ML 86) lines 1–10: 23
IG I³ 104 (= ML 86) lines 3–8: 98
IG I³ 104 (= ML 86) line 8: 96
IG I³ 104 (= ML 86) line 10: 93
IG I³ 104 (= ML 86) lines 11–13: 135
IG I³ 104 (= ML 86) lines 23–9: 26
IG I³ 104 (= ML 86) line 27: 93
IG I³ 104 (= ML 86) lines 37–8: 26
IG I³ 240K: 105 n.41
IG I³ 364 lines 8–9: 219 line 37
IG I³ 1185: 105 n.41
IG I³ 241 line 10: 112 n.54
IG I³ 241 line 33: 112 n.54
IG I³ 241 line 217: 112 n.54
IG I³ 241 line 317: 112 n. 54
IG I³ 241–30: 112
IG II² 10 (= SEG 30.54) line 8: 70 n.4, 131
IG II² 28: 122
IG II² 43 (= RO 23): 122, 188 n.14
IG II² 43 (= RO 23) lines 5–9: 188
IG II² 43 (= RO 23) lines 17–26: 188
IG II² 43 (= RO 23) lines 27–48: 188
IG II² 43 (= RO 23) lines 42–9: 188
IG II² 43 (= RO 23) lines 49–68: 188
IG II² 43 (= RO 23) lines 58–9: 188
IG II² 43 (= RO 23) lines 58–60: 188 n.19
IG II² 43 (= RO 23) lines 59–60: 188
IG II² 43 (= RO 23) lines 62–4: 188
IG II² 43 (= RO 23) lines 64–5: 188
IG II² 43 (= RO 23) lines 69–79: 188
IG II² 43 (= RO 23) lines 69–80: 188
IG II² 43 (= RO 23) lines 80–1: 188
IG II² 43 (= RO 23) lines 81–2: 188
IG II² 43 (= RO 23) lines 71–2: 188
IG II² 43 (= RO 23) lines 73–4: 188
IG II² 43 (= RO 23) lines 75–8: 188
IG II² 43 (= RO 23) lines 75–9: 188
IG II² 101 (= RO 39) lines 65–6: 77 n.26

INDEX LOCORUM

IG II² 111 (= RO 39): 122
IG II² 111 (= RO 39) lines 57–61: 83 n.49
IG II² 140: 209, 210 n.10
IG II² 174: 122
IG II² 204: 122
IG II² 244: 210 n.10
IG II² 320: 209
IG II² 333I: 209
IG II² 1183 lines 16–24: 208 n.6
IG II³ 281 line 3: 199
IG II³ 320: 210 n.10
IG II³ 327: 210 n.10
IG II³ 355: 210 n.10
IG II³ 452: 210 n.10
IG II³ 445: 210 n.10
IG II³ 447: 210 n.10

IMagnesia am Sipylos I: 201
Inscr. Erythr. 10 lines 1–9: 199
Inscr. Erythr. 10 lines 18–21: 199
IPArk 16: 202
IPArk 16 lines 11–13: 202
IPArk 24 (=SEG 25.447): 194
Milet. I 3 148: 201, 182 n.4
Milet. I 3.150 lines 36–9: 202
RO 88: 173
SEG 26.25 lines 44–7: 93
SEG 26.72: 210 n.10
SEG 29.1130 esp. lines 11–22: 182 n.4, 201
SEG 30: 1119: 200
SEG 36.170 (= Tod 201 = RO 85B): 199

SEG 36.170 (= Tod 201 = RO 85B) lines 1–10: 199
SEG 36.170 (= Tod 201 = RO 85B) lines 5–12: 199
SEG 36.170 (= Tod 201 = RO 85B) lines 21–2: 199
SEG 36.170 (= Tod 201 = RO 85B) line 30: 199
SEG 36. 750: 199
SEG 52.104: 210 n.10
SEG 57.576: 192 n.21
Syll.³ 306 (= RO 10): 193 n.24
Syll.³ 306 (= RO 10) lines 3–8: 195
Syll.³ 306 (= RO 10) lines 59–60: 194 n.25

Subject Index

Achaean League, 201–2
Aegospotami, battle at, 46, 60, 100, 119, 130, 150
Aeschines (Athenian orator)
   on democracy, 14
   on *nomothesia*, 96–7, 117–8
   on the trial of Socrates, 170
   participation of in the trial of Ctesiphon, 26
   struggles of with Demosthenes, 128, 223
Aesimus (of Athens), 62
Agesilaus (king of Sparta), 198
Agoratus (of Athens)
   as possible non-citizen, 34, 130–3
   association of with Theocritus, 130
   awards to, 135
   background of, 129
   crime of, 34, 82, 131, 134–6, 138–42, 148–9
   possible democratic credentials of, 34, 134
   special plea of, 137, 149, 214
   trial of, 11, 16, 24, 33–5 81–3, 89, 92, 129–42, 158–9, 207–8, 223
Agrae (deme in Attica), 78
Alcibiades (Athenian politician), 62, 111–12, 172, 177
Alexander (the Great)
   conquests of 27–8
   death of 193–4
   Exiles Decree of, 28, 193
   mediator in local dispute, 201
   reign of, 200
'all the laws' (phrase used by the orator Andocides), 93, 99, 100, 104, 109, 113, 114, 115
American Declaration of Independence, 14
amnestia (amnesty), 182–3, 201–2
anagrapheis (transcribers), 97–100, 105–7, 124, 176
Anaxilaus (of Byzantium), 60
Andocides (Athenian orator)
   as beneficiary of the Amnesty, 115–16
   atimia of, 58
   crime of, 25, 33, 58

   family of, 24
   inserted documents in, 24–8, 34, 117, 119–25
   interpretation of in the nineteenth century, 5
   legal citations of, 24
   on Critias, 48
   on Epichares, 64
   on the Amnesty, 25, 33, 70–5, 83–4
   on the decree of Isotimides, 33, 110–11, 113
   on the legal review, 23, 116–9
   on *nomothesia*, 95–8, 104, 107–10
   on private judgments and arbitrations, 118–19
   on the religious scandals, 110–13
   on the rule of law, 94
   on the statute of limitations, 99
   reliability of, 99, 104, 113–15, 214, 222
   trial of, 25, 33, 89, 92, 177
Anytus (son of Anthemion), 35, 50, 62, 166, 174
Antiphon (Athenian orator), 55, 133–4, 207, 223–4
apagōgē (summary arrest), 133–4
apophasis (denunciation), 164
Archinus (Athenian legislator)
   law of, 50, 88, 131–2, 160, 164–5, 170
   of Koile, 62
Areopagus (court of homicide), 45, 56, 144, 216
Arginusae
   battle at, 60, 62
   generals, 10, 45, 59, 171, 176
Argos (city in the Peloponnese) 62–3, 198
Aristides (Athenian politician), 219
Ariston (tyrant of Cyrene), 197
Aristophanes (Athenian comic playwright)
   on democracy, 217
   on letting bygones be bygones, 184
   on Socrates, 172
   on the trial of Laches, 44
   on vexatious litigation, 44, 53
Aristophanes of Cholleidae, 55
Aristotle (of Stagira, philosopher)

SUBJECT INDEX 251

as possible author of the *Ath. Pol.*, 21–2
on democracy, 74, 95, 206–7, 211, 215–17, 220–2
on nature and virtue, 14
on *timêma*, 85
on vengeance, 128
Artemis Euclea, festival of (at Corinth), 197
asebeia, crime of, 170–2, 177; *see also* impiety
Assembly
    Athenian, 9, 45, 49–50, 52–4, 58, 75, 78, 92, 94–8, 116, 121–3, 160, 162, 208–11
    Dicaean, 192
    Spartan, 54
    Syracusan, 16, 197
atimia (loss of civic rights)
    absence of mention of in the Amnesty, 116
    in connection with the Mutilation, 33
    limitation of civic rights under, 192
    not meaning exile, 58
    relationship to Isotimides' decree, 120–1
    verdicts of under democracy, 119
    verdicts of under the Thirty and their subsequent cancellation, 73–4, 116
Atheniensium vetus exemplum ('the ancient Athenian example'), 4, 181, 212, 225
Attic Stelae (inscription recording families who lost property in the late fifth century), 112
auxêsis, rhetorical technique of, 166
axones (monuments bearing the archaic laws), 96, 114

Bias of Priene (one of the sages of Greece), 184
Börm, H., 9
Bottiaea, in the Thracian Chersonese, 186–7, 191, 201
bribery, 55, 113, 136, 139

calendar, 29–32
Callias (son of Hipponicus), 175
Callibius (Spartan general), 63
Callimachus (of Athens, tried after 403)
    accuser of, 89
    arbitration of, 165
    crime of, 161–2, 166, 169
    oligarchic connections of, 164
    relationship of to the Amnesty, 167–9
    trial of, 16, 22, 27–8, 35, 92, 129, 164–70, 175, 207, 223
Canevaro, M., 104, 121, 210
Carawan, E., 8, 82–3, 114, 116, 131, 155, 161, 166
Cartledge, P., 14
Carugati, F., 9–10
Ceos (island in the Aegean), Athenian treaty with, 188–92
Chabrias (Athenian general), 188–9
Chalcidice (part of the Thracian Chersonese), 186
Chalcis (on the island of Euboea in the Aegean), 62
Charicles (member of the Four Hundred), 112, 178, 218
Chremon (member of the Thirty), 137, 218
Cicero (Roman politician and orator), 4–5, 8, 15–16, 36, 180–1
Cimon (Athenian general and politician), 20, 219
City Party
    abolition of, 83–4, 87
    as victims of the Thirty, 156

Callimachus a member of, 164
enfranchised body under the Thirty, 56
identification of with the Three Thousand, 66, 116
identified by Cloché as political moderates, 6
judges from, 85–7, 145–6
members of who emigrated to Eleusis, 76
oaths sworn by, 136, 143
parleys of with Piraeus Party, 66, 153
relationship of with the Ten, 156
social composition of, 86
class struggle, 17–18, 32, 45, 213, 215
Cleisthenes (sixth-century Athenian lawgiver), 29–30, 53, 107
Cleocritus (herald of the Mysteries), 78
Cleomenes (king of Sparta who rid Athens of tyranny), 43, 65
Cleon (Athenian politician and enemy of Thucydides), 16, 24, 43, 46, 196–7, 207, 220, 225
Cleophon (Athenian politician at the end of the fifth century), 31, 48, 100, 103, 130
Cloché, P., 6–7, 22, 38, 147
Cohen, D., 128
Conon (Athenian general and hero of the early fourth-century Athenian resurgence), 177
contracts
    of amnesty, 7–9, 64, 69, 72, 83, 90, 147, 152, 163, 166, 201, 214
    of loans, 77
    private, 103, 166–7
    public, 167–8
    sanctity of, 166–9
    violation of, 103, 168
Corcyra (former Corinthian colony in the Adriatic), 18, 40, 59
Corinth (city on the Isthmus), 19, 27, 43, 53, 63, 65–6, 68, 186, 197–8
Corinthian War (395–386 BCE), 27, 198
Council (of Five Hundred)
    chosen anew after the democratic victory, 95, 109
    decrees of, 41, 122
    emergency powers of, 110–13
    Epichares a member of during the oligarchy, 64
    in *nomothesia*, 209–10
    in Teisamenus' decree, 121–2
    in the *Ath. Pol.* 95, 210–11
    judicial powers of, 100–1
    under the Thirty, 51–2, 55–7, 64, 149, 164
counterrevolution, 46
covenants of reconciliation
    at Athens, 5, 7–8, 39, 71–2, 75–89, 92, 108–9, 116, 136–7, 143, 160, 164, 167
    at Ceos, 189–90
crisis
    at Corcyra, 18
    at Rome, 180–1
    military, 31
    of debt, 195
    of democracy, 9
    of oligarchy, 32
    of religion, 172
    political, 182, 203, 205

Critias (leader of the Thirty Tyrants at Athens)
  as admirer of Sparta, 48
  as associate of Eratosthenes, 150–1, 156
  as atheist, 47, 174–6, 178
  as enemy of Theramenes, 59, 62, 155
  as extremist, 24, 32, 52, 56, 58–9, 62, 143
  as legislator, 56
  as opponent of rhetoric, 56
  as philosopher, 171
  as proponent of oligarchy, 47–8, 173
  as pupil of Socrates, 47, 170–1, 177–8
  as supporter of the Four Hundred, 48
  death of, 64, 143
  death penalties because of, 58–9
  excesses of, 149
Curtius (Quintus Curtius Rufus, Roman historian), 28, 193
Cypselus (tyrant of Corinth), 19, 43

debt
  bondage for, 18
  private, 18, 58, 194–5
  public, 87, 142, 188
  slavery for, 18
decrees
  awarding immunity to Epicerdes, 26–7
  body of, 224
  citation of, 23, 119
  distinct from laws, 33–4, 91–6, 110–11, 211
  enactment of, 41
  honorary, 131
  inscription of, 107
  inserted into speeches, 25–6, 34, 114, 120–6
  judicial, 10
  of Cyrene, 197
  of demes, 122
  of Demophantus see Demophantus
  of Dicaea, 192–3
  of Dionysius of Syracuse, 197
  of Elis, 199
  of Erasinides, 130
  of Isotimides see Isotimides
  of Mytilene, 199
  of Patrocleides see Patrocleides
  of Nakone see Nakone
  of Polyperchon see Polyperchon
  of Samos, 196
  of Sparta, 198
  of Tegea, 24, 193–4
  of Teisamenus see Teisamenus
  of Temnus and Clazomenae, 201
  of Thasos, 197
  of the Second Athenian Confederacy, 199
  of the Thirty, 71
  on amnesty, 6, 72, 186–204
  on appointment of *nomothetai*, 209
  on *atimia* see *atimia*
  on Bottiaea, 186–7
  on citizenship, 34, 130–2, 187
  on emotion, 212
  on exiles see Alexander (the Great), Exiles Decree of
  on Iulis, 188–92
  on Paros, 198
  on Phlius, 198
  on property rights, 130
  on publication of laws, 104–5
  on Selymbria, 196
  on the disrepair of temples see Temples Decree
  prefacing laws, 75, 98–9, 123
  prescripts to, 210
  records of, 24
Delian League (otherwise known as the Athenian Confederacy), 40
Delphi (oracle at), 173, 185
Demeter (sanctuary of), 76, 78, 113
democrats
  at Corcyra, 40
  at Phyle, 34, 59, 149
  at Piraeus, 63, 156
  benefits for under the Amnesty, 71–3, 136–7, 161
  committed to the rule of law, 12–3, 39, 45–6, 93, 115, 156, 160, 216, 222
  constraints on under the Amnesty, 32, 69, 78, 80, 135, 138, 146, 159, 166–7, 171
  courts of, 145
  moral example of, 35, 167, 177
  opposed by Socrates, 176
  persecuted by the Thirty, 61, 86, 100, 139, 159
  reliant on Athens, 18, 40
  support of by Corinth and Thebes, 65
  victorious at Athens, 2, 32, 38, 41, 69–71, 114, 147, 157, 160, 164–5
  war debts of, 87
Demophantus (decree of), 25, 119–20
demos (the people), 7, 41–2, 46
Demosthenes (Athenian general), 44
Demosthenes (orator)
  litigation of, 223
  on abuse, assault, and slander, 117
  on democracy, 16
  on friendship and enmity, 184
  on *paragraphē*, 162
  on political dissent, 47
  on the rule of law, 93
  on the aim of *nomothesia*, 93
  on the legal issue in court, 166
  on the trial of Ctesiphon, 26
  showing lack of vindictive motive, 128
  trial of for slander, 161
diaitai (out-of-court settlements)
  epi rhētois (on fixed terms), 164, 207
  meaning 'out-of-court' settlement, 162, 207
διαλλαγαί (exchanges) 70–1
diallaktai (commissioners) 68, 163
διαλύσεις (treaty), 70
diamartyria (right of appeal to the archon in the event of frivolous litigation), 162, 207
Dicaea (amnesty legislation of), 192–5
dikē, (private lawsuit)
  dikē phonou (homicide trial by private lawsuit), 35, 80, 82, 134, 142–3
  meaning private lawsuit, 186

SUBJECT INDEX 253

Diocleides, 112
Diocles (law of), 99
Diodorus (Siculus)
   as a source for the Amnesty, 5, 144
   on Dionysius I of Syracuse, 197
   on the Macedonian edict to oust oligarchies, 201
Dionysodorus (Athenian general and victim of the Thirty), 55, 129–30, 139–41
Dionysius (tyrant of Syracuse), 197, 225
Dorjahn, A., 6
Dow, S., 96, 98, 103–4, 106, 121
Draco (seventh-century Athenian lawgiver)
   as archaic lawgiver, 211
   homicide law of, 23, 75, 82, 93, 95–7, 99–100, 104, 122, 134
   on justifiable homicide, 26
   ordinances (*thesmoi*) of, 109, 114–15, 121–3
   prescript to the homicide law of, 97, 100, 124
   transcription of the laws of, 99
Dracontides (Athenian politician who urged peace with Sparta in 404), 50, 52

economy, 12, 168
Eleusinian Mysteries
   general, 76, 78, 111
   Greater, 78–9
   Lesser, 78
   Profanation of, 110–11
Eleusis (in western Attica)
   assessment of, 79
   confinement to, 78–9
   debarment from, 76, 78
   dissolution of, 33, 71, 74, 101, 144–5, 147, 152
   homicide jurisdiction regarding, 76–7, 80–2
   migration to, 63, 87, 144, 152–3
   natives of, 77–8
   obligations of to the alliance, 77
   oligarchic enclave at, 5–8, 39, 63, 73–87, 112, 135, 152–5, 159
   property holders at, 77
   relationship of with Athens, 107, 147
   separate treaty with, 8, 23, 70
   special provisions for, 69–71, 76–80
   temple of Demeter at, 75–6, 78
Eleven (under democracy), 139
Eleven (under oligarchy)
   admissibility of action against, 147
   Agoratus not a member of, 80, 137–8, 140
   as enemies of the people, 84, 157
   crimes of, 82
   exemption of from the Amnesty, 32, 54, 71, 76–7, 82–4, 137, 141, 146–7, 158–9
   public audits of, 86, 146–7
Elis (in the western Peloponnese), 40, 43, 199
embezzlement, crime of, 55
endeixis (public indictment)
   as a process to try crimes against the state, 82, 138–9, 208
   as distinct from *apagôgê*, 133–4
   for homicide, 35, 80, 133, 138, 142, 208
   meaning arrest, 133
   trial of Agoratus by, 129–34, 138, 208
ἐπ' ἀνδρί, 93–4

ἐπ' αὐτοφώρῳ, 131, 133, 139
Ephebic Oath, 173
Ephialtes (fifth-century Athenian lawgiver), 45, 56, 219
ephors (Spartan magistrates, imitated at Athens under the oligarchy), 48, 54, 66, 143, 198
Epichares
   accuser of Andocides, 120
   of Dikaia, 192
   of Lamptra (of the Ten), 64, 151, 153
epieikeia (type of legal argument), 142
epôbelia (penalty for loss in litigation), 208
equality
   before the law, 3, 13–14, 93
   contractual, 69, 83
   economic, 15, 219
   judicial, 14
   of birth, 14
   of speech, 14
   political, 14
   racial, 215
Eratosthenes (member of the Thirty Tyrants, put on trial after 403)
   association of with Eleusis, 147, 151–6
   association of with the Ten, 153–6
   association of with the Thirty, 34, 137, 142–3, 218
   audit of, 159
   crime of, 143–4, 146–50
   enmity of towards Polemarchus, brother of Lysias, 50
   Lysias' opposition to, 24, 50
   possible democratic credentials of, 149
   trial of, 11, 24, 33–5, 84, 86, 89, 92, 129–57, 223
Eresus (*stasis* at), 200–1
Ergocles (one of the democratic opponents of the Thirty), 62
Eucleides (archonship of in 403/2), 30, 39, 76, 99–100, 110, 121, 132
Eucrates (victim of the Thirty), 55
Eumolpidae (priestly family), 76, 78
Eurymedon (Athenian general), 44
European Enlightenment, 5
Euxitheus, trial of for homicide, 134

Filonik, J., 221–2
Four Hundred (oligarchy of 411 BCE)
   fraudulent practices of, 219
   Nicomachus' possible association with, 101–2
   overthrow of, 48, 52, 94
   Peisander's association with, 112
   Theramenes' association with, 49
   resistance of Leon of Salamis to, 55
forgiveness
   moral, 10
   political 6–8, 10–11, 16–17, 73, 183, 188, 195
freedom
   from recrimination, 87
   of self-determination, 32
   of the Greeks, 61
   religious, 15
   restoration to, 195
   to speak one's mind, 14
Frohberger, H., 153, 155
furtum manifestum, 134

graphē (a public process of litigation at Athens)
  asebeias, 175
  meaning of, 82
  nomon mē epitēdeion theinai, 209
  paranomōn, 208
Gray, B., 9
Großer, R., 5

Halipedon, battle at, 65
Hansen, M. H., 14, 122–3, 133–4
Harpalus, trial of, 144
Harris, E. M., 15, 104, 121, 128, 134, 161, 219
Herms (inscribed plaques in the likeness of the god Hermes)
  as sacred objects, 111
  mutilation of (*hermokopeia*), 33, 48, 110–13
Herodotus (of Halicarnassus, Greek historian), 12, 19, 43, 183–5
Hippias
  eldest son of Peisistratus and last tyrant of Athens, 43, 55, 65, 112, 175
  of Elis, 175
  of Thasos (victim of the Thirty), 55
Hippocles (member of the Ten), 64, 151, 153
Hippolytus (mythical son of Theseus and stepson of Phaedra), 134
homicide
  accessory, 80, 134–5
  at Alipheira, 194–5
  at Dicaea, 192–3
  Athenian law of, 22, 23, 26, 33–4, 75, 136, 211
  categories of, 33, 80, 131
  Eratosthenes (trial of), 143–4, 146
  inscribed copy of Draco's law of, 75, 82, 93, 96, 100, 122, 135
  jurisdiction over, 7, 77, 80–1
  justifiable, 26
  own-hand, 33–5, 80–1, 131, 134–6, 193
  past and future cases of (from the time of Eucleides), 76, 80–1
  private action for (by *dike*), 35, 80, 138
  public action for (by *endeixis* or *apagōgē*), 133–4
  statute of limitations prohibiting action for, 208
Homonoia (like-mindedness), 2, 29, 101, 219
hoplite
  census group, 50, 57
  democracy, 48
  military organisation, 63
Hyperbolus (Athenian politician), ostracism of, 44

impiety, crime of, 98, 110, 113, 170, 172, 174, 176
isēgoria (equality of speech) 14
Isocrates (Athenian orator), 22, 24, 27–8, 73, 88, 177, 183–4, 198, 217, 221
isogonia (equality of birth), 14
isonomia (equality before the law), 14
Isotimides, decree of, 33, 110–11, 113, 119–20, 122, 124

Judicial Oath, 97, 224
Julius Caesar (Roman politician), assassination of, 180
justice
  absence of, 59, 145, 156
  as fairness, 213
  as freedom, 215
  judicial, 192, 213
  legal, 4, 10–15, 36–9, 60, 89, 134, 142–3, 150, 156–7, 173–9, 199, 212–15, 224
  miscarriages of, 36, 60
  of democracy as distinct from that of oligarchy, 89, 156
  righteousness, 134, 142, 156, 172–4, 176, 203, 215
  social, 40–2, 45

kakourgoi (malefactors), 133
Kerykes (priestly family), 24, 76, 78
Keyt, D., 221–2
Köhler, U., 82
kyrbeis (monuments bearing the archaic laws), 99, 101, 105

La'da, C., 9
Laches (Athenian general), 44
Lamian War (fought in 322 BCE after the death of Alexander the Great), 2
Lanni, A., 11, 15
lawcourts
  abuse of, 99–101, 108, 126–9, 148, 173, 191, 195, 200, 207, 213, 215
  at Piraeus, 77
  authority of, 2, 125, 212, 215
  avoidance of frivolous litigation in, 15, 32–3, 37, 44–6, 59–69, 162–3, 203, 223–4
  debarment from serving in, 58, 80, 82
  democratic, 2–4, 19, 23, 25, 118–19, 212–13
  enforcement of the rule of law in, 3, 10, 15, 17, 32–6, 96, 127–30, 140, 157, 203, 207, 213–14
  equal access to, 14, 80–1
  of homicide, 7, 81, 134
  prosecutors as defendants in, 35; *see also paragraphē*
  retaliatory action in, 4, 6, 82, 103, 108, 126–9, 160
  subversion of, 2, 32, 215
  under the Thirty, 32, 118
laws
  abrogation of, 45, 56, 103, 109–10, 209
  ancestral, 48, 52, 56–7, 61, 72, 95, 99, 104–7, 109–10, 114–25, 211
  application in the courts, 3, 99–100, 110, 120, 132, 224
  body of, 92–3, 95, 97–9, 104, 109–10, 113–19, 127, 167, 173, 221–2, 224
  bogus, 100, 103, 105, 109–10, 209
  citation of, 23–4, 26, 70, 109, 114
  code of, 107, 206, 209
  consultation of, 206
  distinct from constitutions, 219
  enactment of, 16, 72, 75, 93, 96, 109–10, 114–23, 163, 208–10
  entrenchment of, 205, 211
  of Critias outlawing the teaching of rhetoric, 56
  of Ephialtes on the Areopagus, 56
  of the Thirty, 56
  on abuse, 117
  on children, 117
  on citizenship, 118
  on dowries, 211
  on inheritance, 118, 211

on neutrality, 211
on politicians, 117
on private individuals, 117
on procedure, 175
on seizure, 114, 116
on sacrifices, 56, 105–6, 211
on slander, 117, 211
on tyranny, 211
on vexatious litigation, 169, 207–8
prescripts to, 210
proposed, 93, 208
publication of, 28, 34, 45, 72, 90, 93–4, 96–9, 101, 103–7, 109–10, 113–25, 127, 175, 209
records of, 24, 72, 75, 90, 93, 97–100, 105–7, 109–10, 117–23, 209
scrutiny of, 8, 33, 97, 99, 101, 109–10, 114–25, 127, 141, 209–10, 213, 216
unwritten, 94, 109, 111, 117, 211, 224
laying of information against (*mēnusis*), 129
Leon of Salamis (victim of the Thirty), 55, 171, 218
liability
 of Agoratus, 139
 private, 142
 public, 139, 141–2
 to indemnity, 87
liberty
 as a normative value, 10
 Sparta's support for, 14, 32, 43, 65
 of thought and expression, 232
Lintott, A. W., 220
litigation
 lawful, 31, 76, 126–9, 131, 138, 141, 160–2, 170, 192–3, 206–7, 213, 223–4
 vexatious, 2, 6, 33, 35–6, 44, 60–1, 88, 116, 127–8, 131, 133, 135, 148, 158–66, 176, 182, 187, 191–2, 195–6, 200, 202–3, 206, 208, 212
logistai (accounting officers), 98
Loening, T. C., 6–8, 89, 130–2, 135, 169
Loeper, R., 53–4
Long Walls (defence system around Athens) 48, 130
Loraux, N., 7
Luebbert, J., 5
Lycon (accuser of Socrates), 174
Lycurgus
 Athenian orator, 127, 167
 son of Lycomedes (executed by the Thirty), 55, 218
 Spartan lawgiver, 219
Lycus (son of Thrasybulus), 62
Lysander (Spartan general), 32, 38, 43–4, 49–54, 61, 63–7, 215
Lysias (Athenian orator)
 as victim of the Thirty, 148–9
 family background of, 24
 lost speeches of 23–4, 73
 on the Amnesty, 70, 81–2, 84–6
 on the *anagrapheis*, 100, 122, 142
 on the citizenship of Agoratus, 133
 on the death of Polemarchus, 149
 on the dereliction of duty by Nicomachus, 104–5
 on the scrutiny of laws, 117–8, 121–4
 on the Ten, 153, 156
 on the Thirty, 49–51, 58–9, 68, 73, 153

opposition to Eratosthenes of, 24
opposition to Theramenes of, 32, 53, 59
prosecution of Agoratus, 81
prosecution of Eratosthenes, 145–57
reliability of 21–4, 26, 32–4, 49–50, 53
vindictive language of, 89, 148, 184

MacDowell, D. M, 115, 120, 147
magistrates
 accountability of, 36, 213
 authority of, 17, 32, 95, 122, 213
 crowns for, 26
 instructed not to use unwritten laws, 109–10
 jurisdiction of, 116, 162
 rotation of, 211
Magnesia
 on the Maeander, 201
 on the Sipylus, 201
Mann, C., 219
Marxism, 17–18, 32, 213
Megara
 oligarchic coup at, 196–7
 town to the west of Athens, 24, 62
Meletus (accuser of Socrates), 174–5
μὴ μνησικακεῖν
 adopted by Cicero, 180
 applicability of to non-citizens, 133, 140
 as a bar to court action, 1, 6, 16–17, 103, 108, 116, 103, 108, 142, 158, 183–201
 as a covenant, 71, 76, 83, 103, 159
 as an ideological commitment, 7
 as an oath, 72, 116
 as a moral commitment, 16
 as a sealing pledge, 8, 82
 at Athens, 71–2, 126, 156
metics (resident aliens)
 application of the Amnesty to, 133
 exclusion of from the definition of citizenship, 215
 execution of by Critias, 59
 persecuted by the Thirty, 56, 148, 149
 property of confiscated under the oligarchy, 59
Methymna, *stasis* at, 198–9
Metroon (Athenian state archive), 93, 114, 117
Miletus (in western Asia Minor), *amnestia* at, 202
monarchy, as a political system, 12–3, 206
Munychia (battle at), 64, 130
Mytilene (on the island of Lesbos off the coast of Asia Minor), *stasis* at, 198–9

Nakone (Greek-speaking city in Sicily), 9, 200, 212
Németh, G., 54
Nepos (Cornelius, Roman biographer), 73
Niceratus (son of Nicias), 55–6, 65, 218
Nicias (victim of the Thirty), 55
Nicomachus (leader of the *anagrapheis*)
 accuser of, 101–3
 commission of, 92, 98–101, 106, 176
 connection (possible) of with inscribed fragments, 105–7
 plaint against, 92, 100–1, 103–4
 political complexion of, 101–2
 sources of authority for, 104–5
 trial of 34, 89, 92, 97–107, 132

Nicomenes (victim of the Thirty), 55
Nicophon (law of), 93
νόμοι (laws) 70, 108–9, 118; *see also* laws
nomothesia (law-making)
  beginning of, 101
  democratic character of, 210
  importance of for the rule of law, 208
  in the decree of Teisamenus, 121
  process of, 36, 93–6, 205, 208–11
  purpose of, 93
  silence of the *Ath. Pol.* about, 95
  sources for, 208–9
nomothetai (lawmakers), 92, 94, 96, 99–100, 115, 117–18, 121, 123, 209–11

Oath of Reconciliation, 1, 5, 8, 30, 51, 96, 137, 162, 194
Ober, J., 216
oblivion, attitude of towards the past, 7–8, 180, 203
ochlos, ('mob' as opposed to 'people' in a legal sense), 41
Old Oligarch
  as a nickname, 40
  as a political theorist, 43, 53, 55, 173, 216, 218
oligarchy
  as a mode of government, 11–12, 16, 20, 47, 50–6, 59, 62, 85–8, 136, 146, 174, 218
  as a party or side, 2, 40–1, 85–8, 133, 136, 143, 154, 178, 218
  as a period in Athenian history, 13, 34, 53, 64, 68–9, 73, 79–80, 95, 98–9, 128–30, 136, 138, 156, 158, 164–6, 170–1, 174, 176, 224
  as a regime, 3, 17, 19, 24, 32, 34–5, 39, 46, 48–50, 52–5, 59, 62–5, 68–70, 73, 85, 102, 112, 128, 133, 140, 143, 145, 150, 153–4, 158, 164, 184, 212, 216, 218
  extreme, 50–2, 59, 150, 153–4, 156
  moderate, 6, 32, 43, 50–2, 59, 149–50
  support for among citizens, 10, 20, 47, 85–6, 102, 133, 136, 196, 218
ὅρκοι καὶ συνθῆκαι (oaths and covenants), 74, 185
Orchomenus (town in the Peloponnese), 202
Oropus (town on the border between Athens and Thebes), 62
ostracism (an older method of exile without trial), 31, 44

Pamphilus (a member of the Piraeus Party), 164
Paoli, U. E., 161
paragraphê (turning the tables in litigation), 27, 35–6, 131, 136, 159–65
Parker, R., 172
Paros (island in the Aegean), *stasis* at, 198
Patrocleides (decree of), 25, 119
Patrocles (member of the City Party), 164–5
Pausanias
  antiquarian, 202
  king of Sparta, 44, 65–8
Peisander (member of the Four Hundred), 112–13
Peisistratus (tyrant of Athens), 19, 29, 43, 53, 112, 197
Peloponnesian League (led by Sparta), 63, 65–6, 196
Peloponnesian War (431–404 BCE)
  class conflict during, 17
  duration of, 2, 4
  effect of in defining *stasis*, 18–19, 40
  effect of in dividing Greece, 27, 40, 183

effect of upon Athens, 44–6, 53
effect of upon Sparta, 43
time of, 31, 186, 219
Pelloso, C., 172
Perdiccas
  citizen of Dicaea
  king of Macedon, 186
Periander (tyrant of Corinth), 43
Pericles (Athenian general and politician)
  association of in political clubs (*hetaireiai*), 20, 60–1
  citizenship law of, 118
  death of, 43–4, 61
  Funeral Oration of, 14, 93, 127
  successors of, 60
  time of, 31
  war strategy of, 47
Persia
  debate at, 12
  enmity of Isocrates towards, 27
  Greek campaign against, 68
  support of against Sparta, 197
  support of towards Sparta, 46, 65–6, 196
  support of towards the Four Hundred, 46
  invasion of Greece by, 49, 183–5, 203
  withdrawal of from Greece, 219
Pheidon (of the Ten), 64, 84, 143, 147, 150–6, 64
Phillips (D. D.), 130, 132
Philopoemen (Achaean general), 201
Phlius (*stasis* at), 198
Phormio (Athenian general), 44
Phormisius (oligarchic sympathiser), 50
Phrynichus
  member of the Four Hundred, 48, 52, 130–1, 134
  playwright, 184
Phyle (town in Attica), democratic victory at, 34, 59–60, 62, 130–2, 149
Piérart, M., 96
Piraeus Party
  abolition of, 83–4, 87, 157
  Agoratus latterly a member of, 87, 136
  judges at Piraeus, 85
  negotiations of with City Party, 151–3
  opponents of Sparta, 66
  opponents of the Ten, 64
  opponents of the Three Thousand, 66, 130
  Pamphilus a member of, 164
Piraeus Ten, 85
Plato (Athenian philosopher, pupil of Socrates, teacher of Aristotle)
  foundation by of the Academy, 53
  on *asebeia*, 171
  on Critias, 171
  on Polemarchus 24
  on Socrates, 29, 159, 170–5, 178
  on the trial of the Arginusae generals, 45
  philosophical theories of, 55, 173
  views about democracy, 14, 173, 217, 221
plêthos (the 'mass'), 41
Polemarchus (brother of Lysias), 24, 142, 148–9
Polycrates (anti-Socratic pamphleteer), 172, 177
Polyperchon (Macedonian general), 201

SUBJECT INDEX 257

Potidaea (town in the Thracian Chersonese), 186
probouleuma (legal proposal and first stage in the
    nomothesia process), 209
property
    private, 56–8, 60, 70, 73, 76–9, 87–8, 112, 130,
        142, 148, 161, 163, 166, 192–3, 196, 199,
        201–2
    public, 64
    qualification, 85–7, 211, 217
    rights, 166, 188–9
prytaneia (court fee imposed to reduce vexatious
    litigation), 162, 165, 208
prytanic officers (or prytaneis), 95–6, 210
prytany (one-tenth of the solar year and basis of the
    Cleisthenic calendar), 30
psêphismata, 75, 110, 208
Ptolemaic Egypt (305–30 BCE), 9
Pythodorus (Athenian general), 44

rape, 82, 211
Rauchenstein, R., 146
res iudicata (literally, 'matter tried')
    at Miletus, 206
    meaning of, 25, 83, 176, 207
    observation of, 164, 214, 216, 224
    violation of, 131, 159, 161
revolution
    provoked by foreign intervention, 2
    of the earth around the sun, 29
    of the Four Hundred, 101, 219
rhetoric
    and the rule of law, 206
    of Andocides, 25, 116, 138
    of Isocrates, 28, 35, 166, 169
    of Lysias, 21, 50, 53, 132, 140, 145, 156
    of Socrates' accusers, 170
    outlawing teaching of see laws, of Critias outlawing
        the teaching of rhetoric
Rhinon son of Charicles (member of the Ten), 64,
    84, 164
Rhodes, P. J., 96, 219
Robertson, N., 103–4, 114, 120–1, 123
Rome, 4, 180, 202
Rubinstein, L., 8
rule of law
    absence of, 11, 30, 36
    as a precondition of democracy, 31, 39, 90–1, 94–6,
        107–8, 178, 205–6, 208, 211, 213, 216
    Athenian commitment to, 12, 15, 29–31, 36
    conflict of with tyranny, 19
    definition of, 3, 93–4, 206
    differences of between ancient and modern notions,
        10, 94
    effect of upon litigation, 30, 206
    enforcement of through the courts, 17, 32–3, 36, 92,
        127–8, 140, 156–7, 213–4
    enforcement through the scrutiny of laws, 127, 141
    evidence for, 29, 35, 140
    respect for in the Amnesty, 126, 212
    restoration of, 2, 13, 15, 36–7, 46, 92
    suppression of under the Thirty, 17, 32, 92, 215

sacrificial calendar
    as part of a possible law code, 56, 105
    contents of, 98
    discovery of, 103
    inscribed in Nicomachus' first term, 176
    inscribed lettering upon, 106
    made up of inscribed opisthographic fragments, 34, 98
    redacted from the archaic laws, 103–4
    suggested publication at the Stoa, 121
Samos (island in the Aegean off the coast of Asia Minor),
    40, 53, 62, 196
Schöll, R., 96
Shear, J. L., 7, 106
Shear, T. L., 123–4
Sickinger, J. P., 117
slander
    at Dicaea, 193
    law against, 117
    of Lysias 24, 50, 98
    of Socrates' accusers, 175
    of the sycophants, 44
    prosecution of Demosthenes for, 161
slavery, 12, 208, 221
Socrates (Athenian philosopher and teacher of Plato)
    admissibility of the trial of, 178
    association of with Alcibiades, 172, 177
    association of with Critias, 47, 170–3
    association of with oligarchy, 177
    bad reputation of, 172–2, 175, 177
    cautioned by Critias for teaching rhetoric, 178
    character of, 174
    condemnation of, 178
    death of, 170–1
    innocence of, 170
    philosophical theories of, 55, 171–4
    plaint against, 35, 171–2, 176
    Polycrates on, 177–8
    speech in self-defence of, 29, 173–6
    trial of, 16, 24, 29, 35, 89, 129, 159–60, 170–8, 207, 213, 225
Solon (lawgiver of Athens)
    axones of, 114
    census classes of, 57
    constitution of, 219
    kyrbeis of, 101
    laws of, 57, 95, 99, 104–6, 109, 114–15, 121–3, 211
    laws postdating, 105, 114, 118, 123
    mentioned by Aristotle, 219
    predictions of about the rule of law, 204
    seisachtheia of, 18
    weights and measures of, 122
Sophocles (fifth-century Athenian playwright), 44, 184
Sparta
    as champion of Greek liberty, 32, 43, 61, 65, 215
    Athenian negotiations with, 45–53, 66–74
    campaign of against Persia, 7, 63, 184
    Critias' attitude towards, 178
    fleet of at Arginusae, 45
    interests of in the Aegean, 188
    opposition of to Athens, 2, 30, 32, 38, 46–51, 90, 130,
        183, 213, 215
    political system of, 14, 17–18, 32, 47–9, 54, 219–20

Sparta (cont.)
  relations of with the Achaean League, 201
  relations of with Corinth, 197–8
  relations of with Macedon, 193
  relations of with Phlius, 198
  support of towards the Ten, 143, 152
  support of towards the Thirty, 2–3, 18–19, 32, 38–40, 44–55, 63, 215
  trial of Anaxilaus of Byzantium by, 60
  Xenophon's attitude towards, 21
stasis (civil conflict)
  at Alipheira, 194–5
  at Athens, 38–67, 79, 115
  at Corcyra, 18, 59–60
  at Dicaea, 17, 192–3
  at Iulis, 188–92
  at Nakone, 17
  at Tegea, 193–4
  banishment of, 42
  due to foreign intervention, 2
  in Greece, 186
  in the time of Peisistratus, 19
  intra-elite 9, 19
  Marxist interpretation of, 17–18
  non-Marxist interpretation of, 215
  reconciliation in the aftermath of, 196
  tyranny as a remedy of, 18
statute of limitations
  barring litigation for crimes predating Eucleides, 2, 30, 99–100, 213
  on homicide, 208
  on private actions in the fourth century, 118, 207
stêlai, wall of, 34, 103–4, 106, 120–4, 176
Stoa Basileios, 28, 114, 124, 127
Stone, I., 171
Strombichides (Athenian general and victim of the Thirty), 55, 130
συκοφάντειν, meaning of, 108, 160
sycophants
  abuse of the courts by 2, 17, 157
  recrimination against under the Thirty, 44, 54–5, 61
  reliance upon under the Thirty, 88, 108
symbolai, 107
Syracuse
  alliance of with Sparta, 24, 46, 196
  Athenian expedition against, 16, 43, 225
  democracy of, 207, 220
  tyranny of Dionysius I at, 197, 225

Tegea (amnesty decree of), 28, 193–5
Teisamenus (decree of), 25, 34, 98, 103–4, 106, 114, 117, 119–24
Temples Decree, 183, 203
Ten (tyrants at Athens who succeeded the Thirty), 11, 32, 83, 212
Thalheim, T., 80–1
Theatre of Dionysus (on the southern side of the Athenian Acropolis), 112
Thebes (city in Boeotia in central Greece), 62–3, 65–6, 68, 188
Themistocles (Athenian general and politician), 219
Theocritus (Athenian oligarch), 130

Theramenes (Athenian oligarch)
  bargaining of with Sparta, 50–3, 130
  involvement of in the selection of the Thirty, 54
  Lysias' attitude to, 49, 143, 150
  political attitudes of, 32, 48–53, 62, 143, 153
  predictions of about the collapse of the Thirty, 61
  proposed replacement of by Thrasybulus, 63
  prosecution of the Arginusae generals by, 60
  relationship of with Critias, 59, 155
  support of for the Four Hundred, 52
  trial of 32, 51–4, 59–60
  Xenophon's attitude to, 21, 62
Theramenes papyrus, 50
Theseus (mythical king of Athens), 14, 134
Thibron (Spartan harmost, dismissed for mismanaging the war in Asia), 60
Thirty (tyrants)
  abolition of sacrifices under, 176
  actions of against the sycophants, 44
  Agoratus not a member of, 35, 134–41, 158, 223
  banned from the city, 71
  chronology of, 51–2
  confiscation of property by, 46, 56, 148, 218
  crimes committed in the time of, 33, 70
  Critias the leader of, 170
  defeat of, 32, 37, 60, 215
  denunciation under, 88, 134, 139
  deposition of by the Three Thousand, 64, 143
  dispatch of the Three Thousand, 62–3
  elimination of political opponents, 32, 54–7, 145
  Eratosthenes a member of, 34, 143–9, 159
  execution of Diognetus brother of Nicaretus by, 65
  execution of Dionysodorus, 129
  execution of Leon of Salamis by, 55
  execution of Theramenes by, 62
  exemplary punishment of, 11
  exempt from the Amnesty, 74, 76–7, 80, 82–3, 139, 169
  imposed by Sparta, 32, 53, 61, 63, 66–7, 90
  installation of, 48, 53–4, 60, 80, 90, 138
  legislation of, 51–2, 56–7, 97
  law code under, 103–5
  link to Socrates, 55, 170–8
  name of, 2
  Pheidon a member of, 153–6
  public audits of, 86, 146–7
  reversal of the measures of, 37, 71, 82, 118, 205
  rise of, 10, 17, 32, 39, 46, 60–1, 126, 213, 215
  selection of Council of Five Hundred under, 51
  selection of the Three Thousand under, 57
  support for, 32, 45–6, 53, 57–8
  suppression of the courts under, 2, 13, 15, 32, 37, 39, 98
  transactions under, 88
  the orators on, 22
  Theramenes a member of, 50
  trial of Theramenes by, 49
  withdrawal to Eleusis of, 143, 150–3, 156
  Xenophon on, 21

SUBJECT INDEX

Thrasybulus
  son of Lycus, 24–5, 35, 38, 62–4, 66–7, 69, 74, 78, 134, 150, 166, 177
  of Calydon, 130
  of Collytus, 62
Three Hundred, 101
Three Thousand
  aided by Sparta, 64
  approached by King Pausanias of Sparta, 66
  as early supporters of the Thirty, 58
  failure to be enlisted among, 88
  identified with the City Party, 57, 116
  installation of, 62
  instructed to make peace with the Piraeus Party, 65
  lose faith in the Thirty, 64
  modelled on the Spartan system, 54
  opposed by Theramenes, 59
  opposition to, 63
  resistance of to the democrats, 68–9
  social composition of, 57
Thucydides (son of Olorus and Greek historian)
  exile of, 59
  on Andocides, 24–5
  on Megara, 196
  on oligarchy, 216–7
  on Pericles, 14
  on Pericles' successors, 44
  on political trials, 60
  on Samos, 196
  on *stasis*, 18–19, 42, 59
  on *nomothetai*, 94
  on the *hermokopeia*, 111–12
  on the Peloponnesian War, 40–3
  text of, 20–1
Timagoras (Athenian politician tried and executed for disloyalty) 60
timêma (either 'property qualification', or 'security' or 'penalty' or 'rateable property'), 85
τιμωρεῖσθαι, range of possible meanings of, 108–9
Todd, S. C., 7, 51, 54, 132, 145
transcribers of laws *see anagrapheis*
transitional justice, 11
tyranny
  and the rule of law, 19
  as a mode of government, 61
  as a remedy of *stasis* 18, 225
  as the antithesis to democracy, 92, 213
  at Mytilene and Methymna, 198
  at Orchomenus, 201–2
  at Syracuse, 197
  early laws against, 211
  of Cypselus and Periander, 43
  of the Peisistratids, 29
tyrants
  at Eresus, 200
  ideological motivation of, 18
  opposition of King Cleomenes of Sparta to, 65
  part of the nomenclature of the Thirty, 2, 13, 30, 143
  the reign of at Athens, 112
  unelected, 211

vengeance
  as an act of war, 63, 203
  as ignoble, 6, 128, 184
  as illegal, 32, 73, 194
  as politically partisan, 89, 109, 129, 184, 194
  in legal language, 89, 140, 157; *see also* τιμωρεῖσθαι

Waterfield, R., 171
Wolpert, A., 7
Wolff, H.-J., 161

Xenophon (Greek historian)
  as a source for the Amnesty, 5, 21–2, 71–2, 74, 84, 144
  attitude of to oligarchy, 24, 48, 217
  attitude of to Sparta 16, 43, 48
  attitude of to Theramenes, 59, 62
  on Cleocritus the Herald, 78
  on democracy, 16, 217
  on Eleusis, 101
  on King Pausanias of Sparta, 65
  on Socrates, 170–7
  on Spartan negotiations with Athens, 70
  on the massacre at Corinth, 197–8
  on the trial of Theramenes, 59–61
Xenophon of Kourion (victim of the Thirty), 55

Zaleucus (Locrian lawgiver), 211
zeugitai (census class), 57
Zeuxippus (Boeotian exile restored to rights), 202–3

War were related by the historian Xenophon in his *History of Greece*. This is a problematic work, not least because Xenophon is notoriously selective with his detail and, often to an infuriating degree, omits key information which we would dearly like to have had at our disposal.[62] Xenophon's narrative is crucial for the events of 404/3 and is the most reliable and complete source for the Thirty, but his usefulness peters out once we get to the Reconciliation Agreement and the events that followed. Xenophon's interest in the internal affairs of Athens is important from the point of view of Greek history more widely, but once democracy is restored in 403, Xenophon shows little interest in democracy *sui causa*, and therefore has little of use or importance to say about how democracy was re-established at Athens. Xenophon has often in the past been caricatured as an uncritical admirer of Sparta and her political institutions, but more recent studies have drawn attention to the frequency with which Xenophon is willing to criticise Sparta.[63] The account of the Thirty is by no means encomiastic, and while some may find fault with the soft treatment of Theramenes, it is important at the same time not to be misled by the rhetoric of Lysias (see below), who had special reasons for condemning all oligarchs regardless of nuance. Xenophon is frustrating when it comes to the Reconciliation itself, and thanks to his lacunose narrative, scholars, especially in the nineteenth century, debated needlessly as to whether there was an Oath of Amnesty in 403. A judicious approach to his text should warn against more recent efforts to speak of an 'evolving agreement', for which there is little good evidence.[64]

The most important source for the Treaty of Reconciliation is the thirty-ninth chapter of the Aristotelian *Ath. Pol.*, discovered on papyrus scroll in Egypt in 1890. Since its discovery in the last decade of the nineteenth century, scholars have debated back and forth whether this treatise was by Aristotle or by a pupil.[65] The Aristotelian *Ath. Pol.* is of varying reliability, and because of its

---

[62] For authoritative overviews of the use and reliability of Xenophon as a historian, see Andersen (J. K.) 1974; Dillery 1995.

[63] See, for example, Humble 1999, who observes that the critique of Spartan policy at X. *Lac.* 14 is no mere deviation but can be brought in line with many of the critical remarks made by Xenophon elsewhere.

[64] Most recently, that approach has been canvassed by Carawan (2013), who claims that there was more than one legislative package spread over a two-year interval through which the Amnesty was legally enshrined; as shown in Chapter 3, the evidence supporting that approach is minimal.

[65] For an overview of scholarship since the nineteenth century and discussion of the problems of authorship, see Rhodes 1981. To disengage from the suggestion that the *Ath. Pol.* is a mere mouthpiece for Aristotelian political theory, Rhodes argues tendentiously that the work is not by Aristotle but, in so doing, confuses two questions, the first of authorship, the second of historical reliability. As more recent scholarship has shown, even if not by Aristotle but by a pupil, the *Ath. Pol.* is significantly indebted to the Aristotelian school; see Bertelli 2018 for a more up-to-date discussion and critique of surrounding scholarship.

mistreatment of certain key historical episodes, most memorably the period of the so-called 'Ephialtic reforms' of 462/1, it is superficially tempting to underestimate it as a source for Athenian history more widely.[66] That would be a mistake, because other portions of the text, notably what it has to say for the revised constitution of 403, are not as feeble as some have suggested, and indeed its account of the fourth-century democracy is largely confirmed by the evidence of the orators.[67] Unlike Xenophon, *Ath. Pol.* shows no interest in Athens as a political power in relation to the rest of Greece and is far more interested in its internal nature. For all its manifold faults and defects, *Ath. Pol.* is the best and most trustworthy source for the treaty of 403 to which the two sides of the civil conflict swore, and though some recent scholars have challenged its authority, there is no good reason to doubt that behind the account at *Ath. Pol.* 39 stands a reliable documentary tradition.[68] Even though most scholars and historians since Cloché have accepted its authority for the events of 403, the passage is not without its problems, the most important of which is a serious textual corruption at 39.5 for which restorations to date have never been satisfactory. The majority has thought that this refers to exemptions made for own-hand homicide, but as shown more recently, none of that is compatible with what else we know from the orators about the nature of Athenian homicide law.[69] As argued in Chapter 3, the best way to deal with the rogue evidence is to remove it. Similarly, textual readings for the provisions on dikastic composition require emendation (see Chapter 3). The evidence of *Ath. Pol.* has been supplemented by the discovery of papyrus fragments from Lysias' otherwise lost speech *Against Hippotherses*, which refers to covenants not included in *Ath. Pol.* 39, and from a reference in Isocrates' eighteenth speech, *Against Callimachus*, to agreements which the author of the *Ath. Pol.* did not clearly elucidate. It would be foolhardy, therefore, to assume that the account at *Ath. Pol.* 39 is an unvarnished reproduction of a copy of a treaty which came down in the archives from 403, and a closer reading indicates that the passage follows a preconceived narratological structure, stressing what was innovative in the Reconciliation Agreement and counterposing that over and against the *status quo ante*. Even if the account is not exhaustive or unproblematic, this is

---

[66] For recent demonstration that the twenty-fifth chapter of *Ath. Pol.* covering events of the mid-fifth century is historically worthless, see now Zaccarini 2018; Harris 2019a. For discussions of the so-called 'constitution of Draco', see Verlinski 2017.

[67] On this, see Canevaro and Esu 2018. See further the opening remarks in Chapter 4.

[68] For the documentary reliability of *Ath. Pol.* 39, see Scheibelreiter 2013, and further, Chapter 3.

[69] At Joyce 2008: 314, I mistakenly followed the majority view that own-hand homicide (*autocheir*) was treated differently, following the restoration of Thalheim of *Ath. Pol.* 39.5. I now no longer believe this; for recent demonstration that this exemption was not made, see Harris 2015b.

not reason to reject it wholesale, or to suggest that it telescoped two separate amnesty treaties, one contracted in 403 touching Eleusis, one in 401 touching a newly integrated Athenian polity which drew no further distinction between the democratic state and the oligarchic rump which had been carved out in 403 and eliminated in 401.

The Attic orators furnish vital evidence for the period of the Thirty and what followed, and for the period after 403 they come significantly into play, especially when we turn to the trials which took place in the immediate aftermath of the Reconciliation (Chapters 4, 5, 6). The degree to which orators can be relied upon as historical evidence for the fourth century is never an easy matter to resolve, and caution must be taken before engaging in broad generalisations. Nevertheless, four guiding principles on how to treat the evidence of orators can be adduced:

1. Statements that are supported by relevant evidence can be regarded as reliable.
2. External evidence, such as the evidence provided by epigraphy, can corroborate an orator's remark or interpretation of fact.
3. While we can trust a statement of fact that is corroborated by relevant evidence, nothing compels us to accept the speaker's interpretation of the fact.
4. Documents inserted into the MSS of orators should not be trusted and can only be defended if there are conclusive external reasons to do so.[70]

By relevant evidence, we mean the evidence which an orator can cite of laws, decrees, court verdicts, or other transcripts of documents which might support a particular case. Thus, when orators refer to the Amnesty, if they can cite a clause in the agreement which sustains the case they are advancing before the court, unless we have a reason to believe otherwise, we should take as a working hypothesis that the clause cited is genuine, without being committed necessarily to accept the way in which an orator interprets that clause legally or historically. Our period is replete with the evidence of inscriptions, in particular the prescript to the homicide law of Draco (*IG* I³ 104 lines 1–10) which can be adduced to confirm the interpretation given by Lysias, and refute that given by Andocides, about the process of legal review at the end of the fifth century. The third criterion is of particular importance once we turn to consider

---

[70] This is a modification of rules adduced by Harris (1995: 15–16) in discussion of the methodological problems which arise from the exchange between Demosthenes and Aeschines in the second half of the fourth century, later supplemented by Canevaro (2013b). For our period, this type of exchange does not happen, and so the full list of criteria adduced by Harris may not apply to our evidence.

how the Amnesty is understood within the oratorical tradition. As the case of Andocides shows, genuine laws might be cited, even if the argument which the orator chooses to build upon the basis of that evidence might be thought legally or historically questionable. As we shall see, many of the transcripts of laws and decrees inserted into the MSS of orators, such as in the first speech of Andocides, *On the Mysteries*, are forgeries, and it is crucial therefore not to attempt to reconstruct history based upon those fraudulent documents, as has been done extensively in the past. None of this is to deny that Andocides was able to cite genuine texts; the problem is that the transcripts of those texts which survive to us are not genuine but have been inserted by errant scribes and editors.

These guiding principles will be useful when we treat the three main oratorical sources for our period, Lysias, Andocides and Isocrates. Most important is Lysias, born sometime in the middle of the fifth century and died soon after 380, perhaps close the age of eighty. Lysias was the son of a Syracusan man called Cephalus, who came to Athens at some point in the 440s, the father of the Polemarchus, Lysias' elder brother, whose house provides the lavish scene of the dialogue of Plato's *Republic*. We know from the twelfth speech, *Against Eratosthenes*, that Lysias and Polemarchus were both wealthy residents (Lys. 12.20). During the period of the Thirty, they were arrested, his brother killed by hemlock, but Lysias escaped to Megara and later returned with Thrasybulus. Lysias is an artful slanderer, and much of his speechwriting is infused with bombast. Unlike Xenophon, who maintained a clear-cut distinction between the extremist wing of the oligarchy led by Critias and its more moderate proponents, Lysias tears down that distinction in an effort to show that his long arch-rival, Eratosthenes, charged with the murder of his brother Polemarchus, could not plead a case of moderation under the oligarchy.[71] The evidence of Lysias is reductive, whereas the more nuanced approach of Xenophon is to be preferred. Three Lysianic speeches come into play in our survey, that *Against Eratosthenes* (12), that *Against Agoratus* (13) and that *Against Nicomachus* (30). The first two were delivered shortly after 403, though scholars disagree when precisely (see Chapter 5), whilst the third we can date precisely to 399, the same year as the trial of Socrates. The third furnishes vital evidence for an obscure process, the legal redaction which followed the restoration of democracy, particularly that this was a controlled democratic process and not subject to the whim of clever legal manipulators (see further Chapter 4).

For the last-mentioned event the orator Andocides features heavily in discussion. Born sometime in the 440s and Lysias' contemporary, Andocides came from the noble line of the Kerykes, who traced their ancestry back to Odysseus

---

[71] See further Chapter 2.

(Plu. *Alc.* 21; And. 1.141). His name first appears in history with the infamous religious scandals of 415, related in the sixth book of Thucydides' *History* and subsequently by Andocides himself in his speech of self-defence in around 400, *On the Mysteries*, after which event fifteen years earlier he went into voluntary exile. After the victory of Thrasybulus in 403, he returned to Athens in the hope that the measures which had forced him into exile no longer had effect (And. 1.132). The first speech of Andocides, *On the Mysteries*, is a fiendishly difficult text to interpret since the orator tries to telescope two entirely separate issues, the democratic restoration and the abrogation of certain measures passed when Athens was still a democracy, before 404. If Andocides is taken at face value, the Amnesty of 403 was a *carte blanche* which effectively eradicated any court judgment prior to 403. If this were true, we would have to imagine that the events of 403 marked a 'year zero' at which the entire criminal docket at Athens was wiped clean. As other historical sources show, the main purpose of amnesty was to ensure that any crime committed prior to 403 *which had not already been prosecuted* was no longer actionable after 403.[72] This was not an injunction to a clean slate, despite the inferences which Andocides makes himself. As argued in Chapters 3, 5 and 6, the principle of *res iudicata*, which upheld court decisions taken in time of democracy, was upheld after 403. In law, if Andocides had been guilty of the crimes of 415, which in any case he denies, and then convicted, the conviction against him stood after 403. The speech *On the Mysteries* is an intriguing piece of sophistry, but as argued in Chapter 4, once the rhetorical labyrinth is carefully negotiated, its historical value falls into serious question.

Andocides is a problem for another reason. The first speech contains three documents purporting to be transcripts of decrees proposed by Patrocleides (§§77–9), Teisamenus (§§83–4) and Demophantus (§§96–8) towards the close of the fifth century. Recent studies of these inserted texts have disproven their authenticity beyond reasonable doubt. Most scholars have now endorsed the results of those studies.[73] How inserted documents are

---

[72] See further Chapters 3, 5 and 6, but also see Joyce 2008 and 2015.
[73] For a list of scholars who have sided with scepticism, see Canevaro and Harris 2016–17: 10 n. 3, to which should be added Dilts and Murphy in the OCT of Antiphon and Andocides, and Liddel 2020. Sommerstein (2014) endorsed Canevaro and Harris 2012 on the decrees of Patrocleides and Teisamenus and on the shorter documents, but his attempt to defend the authenticity of the Demophantus decree was refuted in detail in Harris (2013–14), with additional evidence against authenticity. Hansen (2015) attempted to defend the authenticity of the decree of Patrocleides and again (2016) attempted to defend the authenticity of the decree of Teisamenus. Both these articles were refuted in detail by Canevaro and Harris (2016–17) with additional evidence against authenticity, whose analysis was endorsed by Dilts/Murphy and Liddel. Carawan (2017) argues that the three documents in Andocides are forgeries, but that they are a patchwork of reliable information taken from writers like Craterus. This view is refuted in detail by Harris (2021).

authenticated is a subdiscipline *sui generis*, which involves knotty questions of stichometry which extend well beyond the remit of this study.[74] Yet a brief outline of the methodology may be provided. The correct methodology is to compare what the orator says about a document with the content of the document quoted, and then by comparative assessment decide whether the document can be defended on its own internal merits and by reckoning with what the orator states about it. This has five major components. First, the texts should be studied on their merits without the attempt to remove components which do not appear to fit. To amend documents to make them fit is simply to beg the question about authenticity. Secondly, the summaries and paraphrases of the documents in the orator in whose speech they appear must be measured up against the content of the quoted document. If the two do not match up, serious questions can be raised against authenticity. Thirdly, if the content of the document conforms to the summary in the orator, this is no guarantee for authenticity, as a later editor may have modelled a summary on what the orator himself states. Fourth, if information appears in the document which cannot be found in the orator's summary, this does not prove authenticity unless external evidence, most importantly that of inscriptions, corroborates the information. Finally, the language of the inserted document needs to correspond to the known language of fifth- and fourth-century legal texts if its authenticity is to be corroborated. If the language of the text does not correspond to what else we know of the language of Athenian decrees, it is a forgery.

Some examples of this methodology can be adduced from documents which appear from outside our immediate period. Aeschines and Demosthenes both refer to three laws in the trial of Ctesiphon in 330: the law requiring audit (Aeschin. 3.17–22; D. 18.111–18); the law about crowns for magistrates (Aeschin. 3.11, 31; D. 18.111–18); and the law about crowns in the theatre (Aeschin. 3.35–6; D. 18.120–2). The two orators interpret the terms differently, but they do not disagree on the summary of their contents.[75] The same confidence in the authority of the orators can be established by comparison of what Lysias (1.30–5) and Demosthenes (23.55) say about the provisions in the Draconian law on justifiable homicide. Demosthenes' summary of the Draconian law at D. 23.37–8, 60–1 is confirmed by the epigraphic remnants at *IG* I³ 104 lines 23–9, 37–8. A similar case where external fragments of inscriptions confirm the reading of Demosthenes is the decree awarding immunity to

---

[74] For a general discussion of the methodological problems entailed in the assessment of the documentary material, see Canevaro and Harris 2012: 98–100; Canevaro 2013b: 27–36; Canevaro 2018: 72–81.

[75] For a more detailed discussion of the sources and related evidence, see Canevaro and Harris 2012: 99.